Lecture Notes in Business Information Processing 549

LNBIP reports state-of-the-art results in areas related to business information systems and industrial application software development – timely, at a high level, and in both printed and electronic form.

The type of material published includes

- Proceedings (published in time for the respective event)
- Postproceedings (consisting of thoroughly revised and/or extended final papers)
- Other edited monographs (such as, for example, project reports or invited volumes)
- Tutorials (coherently integrated collections of lectures given at advanced courses, seminars, schools, etc.)
- Award-winning or exceptional theses

LNBIP is abstracted/indexed in DBLP, EI and Scopus. LNBIP volumes are also submitted for the inclusion in ISI Proceedings.

Yiliu Paul Tu · Maomao Chi
Editors

E-Business

Generative Artificial Intelligence and Management Transformation

24th Wuhan International Conference on E-business, WHICEB 2025
Guangzhou, China, June 6–8, 2025
Proceedings, Part I

Springer

Editors
Yiliu Paul Tu
University of Calgary
Calgary, AB, Canada

Maomao Chi
China University of Geosciences
Wuhan, China

ISSN 1865-1348 ISSN 1865-1356 (electronic)
Lecture Notes in Business Information Processing
ISBN 978-3-031-94183-2 ISBN 978-3-031-94184-9 (eBook)
https://doi.org/10.1007/978-3-031-94184-9

This Springer imprint is published by the registered company Springer Nature Switzerland AG
The registered company address is: Gewerbestrasse 11, 6330 Cham, Switzerland

Welcome Message from the AIS President

I am delighted to welcome you to the proceedings of the 24th Wuhan International Conference on E-Business (WHICEB). The conference provided an excellent forum for faculty and students to build friendships and share creative ideas and findings. Local conferences are an important part of our community because they provide opportunities for faculty and students to come together, form friendships, and exchange ideas. By fostering such relationships and ideas, WHICEB cultivates high quality scholarship in China, in Asia, and around the globe.

On behalf of the Association for Information Systems (AIS), I would like to thank the conference organizers, Jing Zhao, from the China University of Geosciences, Jüergen Seitz from Baden-Wüerttemberg Cooperative State University in Heidenheim, Germany, and Doug Vogel from Harbin Institute of Technology, for their service to the conference and to the Information Systems community. The conference organizers assembled a world-class conference committee, attracted a strong set of globally recognized publication outlets, and attracted significant global sponsorship to ensure that the conference, and to ensure that the conference is an ongoing success.

The AIS is honored to count WHICEB as an affiliated conference. The past two years have been very different ones for this conference, and the world as a whole. The conference provides an excellent example of how a group of scholars can come together and have a lasting impact on the quality of research that is necessary to advance the Information Systems discipline.

As AIS President, I also want to personally invite you to join the Association and participate in AIS activities. In addition to WHICEB, AIS offers many high-quality conferences, including the International Conference on Information Systems (ICIS), the Pacific Asia Conference on Information Systems (PACIS), the Americas Conference on Information Systems (AMCIS) and the European Conference on Information Systems (ECIS).

As AIS President, I personally invite each of you to familiarize yourself with the Association. We offer a growing set of digital services, such as the eLibrary, where the WHICEB conference proceedings will be available to download, webinars on research methods, research exchanges, career management, and access to workshops that can help develop your skills for research and teaching. For AIS members and non-members alike, I urge you to visit www.aisnet.org to learn more about the benefits of membership.

WHICEB is a very important, longstanding conference in the Information Systems field. The AIS is very proud to be affiliated with WHICEB and we look forward to many rewarding years of partnership together.

Best wishes for your conference.

Andrew Burton-Jones

Preface

The Wuhan International Conference on E-Business (WHICEB), an AIS-affiliated annual conference, took take place from June 6–8, 2025, in Guangzhou. WHICEB is dedicated to advancing scholarly research and fostering networking opportunities within the e-business sector and related fields. Our goal is to catalyze academic inquiry and business innovation by facilitating discussions on e-business, global finance, and the imperative for ongoing innovation. This conference aims to showcase cutting-edge research, solutions, and methodologies that leverage the Internet as a powerful tool for global commerce. The digital age presents a myriad of challenges, from technological hurdles to behavioral adaptations, marketing strategies to data analytics, and concerns over efficacy to security. In recent years, the ABCD Technology—big data, cloud computing, artificial intelligence, and blockchain—has sparked a new wave of innovation across manufacturing, business, education, and personal life sectors. This digital and intelligent transformation is paving the way for a novel digital economy growth model, redefining "Internet Plus" applications, and enabling businesses to reinvent their models from the ground up. In response to this digital and intelligent trend, companies are actively engaging with new challenges, thereby generating numerous research opportunities.

This year's conference theme, "Generative Artificial Intelligence and Management Transformation," was designed to ignite robust academic and corporate engagement by integrating e-business and information technology in our increasingly digital and intelligent landscape, alongside fresh insights and discoveries in service, marketing, and operational management reform. The conference sought to highlight groundbreaking scientific research in fields enabled by artificial intelligence, foster cross-disciplinary studies, and share experiences from various nations and regions. The proceedings encompass 18 tracks and will be indexed appropriately. The selected best papers from the proceedings will be recommended to international academic journals including but not limited to the following: Electronic Commerce Research and Applications, Electronic Markets, Electronic Commerce Research, Internet Research, Journal of Organizational and End User Computing, Journal of Information & Knowledge Management, International Journal of Networking and Virtual Organizations, and Journal of Systems and Information Technology.

The research papers in the proceedings went through a double-blind peer review process. Papers were accepted based upon a clear research methodology and contributions to the knowledge of e-business including but not limited to case study, experiment, simulation, or survey. The efforts made by our track chairs in reviewing submissions, which ensured the quality of the proceedings, are really appreciated. On behalf of the conference organization, we thank them for their professional diligence. They are: *Yi Wang, Yuan Sun, Si Shi, and Jindi Fu*, Artificial Intelligence and New Ways of Working; *Chunmei Gan, Weijun Wang, and Ming Yi,* Conversational Artificial Intelligence and Information Behavior; *Dongxiao Gu, Yiming Zhao, Ying Yang, and Xuejie Yang*, Data Analytics and Digital Governance; *Guoyin Jiang, Xiaodong Feng, and Jing Ma*,

Data Intelligence and Social Computing on Digital Platforms; *Zhongyun (Phil) Zhou, Yongqiang Sun, Wei Hu, Zhenya "Robin" Tang, and Qun Zhao,* Digital Enablement and Digital Governance; *Xiaobo (Bob) Xu, Chenwei Li, and Fei Ma,* Digital Innovation and Social Impact; *Wei Zhang, Chunping Deng, and Xiaohao Zhou,* Digital Technologies for Sustainable Development; *Ping Wang, Xiuyan Shao, and Cong Cao,* Disruptive Technologies and Digital Transformation; *Xiaoling Li, Lu Wang, and Qing Huang,* E-business Strategy & Online Marketing; *Rong Du, Hongpeng Wang, and Peng Wang,* Emerging e-Commerce Initiatives Enabled by Advanced Technologies; *Nannan Xi, Hongxiu Li, Juan Chen, and Juho Hamari,* Engaging Technologies; *Gang Wang, Wei Xu, and Jingling Ma,* Generative AI-Enhanced Risk Analytics and Modelling; *Zhaohua Deng, Tailai Wu, Jia Li, and Junjie Zhou,* Healthcare Service and IT Management; *Ling Zhao, Zilong Liu, and Aihui Chen,* Human-AI Integration in Organizations; *Shaobo Wei, Xiayu Chen, and Hua Liu,* Next-Gen Technologies and Social Commerce; *Nan Zhang, Zilong Liu, and Bailing Liu,* Privacy and Security in Artificial Intelligence Generated Content; *Zhao Du, Shan Wang, Fang Wang, and Ruoxin Zhou,* Transformative Digital Innovations: Education, Sports, and Entertainment; *and Maomao Chi, Zhen Zhu, and Haiyan Ma,* General IS and Digital Business Topics.

This year, we received a total of 324 submissions, from which 92 papers have successfully secured acceptance for publication. This results in an acceptance rate of approximately 28.39%. Our proceedings are structured across three volumes. Each paper included in these volumes has undergone a rigorous review process, involving a minimum of three double-blind reviews conducted by members of the Editorial Board of the Proceedings. Again, we express our sincere appreciation to all members of the Editorial Board for their invaluable contributions, unwavering support, and dedicated efforts throughout this process.

Yiliu Paul Tu
Maomao Chi

Organization

Conference Hosts

School of Economics and Management, China University of Geosciences, Wuhan, China
Baden-Württemberg Cooperative State University Heidenheim, Germany

Organizers

School of Management, Guangdong University of Technology, China
Center for International Cooperation in E-Business, China University of Geosciences, Wuhan, China

Sponsors (Alphabetical Order)

Association for Information Systems (AIS)
China Association for Information Systems (CNAIS)
China Information Economics Society
Wuhan University of Communication

Conference Co-chairs

Jing Zhao	China University of Geosciences, Wuhan, China
Juergen Seitz	Baden-Württemberg Cooperative State University Heidenheim, Germany
Doug Vogel	Harbin Institute of Technology, China

Publication Chairs and Proceedings Editors

Yiliu (Paul) Tu	University of Calgary, Canada
Maomao Chi	China University of Geosciences, Wuhan, China

Program Committee

Chairs

Weiguo (Patrick) Fan	University of Iowa, USA
Zhen Zhu	China University of Geosciences, Wuhan, China
Xiaojie Wu	Guangdong University of Technology, China

Members

Yukun Bao	Huazhong University of Sciences & Technology, China
Zhao Cai	University of Nottingham Ningbo, China
Cong Cao	Zhejiang University of Technology, China
Juan Chen	Anhui University of Finance and Economics, China
Meng Chen	Soochow University, China
Xiayu Chen	Hefei University of Technology, China
Xusen Cheng	Renmin University of China, China
Zhaohua Deng	Huazhong University of Sciences & Technology, China
Rong Du	Xidian University, China
Zhao Du	Beijing Sport University, China
Xiaodong Feng	Sun Yat-sen University, China
Dongxiao Gu	Hefei University of Technology, China
Juho Hamari	Tampere University, Finland
Qing Huang	Chongqing Technology and Business University, China
Zhongyi Hu	Wuhan University, China
Lin Jia	Beijing Institute of Technology, China
Guoyin Jiang	University of Electronic Science and Technology of China, China
Xiaoling Jin	Shanghai University, China
Hongxiu Li	Tampere University, Finland
Jia Li	East China University of Science and Technology, China
Xiaoling Li	Chongqing University, China
Xixi Li	University of Science and Technology Beijing, China
Hefu Liu	University of Science and Technology of China, China

Yuxiang Zhao	Nanjing University of Science and Technology, China
Haichao Zheng	Southwestern University of Finance and Economics, China
Zhongyun Zhou	Tongji University, China
Ling Zhao	Huazhong University of Sciences & Technology, China
Weiyong Zhang	Old Dominion University, USA
Ruoxin Zhou	University of International Business and Economics, China
Bin Zhu	Oregon State University, USA

Session Chairs

Kanliang Wang	Renmin University of China, China
Jinghua Xiao	Sun Yat-sen University, China
Rong Du	Xidian University, China
Xiangbin Yan	Guangdong University of Foreign Studies, China
Yi Jiang	China University of Geosciences, China

Organization Committee

Chair

Yao Zhang	China University of Geosciences, Wuhan, China

Secretary-General

Fei Wang	China University of Geosciences, Wuhan, China

Members

Songhua Du	Guangdong University of Technology, China
Jie Zhao	Guangdong University of Technology, China
Pei Liang	Guangdong University of Technology, China
Xiaohao Zhou	China University of Geosciences, Wuhan, China
Yating Peng	China University of Geosciences, Wuhan, China
Jing Wang	China University of Geosciences, Wuhan, China
Qian Zhao	China University of Geosciences, Wuhan, China

International Advisory Board

European

Editorial Board of the Proceedings

Artificial Intelligence and New Ways of Working

Conversational Artificial Intelligence and Information Behavior

Data Analytics and Digital Governance

Data Intelligence and Social Computing on Digital Platforms

Guoyin Jiang	University of Electronic Science and Technology of China, China
Xiaodong Feng	Sun Yat-sen University, China
Jing Ma	University of Electronic Science and Technology of China, China

Digital Enablement and Digital Governance

Zhongyun (Phil) Zhou	Tongji University, China
Yongqiang Sun	Wuhan University, China
Wei Hu	Tongji University, China
Zhenya (Robin) Tang	University of Northern Colorado, USA
Qun Zhao	Ningbo University, China

Digital Innovation and Social Impact

Xiaobo (Bob) Xu	Xi'an Jiaotong-Liverpool University, China
Chenwei Li	Xi'an Jiaotong-Liverpool University, China
Fei Ma	Chang'an University, China

Digital Technologies for Sustainable Development

Wei Zhang	University of Massachusetts Boston, USA
Chunping Deng	Beijing Technology and Business University, China
Xiaohao Zhou	Guangdong University of Technology, China

Disruptive Technologies and Digital Transformation

Ping Wang	Central China Normal University, China
Xiuyan Shao	Southeast University, China
Cong Cao	Zhejiang University of Technology, China

E-Business Strategy and Online Marketing

Xiaoling Li	Chongqing University, China
Lu Wang	Zhongnan University of Economics and Law, China
Qing Huang	Chongqing Technology and Business University, China

Emerging e-Commerce Initiatives Enabled by Advanced Technologies

Rong Du	Xidian University, China
Hongpeng Wang	Lanzhou University, China
Peng Wang	Northwestern Polytechnical University, China

Engaging Technologies

Nannan Xi	Tampere University, Finland
Hongxiu Li	Tampere University, Finland
Juan Chen	Anhui University of Finance and Economics, China
Juho Hamari	Tampere University, Finland

Generative AI-Enhanced Risk Analytics and Modelling

Gang Wang	Hefei University of Technology, China
Wei Xu	Renmin University of China, China
Jingling Ma	Zhejiang University of Finance and Economics, China

Healthcare Service and IT Management

Zhaohua Deng	Huazhong University of Science & Technology, China
Tailai Wu	Huazhong University of Science & Technology, China
Jia Li	East China University of Science and Technology, China
Junjie Zhou	Shantou University, China

Human-AI Integration in Organizations

Ling Zhao	Huazhong University of Science & Technology, China
Zilong Liu	Dongbei University of Finance & Economics, China
Aihui Chen	Tianjin University, China

Next-Gen Technologies and Social Commerce

Shaobo Wei	Hefei University of Technology, China
Xiayu Chen	Hefei University of Technology, China
Hua Liu	Anhui University, China

Privacy and Security in Artificial Intelligence Generated Content

Nan Zhang	Harbin Institute of Technology, China
Zilong Liu	Dongbei University of Finance & Economics, China
Bailing Liu	Central China Normal University, China

Transformative Digital Innovations: Education, Sports, and Entertainment

Zhao Du	Beijing Sport University, China
Shan Wang	Edwards School of Business, University of Saskatchewan, Canada
Fang Wang	Lazaridis School of Business & Economics, Wilfrid Laurier University, Canada
Ruoxin Zhou	University of International Business and Economics, China

General IS and Digital Business Topics

Maomao Chi	China University of Geosciences, Wuhan, China
Zhen Zhu	China University of Geosciences, Wuhan, China
Haiyan Ma	China University of Geosciences, Wuhan, China

Best Paper Award and Journal Publication Committee

Chairs

Yiliu (Paul) Tu	University of Calgary, Canada
Maomao Chi	China University of Geosciences, Wuhan, China

Members

Alain Chong	University of Nottingham Ningbo China, China
Chris Yang	Drexel University, USA

Sponsoring Journals (Alphabetical Order)

Electronic Commerce Research
Electronic Commerce Research and Applications
Electronic Markets-The International Journal on Networked Business
Internet Research
Journal of Database Management
Journal of Organizational and End User Computing
International Journal of Networking and Virtual Organizations
Journal of Systems and Information Technology

Contents – Part I

Data Analytics and Digital Governance

Data Intelligence and Social Computing on Digital Platforms

Contents – Part II

E-Business Strategy and Online Marketing

Engaging Technologies

Contents – Part III

Privacy and Security in Artificial Intelligence Generated Content

Transformative Digital Innovations: Education, Sports, and Entertainment

General IS and Digital Business Topics

Artificial Intelligence and New Ways of Working

Research on the Influence of Technology Shock Awareness on Job Reinvention of Older Employees in the Age of Digital Intelligence

Na Zhang[1] and Ying Xiong[2](✉)

[1] School of Economics and Management, China University of Geosciences, Donghu New Technology Development Zone, No. 68, Jincheng Street, Donghu New Technology Development Zone, Wuhan 430078, China

[2] School of Economics and Management, China University of Geosciences, No. 388, Lumo Road, Hongshan District, Wuhan 430074, China

thamansa@126.com

Abstract. The convergence of the two waves of "digitization" and "aging" is a distinctive feature of contemporary society, and the updating of technological products has caused older employees to face the digital divide, which affects their workplace environments, psychological states, and work behaviors. Based on resource preservation theory and stress cognitive evaluation theory, this study examines the influence mechanism of technology shock awareness on older employees' job reinvention in the digital age. Through stratified regression and Bootstrap analysis of 303 questionnaires, it was found that technology shock awareness significantly positively affected job reinvention of older employees, including convergent job reinvention and defensive job reinvention, with job insecurity mediating. In addition, perceptions of organizational support positively moderated the positive effect of job insecurity on convergent job reinvention while weakening the impact on defensive job reinvention. This study enriches the research on technology shock awareness and job reinvention for employee management and corporate practices in the digital age.

Keywords: Digital technology shock · Older employees · Job insecurity · Convergent job reinvention · Defensive job reinvention

1 Introduction

Advances in medical technology have extended the average life expectancy of human beings, and population aging has become one of the significant challenges for the state, society, and enterprises. The eleventh meeting of the Standing Committee of the China People's Congress formally approved the decision to gradually postpone the mandatory retirement age, which means that older employees will occupy an important place that cannot be ignored in the labor market. For a long time, it has been stereotyped that older employees' cognition, motivation, and capacity decline with age and that they are gradually entering the "decline period" of their careers [1], and many views regarding

Y. P. Tu and M. Chi (Eds.): WHICEB 2025, LNBIP 549, pp. 3–15, 2025.
https://doi.org/10.1007/978-3-031-94184-9_1

"aging" as a crisis, while ignoring their unique value and extraordinary potential. Older employees are in the golden period of integrating knowledge reserves and practical experience, and their rich experience and skills are scarce strategic resources and essential factors for enterprises to obtain competitive advantages.

As the world economy steps into the "Industry 4.0 era", artificial intelligence technology, as the core driving force of emerging industrial change, is accelerating the pace of "freeing the brain and hands" of human beings and has become an essential factor affecting employees' psychological state and work patterns [2]. Older employees are subject to the constraints of technology, system, culture, and their factors. They are prone to digital technology fallout and the fear of uncertainty about their value and ability, which subsequently brings about the fear of digital tools such as artificial intelligence, robots, and algorithms replacing their work [3], i.e., the sense of technological shock that further trigger psychological insecurity where career continuity is difficult to ensure. Resource conservation theory states that individuals can respond to environmental changes by protecting, acquiring, and accumulating resources, forming a "value-added spiral" mechanism. Therefore, older employees' perceived threat to career stability may prompt them to adapt their work tasks, contents, roles, and relationships, i.e., older employees' job reinvention will be evoked.

However, how and what kinds of reshaping behaviors of older employees are affected by digital technological change? The cognitive appraisal theory of stress suggests that stressors in the organizational environment affect individual behavioral outcomes and that employees differentiate their cognitive appraisal of their stressors based on their job stability, amount of resources, and amount of information. Concerns about technological change and perceived threats of job insecurity are seen as potential psychological stressors with both positive and negative attributes. Therefore, the job reinvention triggered by the impact of technological change and career threat is a dynamic mechanism that can trigger either "problem-solving" oriented convergent job reinvention or "obstacle-reducing" oriented defensive job reinvention [4]. In addition, Qiao et al. [5] found that when individuals face external pressures, they will have different levels of stress reactions, such as "threat" or "challenge", and organizational support will have a significant impact on individual role behavior. Therefore, this study suggests that organizational support may be key in determining the relationship between technology shock awareness, job insecurity, and convergent and defensive job reinvention. The specific research framework is shown in Fig. 1.

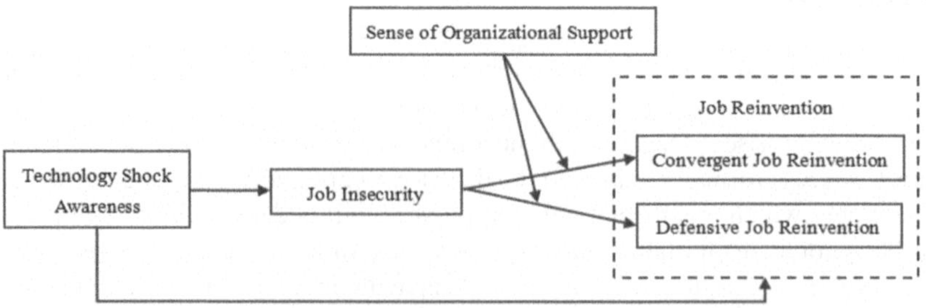

Fig. 1. Research framework model

2 Model Construction and Hypotheses Development

2.1 Technology Shock Awareness and Job Reinvention

Artificial intelligence technology is leading a new technological revolution, with some scholars predicting that one-third of jobs will be replaced by innovative technology and artificial intelligence by 2025, with a particularly significant substitution effect on women, older people, and less-educated and lower-income groups [6]. This means that corporate employees will face serious challenges, and their cognition and behavior will be affected by technological innovations and the development of digital technology. The introduction of digital technology places higher demands on employees' job skills, and employees need to take the initiative to change their job skills to adapt to organizational changes and perform better.

It has been found that when working conditions are poor or are faced with environmental uncertainty, employees adapt their work and exhibit extra-role behaviors through job reinvention. Resource conservation theory states that the loss of resources increases individuals' stress, prompting them to increase resource acquisition or minimize resource loss. In the face of perceived uncertainty due to advances in digital technology, employees may need to put more effort into approaching their work and acquiring resources through job reinvention to cope with the competency-job mismatch problem as well as the turbulent environment of the organization. Older employees have more resources than younger employees due to their long years of experience and knowledge, which facilitates them to make work behavior changes and pursue social work resources [7]. Therefore, technological shocks may motivate older employees to be more active in reaching out to external resources and accelerating the effectiveness of digital skills and knowledge [8], which may facilitate job reinvention behaviors. Based on these findings, the following hypothesis is proposed:

Hypothesis 1: Technology shock awareness significantly positively affects job reinvention among older employees.

2.2 The Mediating Role of Job Insecurity

Introducing digital intelligence technologies, especially artificial intelligence AI, often brings new work pressures and challenges. These pressures stem from the need to learn new technologies and concerns about career stability and growth. According to theoretical studies, anticipated organizational change is a prerequisite for job insecurity and has a magnifying effect. Scholars have argued that intelligent technologies and artificial intelligence will change the nature of work in the industry. Therefore, employees aware of smart technological changes will feel threatened in the face of these changes. For example, Ashford et al. noted that significant organizational changes such as mergers, layoffs, and new technologies tend to increase employees' perceived uncertainty and insecurity by threatening the psychological contract between the employee and the company. Nam (2019) also suggested that the degree of an individual's preparedness for the future environment affects their job insecurity perception. In addition, scholars such as Lingmont and Alexiou [9] further verified that perceptions of STARA lead to skepticism among workers, weakening job security and depleting mental resources. Based on these studies, the impact of digital intelligent technologies has led employees to anticipate technological innovations in their organizations and thus perceive higher levels of job insecurity. The following hypothesis is proposed:

Hypothesis 2: Technology awareness shock significantly positively affects job insecurity among older employees.

In the era of the digital economy, emerging digital technology changes are increasing employee stress, and job insecurity has become an essential stressor in the workplace [10], significantly affecting employees' psychological state and work behavior. Faced with the fear of unemployment and the threat of future job stability, employees may be motivated to change work tasks, increase work communication, and shift work perceptions to reduce the risk of unemployment or performance decline.

The cognitive appraisal theory of stress states that individuals differ in how they perceive and assess stressors in the organizational environment, which affects their behavioral outcomes. Job insecurity is a subjective feeling that emphasizes the interaction between the external environment and the employees and is closely related to the work environment, conditions, and personal resources. These differences lead to different levels of cognitive appraisal of job insecurity among employees. The cognitive appraisal theory of stress classifies the results of stressor assessment into two categories: "threatening" and "challenging" [11]. When individuals face pressure, challenging pressure assessment is likely to trigger active adaptation behavior, while threatening pressure assessment is more likely to trigger passive withdrawal behavior.

The cognitive evaluation of job insecurity is influenced by the stability of the work situation, the amount of available resources, and the amount of information. Employees with a stable work environment, abundant work resources, strong personal ability, and good development prospects tend to regard job insecurity as challenging. In contrast, older employees with rich experience and seniority and more external resources are more likely to consider job insecurity as a challenging assessment, which motivates them to adopt convergent job reinvention, such as expanding work tasks, exploring external perceptions, enriching interpersonal relationships, and upgrading their skills, etc. Relevant studies have also shown that when the external environment brings excellent benefits and confidence in overcoming stress, individuals' perception of job insecurity changes from passive and depletion to positive and challenging, stimulating the willingness to remodel work autonomously.

However, stressors have two-sided attributes that can stimulate both positive and negative responses in individuals. When employees perceive job insecurity as an obstructive need, this perception consumes their energy and resources, leading them to adopt avoidant defensive behaviors such as reducing the amount of work and lowering the difficulty of work, i.e., defensive job reinvention. Compared with younger employees, older employees are more likely to be out of touch with the information age, become "digital orphans" or "digital refugees", and are more sensitive and vulnerable to the technological job insecurity brought about by digital intelligent technologies. This heightened sensitivity and vulnerability exacerbate negative perceptions of job insecurity, leading employees to adopt negative attitudes and behaviors for strategic coping, stimulating defensive job reinvention. Based on the above, this study proposes the hypothesis:

Hypothesis 3: Job insecurity has a significant positive effect on older employees' convergent job reinvention.
Hypothesis 4: Job insecurity has a significant positive effect on older employees' defensive job reinvention.

In short, advances in automation and intelligent technologies are reshaping traditional working methods, making them data-driven and intelligent [12]. Emerging job skill requirements and business processes, among others, are placing higher demands on employees' work, and technological innovations in firms have become one of the primary sources of job insecurity for employees. In this context, employees are motivated to adjust the content and form of their work to maintain resource reserves, adapt to the organizational environment, and rediscover the meaning of their work. Job insecurity thus becomes a plausible path to explain how technological shocks affect the reshaping of employees' work. Therefore, the hypothesis is proposed:

Hypothesis 5: Job insecurity mediates the relationship between technology shock awareness and job reinvention among older employees.

2.3 The Moderating Role of Sense of Organizational Support

Organizational support is a positive social resource that mitigates the adverse effects of resource loss on employees and enhances their ability to give positive feedback about their work. A high sense of organizational support enhances employees' self-efficacy and makes them believe they can cope with challenges at work. This confidence helps employees to adopt proactive job reinvention behaviors rather than passive responses to job insecurity. In addition, the sense of organizational support enhances employees' commitment, motivating them to contribute to the organization and make positive job adjustments, which promotes positive job reinvention behaviors by reducing job stress and enhancing job satisfaction [13].

This study argues that the sense of organizational support enhances the positive effects of job insecurity on convergent job reinvention and attenuates its impact on defensive job reinvention. Organizational support provides older employees with the necessary external resources to help them learn new knowledge and acquire new skills. A high sense of organizational support enables older employees to access resources promptly despite technological shocks, clarifies new job requirements, replenishes depleted mental resources, and creates a resource-gaining effect that stimulates self-confidence and positive behaviors. On the contrary, if employees perceive insufficient organizational support, it will lead to difficulties in solving the problems they encounter in technological change promptly, exacerbate the sense of resource depletion, impede the adequate performance of work and career expectations, and prompt employees to adopt negative behaviors to cope with the uncertainty of the external environment and resource depletion. Based on this, this paper proposes:

Hypothesis 6: The sense of organizational support positively moderates the impact of job insecurity on older employees' convergent job reinvention. As the level of organizational support increases, the positive effect of job insecurity on convergent job reinvention increases.

Hypothesis 7: The sense of organizational support negatively moderates the effect of job insecurity on older employees' defensive job reinvention. As the level of organizational support increases, the positive impact of job insecurity on defensive job reinvention subsequently diminishes.
Hypothesis 8: Sense of organizational support moderates the indirect relationship between technology shock awareness and convergent and defensive job reinvention through job insecurity.

3 Research Methodology

3.1 Research Samples and Procedures

This study used questionnaire research to collect data, mainly utilizing the Credamo platform to distribute the questionnaires while inviting employees to fill them out at two technology-based companies focusing on smart technologies. The study samples were drawn from working employees aged 40 and above from 28 provinces in China, including Shandong, Hubei, Zhejiang, and Sichuan, covering job types such as production, technology, R&D, management, and general grassroots positions. The questionnaires were distributed in two phases with a one-week interval. The T1 phase collected demographic information, measured technology shock awareness and assessed the sense of organizational support variables. We distributed 500 questionnaires, and 387 valid questionnaires were retrieved, with a validity rate of 77.40%. The T2 phase collected the variables of job insecurity, convergent job reinvention, and defensive job reinvention. A total of 387 questionnaires were distributed, and 303 valid questionnaires were finally collected, with a validity rate of 78.29%.

3.2 Measuring Tool

This study measured the variables using mature scales widely used by foreign scholars and appropriately revised based on the local application in China. All the variables were measured using a five-point Likert scale.

Technology shock awareness: Drawing on the study of Xu Guanglu et al. (2023), a four-question item scale developed by Li et al. (2019) was used, such as "I think there is a high probability that my job will be replaced by digital technology" ($\alpha = 0.857$, CR $= 0.864$, AVE $= 0.614$).

Job insecurity: The 7-item job insecurity scale developed by Hellgren (1999) was used, which includes four reverse items, such as "I may be at risk of having to leave my current job." ($\alpha = 0.916$, CR $= 0.916$, AVE $= 0.610$).

Convergent job reinvention: The scale developed by Tims et al. (2013) was used, and the original scale consisted of three dimensions with a total of 15 items, of which 12 items were selected as representative considering the length of the questionnaire and the fact that some of the questions had similarities. For example, "I learn new things from my work" ($\alpha = 0.950$, CR $= 0.900$, AVE $= 0.600$).

Defensive job reinvention: The Tims et al. (2013) development scale was used, and as the convergent job reinvention, the four items with the highest loadings for this dimension were selected as representative, such as "I allow myself to minimize contact with those who affect me emotionally" ($\alpha = 0.858$, CR = 0.945, AVE = 0.591).

Sense of organizational support: Eisenberger's (1986) perceived organizational support scale was used, based on real-world scenarios, resulting in the selection of six high-loading representative items, such as "The organization considers and values the opinions and suggestions I make" ($\alpha = 0.907$, CR = 0.833, AVE = 0.655).

4 Results

Due to the subjective nature of the questionnaire filled out by employees on their own, this study used Harman's one-way analysis of variance to test the problem of homogeneous bias. The results were obtained that the initial eigenvalues of the five factors were greater than 1, and the variance explained ratio of the first factor was 35.54%, which was lower than the research standard value of 40%, indicating that there is no serious problem of covariance among the variables.

The study used SPSS 20.0 to test the reliability and validity of the data, and the results showed that the Cronbach's α values of all variables were above 0.8, and the scales had high reliability; the CR values were all greater than 0.8, and the internal consistency of the sample data was better; and the AVE values were above 0.5, and there was good convergent validity. Validated factor analysis was conducted using AMOS 24.0, and it can be seen from Table 1 that the five-factor model is optimally fitted and the variables can be effectively differentiated ($\chi2 = 557.75$; df = 485; $\chi2$/df = 1.15; RMSEA = 0.02; SRMR = 0.03; IFI = 0.98; TLI = 0.98; CFI = 0.98).

Table 1. Results of validation factor analysis

Model	Combination	$\chi2$	df	$\chi2$/df	RMSEA	SRMR	IFI	TLI	CFI
Five-factor	A; B; C; D; E	557.75	485	1.15	0.02	0.03	0.98	0.98	0.98
Four-factor	A; B; C; D + E	1037.03	489	2.12	0.06	0.07	0.91	0.90	0.91
Three-factor	A; B; C + D + E	1837.45	492	3.74	0.09	0.10	0.78	0.77	0.78
Two-factor	A; B + C + D + E	2795.83	494	5.66	0.12	0.13	0.63	0.60	0.63
One-factor	A + B + C + D + E	3184.33	495	6.43	0.13	0.14	0.57	0.53	0.56

Note(s): *A* technology shock awareness, *B* job insecurity, *C* sense of organizational support, *D* convergent job reinvention, *E* defensive job reinvention, the same as below.

The results of the descriptive statistics and correlation analysis are shown in Table 2, which indicates that there is a significant positive correlation between technology shock awareness and job insecurity ($r = 0.36$, $p < 0.01$), convergent job reinvention ($r = 0.39$, $p < 0.01$), and defensive job reinvention ($r = 0.25$, $p < 0.01$); and job insecurity was positively correlated with both convergent job reinvention ($r = 0.42$, $p < 0.01$) and defensive job reinvention ($r = 0.21$, $p < 0.01$) and was significant at the 0.01 level. In addition, the sense of organizational support was correlated with job insecurity, convergent job reinvention, and defensive job reinvention.

Table 2. Results of descriptive statistics and correlation analysis of variables

Variable	1	2	3	4	5	6	7	8	9	10
1 Age	–									
2 Gender	−0.07	–								
3 Education	−0.60**	0.02	–							
4 Years of working experience	0.92**	−0.04	−0.55**	–						
5 Position	0.10	−0.02	−0.11	0.07	–					
6 Technology shock awareness	−0.10	−0.01	0.09	−0.15*	0.04	–				
7 Job insecurity	−0.02	−0.09	0.06	−0.04	0.06	0.36**	–			
8 Sense of organizational support	−0.06	−0.02	0.15*	−0.08	0.05	0.41**	0.36**	–		
9 Convergent job reinvention	−0.02	−0.08	0.11	−0.02	0.06	0.39**	0.42**	0.44**	–	
10 Defensive job reinvention	0.01	−0.13*	0.06	−0.04	0.02	0.25**	0.21**	0.34**	0.30**	–
Mean	2.47	1.51	2.48	2.27	2.46	3.32	3.29	3.45	3.37	3.17
Standard deviation	1.01	0.50	0.80	0.97	0.98	0.98	0.96	0.97	0.95	1.02

Note(s): N = 303, ***$p < 0.001$, **$p < 0.01$, *$p < 0.05$, the same as below

As the data in Table 3 show, technology shock awareness positively affects the composite variable of job reinvention. From the combination of Model 3 and Model 7, technology shock awareness has a significant positive effect ($\beta = 0.39$, $p < 0.001$) on both convergent and defensive job reinvention ($\beta = 0.24$, $p < 0.001$). The data support hypothesis 1. In addition, the data from Model 2 in Table 3 showed a positive effect of technology shock awareness on employees' job insecurity ($\beta = 0.36$, $p < 0.001$), and hypothesis 2 was supported. Model 4 showed that job insecurity had a significant positive effect on convergent job reinvention ($\beta = 0.41$, $p < 0.001$) after controlling for relevant variables. The data from Model 8 in Table 3 indicated that job insecurity also had a significant positive effect on defensive job reinvention ($\beta = 0.19$, $p < 0.01$), and hypotheses 3 and 4 were supported.

To address the mediating role of job insecurity, this study used the Bootstrapping command to test the mediating effect with a confidence level interval of 95%. The results show that the indirect effect value of influencing older employees' convergent job reinvention behavior is 0.11, the confidence interval is [0.06, 0.17], and the interval excludes 0. The indirect effect value of influencing older employees' defensive job reinvention behavior is 0.05, the confidence interval is [0.01, 0.10], and the interval excludes 0. The mediating effect is significant, indicating that job insecurity has a mediating effect

Table 3. Results of regression analysis

Variable	Job insecurity		Convergent job reinvention			
	Model 1	**Model 2**	**Model 3**	**Model 4**	**Model 5**	**Model 6**
Control variable						
Age	0.17	0.09	−0.08	−0.07	−0.11	−0.09
Gender	−0.09	−0.09	−0.08	−0.04	−0.05	−0.06
Education	0.08	0.06	0.13	0.12	0.11	0.07
Years of experience	−0.17	−0.05	0.19	0.13	0.20	0.13
Position	0.06	0.05	0.05	0.05	0.04	0.02
Independent variable						
Technology shock awareness		0.36***	0.39***		0.28***	
Mediator variable						
Job insecurity				0.41***	0.31***	0.24***
Moderator variable						
Sense of organizational support						0.32***
Interaction term: B × C						0.15**
Adj R2	0.02	0.14	0.17	0.19	0.25	0.30
ΔR2	0.02	0.12	0.15	0.16	0.08	0.11
F	1.31***	8.25***	10.33***	11.40***	14.37***	15.45***

Continued from Table 3.

Variable	Job insecurity		Defensive job reinvention			
	Model 1	**Model 2**	**Model 7**	**Model 8**	**Model 9**	**Model 10**
Control variable						
Age	0.17	0.10	0.21	0.23	0.19	0.19
Gender	−0.09	−0.09	−0.13	−0.11	−0.12	−0.10
Education	0.08	0.06	0.07	0.07	0.06	0.03
Years of experience	−0.17	−0.05	−0.16	−0.21	−0.15	−0.17
Position	0.06	0.05	0.01	0.01	0.00	0.00
Independent variable						
Technology shock awareness		0.36***	0.24***		0.20**	
Mediator variable						
Job insecurity				0.19**	0.12*	0.13*
Moderator variable						
Sense of organizational support						0.30***

(*continued*)

Table 3. (*continued*)

Interaction term: B × C						−0.13*
Adj R2	0.02	0.14	0.09	0.07	0.10	0.156
ΔR2	0.02	0.12	0.06	0.04	0.01	0.09
F	1.31***	8.25***	4.70***	3.54**	4.66***	6.84***

between technology shock awareness and convergent job reinvention and defensive job reinvention, and hypothesis 5 was supported.

As shown in Model 6 of Table 3, the positive effect of the interaction term between job insecurity and sense of organizational support on convergent job reinvention was significant ($\beta = 0.15$, $p < 0.01$); Model 10 indicated that the negative impact of the interaction term on defensive job reinvention was significant ($\beta = -0.13$, $p < 0.05$), and Hypotheses 6 and 7 were supported. To further clarify the magnitude of the moderating effect, simple slope moderating effect plots were made, as shown in Figs. 2 and 3. Figure 2 shows that the slope of the graph increases significantly from the low level of perceived organizational support to the high level, indicating the positive moderating effect of job insecurity on convergent job reinvention, further validating Hypothesis 6. Similarly, the apparent difference in slopes in Fig. 3 validates the negative moderating effect of perceptions of organizational support on defensive job reinvention, further supporting hypothesis 7.

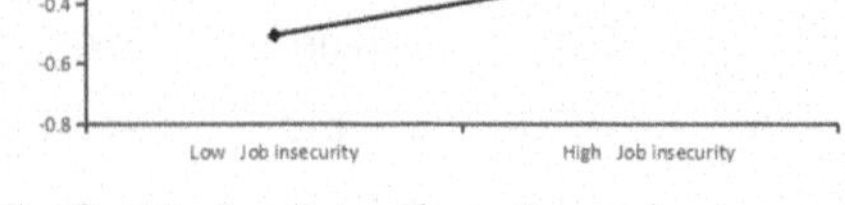

Fig. 2. Moderating effect of perceived organizational support on the job insecurity-convergent job reinvention

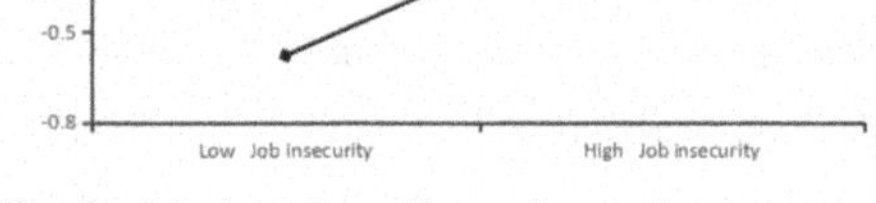

Fig. 3. Moderating effect of perceived organizational support on job insecurity-defensive job reinvention

This study further conducted a moderated mediated effects test with the help of model 14 of PROCESS with Bootstrap repeated sampling number of 5000, and the results are shown in Table 4. At lower levels of perceived organizational support, technology shock awareness has no significant indirect effect on convergent job reinvention (indirect effect value = 0.03, 95%CI = [−0.03, 0.09]). When perceived organizational support is high, technology shock awareness has a significant indirect effect on convergent job reinvention via job insecurity (indirect effect value = 0.12, 95%CI = [0.06, 0.19]). Similarly, the data in Table 4 confirm the significant indirect effect of technology shock awareness on defensive job reinvention through job insecurity at low levels of organizational support (indirect effect value = 0.10, 95%CI = [0.03, 0.18]). Thus, it can be found that there is a difference in the mediating effect of job insecurity at different levels of perceived organizational support. Hypothesis 8 was supported.

Table 4. Sense of organizational support moderates indirect effects

Path	Moderator variable	Indirect effect value	Standard error	95% Confidence interval	
				Lower limit	Upper limit
Technology shock awareness —Job insecurity —Convergent job reinvention	Low organizational support	0.03	0.03	−0.03	0.09
	High organizational support	0.12	0.04	0.06	0.19
	Difference	0.09	0.04	0.01	0.18
Technology shock awareness —Job insecurity —Defensive job reinvention	Low organizational support	0.10	0.04	0.03	0.18
	High organizational support	−0.01	0.03	−0.07	0.05
	Difference	−0.10	0.05	−0.22	−0.01

5 Conclusion and Discussion

This study explored the effects of technology shock awareness on the cognition and behavior of older employees, identifying the mediating role of job insecurity and the moderating role of the sense of organizational support. The research result found that technology shock awareness positively affects older employees' job reinvention, and technology shock awareness increases older employees' convergent job reinvention and defensive job reinvention behaviors by influencing employees' sense of insecurity. Employees' perceived organizational support moderates job insecurity. The relationship between convergent job reinvention and job insecurity-defensive job reinvention is such that when the level of perceived organizational support is high, the positive effect of job insecurity on convergent job reinvention is more substantial. In contrast, the positive effect of defensive job reinvention is weaker.

5.1 Theoretical Contributions and Practical Implications

The theoretical contribution lies in: Firstly, focusing on the job reinvention behaviors of a particular group of older employees based on the context of an aging workforce expands the understanding of how the development of digital technology affects the outcomes of employees' roles; Secondly, it enriches the results on employees' job reinvention, explores the influencing factors of job reinvention from the level of individual subjective perception, and verifies the mediating role of job insecurity between the technology shock awareness and job reinvention behaviors; Thirdly, based on the dual perspective of "resource-pressure", we explore the mechanism and boundary conditions of the technology shock awareness within the enterprise on the convergent and defensive job reinvention behaviors of the employees, and reveal the influence of the organizational context on the employees' cognitive assessment of the stressors, which provides new perspectives for the research in the field of job insecurity.

Technology impact awareness has a double-edged sword effect on job reshaping, so enterprises need to help managers recognize the dual attributes of technology shock awareness and provide conditions for employees to adapt to job changes actively. On the one hand, correctly guide employees' cognition on the impact of intelligent technology on employment. By strengthening publicity and training on the process and purpose of technological change, activating individual digital self-efficacy, promoting self-driven learning, and encouraging older employees' awareness of the positive effects brought about by technological change, digital worries and psychological threats due to technological shocks are reduced. On the other hand, moderating effects analysis shows that organizational support is essential in stimulating employees' convergent job reinvention or defensive job reinvention. Under the high organizational support level, enterprises can further optimize internal resource allocation and amplify the active adaptation behavior of older employees in the face of technological shocks; under the low organizational support level, enterprises can increase the frequency of communication with employees and pay more attention to the emotional needs and feelings of employees in the process of change, to make employees realize the win-win effect brought by technological introduction, thus weakening to a certain extent the passive retraction behavior of employees in the face of technological shocks.

5.2 Limitations and Future Perspectives

There are also several limitations in this study. First, only factors such as age, gender, education, and position are selected as control variables, ignoring the influence of potential factors such as technological complexity and the enterprise's digitalization level on the inferred results. We suggested that future research could compare the differences between employees in traditional industries and non-technical positions to explore the impact of technology shock awareness on employees' work behavior more deeply. Second, the data mainly comes from questionnaires, a relatively single source. In the future, experimental and sampling methods can be added to diversify the data sources. Third, this study focuses on the group of older employees, and in the future, the relationship between technology shock awareness and the job reinvention behavior of new-generation employees can be explained in depth.

References

1. Wang, Z.J., Zhang, L.Y., Yang, Y.Y.: Job crafting in late career stage and successful aging at work. Adv. Psychol. Sci. **09**, 1643–1655 (2019) (in Chinese)
2. Umair, A., Conboy, K., Whelan, E.: Examining technostress and its impact on worker well-being in the digital gig economy. Internet Res. **33**(7), 206–242 (2023)
3. Brougham, D., David, P., Haar, J., Jarrod.: Smart technology, artificial intelligence, robotics, and algorithms (STARA): employees' perceptions of our future workplace. J. Manag. Organ. **24**(2), 239–257 (2018)
4. Wang, Q.Q., Liu, J., Yuan, Y.W.: Exhaustion or engagement? The double-edged sword effect of prevention-oriented job crafting. Nankai Manag. Rev., 1–22 (2024) (in Chinese)
5. Qiao, Y.S., Qiao, R.S., Chen, L.H.: The influence of participative leadership on team performance: the multilevel chain mediating effect of perceived organizational support and subordinates' moqi. Manag. Rev. **35**(3), 196–206 (2023) (in Chinese)
6. Wang, C.C., Nie, Y.F.: Research progress on the effects of digital economy on employment. Econ. Dyn. **4**, 134–149 (2023) (in Chinese)
7. Zacher, H., Kooij, D.T., Beier, M.E.: Successful aging at work: empirical and methodological advancements. Work Aging Retire. **4**(2), 123–128 (2018)
8. Zhu, Y.Y., Zhang, M.F.: The double-edged sword effect of technology shock awareness on manufacturing employees' proactive skill development: a study based on SEM and fsQCA. Sci. Technol. Progr. Countermeasures, 1–12 (2024) (in Chinese)
9. Lingmont, D.N.J., Alexiou, A.: The contingent effect of job automating technology awareness on perceived job insecurity: exploring the moderating role of organizational culture. Technol. Forecast. Soc. Chang. **161**, 120302 (2020)
10. Lin, W., Shao, Y., Li, G., Guo, Y., Zhan, X.: The psychological implications of COVID-19 on employee job insecurity and its consequences: the mitigating role of organization adaptive practices. J. Appl. Psychol. **106**(3), 317–329 (2021)
11. Zhang, Y., Zhang, Y., Ng, T.W., Lam, S.S.: Promotion-and prevention-focused coping: a meta-analytic examination of regulatory strategies in the work stress process. J. Appl. Psychol. **104**(10), 1296–1323 (2019)
12. Wang, B.C., He, M.M., Zhao, J.Y.: Impact of job autonomy on business model innovation in the digital era. Stat. Inform. Forum. **1-10** (2024) (in Chinese)
13. Kurtessis, J.N., Eisenberger, R., Ford, M.T., Buffardi, L.C., Stewart, K.A., Adis, C.S.: Perceived organizational support: a meta-analytic evaluation of organizational support theory. J. Manag. **43**(6), 1854–1884 (2017)

Advertising or Freemium: The Revenue Model Decisions for Competing Artificial Intelligence-Based Platforms

Siyuan Wang[1(✉)], Lin Wang[1,2(✉)], Zhiyong Li[1,2(✉)], and Donghan Wang[1,2(✉)]

[1] School of Economics and Management, Communication University of China, Beijing 100024, China
202219063020@mails.cuc.edu.cn, {carolinewang,zyli, dhwang}@cuc.edu.cn

[2] State Key Laboratory of Media Convergence and Communication, Communication University of China, Beijing 100024, China

Abstract. Artificial intelligence (AI) has gained significant prominence in technological development, resulting in an increasing prevalence of AI-based platforms. These platforms typically employ either an advertising-based revenue model offering basic services, versus a freemium model providing free basic services alongside premium paid features. We develop a game-theoretic framework to analyze strategic revenue model selection in duopoly AI platform competition. The analysis demonstrates that when premium service quality is sufficiently low (high), competing platforms are compelled to adopt homogeneous advertising-based (freemium) models. At intermediate quality levels, platforms achieve equilibrium through differentiated revenue model adoption.

Keywords: AI platforms · Data network effect · Freemium · Advertising · Competition · Game theory

1 Introduction

With the rapid development of Artificial Intelligence (AI) technologies, AI applications have increasingly become an integral part of various industries and platforms. This technological penetration manifests in four key domains: social media platforms (e.g., TikTok, Instagram) employing AI-powered recommendation systems; video processing platforms (e.g., Vimeo); creative design tools (e.g., Figma, Canva); intelligent office suites (e.g., Sana AI, Otter AI). These implementations systematically harness AI capabilities to optimize user engagement metrics and augment core product functionalities.

The exponential advancement of AI technologies has precipitated their ubiquitous integration across industrial and digital platform ecosystems. The data network effect denotes a self-reinforcing mechanism wherein platform value exhibits positive correlation with cumulative user data acquisition. Through iterative data refinement cycles,

Y. P. Tu and M. Chi (Eds.): WHICEB 2025, LNBIP 549, pp. 16–26, 2025.
https://doi.org/10.1007/978-3-031-94184-9_2

platforms achieve dual optimization: service quality enhancement via machine learning pipelines, and consumer surplus maximization through personalized feature adaptation. The service quality improves with the increasing amount of data, creating a positive feedback loop. These network effects critically determine platform operators' revenue model selection through the lens of dynamic game theory. The strategic dichotomy in revenue model adoption is empirically evidenced across platform markets. Within the office software market, a salient example is evident in the competition among Sana AI, Otter.ai, and Gamma. Sana AI's pricing stratification comprises: Free Tier (10 meetings/month): 5-member limit; Team Tier ($30/user/month): Open AI and Claude model selection; Enterprise Tier: Extended range of LLMs. Similarly, Otter.ai offers a basic free version but charges for enhanced team features and more transcription through its Pro and Business plans. Gamma also provides a free basic version, with its paid Plus and Pro versions delivering more advanced AI editing services. This strategic landscape reveals a binary equilibrium: platforms converge on either advertisement-subsidized or feature-tiered freemium monetization frameworks.

How do duopolistic platforms achieve profit maximization through strategic pricing calibration across heterogeneous revenue model configurations? What equilibrium selection mechanisms govern platform operators' revenue model adoption under Nash bargaining frameworks? To answer these questions, we develop a game-theoretic model to investigate the revenue model decisions for competing AI-based platforms. We find that the advertising (freemium) model is dominant for each platform when the quality of the premium service is too low (high).

The contribution of this paper lies in offering a novel perspective on the revenue model decisions for competing platforms in the context of the growing prominence of artificial intelligence, providing theoretical support and practical in-sights for platform strategy in the rapidly evolving AI-driven market.

2 Literature Review

Three streams of research are closely related to our study. The first stream is the work on AI product. In the field of artificial intelligence, the highbrow debate is not just the nature of intelligence but a practical discussion of revenue models. Jacobides et al. (2021) distinguish between AI enablement, AI production, and AI consumption and analyze the emerging patterns of co-specialization between firms and communities. They also point out that a small number of Big Tech firms dominate top academic institutions in AI research. Following the previous literature, our paper carries out research on AI products and deeply analyze their revenue model decision-making mechanism in the context of big data and AI era.

The second stream of research related to our study is the work that examines the effect of data network effect. AI Flywheel effect designates a virtuous cycle by which as an ML product is adopted and new user data are fed back to the algorithm, the product improves, enabling further adoptions. Firms can boost its profit by increasing the product's capacity to acquire usage data only up to a certain level (Gurkan and de Véricourt, 2022). Gregory et al. (2021) claim the definition of data network effects, which is the more that the platform learns from the data it collects on users, the more valuable the platform becomes to each user. They also develop a model of data network effects to prove that there is a positive direct relationship between the AI capability of a platform and the value perceived in the platform by its users—a relationship that is moderated by platform legitimation, data stewardship and user centric design. Our paper is built on the previous literature but focuses on the decision-making process regarding revenue models for AI-based platforms.

The third stream of work related to ours is the study of revenue model decisions. Our model builds on the theoretical literature on freemium and advertising revenue models. Freemium revenue models are characterized by the simultaneous existence of free and premium versions of the same product (Mei et al., 2022). Shi et al. (2019) points out that the asymmetry in network effects is the necessary conditions for the optimality of freemium. In our paper, we study AI-based platforms with data network effects. Gardete and Guo (2020) strengthen that in-formative advertising can not only increase consumers' expected value, but also induces more information acquisition and thus hurts the firm's ability to extract consumer surplus. Latest literatures in advertising models connect the subscription with advertisement. De Valve and Pekeč (2022) demonstrate that platforms profit from the collection between multiple subscription price and advertising quantity pairs. They conclude that platforms can increase revenues by exploiting heterogeneity in consumer disutility for ads. Our paper investigates that under these two kinds of revenue models, how AI-based platforms make choices.

3 Model

We consider a market with two competing platforms: Platforms 1 and 2 that integrate AI (artificial intelligence) into their services. The platforms differ in the taste/fit attribute, which represents the horizontal dimension in the sense that preferences vary across consumers (i.e., horizontal differentiation). The quality determines the intrinsic value derived by consumers from a service, whereas the taste describes a disutility due to the misfit between a consumer's ideal service and that which the consumer consumes.

Platforms. Without loss of generality, platform 1 is located at 0, and platform 2 is located at 1. It is a standard Hotelling model that has been adopted by most of the existing research. Platforms choose modes of financing using either an advertisement revenue model (AM) or a freemium revenue model (FM). Under an AM, a platform acts an intermediary and provides connections between advertisers and consumers. There are two essential ways to charge advertisers for connections. First, the platform can charge a lump-sum fee. Second, it can charge a fee based on the consumer size such as cost per thousand impressions, cost per action, and cost per click-through. In this paper, we focus on the former approach. Under a FM, the platform excludes the advertiser side and serves consumers with free and paid services. Because there are two opinions for each platform, four market configurations are possible; that is as follows.

- Both use an AM, denoted as Case AA.
- Only Platform 1 uses an AM, denoted as Case AF.
- Only Platform 1 uses an FM, denoted as Case FA.
- Both use an FM, denoted as Case FF.

Consumers. Consumers with a unit mass are uniformly distributed along a unit line in terms of their preferences. A consumer's location represents his ideal service. When a consumer purchases a service that does not perfectly match his ideal taste, he will incur a misfit cost, which increases with the distance between the location of his ideal service and the service he buys. For the sake of convenient calculation, we normalize the unit misfit cost for using the basic service to 1. Since the premium service is a whole unit and includes a basic service and an add-on service, more functionalities cause consumers to incur more learning and implementation costs. These characteristics imply that a consumer's unit misfit cost for the premium service (denoted by β) is more than that of using the basic service. Following the previous literature (Li et al., 2020), we assume >1. In addition, if platforms use an FM, the overall value of basic and premium services is denoted by s. If platforms use an AM, the intrinsic value of basic service is denoted by v .

The nature of data network effects is that the more that the platform learns from the data it collects on users, the more valuable the platform becomes to each user and the more utility the consumers will derive. Following the previous literature (Gregory et al. 2021), we assume that platforms equipped with Artificial Intelligence (AI) service functionalities can leverage data network effects to enhance quality. Due to the relatively lower quality of data disclosed by users in the advertising model, the quality improvement is less than that in the freemium model. Consequently, we define the enhanced quality for platform i adopting AM as $v\left(1+D_i^z\right), i \in \{1,2\}, z \in \{AA, AF, FA, FF\}$, and the enhanced qualities of basic service and premium service for platforms adopting i FM as $v\left(1+\alpha D_i^z\right)$ and $s\left(1+\alpha D_i^z\right)$, respectively, where α means intensity of data network effects, $\alpha > 1$.

When platform i adopts an FM, there are two options for consumers: a free basic service and a paid premium service with price $p_i^k, k \in \{AF, FA, FF\}$. However,when platform i adopts an AM, using free basic service is the consumers' only option. Different from the former basic service, the latter includes embedded advertisements, which causes consumers to incur some nuisance costs, denoted by $\xi\psi Q_i^j, j\in\{AA, AF, FA\}$, where ψ measures the disutility incurred by a consumer from interacting with an advertisement, ξ is the expected probability for the display of each advertisement, and Q_i^j is platform i's advertiser demand. Thus, $\xi\psi$ is the expected strength of the cross-side network effects. For simplicity, let $\xi\psi$ be b.

Each consumer uses only one type of service provided by the competing platforms and participates in the platform that gives him the most nonnegative utility. It is appropriate for our setting because of consumer' limited online time and inherent preference for a specific platform. In addition, if the consumer side is multi-homing, each platform will become a local monopoly. This setting is not our focus.

We define a consumer's net utility as the total utility from consuming the service upgraded by data minus the service's price. If the platform uses an FM, its consumer's total utility is the sum of a base utility from consuming the service. If the platform uses an AM, its consumer's total utility should continue to add the negative cross-side network utility derived from advertisements. Following the existing literature (Li et al., 2020), we use the rational/fulfilled expectations equilibrium concept, which means that the agents' (i.e., consumers' and/or advertisers') expected network size is equal to the actual network size in equilibrium. Consumer surplus is summarized as follows.

When both platforms adopt AM, the surpluses are as follows:

$$U_1 = v\left(1 + D_1^j\right) - x - bQ_1^j \tag{1}$$

$$U_2 = v\left(1 + D_2^j\right) - (1 - x) - bQ_2^j \tag{2}$$

When platform 1 adopts an AM, whereas platform 2 opts for an FM, surplus Eq. (1) is the consumer surplus of using platform 1's basic service. The consumer surplus of using platform 2's premium service (denoted by U_{2F}) and that of using its basic service (denoted by U_{2f}) are:

$$U_{2F} = s\left(1 + \alpha D_2^j\right) - \beta(1 - x) - p_2 \tag{3}$$

$$U_{2f} = v\left(1 + \alpha D_2^j\right) - (1 - x) \tag{4}$$

When platform 2 adopts an AM, whereas platform 1 opts for an FM, surplus Eq. (2) is the consumer surplus of using platform 1's basic service. The consumer surplus of using platform 1's premium service (denoted by U_{1F}) and that of using its basic service (denoted by U_{1f}) are

$$U_{1F} = s\left(1 + \alpha D_1^j\right) - \beta x - p_1 \tag{5}$$

$$U_{1f} = v\left(1 + \alpha D_1^j\right) - x \tag{6}$$

When both platforms adopt FM, surplus Eqs. (5) and (6) are the consumer surpluses of using platform 1's premium and basic services, respectively; and surplus Eqs. (3) and (4) are the consumer surpluses of using platform 2's premium and basic services, respectively.

Advertisers. A unit mass of advertisers show their products/services with advertisements through platforms. Consistent with the existing studies on two-sided markets (Li et al., 2020), each advertiser is seen as selling a distinct product or service and, thus, the competition among advertisers is not considered in the model. Advertisers pay w_i^j to access customers. In addition, advertisers incur different fixed costs f of advertising goods through the platform. The costs satisfy a uniform distribution with support [0, 1].

For advertisers, more consumers may enable an advertiser to yield more profits. In other words, there are positive cross-side network effects for advertisers. Similar to the previous literature (Li et al., 2020), we model cross-side network effects as a function of the network size. An advertiser derives an expected payoff eD_i^z for using platform i's service, where e is the strength of the cross-side network effects on the advertiser side, which presents the benefit derived by an advertiser from the participation of each consumer. To summarize, the profit of platform i's advertiser is given by $U_i^A = eD_i^z - f - w_i^j$. Following the previous literature (Li et al., 2020), we assume advertisers are multi-homing, and if $U_i^A \geq 0$, an advertiser participates in platform i. In essence, when both platforms use AM, our setting is essentially a model of competitive bottlenecks (Zhang et al., 2022).

As illustrated in Fig. 1., the model has three stages. In stage 1, competing platforms decide which revenue model to choose. In stage 2, platforms determine the price w_i^j for advertisers and price p_i^k for consumers. In stage 3, consumers and advertisers decide which platform to join. All notations are summarized in Table 1.

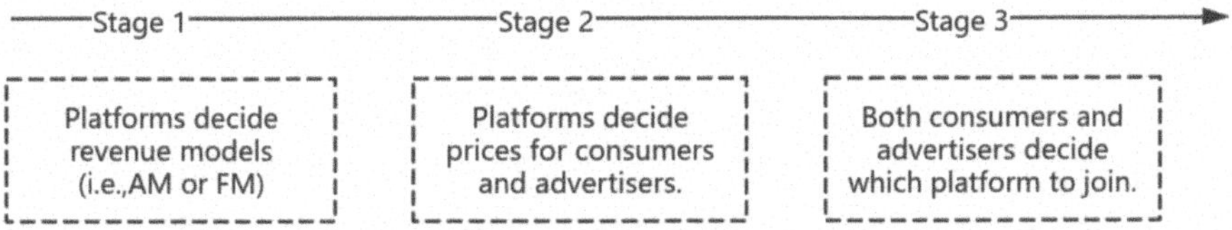

Fig. 1. Sequences of events

Table 1. Summary of notations

Decision variables	
p_i^k	Price of premium service sold by platform i when the options regarding service provision are given by k, where $i \in \{1, 2\}$ *and* $k \in \{AF, FA, FF\}$
w_i^j	Price of advertising service sold by platform i when the options regarding Service provision are given by j, where $i \in \{1, 2\}$ *and* $j \in \{AA, AF, FA\}$
Other variables	
D_i^z	Platform i's consumer demand, where $i \in \{1, 2\}$ *and* $z \in \{AA, AF, FA, FF\}$
Q_i^j	Platform i's advertiser demand, where $i \in \{1, 2\}$ *and* $j \in \{AA, AF, FA\}$
π_i^z	Platform i's profit, where $i \in \{1, 2\}$ *and* $z \in \{AA, AF, FA, FF\}$
U_i^A	Payoff of the advertiser on platform i, where $i \in \{1, 2\}$
Parameters	
v	Intrinsic value of platform i's basic product
s	Overall intrinsic value of platform i's basic and premium services
f	Advertiser' fixed cost for providing its product or service through a platform
α	Intensity of data network effects for an additional consumer data to service quality
b	Intensity of network effects for an additional advertiser to consumers
e	Intensity of network effects for an additional consumer to advertisers
β	Unit misfit cost for using the premium service

4 Equilibrium Analysis

When both platforms adopt AM, the equilibrium outcomes are summarized in the following lemma.

Lemma 1 In the case AA, the equilibrium prices are

$$w_1^{AA} = \frac{e(be - v + 1)}{3be - 4v + 4},$$

$$w_2^{AA} = \frac{e(be - v + 1)}{3be - 4v + 4},$$

the equilibrium demands are

$$Q_1^{AA} = \frac{e[be - 2(v - 1)]}{6\text{be} - 8(v - 1)},$$

$$Q_2^{AA} = \frac{e[be - 2(v - 1)]}{6\text{be} - 8(v - 1)},$$

and the equilibrium profits are

$$\pi_1^{AA} = \frac{e^2[be - 2(v - 1)][be - (v - 1)]}{2[3be - 4(v - 1)]^2},$$

$$\pi_2^{AA} = \frac{e^2[be - 2(v - 1)][be - (v - 1)]}{2[3be - 4(v - 1)]^2}.$$

When platform 1 adopt the AM while platform 2 adopt the FM, the equilibrium outcomes are summarized in the following lemma.

Lemma 2 In the case AF, the equilibrium prices are

$$w_1^{AF} = \frac{e(\alpha v - 1)}{2(\alpha v + v - 2)},$$

$$p_2^{AF} = \frac{(s - v)\{(-4\alpha^2 - 6\alpha - 2)v^2 + [(be + 2)\alpha^2 + (4be + 14)\alpha + 2be + 8]v - 3\alpha be - 4be - 4\alpha - 8\}}{4[(\alpha + 1)v - 2][(-\alpha - 1)v + be + 2]},$$

the equilibrium demands are

$$Q_1^{AF} = \frac{e(\alpha v - 1)}{2(\alpha v - be + v - 2)},$$

$$D_2^{AF} = \frac{(s - v)\{(-4\alpha^2 - 6\alpha - 2)v^2 + [(be + 2)\alpha^2 + (4be + 14)\alpha + 2be + 8]v - 3\alpha be - 4be - 4\alpha - 8\}}{4[(\alpha + 1)v - 2][(-\alpha - 1)v + be + 2](\beta - 1)},$$

and the equilibrium profits are

$$\pi_1^{AF} = \frac{e^2(\alpha v - 1)^2}{4(\alpha v + v - 2)(\alpha v - be + v - 2)},$$

$$\pi_2^{AF} = \frac{(s - v)^2\{(-4\alpha^2 - 6\alpha - 2)v^2 + [(be + 2)\alpha^2 + (4be + 14)\alpha + 2be + 8]v - 3\alpha be - 4be - 4\alpha - 8\}^2}{16[(-\alpha - 1)v + be + 2]^2[(\alpha + 1)v - 2]^2(\beta - 1)}.$$

When both platforms adopt FM, the equilibrium outcomes are summarized in the following lemma.

Lemma 3 In the case FF, the equilibrium prices are

$$p_1^{FF} = \frac{(\alpha + 2)(s - v)}{4},$$

$$p_2^{FF} = \frac{(\alpha + 2)(s - v)}{4},$$

the equilibrium demands are

$$D_1^{FF} = \frac{(\alpha + 2)(s - v)}{4(\beta - 1)},$$

$$D_2^{FF} = \frac{(\alpha + 2)(s - v)}{4(\beta - 1)},$$

and the equilibrium profits are

$$\pi_1^{FF} = \frac{(\alpha + 2)^2(s - v)^2}{16(\beta - 1)},$$

$$\pi_2^{FF} = \frac{(\alpha + 2)^2(s - v)^2}{16(\beta - 1)}.$$

Based on the above lemmas, we can derive the condition under which different revenue model profiles are Nash Equilibria.

Proposition 1 Market Equilibria under Different Conditions:

- Case AA is an equilibrium in which both platforms adopt AM, if and only if $s < v + k_1\sqrt{\beta - 1}$.
- Case AF or Case FA is an equilibrium in which only one platform adopts AM, if and only if $\min\{v + k_1\sqrt{\beta - 1}, v + k_2\sqrt{\beta - 1}\} < s < \max\{v + k_1\sqrt{\beta - 1}, v + k_2\sqrt{\beta - 1}\}$.
- Case FF is an equilibrium in which both platforms adopt FM, if and only if $s > v + k_2\sqrt{\beta - 1}$.

where
$k_1 = \frac{4e\sqrt{[be-2(v-1)][be-(v-1)]}[(\alpha+1)v-2][(-\alpha-1)v+be+2]}{\sqrt{2}\{(-4\alpha^2-6\alpha-2)v^2+[(be+2)\alpha^2+(4be+14)\alpha+2be+8]v-3\alpha be-4be-4\alpha-8\}[3be-4(v-1)]}$,
and $k_2 = \frac{2e(1-\alpha v)}{(\alpha+2)\sqrt{(\alpha v+v-2)(\alpha v-be+v-2)}}$. This is graphically shown in Fig. 2.

Figure 2 illustrates that when β remains constant, the market equilibrium transitions through different states depending on the value of s. Specifically, the equilibrium is AA when s is relatively low, shifts to either FA or AF under moderate values of s, and ultimately settles into FF as s becomes sufficiently large.

When premium service quality s is low, competing platforms will simultaneously opt for the advertising model. Social media platforms such as TikTok, Facebook, and

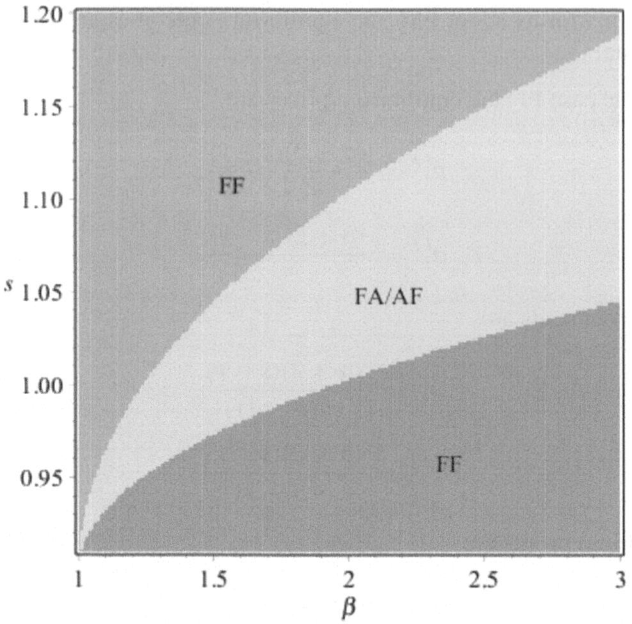

Fig. 2. Market equilibria*Note.* Parameter values are $\alpha = 1.2$, $v = 0.9$, $b = 3$, $e = 1$.

Instagram exemplify this behavior. These platforms offer free access to their core services but rely on advertisement to generate revenue. The minimal quality advantage of premium services in this context stems from the fact that the differences between free and paid features are not as pronounced as in freemium models. Instead, platforms choose to monetize user data and attention through advertisements, capitalizing on their vast user base and engagement metrics to attract advertisers.

When premium service quality s is high, competing platforms will simultaneously adopt the freemium model. This equilibrium pattern is empirically validated in the office SaaS sector, exemplified by the tripartite competition between Sana AI, Otter.ai, and Gamma. These platforms provide free basic versions to individual users but charge for advanced features that significantly enhance user experience. Sana AI's pricing stratification comprises: Free Tier (10 meetings/month): 5-member limit; Team Tier ($30/user/month): Open AI and Claude model selection; Enterprise Tier: Extended range of LLMs. Similarly, Otter.ai provides a basic free version, but its Pro and Business plans offer enhanced team collaboration features and additional transcription capacity, which significantly improve productivity. Gamma follows a similar approach, offering a free basic version while its Plus and Pro plans provide more advanced AI-powered editing tools, delivering a clear quality advantage. In the office software market, the high quality of these premium services creates strong incentives for users to opt for the paid versions, making the freemium model a highly effective strategy for these platforms to monetize their offerings.

However, when premium service quality s is medium, competing platforms will choose different revenue models, with one platform selecting the advertising model and the other opting for the freemium model. Within the video platform market, Vimeo's subscription member count in the second quarter of 2021 increased by 17% compared to the same period in the previous year. Vimeo provides users with the ability to upload, store, and share videos, while its freemium model offers additional value through premium services such as increased storage capacity and advanced video management features. These features provide users with a clear quality advantage over the free version, making the freemium model a suitable choice for Vimeo's revenue generation. In contrast, platforms like TikTok and Instagram, which are also video-sharing services, primarily rely on advertising as their main revenue source. For example, the advertising revenue accounts for approximately 80% of TikTok's annual total income. This is because the quality advantage offered by premium services in these platforms is relatively minimal. While both TikTok and Instagram allow users to upload and share videos for free, the differences in functionality between the free and paid versions do not provide enough of a competitive edge to justify widespread adoption of the freemium model. As a result, these platforms opt for advertising-based monetization, capitalizing on their large user bases and high engagement to generate revenue from advertisers.

5 Conclusion and Limitations

Grounded in the technological proliferation of AI, this research develops a game-theoretic duopoly framework to analyze strategic revenue model selection (advertising vs. freemium) in competing AI platforms. Our model innovates the traditional consumer utility function by introducing data network effect which is characteristic in AI-based platforms.

This study provides important implications for both research and practice. Our analysis reveals that data is an important resource for AI-based platforms, that is, the more data platforms collect from users, the higher quality of products platforms can provide. There are two main revenue models for platforms to decide: freemium and advertising. Our result implies that the advertising (freemium) model is dominant for each platform when its service quality improved by data network effect is too low (high). Therefore, platform managers should be aware that the level of improved quality is vital in determining revenue models.

Our findings offer practical implications for AI-based platforms. Social media platforms like TikTok and Facebook ought to adopt advertising revenue model, allowing them to profit from advertisers. Office software platforms such as Sana AI and Otter.ai should endeavor to improve the quality and adopt freemium revenue model, enabling them to profit from freemium service. By tailoring their strategies according to the improved quality, platforms can optimize their operations, enhance user satisfaction, and achieve better performance.

This study has several limitations that provide opportunities for future research. On the one hand, this study considers data network effect to innovate the consumer utility function. Future studies could extend the model by considering other characteristics of AI-based platforms. On the other hand, future studies could investigate the impact of different models of data ownership and product copyright on the revenue models of competing AI-based platforms.

Acknowledgments. This research is supported by research grant from the National Natural Science Foundation of China (No. 72472143), the Key Program of National Natural Science Foundation of China (No. U21B20102).

References

De Valve, L., Pekeč, S.: Optimal Price/advertising menus for two-sided media platforms. Oper. Res. **70**(3), 1629–1645 (2022)

Gardete, P.M., Guo, L.: Prepurchase information acquisition and credible advertising. Manag. Sci. **67**(3), 1696–1717 (2020)

Gregory RW, Henfridsson O, Kaganer E. The role of artificial intelligence and data network effects for creating user value. Acad. Manag. Rev., 2021, 46(3): 534-551

Gurkan, H., de Véricourt, F.: Contracting, pricing, and data collection under the AI flywheel effect. Manag. Sci. **68**(12), 8791–8808 (2022)

Jacobides, M.G., Brusoni, S., Candelon, F.: The evolutionary dynamics of the artificial intelligence ecosystem. Strat. Sci. **6**(4), 412–435 (2021)

Li, Z., Nan, G., Li, M.: Advertising or freemium: the impacts of social effects and service quality on competing platforms. IEEE Trans. Eng. Manag. **67**(1), 220–233 (2020)

Mei, X., Cheng, H.K., Bandyopadhyay, S., Qiu, L., Wei, L.: Sponsored data: smarter data pricing with incomplete information. Inf. Syst. Res. **33**(1), 362–382 (2022)

Shi, Z., Zhang, K., Srinivasan, K.: Freemium as an optimal strategy for market dominant firms. Mark. Sci. **38**(1), 150–169 (2019)

Zhang, C., Chen, J., Raghunathan, S.: Two-sided platform competition in a sharing economy. Manag. Sci. **68**(12), 8909–8932 (2022)

Conversational Artificial Intelligence and Information Behavior

How AI Shopping Assistants' Interactivity Affects Consumers' Intention to Accept Product Recommendation: The Boundary Condition of Need for Cognition

Yuling Hu[1], Sihong Li[1], Hui Li[1], and Min Zhang[2](✉)

[1] School of Information Management, Wuhan University, Wuhan 430072, China
[2] Center for Studies of Information Resources, Wuhan University, Wuhan 430072, China
zhangmin@whu.edu.cn

Abstract. Understanding the interactivity of artificial intelligence shopping assistants (AISAs) for consumer service is essential to realize the potential of this technology. However, the effectiveness of interaction between AISAs and consumers in triggering purchasing decisions is unclear. This study examines what kind of functional characteristics are presented by the interactivity of shopping assistants and the perception of user value they elicit. It reveals the effect of interaction form (multi- vs. uni-modal) and interaction style (task- vs. social-oriented) on consumers' intention to accept recommendations by AISA through behavior experiments, which reveals the psychological mechanism and the boundary condition required for this to occur. The results show that the interaction form and style have a similar positive effect on consumers' intention to accept a product recommendation. In accordance with consumption value theory, the study demonstrates that the impact of interactivity on the intention to accept recommendations is mediated by functional and emotional values. Consumer characteristics play a moderating role in the influence mechanism, indicating that the effect is only operative when consumers' need for cognition is low. These findings contribute to the theoretical study of consumer digital assistance in the context of online shopping and provide insights for marketing strategies designed to enhance purchase intention for products recommended by AISAs.

Keywords: AI shopping assistant · AI interactivity · online shopping · need for cognition

1 Introduction

An artificial intelligence shopping assistant (AISA) is defined as an AI-powered algorithmic digital assistant that uses Natural Language Processing (NLP) to converse with consumers in e-commerce. The application of AISAs and their associated research have attracted considerable attention from a range of industries [1]. A significant majority (88%) of consumers have indicated that they expect businesses to integrate AISAs into

Y. P. Tu and M. Chi (Eds.): WHICEB 2025, LNBIP 549, pp. 29–39, 2025.
https://doi.org/10.1007/978-3-031-94184-9_3

their decision-making processes to facilitate the selection of the optimal product and brand. Assimilating AISAs into natural user interfaces allows to provide appropriate and timely product recommendations for consumers based on personalized information, which can reduce consumers' decision time and enhance efficiency and nurture relationships between companies and consumers [2].

There is a paucity of integrative research on AISA interactivity. The majority of extant studies concentrate on singular interaction characteristics of AI chatbots, including interaction style [3, 4], interaction mode and message interactivity. Interacting with chatbots has been shown to provide customers with a more positive user experience, which has been demonstrated to result in higher persuasive results [5].

The previous studies have focused on consumer interactions [3] and the role of AISAs in consumer purchase decisions [6], attitude [7], acceptance [8], satisfaction [9]. However, research into the accept intention to recommendations has been limited. The key function of AISAs is to provide product recommendations to improve efficiency and increase conversion rates. Nonetheless, a gap remains in the research on how interactive features determine consumer accept intention to recommendation by AISAs.

Contemporary research concentrates on demographic characteristics such as Internet competence [3], and usage experience [7], yet it falls short in terms of addressing consumers' internal cognitive processes. Chattaraman [3] identified the moderating effect of older consumers' internet competency in leading to benefits. The results showed that gender moderated the relationship of perceived interactivity and purchase intention [6]. However, need for cognition emerges as a pivotal individual variable that exerts a substantial influence on purchase intention.

Based on the above analysis, this study examines AISAs' interactivity and whether it impacts intention to accept recommendations among Chinese consumers. The following research questions (RQs) have emerged from the literature review:

RQ1: Do existing research findings in the service domain regarding AI assistants apply to intention to accept recommendations in online shopping?
RQ2: What are the main dimensions of AISAs' interactivity and how do they impact consumers' intention to accept recommendations?
RQ3: What is the effect of consumer characteristics on the intention to accept recommendations offered by AISAs?

To address these inquiries, this study developed a model assessing how interaction features in AISAs impact intentions to accept recommendations. To validate our research model and associated hypotheses, the study focused on examining the role of perceived value as a mediator for AISAs while also considering how consumer characteristics moderate the relationship between interactivity and acceptance of purchase recommendations. The results yield both theoretical insights and practical implications for advancing AISA technologies.

2 Literature Review

Recent studies have explored interactions between AISAs and consumers, using theories like technology acceptance model [7–10] and the use and gratification theory [8] to illustrate the effects of AISA attributes and properties on consumer attitudes and behavior intentions. Expectation Confirmation Theory has been used to explore what factors may contribute to the continuance usage of AISAs [9]. Research has focused on antecedents related to information (e.g., information quality and quantity) [6], technology (e.g., relative advantage and perceived intelligence) [7, 10], and communication (e.g., anthropomorphism and discomfort) [10, 11], as well as consequences like satisfaction [2], trust [11], attitude [7, 10], acceptance [8], and continuance usage intention [2, 10] and purchase intention through AISAs [6, 11].

AISAs differ from other high-tech products for strongly interacting with their users. The interaction between users and AISAs includes message interaction, information exchanges, and socio-emotional interaction, which build up a parasocial relationship [2]. This underscores the importance of investigating how users develop behavior intention toward AISAs in terms of their interactivity. Existing research has explored interactivity from the perspectives of functions (functional features of interactivity), processes (information exchange and responsiveness), and perceptions (control, two-way communication, and time). Given the rise of AISAs, this study examines their interactive aspects, focusing on interaction form and style. Interactivity is defined as the technical characteristic enabling human-to-machine interactions, with interaction forms improving usability and styles enhancing communication. Previous studies have examined interaction styles' effects on consumer behavior intentions [3].

3 Hypothesis Development and Theoretical Model

3.1 The Effect of AISA Interactivity

Interaction form refers to how information is represented during humans-computer interaction. A uni-modal form uses the same single modality, while a multi-modal form uses at least two distinct modalities (e.g., text, images, gestures). The extant literature has provided support for the notion that visual stimuli, such as images and pictures, can facilitate the processing of image-related information within the human brain. Furthermore, the use of images has been demonstrated to exert a significant influence on consumer preferences. As such, this research aims to ascertain whether multi-modal interfaces offer optimal user experiences through comprehensive and intuitive interactions. Consequently, we propose the following hypotheses:

H1: The multi-modal (vs. uni-modal) interaction form of AISAs positively affects consumers' intention to accept recommendations.

The interaction style signifies the unique patterns of dialogue employed by the AISAs, demonstrated through the purposeful use of linguistic diversity. Interaction styles of AISAs are categorized into two primary types: social-oriented and task-oriented [3, 4]. Social-oriented styles emphasize social interactions through greeting rituals, informal conversation, emotional support, and positive expressions. Task-oriented styles focus on formal approach and goal-driven conversations related to the task ahead [4]. AISAs with a social-oriented interaction style engage consumers more and lead to higher satisfaction than task-oriented ones. In light of the aforementioned evidence, we put forth the following hypotheses for consideration:

H2: The social-oriented (vs. task-oriented) interaction style of AISAs has a positive impact on consumers' intention to accept recommendation.

3.2 The Mediation Roles of Consumption Values

The consumption value theory, as proposed by Sheth, emphasizes a comprehensive understanding of perceived value that encompasses both utilitarian and hedonic dimensions. In this study, the functional value of a product can be defined as the degree to which consumers are able to complete tasks more conveniently as a result of the product's inherent characteristics or attributes. Emotional value refers to a pleased or hedonic experience from product utilization that satisfies consumers' sentimental needs.

In terms of interaction form, the picture form performs better in terms of consumer perception of helpfulness and usefulness. As a means of facilitating information processing and enhancing memory, pictures play a critical part in affecting consumers' recall and cognitive responses. Pictures display informative cues more vividly and clearly than text; thus, consumers are more attracted to recommendations and concentrate on decision-making. Therefore, the interaction form of AISAs can significantly impact consumers' perceived functional and emotional values. In light of the aforementioned discussion, we put forth the following hypotheses:

H3a: Consumers' perceived functional value mediates the positive effect of the interaction form of AISAs and consumers' intention to accept recommendations.
H3b: Consumers' perceived emotional value mediates the positive effect of the interaction form of AISAs and consumers' intention to accept recommendations.

In terms of interaction style, researchers have explored the impact of different consumers' interaction-style preferences on their behavior in different contexts. De Cicco [1] showed that consumers interacting with a social-oriented (vs. task-oriented) AISA for food ordering reported higher enjoyment and a stronger desire for future interactions. It can be reasonably deduced that the social-oriented interaction style of AISAs has the potential to significantly influence consumers' perceptions of both functional and emotional value. Based on the aforementioned discussion, the following hypotheses are proposed:

H4a: The perceived functional value of consumers mediates the positive effect of the interaction style of AISAs on consumers' intention to accept recommendations.
H4b: The perceived emotional value of consumers mediates the positive effect of the interaction style of AISAs on consumers' intention to accept recommendations.

3.3 The Moderating Mediation Role of the Need for Cognition

The Need for Cognition (NFC) measures how individuals seek and process information when forming attitudes. High NFC indicates a preference for deep, analytical thinking, while low NFC suggests a reliance on less effortful processes. This aligns with the Elaboration Likelihood Model (ELM), which proposes two persuasion pathways: central route processing for high NFC individuals and peripheral cues for low NFC individuals. Thus, low NFC individuals are more influenced by interaction features of AISAs.

Low NFC individuals focus on design elements and interaction styles in persuasive web interfaces. They feel higher consumption value and purchase intentions when interacting with multi-modal AISAs than uni-modal ones. Conversely, high NFC consumers demonstrate minimal discernment regarding the interaction form and report negligible variance in the perceived consumption value across different interaction modalities. Based on these findings, we put forth the following hypothesis:

H5: NFC moderates the effect of interaction form of AISAs on consumers' intention to accept recommendations through perceived functional value.
H6: NFC moderates the effect of interaction form of AISAs on consumers' intention to accept recommendations through perceived emotional value. Specifically,

High NFC individuals prefer cognitive messages, whereas low NFC individuals favor affective messages. Specifically, low NFC consumers show higher purchase intentions with AISAs using socio-emotional and affective styles (Fig. 1). High NFC individuals enjoy analytical elaboration and see little difference in consumption values across diverse styles. Based on this, we proposed the following hypothesis:

H7: NFC moderates the effect of interaction style of AISAs on consumer's intention to accept recommendations through perceived functional value.
H8: NFC moderates the effect of interaction style of AISAs on consumer's intention to accept recommendations through perceived emotional value. Specifically,

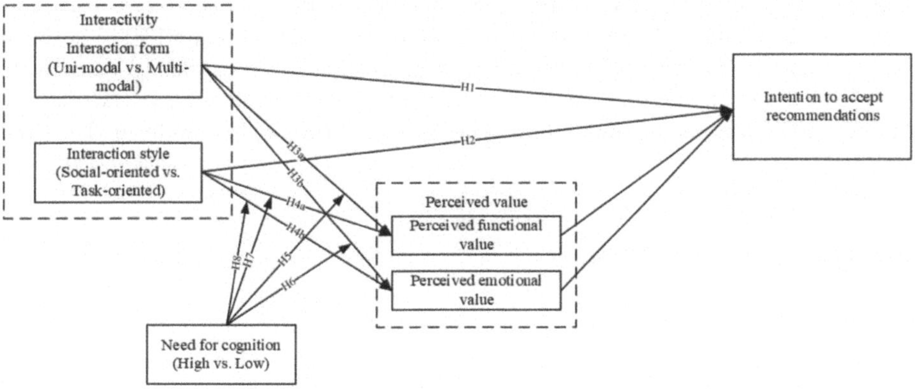

Fig. 1. Research framework of this study.

4 Methodology

This study was conducted to test the hypothesis. The study examined the effect of perceived value on the relationship between interactivity and intention to accept recommendations. The study used self-report questionnaires to examine human–computer interaction. In the declarative study, participants completed questionnaires about their perceptions of value and intention to accept purchase recommendations.

Experimental Design and Stimuli. A laboratory experiment tested the hypotheses using a 2 (interaction form: uni- vs. multi-modal) × 2 (interaction style: social vs. task-oriented) between-subjects design. The study used a mobile phone as the experimental product to investigate the impact of interaction form and style. Interaction form was manipulated with and without pictures [12], while interaction styles included social (informal, small talk) and task-oriented (formal, goal-focused) approaches [3]. Appendix illustrates these manipulations.

Participants and Experimental Procedure. We recruited an additional cohort of 160 participants from a university in central China. Subjects had normal vision and were excluded if they were color blind or had color weakness. They were right-handed. Of the 160 subjects, 85 were women and 75 men, aged 18 to 40. Each had previously shopped online. Prior to the experiment, all participants provided informed consent by signing a consent form. Subjects were remunerated for their participation. Participants read a pre-prepared dialogue in a dynamic prototype format to ensure internal validity. The dialogue involved a greeting, a request for a mobile phone recommendation, a product recommendation, a request for details, and product descriptions. After interacting with an AISA, participants completed an 18-item NFC survey [18] and were categorized into high NFC ($M = 5.672$, $SD = 0.423$) and low NFC ($M = 3.620$, $SD = 0.932$) groups. They also answered a questionnaire about personal info, online shopping experience, product adoption intention, and interaction form/style perception, and rated their likelihood of purchasing the product.

Measures. The study used a 7-point Likert scale (*1 = strongly disagree,7 = strongly agree*). Scales included functional value (3 items from Chattaraman [3]), emotional value (3 items from Davis [13]), intention to accept recommendations (4 items from Ji [14]), NFC (18 items from Cacioppo and Petty [15]), interaction style (social- vs. task-oriented) from Chattaraman [3], and interaction-form (uni- vs. multi-modal) from Cian [12].

5 Results

This study examined the effects of interaction form and style on intention to accept recommendations (H1, H2), and tested the mediating effect of perceived value (H3, H4). Moderated mediation analysis based on 5000 bootstrapped samples was used (H5, H6, H7, H8; see Table 1; Fig. 2).

Manipulation Check. Results from independent sample T-tests indicated that the social-oriented group scored significantly higher ($M_{social\text{-}oriented} = 6.033$, $SD = 0.594$) than task-oriented group ($M_{task\text{-}oriented} = 3.804$, $SD = 0.980$; $t = 17.391$, $p < 0.001$) on interaction style scores. The multi-modal group scored significantly higher ($M_{multi\text{-}modal} = 6.594$, $SD = 0.601$) than the uni-modal group on the interaction form scores ($M_{uni\text{-}modal=}1.300$, $SD = 0.440$; $t = 63.555$, $p < 0.001$). The manipulation was successful.

Hypotheses Testing. The one-way ANOVA verified interaction form significant affects intention to accept recommendations ($M_{multi\text{-}modal=}5.616$, $SD = 0.805$; $M_{uni\text{-}modal} =$

Table 1. Model coefficients for the PROCESS Model 8.

Variable	Functional Value		Emotional Value		Intention to Accept Recommendations	
	b (se)	t	b (se)	t	b (se)	t
Interaction form	0.744(0.217)	3.430***	0.813(0.232)	3.503***	0.245(0.124)	1.979*
Interaction style	0.657(0.222)	2.964**	1.097(0.227)	4.837***	0.139(0.130)	1.068
Interaction form × NFC	−0.658(0.308)	−2.134*	−0.646(0.330)	−1.959	−0.365(0.171)	−2.139*
Interaction style × NFC	−0.332(0.313)	−1.061	−0.666(0.321)	−2.076*	−0.317(0.174)	−1.827
Functional value					0.498(0.062)	7.969***
Emotional value					0.382(0.058)	6.538***

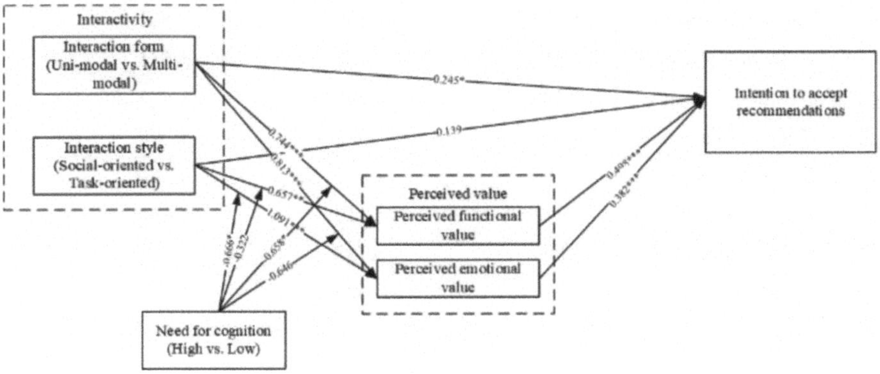

Fig. 2. Results of the research model.

5.134, SD = 1.274; t = 2.856, $p = 0.005 < 0.01$). The interaction style significantly affects intention to accept recommendations ($M_{social\text{-}oriented}$=5.588, SD = 0.798; $M_{task\text{-}oriented}$=5.163, SD = 1.289; t = 2.508, $p = 0.013 < 0.05$). H1 and H2 are supported.

Mediation effect. The results show that perceived functional value mediates the impact of interaction form on intention to accept recommendations (b = 0.239, 95% CI = [0.062, 0.457]), and perceived emotional value mediates the impact of interaction form on intention to accept recommendations (b = 0.196, 95% CI = [0.053, 0.386]). Perceived functional value mediates the impact of interaction style on intention to accept recommendations (b = 0.209, 95% CI = [0.034, 0.419]), and perceived emotional value mediates the impact of interaction form on intention to accept recommendations ($b = 0.263$, 95% CI = [0.097, 0.497]). H3a, H3b, H4a and H4b are supported. Functional value (path coefficient = 0.498) has a stronger impact on intention to accept recommendations than emotional value (path coefficient = 0.382) (see Table 1).

Moderation effect. We tested the moderation effect of NFC (high = 1, low = 0) on the impact of interaction form and style on intention to accept recommendations (see Table 2). The interaction form × NFC interaction effect was significant ($F = 10.497$, $p = 0.001 < 0.01$). Multi-modal interaction form increased intention to accept recommendations for low NFC participants ($M_{\text{multi-modal}} = 5.531$, $M_{\text{uni-modal}} = 4.587$, $F = 17.929$, $p < 0.001$) but not for high NFC participants ($M_{\text{multi-modal}} = 5.700$, $M_{\text{uni-modal}} = 5.681$; $F = 0.007$, $p = 0.933 > 0.05$). The interaction style × NFC interaction effect was significant for intention to accept recommendations ($F = 5.701$, $p = 0.018 < 0.05$). Social-oriented interaction style increased intention to accept recommendations for low NFC participants ($M_{\text{social-oriented}} = 5.456$, $M_{\text{task- oriented}} = 4.550$, $F = 16.104$, $p < 0.001$) but not for those with high NFC ($M_{\text{social-oriented}}$=5.757, $M_{\text{task-oriented}} = 5.639$; $F = 0.275$, $p = 0.601 > 0.05$).

Table 2. Comparison of moderation effects across low and high NFC groups.

NFC	Interaction	Emotional value	Functional value	Intention to accept recommendation
Low	Uni-modal form	4.392	4.850	4.587
Low	Multi-modal form	5.217	5.608	5.531
High	Uni-modal form	5.333	5.792	5.681
High	Multi-modal form	5.525	5.933	5.700
Low	Task-oriented style	4.190	4.857	4.550
Low	Social-oriented style	5.281	5.519	5.456
High	Task-oriented style	5.667	5.733	5.639
High	Social-oriented style	5.244	6.029	5.757

Moderated mediation. For interaction form, NFC moderated the mediation of perceived emotional value ($b = -0.491$, 95% CI = [−1.005, −0.007]) and functional value ($b = -0.515$, 95% CI = [−1.062, −0.001]) between the interaction form of AISA and intention to accept recommendation, supporting H5 and H6 (see Table 3). For interaction style, NFC moderated the mediation of perceived emotional value ($b = -0.5339$, 95% CI = [−1.0854, −0.0232]), supporting H8, but did not moderate in the mediation of functional value ($b = -0.2950$, 95% CI = [−0.8205, 0.2113]), failing to support H7 (see Table 4).

Table 3. Conditional indirect effects of interaction form on intention to accept recommendations.

	NFC level	b	se	CI_{95}
Mediator: Functional value	Low	0.370	0.141	[0.134,0.692]
	High	0.043	0.110	[−0.169,0.270]
Mediator: Emotional value	Low	0.310	0.122	[0.101,0.567]
	High	0.064	0.085	[−0.100,0.245]

Table 4. Conditional indirect effects of interaction style on intention to accept recommendations.

	NFC level	b	se	CI_{95}
Mediator: Functional value	Low	0.339	0.148	[0.090,0.677]
	High	0.168	0.110	[−0.043,0.389]
Mediator: Emotional value	Low	0.418	0.148	[0.165,0.739]
	High	0.164	0.091	[0.011,0.367]

6 Discussion

Discussion of the Results. This study examined how interaction form and style affect consumers' acceptance of AISA recommendations, finding that both positively influence functional and emotional value perceptions, which in turn boost intentions to accept recommendations. NFC moderates these effects. Firstly, both the form and style of interaction affect users' intention to accept recommendations. Although research on this topic is limited, this finding is consistent with the effects of social-oriented AISAs in the consumer service systems [3]. Social-oriented interaction styles lead to higher acceptance intentions than task-oriented styles. Secondly, the effect of interaction form and style on the behavior intentions follows two paths: functional and emotional values. Functional value has a greater impact on consumer behavior than emotional value, likely due to limited experience with AISAs, which underscores the functional value of human–AI interaction to complete the shopping task. Thirdly, NFC can act as a moderator in mediating perceived value between the interactivity of AISAs and the intention to accept recommendations. Specifically, low NFC consumers show stronger acceptance intention from multi-modal and social-oriented AISAs, highlighting differences in perceived value.

Implications for Theory. This study has significant theoretical implications. It contributes to the expansion of the theory regarding the intention to accept recommendations and pre-purchase stage from an AISA by elucidating behavioral intentions through the lens of the widely-accepted ELM in AISAs.

Firstly, the study clarifies the interactivity of AISAs from the perspective of their functional capabilities, augmenting existing knowledge on AISAs and conversational commerce. It reveals multi-dimensional interactivity and lays a foundation for future research on human–AI interaction. Secondly, the study identifies the psychological mechanism by which interactivity affects consumers' intention to accept recommendations based on consumer values theory. The results align with previous findings that the perceived value of AI applications influences consumers' online purchase intentions. This offers a new perspective on the perceived functional and emotional values associated with AISAs interactivity. Thirdly, the analysis shows that NFC, a personalized consumer characteristic, can explain when the effect of interactivity is established. This finding extends existing literature by highlighting the moderating effect of NFC on recommendations acceptance, which was previously overlooked.

Implications for Practice. First, E-commerce platforms can boost recommendation adoption by offering AISAs with personalized interaction forms and styles. This study shows that a social-oriented interaction style and multi-modal interaction form are the best choice for e-commerce platforms when developing or procuring AISAs. Secondly, both major platforms and smaller merchants should focus on AISA design and conversational marketing. Merchants can enhance consumer value perception and recommendation acceptance by designing AISAs based on consumer needs and setting up engaging dialogues. These interactions make consumers feel pleasure while receiving recommendations and personalized info, boosting consumption value. Lastly, understanding consumer cognitive needs is key to improving recommendation effectiveness and purchase conversion through targeted marketing. Platform managers should develop versatile, intelligent recommendation styles and conduct themed activities.

Limitations. This study has some limitations and offers future research directions. Firstly, the experimental setup may not fully replicate the authentic user experience when interacting with AISAs in real-world scenarios based on individual needs. Secondly, it did not take the product type into consideration. Our research focused on consumers' personality characteristics, and paid little attention on the differences caused by product types. Furthermore, future studies may benefit from closer collaboration with e-commerce platforms. Such collaborative endeavors would facilitate the gathering of empirical data from users engaged in actual shopping interactions, thereby enhancing the dependability and practical relevance of the research conclusions.

7 Conclusions

This study investigates the interactivity of AISAs influencing consumers' intention to accept recommendations and the psychological mechanism underlying it. This study shows that interactivity from the perspective of functional attributes—interaction form and style—affects consumers' intention to purchase recommended products. Based on consumption value theory, the mediation effect of perceived consumption value is significant, which explains how the interactivity of AISAs affects consumers' intention to accept recommendations. The mediation effect was negatively moderated by the consumer's need for cognition. Our findings not only make meaningful contributions to theory development in human–AI interaction, but they also provide suggestions for product development, marketing strategies, and consumer service by AI shopping-assistant product providers.

Acknowledgement. This research was supported by the National Natural Science Foundation of China under Grant 72474165.

References

1. De Cicco, R., Silva, S.C., Alparone, F.R.: Millennials' attitude toward chatbots: an experimental study in a social relationship perspective. Int. J. Retail Distrib. Manag. **48**(11), 1213–1233 (2020)
2. Minsun, L.P., Jee-Sun.: Do parasocial relationships and the quality of communication with AI shopping chatbots determine middle-aged women consumers' continuance usage intentions? J. Consum. Behav. **842-854** (2022)
3. Chattaraman, V., et al.: Should AI-based, conversational digital assistants employ social- or task-oriented interaction style? A task-competency and reciprocity perspective for older adults. Comput. Hum. Behav. **90**, 315–330 (2019)
4. Cai, N., Gao, S., Yan, J.: How the communication style of chatbots influences consumers' satisfaction, trust, and engagement in the context of service failure. Hum. Soc. Sci. Commun. **11**(1) (2024)
5. Ischen, C., et al.: "I am here to assist you today": the role of entity, interactivity and experiential perceptions in Chatbot persuasion. J. Broadcast. Electron. Media. **64**(4), 615–639 (2020)
6. Sharma, M., et al.: Impact of digital assistant attributes on millennials' purchasing intentions: a multi-group analysis using PLS-SEM, artificial neural network and fsQCA. Inf. Syst. Front. **26**(3), 943–966 (2022)
7. Balakrishnan, J.Y.K., Dwivedi.: Conversational commerce: entering the next stage of AI-powered digital assistants. Ann. Oper. Res. **333**(2), 653–687 (2024)
8. Rese, A., Ganster, L., Baier, D.: Chatbots in retailers' customer communication: how to measure their acceptance? J. Retail. Consum. Serv. **56**, 102176 (2020)
9. Ashfaq, M., et al.: I, Chatbot: modeling the determinants of users' satisfaction and continuance intention of AI-powered service agents. Telematics Inform. **54**, 101473 (2020)
10. Myin, M.T.K., Watchravesringkan.: Investigating consumers' adoption of AI chatbots for apparel shopping. J. Consum. Mark. **41**(3), 314–327 (2024)
11. Yen, C.M.C., Chiang.: Trust me, if you can: a study on the factors that influence consumers' purchase intention triggered by chatbots based on brain image evidence and self-reported assessments. Behav. Inform. Technol. (3), 1–18 (2020)
12. Cian, L., Krishna, A., Elder, R.S.: This logo moves me: dynamic imagery from static images. J. Mark. Res. **51**(2), 184–197 (2014)
13. Davis, F.D.: Perceived usefulness, perceived ease of use, and user acceptance of information technology. MIS Q. **13**(3), 319–340 (1989)
14. Ji, W., Qi, H., Fei, H.: Research on the recommendation persuasion mechanism of intelligent agents to consumers: based on the perspective of social roles. Nankai Bus. Rev. (2024) in Chinese
15. Cacioppo, J.T.R.E., Petty.: The need for cognition. J. Pers. Soc. Psychol. **42**(1), 116–131 (1982)

Can Anthropomorphism Gain an Advantage? The Impact of Virtual Idols' Anthropomorphism on Follower Recognition and Engagement

Jieyu Qiu, Tianmei Wang(✉), Chunliu Gu, and Yaoyao Li

Central University of Finance and Economics, Beijing, China
2023110204@email.cufe.edu.cn

Abstract. Idols typically engage their followers through emotional expressions and interactions. Unlike real human idols, virtual idols are computer-generated avatars that do not exist in the real world. The impact of anthropomorphizing virtual idols' emotions and interactive behaviors on follower reactions is still under investigation. This study analyzes 26,093 videos from 166 virtual idols on the Bilibili platform. The results show an inverted U-shaped relationship between anthropomorphism (both emotion and behavior) and follower recognition and engagement, providing empirical support for the Uncanny Valley hypothesis. Moderation analysis shows that behavioral anthropomorphism flattens the inverted U-shaped relationship between emotional anthropomorphism and follower recognition. Additionally, the moderation effect of the video category reveals that the inverted U-shaped relationship is steeper in entertainment videos compared to daily life videos. This study highlights the importance of balancing emotional and behavioral anthropomorphism when designing virtual idols to optimize follower recognition and engagement.

Keywords: Virtual Idol · Anthropomorphism · Follower Recognition · Follower Engagement · the Uncanny Valley

1 Introduction

In recent years, advancements in motion capture and 3D technology have brought virtual idols from the world of ACGN (Animation, Comics, Games, Novels) into the spotlight, making them one of the most exciting industries today. Virtual idols like Luo Tianyi and A-SOUL are computer-generated avatars with attractive, two-dimensional, and often similar looks and voices. Although they are digital, these idols can gain the affection of followers by anthropomorphizing, that is, behaving more like humans. This approach enhances their vividness but also risks triggering the uncanny valley (UV) effect due to their digital nature. The UV effect refers to the phenomenon where people encounter a character that tries to imitate humans but fails to convincingly display human characteristics, which can lead to negative reactions from the users [1]. How to find the right balance between appealing human-like behavior and unsettling artificiality? This article explores how virtual idols try to act human and how this affects their followers' reactions.

Y. P. Tu and M. Chi (Eds.): WHICEB 2025, LNBIP 549, pp. 40–51, 2025.
https://doi.org/10.1007/978-3-031-94184-9_4

Emotions and interactive behaviors are two crucial aspects of anthropomorphism in virtual idols. Virtual idols can appear emotionally sincere by sharing experiences that resonate with people's feelings, such as discussing personal happy or sad moments [2]. For example, the famous virtual idol "Jiale" shares (or fabricates) her work-related frustrations in videos, which even incites anger among her fans and calls for action against the company she represents. Additionally, virtual idols create a sense of intimacy and exhibit anthropomorphism by imitating human characteristics and interacting with real people in the real world, for instance, asking questions and replying to comments [3]. Appearance and voice also play important roles in the anthropomorphism of virtual beings. Since virtual idols are often designed with similar two-dimensional avatars and voices, their emotional and interactive behaviors represent a higher degree of anthropomorphism. This paper explores the anthropomorphism in the emotional expressions and interactive behaviors of virtual idols.

Research highlights both the positive and negative effects of anthropomorphism in virtual idols. On the positive side, emotional expressions strengthen followers' empathy, trust, and engagement [4]. For instance, when virtual idols share joyful personal stories, they reveal their individuality and attract people to engage in interaction. Sharing negative emotions is often considered intimate and personal, revealing a person's "true" self and enhancing the perception of the virtual idols' authenticity [2]. Furthermore, virtual idols demonstrate human-like interactions, such as asking questions and replying to comments, making the audience feel as if they are interacting with real people [5]. Additionally, according to the Computer as a Social Actor (CASA) framework [6], the anthropomorphic cues of virtual idols activate the audience's perception of human beings, thus gaining the followers' recognition and engagement.

However, the anthropomorphism of virtual idols can also trigger negative reactions. For instance, studies have found that when virtual idols pretend to experience "rape" and express emotions in a superficial manner, they not only fail to garner sympathy but also face criticism and skepticism [7]. This can be explained by the UV hypothesis, which suggests that avatars mimicking human traits but falling short of convincingly replicating them can make viewers feel uncomfortable and even provoke adverse emotional responses [1]. Thus, there's a fine line between achieving anthropomorphism and triggering the UV effect. However, research on how virtual idols manage anthropomorphism in emotional expression and interactive behaviors is scarce, and there's no consensus on how these efforts affect followers' responses.

This paper aims to explore how virtual idols express emotional and behavioral anthropomorphism and its impact on follower reactions (recognition and engagement). The innovation of this study lies in three aspects. Firstly, this study measures the anthropomorphic performance of virtual idols and its impact on followers' recognition and engagement from both emotional and behavioral aspects and explores the interaction between the two. Secondly, this study employs the UV hypothesis, CASA theory, and the similarity-attraction theory, providing insights for improved virtual idol design. Finally, this study uncovers the boundary effect of behavioral anthropomorphism and video categorization in how virtual idols influence follower recognition and participatory behavior, offering a new perspective on understanding the effects of virtual idols' anthropomorphism. This study expands the research scope on virtual idols and holds practical significance for their design.

2 Literature Review

2.1 Anthropomorphism of Virtual Idols

Anthropomorphism refers to the tendency to attribute human-like characteristics, motivations, intentions, or emotions to non-human entities [8]. Virtual celebrities are often portrayed as authentic human-like beings complete with personalities and backgrounds, engaging in interactions with other social media users as if they were real individuals. Research has shown that the anthropomorphism of virtual idols is manifested in their appearance, emotion, and behavior.

In terms of appearance, virtual idols like Hatsune Miku and Luo Tianyi closely resemble real-life idols, showcasing detailed and natural designs that enhance perceived credibility and fulfill users' emotional needs. Emotionally, virtual idols share human-like experiences, from positive anecdotes that highlight individuality to negative emotions that foster intimacy and authenticity [7]. Behaviorally, virtual idols mimic human actions, engaging audiences through interactive exchanges that create a sense of real-time interaction and strengthen affinity with followers [9].

Although existing research have explored the anthropomorphic aspects of virtual humans, they did not explore deeply how the interaction between anthropomorphic cues affects user responses. This gap in knowledge is significant because the way in which different anthropomorphic elements are combined and presented can have a profound impact on how users perceive and engage with virtual entities.

2.2 Follower's Reaction to the Anthropomorphism of the Virtual Being

Anthropomorphism positively impacts followers by fostering emotional connections and enhancing social presence. Human-like traits in virtual beings enable interactive communication that mimics human patterns, enriching the social and emotional context. Anthropomorphic behavior also facilitates parasocial relationships, reshaping cognitive behaviors, such as identifying with virtual personas, and influencing perceptual responses like empathy. In marketing, anthropomorphic communication can reduce consumer resistance and improve interaction behaviors by alleviating defensive attitudes [10].

However, excessive anthropomorphism can trigger negative reactions, as described by the UV theory. When virtual beings appear highly human-like but exhibit mismatched behavior or subtle inconsistencies, they can evoke discomfort or fear. This reaction may stem from perceived threats to human identity, social resources, or job security. Such mismatches can lead to feelings of eeriness and dissatisfaction [11].

While evidence supports the UV hypothesis, findings vary. Some studies confirm that increasing human-likeness decreases positive feelings and heightens unease, while others suggest the UV effect arises only under specific conditions. Therefore, while the theory is well-supported, further empirical research is needed to clarify the specific contexts in which the UV effect occurs.

3 Theory and Hypothesis

3.1 The Effect of Virtual Idol' Anthropomorphism on Follower Recognition and Engagement

Virtual idols exhibiting emotional and behavioral anthropomorphism can enhance followers' recognition and engagement. Emotional anthropomorphism fosters empathy, trust, and connection by allowing followers to relate to virtual idols on a personal level [4]. Similarly, anthropomorphic interactive behaviors, such as responding to comments, bridge the gap between virtual idols and followers, creating a sense of authenticity and human-like interaction. This dynamic strengthens identification with the virtual idols.

According to the CASA theory [6], social cues from virtual idols activate perceptions of human traits, making followers view them as social entities. For example, when virtual idols share emotional posts or engage personally with followers, the connection often mirrors real-world friendships or a sense of belonging. These cues of anthropomorphism make people perceive virtual idols as real humans like themselves, eliciting social responses such as trust and liking. For instance, when users interact with a computer, they are more willing to self-disclose if the computer demonstrates a high degree of reciprocity like that of a human [12]. Furthermore, the similarity-attraction theory suggests that people are drawn to entities resembling themselves [13]. Based on this theory, virtual humans that are more easily perceived as human entities are more attractive. Therefore, people tend to develop positive emotions towards virtual humans that resemble humans in emotion and behavior.

However, according to the UV hypothesis, when the similarity between virtual humans and real humans reaches a certain level, people's reactions to them can suddenly become extremely negative and repulsive. Even a slight difference from humans can appear glaring and jarring, making the virtual entity seem unnaturally rigid and terrifying. Despite their ability to mimic human emotions and behaviors and even exhibit abilities beyond human capabilities, virtual idols, with their two-dimensional appearance and voice, remain inherently computer-generated avatars. Therefore, when virtual humans over-emphasize anthropomorphism either emotionally or behaviorally, this "uncanny" sensation arises, leading to feelings of strangeness or rejection.

In summary, Virtual idols exhibiting appropriate levels of anthropomorphism can resonate with fans, but excessive anthropomorphism may cause fans to perceive them as artificial or unreal, thereby diminishing their sense of recognition and engagement. The hypotheses are proposed.

H1a–H1b: There is an inverted U-shaped relationship between emotional anthropomorphism of virtual idol and follower recognition(a)/engagement(b).
H2a–H2b: There is an inverted U-shaped relationship between behavioral anthropomorphism of virtual idol and follower recognition(a)/engagement(b).

3.2 The Moderating Role of Behavioral Anthropomorphism

Behavioral anthropomorphism can enhance the realism and personality of virtual idols on the basis of emotional anthropomorphism. Specifically, when virtual idols have only moderate levels of emotional anthropomorphism, follower recognition and engagement with them may initially increase but then decrease. However, if virtual idols also display pronounced behavioral anthropomorphism, this combination can enhance their realism and personality, further strengthening follower recognition and engagement. Thus, behavioral anthropomorphism can mitigate the inverted U-shaped relationship between emotional anthropomorphism and follower recognition and engagement. Therefore, the following hypotheses are proposed:

H3a–H3b: Behavioral anthropomorphism of virtual idols positively moderates the impact of emotional anthropomorphism on the follower recognition(a)/engagement(b).

3.3 The Moderating Role of Video Category

Different types of videos have varying impacts on the expressiveness of virtual idols and the reactions of their followers. Daily life videos typically involve everyday life, personal experiences, interpersonal interactions, or emotional experiences, which are more closely related to the audience's real life. In such contexts, virtual idols can more naturally express genuine emotions and behaviors, making it easier for the audience to empathize. On one hand, viewers may feel a sense of closeness due to shared experiences or emotional experiences with virtual idols, thereby enhancing their recognition of virtual beings. On the other hand, viewers may be more willing to share their own emotional experiences or suggestions based on familiar everyday environments, promoting greater audience participation in activities related to virtual idols [14]. In contrast, entertainment videos may pursue entertainment effects more, and viewers may focus more on enjoying the fun brought by the content when watching entertainment videos, without considering the authenticity of virtual idols too much. In such cases, The Daily life scene can flatten the inverted U-shaped relationship between emotional anthropomorphism and follower recognition and engagement.

In summary, the following hypotheses are proposed:

H4a–H4b: Video category moderates the impact of emotional anthropomorphism on the follower recognition(a)/engagement(b).

The theoretical framework diagram is shown in Fig. 1.

4 Research Method

4.1 Data

The data for this study is sourced from Bilibili, a popular platform for virtual idols. Virtual idols were selected based on the Virtual Streamer Directory on Moegirlpedia,[1] a comprehensive ACGN Wiki platform. After matching with Bilibili content creators and

[1] https://mzh.moegirl.org.cn

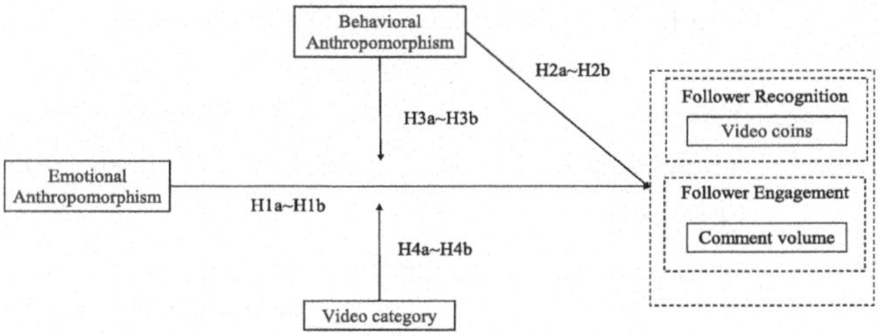

Fig. 1. Theoretical Framework

excluding inactive accounts, 166 active virtual idols were identified. Data collection was completed as of February 2, 2024, and included submission counts, fan numbers, and video details. After extensive data cleaning, we retained information on 166 idols and 26,093 videos.

4.2 Variable Measurement

Dependent Variable: Follower recognition and follower engagement. Coin voting allows viewers to provide direct financial support to the virtual idol, with each coin vote signifying the viewer's affirmation of the virtual idol and contributing to their income. Therefore, we use video coins to represent follower recognition. Follower engagement behavior is gauged by the number of comments, reflecting users' willingness to invest time in expressing their opinions and participating in discussions. To mitigate the impact of extreme values, we applied logarithmic transformations to the two sets of variables.

Independent Variable:

Emotional anthropomorphism: Quantified by analyzing video themes for affective processes (e.g., happy, sweet, bad) using LIWC. The text published by virtual beings on social media lays the emotional foundation of the content, with text titles being a key manifestation of emotional responses [15].
Behavioral anthropomorphism: Measured through comment interactions [9]. Specifically, if the frequency of interactions (i.e., adaptive feedback to fan comments) is higher, we consider the virtual idol to be more humanlike in terms of behavior. Data was collected from the top 50 first-level comments and all second-level comments of each video.
Moderating variable: Video category. We classify virtual idols' dance performances, music videos, etc., as entertainment videos, while their typical chat-based content (e.g., lifestyle, comedy, gaming) is categorized as lifestyle videos.
Control variables: Variables such as video duration, collaboration, release time (dawn, morning, afternoon, evening), and time span from the day the data was crawled (2 February 2024). Individual and year fixed effects control for unobserved time-specific factors. Refer to Table 1 for details.

Descriptive statistics and correlation analysis are shown in Table 2 and Table 3. Correlation coefficients are below 0.6, and VIF values are under 2, indicating minimal multicollinearity concerns.

Table 1. The measurement methods of variables

	Variable	Measurement method
Dependent variable	Recognition	Log (video coins + 1)
	Engagement	Log (comment volume + 1)
Independent variable	Emotional anthropomorphism (EA)	The percentage of words indicating emotion in the video theme
	Behavioral anthropomorphism (BA)	The proportion of virtual idol interactive comments in reviews
Moderating variable	Video category	Entertainment videos such as music, dancing, etc. are 1, while daily life is 0
Control variable	Video duration	Video duration (minutes)
	Collaborative video	Co-created videos are assigned a value of 1, otherwise 0
	Video release time	1 for dawn (0:00 – <6:00); 2 for morning (6:00 – <12:00); 3 for afternoon (12:00 – <18:00); 4 for evening (18:00 – <0:00)
	Time span	Number of days until 2 February 2024 from the date of release of the video

Table 2. Descriptive Statistics (N = 26,093)

Variable	Mean	Std.dev.	Min	Max
Video coins	3084.30	10886.00	0	431,972
Comment volume	434.33	1920.87	0	231,326
EA	3.61	2.87	0	100
BA	0.03	0.07	0	0.6
Video category	0.22	0.41	0	1
Collaborative video	0.14	0.35	0	1
Video duration	64.69	523.86	0.05	28372.5
Video release time	3.03	0.92	1	4
Time span	1260.04	626.30	6	4561

4.3 Results

To test the hypotheses, we used OLS with standardized continuous variables, including individual and time fixed effects (see Table 4). Model 1–4 are used for the test of main effects, while Model 5–8 are used to test the moderating effects.

Table 3. Matrix of correlations

	Video coins	Comment volume	EA	BA	Video category	Collaborative video	Video duration	Video release time	Time span
Video coins	1								
Comment volume	0.566***	1							
EA	0.078***	0.031***	1						
BA	−0.069***	−0.046***	−0.013**	1					
Video category	0.228***	0.103***	0.124***	−0.009	1				
Collaborative video	0.075***	0.022***	0.071***	−0.076***	0.180***	1			
Video duration	−0.016***	−0.014**	0.009	−0.017***	−0.037***	−0.029***	1		
Video release time	0.054***	0.025***	0.075***	−0.027***	0.102***	0.062***	−0.062***	1	
Time span	−0.032***	−0.018***	−0.003	0.056***	−0.110***	−0.160***	0.026***	−0.062***	1

Model 1 shows that there is a significant inverted U-shaped relationship between emotional anthropomorphism and recognition (β_EA = 0.098, $p < 0.01$; β_(EA^2) = −0.005, $p < 0.01$). The extreme point is 9.95 ($p < 0.01$), within the range of standardized values of EA ([−1.26, 33.63])), thus supporting H1a. The results of model 2 show that there is a significant inverted U-shaped relationship between the behavioral anthropomorphism and the follower engagement (β_EA = 0.075, $p < 0.01$; β_(EA^2) = −0.004, $p < 0.01$). The extreme point estimated is 10.27 ($p < 0.01$), which is within the range of standardized values of EA, so H1b is validated. Figure 2(a) shows the inverted U-shaped relationship between emotional anthropomorphism and follower recognition and engagement. Behavioral anthropomorphism also demonstrates a significant inverted U-shaped relationship with follower recognition and engagement, with extreme points at 1.06 and 2.68, respectively, validating H2a and H2b. Figure 2(b) illustrates the inverted U-shaped relationship.

The moderating effect of behavioral anthropomorphism was conducted in model 5–6. In Model 5, β_BA*EA^2 = 0.001, $p < 0.01$, indicating that the inverted U-shaped curve has become smoother. As shown in Fig. 3(a), with increasing BA, the inverted U-shaped relationship between emotional anthropomorphism and follower recognition becomes progressively flatter, and the peak shifts to the right, supporting Hypothesis H3a. Model 6 and Fig. 3(b) show that the degree of the inverted U-shaped relationship between emotional anthropomorphism and follower engagement remains relatively unchanged with increasing BA, and the peak slightly shifts to the right, failing to support Hypothesis H3b.

Finally, we tested the moderating effect of video category. In Model 7, the interaction term was significant (β_ (Video category * EA^2) = −0.009, $p < 0.01$), indicating a steeper inverted U-shaped curve. As shown in Fig. 4(a), when the video category is "daily life," the inverted U-shaped relationship between emotional anthropomorphism and follower recognition is relatively flat; however, when the video category is "entertainment," the curve becomes steeper, supporting Hypothesis H4a. Figure 4(b) displays

Table 4. Regression result

	Model 1	Model 2	Model 3	Model 4	Model 5	Model 6	Model 7	Model 8
Variables	Recognition	Engagement	Recognition	Engagement	Recognition	Engagement	Recognition	Engagement
EA	0.098***	0.075***			0.116***	0.088***	0.086***	0.073***
	(19.15)	(12.88)			(20.22)	(13.29)	(14.99)	(10.74)
EA^2	−0.005***	−0.004***			−0.011***	−0.008***	−0.004***	−0.003***
	(−9.72)	(−6.33)			(−10.63)	(−6.97)	(−7.79)	(−5.29)
BA			0.031***	0.090***	−0.030***	0.022***		
			(3.17)	(8.14)	(−6.18)	(3.98)		
Ba^2			−0.015***	−0.017***				
			(−6.96)	(−7.06)				
BA*EA					0.021***	0.027***		
	Model 1	Model 2	Model 3	Model 4	Model 5	Model 6	Model 7	Model 8
Variables	Recognition	Engagement	Recognition	Engagement	Recognition	Engagement	Recognition	Engagement
					(4.52)	(5.04)		
BA*EA^2					0.001***	0.000		
					(3.11)	(0.95)		
Video category							0.465***	0.316***
							(48.16)	(27.75)
Video category*EA							−0.001	−0.019
							(−0.07)	(−1.35)
Video category*EA^2							−0.009***	−0.005
							(−3.55)	(−1.62)
Collaborative video	0.302***	0.253***	0.318***	0.267***	0.298***	0.252***	0.232***	0.205***
	(27.43)	(19.97)	(28.76)	(21.12)	(27.11)	(19.93)	(21.77)	(16.26)
Video duration	−0.020***	−0.037***	−0.020***	−0.036***	−0.021***	−0.037***	−0.017***	−0.034***
	(−5.81)	(−9.15)	(−5.61)	(−8.98)	(−5.89)	(−9.16)	(−4.94)	(−8.63)
Video release time	0.027***	0.025***	0.029***	0.026***	0.028***	0.025***	0.017***	0.018***
	(6.66)	(5.26)	(7.02)	(5.50)	(6.76)	(5.37)	(4.40)	(3.87)
Time span	0.231***	0.284***	0.240***	0.290***	0.231***	0.286***	0.253***	0.298***
	(10.82)	(11.58)	(11.16)	(11.80)	(10.85)	(11.66)	(12.37)	(12.33)
Constant	−0.121***	−0.108***	−0.119***	−0.100***	−0.116***	−0.104***	−0.179***	−0.146***
	(−9.39)	(−7.26)	(−9.04)	(−6.66)	(−8.95)	(−7.01)	(−14.41)	(−9.97)
Observations	26,093	26,093	26,093	26,093	26,093	26,093	26,093	26,093
R-squared	0.695	0.597	0.692	0.596	0.696	0.598	0.720	0.609
Yearfix	YES	YES	YES	YES	YES	YES	YES	YES
IDfix	YES	YES	YES	YES	YES	YES	YES	YES

a similar trend, but in Model 8, the interaction term's coefficient is not significant, so Hypothesis H4b is not supported.

4.4 Robust Test

Firstly, for each inverted U-shaped relationship, we tested whether the linear relationships on both sides of the extreme point hold. The slopes for emotional anthropomorphism and recognition (left: 0.11, right: −0.23, $p < 0.01$), emotional anthropomorphism and engagement (left: 0.08, right: −0.17, $p < 0.01$), behavioral anthropomorphism and recognition (left: 0.04, right: −0.21, $p < 0.01$), and behavioral anthropomorphism and engagement (left: 0.10, right: −0.19, $p < 0.01$) all passed the U-shape test.

Additionally, we replaced the dependent variable. In this paper, the dependent variable is replaced with the number of video favorites. The robustness of the inverted

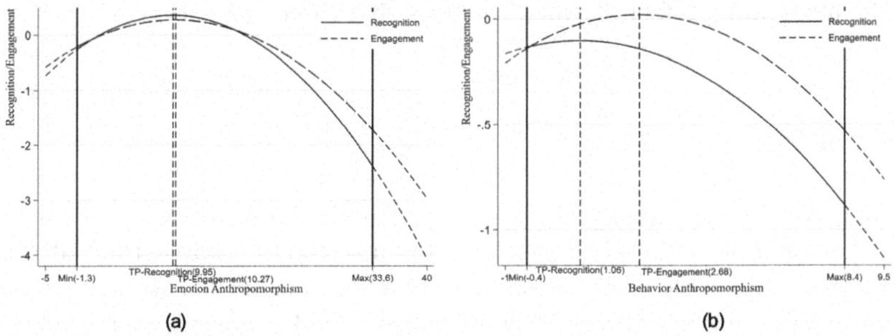

Fig. 2. Inverted U-Shaped Relationship between Anthropomorphism and Recognition and Engagement

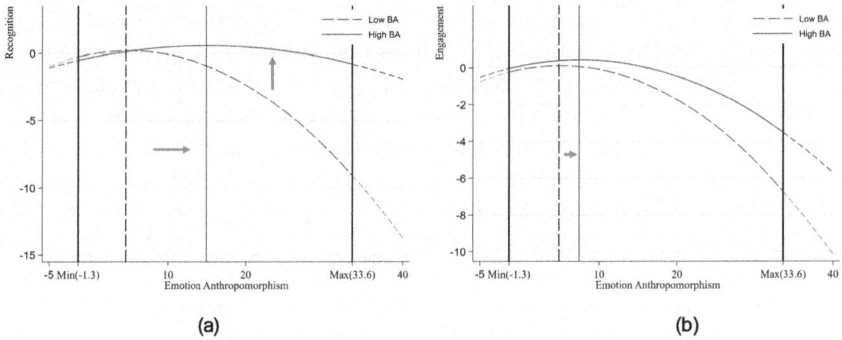

Fig. 3. The Moderating Effect of Behavioral Anthropomorphism on the Inverted U-Shaped Relationship

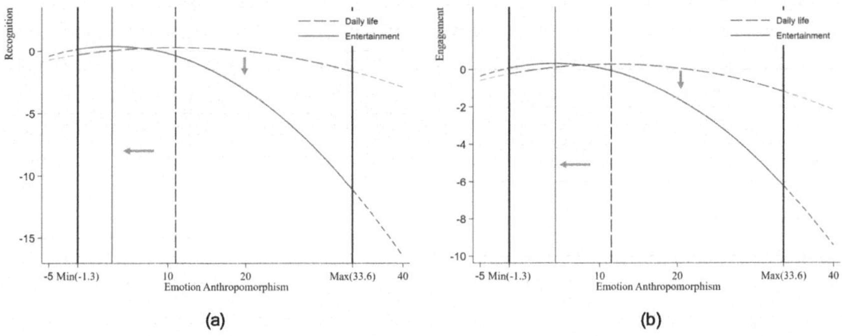

Fig. 4. Moderating Effect of Video Category on the Inverted U-Shape Relationship

U-shaped relationship was tested ($\beta\_(EA) = 0.1095$, $\beta\_(EA\^2) = -0.0064$, $p < 0.01$; $\beta\_(BA) = 0.027$, $\beta\_(BA\^2) = -0.020$, $p < 0.01$), Additionally, the moderating effect of behavioral anthropomorphism was validated ($\beta\_(BA{*}EA\^2) = 0.0016$, $p < 0.01$), as was the moderating effect of video category ($\beta\_(\text{Video category*EA\^{}2}) = -0.018$, $p < 0.01$).

5 Conclusion

In this study, we focused on virtual idols on the Bilibili platform, examining their emotional and behavioral anthropomorphism. This investigation into virtual idol anthropomorphism broadens the scope of related research. Specifically, we delved into how anthropomorphism influences follower recognition and engagement, considering the role of video category. Here are the key findings:

Firstly, there is a significant inverted U-shaped relationship between both emotional and behavioral anthropomorphism and follower recognition and engagement. Specifically, anthropomorphism initially enhances follower recognition and engagement, but excessive levels lead to a decline. This is consistent with previous findings that when "robots" mimic human behaviors exhibit imperfections or inconsistencies [16]. While previous research has explored the UV hypothesis concerning avatar emotional expression and disclosure of sources to avatars, empirical analyses remain scarce.

Secondly, behavioral anthropomorphism significantly moderates the impact of emotional anthropomorphism on follower recognition. This suggests that increasing levels of behavioral anthropomorphism make the inverted U-shaped curve for emotional anthropomorphism and follower recognition smoother. However, the moderating effect on follower engagement is less clear. This is another manifestation of UV: when virtual idols only show anthropomorphism in their emotions but still behave like computers, it may come off as a clumsy imitation, leading to aversion among followers.

Finally, the video category moderates the relationship between emotional anthropomorphism and follower recognition, with entertainment videos making the inverted U-shaped curve steeper compared to daily life videos. In daily life videos, where the scenarios align with the anthropomorphism of virtual idols, their expressions of emotions are more likely to be perceived as genuine, compared to entertainment scenarios.

To make virtual idols more relatable, creators should apply moderate emotional and behavioral anthropomorphism to boost fan recognition and engagement without triggering the uncanny valley effect. Also, balancing these cues is essential for maintaining positive fan reactions. Additionally, they should also consider the content type when performing anthropomorphism. This can guide the design of more relatable and engaging virtual idols.

There are some limitations. Firstly, our approach to measuring anthropomorphism was somewhat simplified, potentially leading to issues such as missing information. Additionally, the study may have been limited by a lack of diversity in the sample of virtual idols and followers. Different demographics and cultural backgrounds might experience and respond to anthropomorphism in varying ways, which could affect the generalizability of the findings.

Acknowledgement. This research was supported by the National Natural Science Foundation of China under Grant 72072194.

References

1. Li, J.: The benefit of being physically present: a survey of experimental works comparing copresent robots, telepresent robots and virtual agents [J]. Int. J. Hum. Comput. Studi. **77**, 23–37 (2015)
2. Chen, S., Boucher, H.C., Tapias, M.P.: The relational self revealed: integrative conceptualization and implications for interpersonal life [J]. Psychol. Bull. **132**(2), 151–179 (2006)
3. Franke, C., Groeppel-Klein, A., Müller, K.: Consumers' responses to virtual influencers as advertising endorsers: novel and effective or uncanny and deceiving? [J]. J. Advert. **52**(4), 523–539 (2023)
4. Mirowska, A., Arsenyan, J.: Sweet escape: the role of empathy in social media engagement with human versus virtual influencers [J]. Int. J. Hum. Comput. Stud. **174**, 103008 (2023)
5. Faddoul, G., Chatterjee, S.: A quantitative measurement model for persuasive technologies using storytelling via a virtual narrator [J]. Int. J. Hum. Comput. Interact. **36**(17), 1585–1604 (2020)
6. Nass, C., Moon, Y., Fogg, B.J., et al.: Can computer personalities be human personalities? [J]. Int. J. Hum. Comput. Stud. **43**(2), 223–239 (1995)
7. Lee, Y.-H., Yuan, C.W.: I'm not a puppet, I'm a real boy! Gender presentations by virtual influencers and how they are received [J]. Comput. Hum. Behav. **149**, 107927 (2023)
8. Epley, N., Waytz, A., Cacioppo, J.T.: On seeing human: a three-factor theory of anthropomorphism [J]. Psychol. Rev. **114**(4), 864–886 (2007)
9. Arsenyan, J., Mirowska, A.: Almost human? A comparative case study on the social media presence of virtual influencers [J]. Int. J. Hum. Comput. Stud. **155**, 102694 (2021)
10. Aaker, J.L.: Dimensions of brand personality [J]. J. Mark. Res. **34**(3), 347–356 (1997)
11. Mende, M., Scott, M.L., van Doorn, J., et al.: Service robots rising: how humanoid robots influence service experiences and elicit compensatory consumer responses [J]. J. Mark. Res. **56**(4), 535–556 (2019)
12. Moon, Y.: Intimate exchanges: using computers to elicit self-disclosure from consumers [J]. J. Consum. Res. **26**(4), 323–339 (2000)
13. van Vugt, H.C., Bailenson, J.N., Hoorn, J.F., et al.: Effects of facial similarity on user responses to embodied agents [J]. ACM Trans. Comput. Hum. Interact. **17**(2), 1–27 (2010)
14. Kim, E., Ratneshwar, S., Thorson, E.: Why narrative ads work: an integrated process explanation [J]. J. Advert. **46**(2), 283–296 (2017)
15. Vempala, A., Preotiuc-Pietro, D.: Categorizing and Inferring the Relationship between the Text and Image of Twitter Posts [M]. (2019)
16. Mathur, M.B., Reichling, D.B., Lunardini, F., et al.: Uncanny but not confusing: multisite study of perceptual category confusion in the Uncanny Valley [J]. Comput. Hum. Behav. **103**, 21–30 (2020)

Exploring the Impacts of Human-Robot Gender Match on Users' Perceptions of Robots

Yong Liu[1](✉), Jiajun Sun[1], Yanqing Lin[2], and Virpi Kristiina Tuunainen[1]

[1] Aalto University School of Business, Espoo, Finland
yong.liu@aalto.fi
[2] Hanken School of Economics, Helsinki, Finland

Abstract. Numerous studies have explored human preferences for male versus female robots, producing inconsistent findings and varied explanations for the manifestation of gender bias towards robots. This study contributes to understanding how user gender and robot gender interact to influence users' evaluations of robots by analyzing over 1100 survey responses on 23 robots, distinguished by their male and female appearances. The findings refute the existence of the same-gender or cross-gender effect. Specifically, we found a general preference for female robots over male robots. In addition, female users report the highest likeability scores for female robots compared to other human-robot gender combinations.

Keywords: Human-Robot-Interaction · Gender · Bias · Gender-Match · Adoption

1 Introduction

Fueled by recent advances in artificial intelligence (AI), AI robots have garnered significant attention in the media. The rapid acceleration of AI robot development, driven by substantial industry investments, has led to predictions that the deployment of these robots in everyday life may be attainable in the near future. However, research on AI robots remains in its early stages, and the academic community has accumulated relatively limited knowledge compared to the swift progress in AI robot development.

In particular, scholars and practitioners have expressed growing concern regarding the design of robot gender and are increasingly focused on understanding how both user and robot gender influence human-robot interaction. Robot gendering can be defined as the attribution of gender to a robotic system through various meanings like voice, name, or physique (Bryant et al. 2020; Robertson 2010). In this vein, robot gendering has been put forward as a key design concept for robot developers and researchers (Bryant et al. 2020). Evidently, determining the gendering design of a robot is a fundamental design question for every robot.

Apart from the robot's gender, the gender of the human who evaluates the robot appears to be an important factor influencing human-robot interaction (e.g., Nomura, 2017). The robot gender and human gender may interact to shape how humans perceive

Y. P. Tu and M. Chi (Eds.): WHICEB 2025, LNBIP 549, pp. 52–61, 2025.
https://doi.org/10.1007/978-3-031-94184-9_5

and interact with a robot. This exhibits an important topic for scholars, leading to a growing body of research on it (e.g., Kislev, 2023; Wagner-Hartl et al. 2022). Nonetheless, conflicting results have often been reported, resulting in a lack of consensus on the existence of gender effects. In the scholarly discussion, a significant debate has been raised about the existence of same-gender versus cross-gender effect. The same-gender (cross-gender) effect refers to individuals' preference for robots of the same (opposite) gender as the users than those of the opposite (same) gender. The study aims to address the following two research questions: (1) Does the same-gender effect or the cross-gender effect exist? (2) Is there a general preference for female robots?

This study aims to contribute to the ongoing debate by analyzing over 1100 survey responses pertinent to 23 robots designed with male or female appearances. In particular, we investigated users' preferences for male or female robots and empirically tested the same-gender versus cross-gender effect. In addition, we explored the possible moderation effect of robot gendering on the relationship between robot anthropomorphism and robot likeability, which are two core variables of the uncanny valley theory. The results add to the discussion on the robot gendering effect by offering new and robust empirical evidence.

The rest of the paper is structured as follows: the next section reviews the past studies, followed by a discussion of the research framework and hypotheses in Sect. 3. Section 4 presents the research methodology, while Sect. 5 discusses the results. The paper concludes by discussing the implications in Sect. 6.

2 Past Studies and Theoretical Basis

Many studies have investigated the impacts of user gender and robot gender on user perceptions of robots, yielding conflicting results (Suzuki and Nomura 2024). For instance, there is a debate about whether people prefer male or female robots. In this vein, Kislev (2023) investigated survey data pertinent to the general attitude of over 11 thousand males and 14 thousand females across 30 European countries toward robots and reported that females develop significantly more negative attitudes toward accepting robots than males. Specifically, they found that women see such robots "more negatively in terms of social norms, psychological health, morality, and functionality" (Kislev, 2023, p. 2230). Likewise, the study of Wagner-Hartl et al. (2022) showed that males' general attitudes toward robots are more positive than those of females.

Several scholars have argued that robot gendering plays a significant role in affecting how users evaluate robots. For instance, a study by Borau et al. (2021) reports a preference for female robots among their study participants. Similarly, Carpenter et al. (2009), in their study of robots designed for in-home use, found that people prefer female robots. Nonetheless, several studies have argued for the existence of a same-gender effect in robot preference, suggesting that users tend to prefer robots of their own gender. For example, Eyssel et al. (2012) examined the impact of robot voice and found that people perceive a strong psychological closeness toward a same-gender robot.

Interestingly, some studies have documented a cross-gender effect, where users show a preference for robots of the opposite gender. For instance, Alexander et al. (2014, p. 2333) studied human-robot collaboration interaction and found that people feel "more comfortable with a robot assigned the other gender". Likewise, Siegel et al. (2009) experimented with using robots to solicit donations from museum visitors and found that participants rated robots of the opposite gender as more credible, trustworthy, and engaging.

Another conflicting point of view resides in the anthropomorphism effect among users of different genders. In this regard, Borau et al. (2021) suggested that female robots are perceived as more human than male robots, which explains people's preference for female robots. Nonetheless, Eyssel et al. (2012) showed that people anthropomorphize robots of the same gender better than those of the opposite gender. McDermott et al. (2020) investigated gender differences in people's perceptions of robot-assisted surgery, reporting that females perceived the surgical process as dehumanizing, while males tended to humanize the process and appear unfazed. It is worth noting that past studies have mostly been conducted with a limited range of robot designs. In this vein, this study attempts to explore a broader spectrum of different robot designs with a large sample size to offer a more comprehensive investigation.

3 Hypotheses Development

As noted above, a heated debate exists regarding the gender effect in human-robot interaction, with conflicting empirical results and controversial theoretical arguments. The studies tested several controversial hypotheses (H1–H4), and a new hypothesis (H5) pertinent to the impact of robot anthropomorphism on robot likeability, which is built upon the same gender effect literature.

3.1 Attitude toward Robots

Past studies indicate that males generally hold a more positive attitude toward using AI robots than females (Kislev, 2023; Wagner-Hartl et al. 2022). McDermott et al. (2020) suggest that males appear more unfazed when interacting with robots compared to females. In line with past studies, we argue that males are more likely to express a positive attitude toward robots and thus perceive robots as more likable. Thus, we posit that:

H1. Males will perceive robots as more likable than females.

3.2 Same-Gender Effect

Psychological studies reveal that people exhibit same-gender preferences for peers, which can be defined as "the degree to which a person prefers to like, befriend or become acquaintances with same-gender peers compared to other-gender peers" (Bukowski and DeLay 2020, p. 1). Such preferences can be observed among males and females across all age groups (Bukowski and DeLay 2020). Thus, we argue that the same gender preference for peers can be extended to robots. In this line, the study of Eyssel et al. (2012) suggests the existence of people's preference for robots of the same gender. Taken together, we hypothesized that:

H2. Males perceive male robots as more likable than female robots.

H3. Females perceive female robots as more likable than male robots.

Evidently, people learn their own gender identity and thus become more familiar with the characteristics of their own gender during their growing up process. Consequently, people should be better able to recognize gender cues that correspond to their own gender. Given that gender cues are also anthropomorphism cues, people can thus more easily anthropomorphize robots of the same gender. In this vein, Eyssel et al. (2012) reported that people anthropomorphize robots with a same-gender voice more strongly than those with an opposite-gender voice. Thus, we posit that:

H4. People perceive robots of the same gender as more human than those of the opposite gender.

3.3 The Moderation Effect of Same-Gender Match

The uncanny valley theory posits that the degree of robot anthropomorphism affects how users perceive the robot's likeability (Mori 1970; Mori et al. 2012). In particular, if "creepy" designs of robots can be avoided, robot anthropomorphism is expected to positively affect perceived robot likeability (see. Mori 1970; Mori et al. 2012). We argue that the impact of robot anthropomorphism on robot likeability could be stronger with a same-gender match between the robot and the user.

Eyssel et al. (2012) indicate that people feel psychologically closer to robots of the same gender. Thomas et al. (2020) imply that affinity bias may exist for human-robot interaction. Specifically, affinity bias describes people's tendency to feel more comfortable when surrounded by people like them (Trainer et al. 2020). In addition, Zogaj et al. (2023) argued that humans would perceive greater psychological closeness and congruence with other individuals of the same gender. Their study reported that a chatbot could have a stronger impact on purchase intention through self-congruence with a same-gender robot than with a robot of the opposite gender.

Given that the same gender match can be associated with greater psychological closeness and congruence (Zogaj et al. 2023), we argue that humans would express greater likeability toward robots of the same gender across different levels of robot anthropomorphism. In other words, for a given level of robot anthropomorphism, an individual would more likely perceive a robot to be likable when the robot is of the same gender as the individual. Accordingly, the same-gender match of the user and the robot should positively moderate the impact of robot anthropomorphism on robot likeability. Thus, we assume that:

H5. The user-robot gender match moderates the impact of robot anthropomorphism on the perceived likeability of the robot. Specifically, the same-gender match will induce a stronger impact of robot anthropomorphism on robot likeability.

4 Research Methodology

While we acknowledge the variations in gender, this study focuses on the binary gender categories of males and females, which allows for simplicity in comparing our results with those of past studies. Specifically, we collected a sample of 1109 questionnaire responses about people's perceptions toward 23 different robot faces with apparent male or female features, as shown in Fig. 1. The robot faces were mostly derived from the work of Mathur and Reichling (2016) or the Internet, following a strict selection criterion similar to that applied in the work of Mathur and Reichling (2016). The selected robot faces are featured with a spectrum of different anthropomorphism levels, increasing the external validity of the results. In the questionnaire, the measure of anthropomorphism is revised from previous studies (Mathur and Reichling 2016), ranging from −100 (very machine-like) to 100 (very humanlike). Given that the robot faces may exhibit certain emotions, the perceived emotion of the robot faces is measured via a scale from −100 (very negative emotion) to 100 (very positive emotion). The measurement of likeability is adapted from the work of Nunamaker et al. (2011) on a 7-point Likert scale that ranges from "*strongly disagree*" to "*strongly agree*".

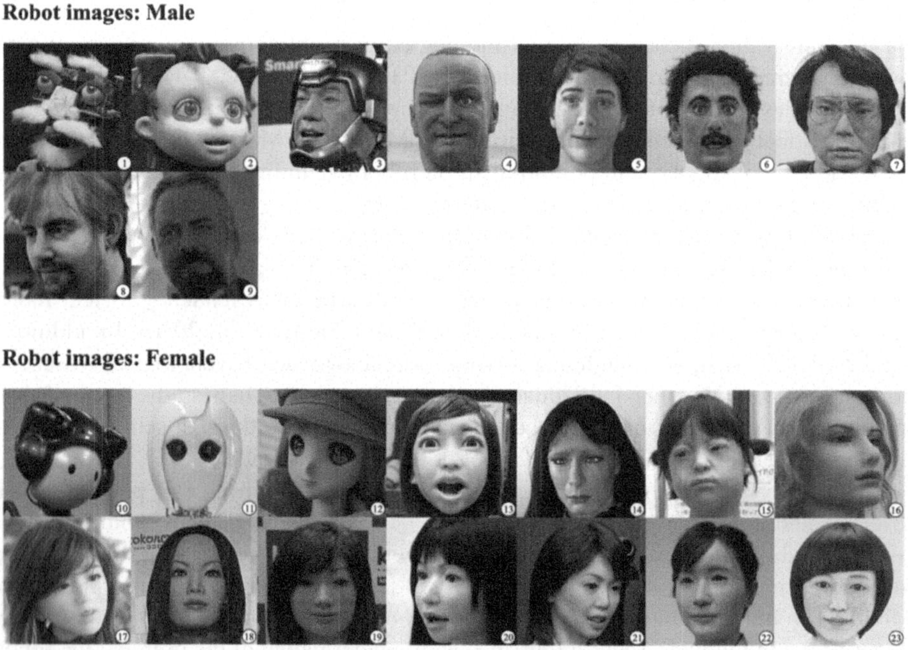

Fig. 1. The Robot Faces Investigated

The experiment participants were recruited from Amazon Mechanical Turk, and they received approximately US$1.60 for completing the experiment. Each robot face received an average of 47.83 evaluation responses ($sd = 2.55$). A total of 9 survey respondents were unwilling to provide gender information or report a gender identity outside the male-female binary, and their responses were excluded from the analysis. This results in a final sample of 1100 responses, in which 659 and 441 responses were identified as males and females. The survey participants were mostly 26–45 years old and held a bachelor's degree or above, as shown in Table 1.

Table 1. Demographic Information of the Experiment Participants

Variable	Category	Frequency
Gender	Male	659
	Female	441
Age	18–25 years old	32
	26–35 years old	490
	36–45 years old	333
	46–55 years old	128
	56–65 years old	77
	66 years old or above	32
	Prefer not to provide	8
Education	Lower than high school	3
	High school	140
	Bachelor's degree	719
	Master's degree or higher	223
	Prefer not to provide	15

5 Results and Discussion

The latent variable score of likeability is used in the analysis. In addition, the values of anthropomorphism were converted to a positive value (plus 101) and then log transformed to achieve a better normal distribution of values. We first compared the perceived likeability scores of male versus female participants, as shown in Table 2. Contrary to our expectations, males did not report a significantly higher likeability score toward robots than females, rejecting H1. Instead, females (5.17) reported a higher average likeability score than males (5.03), albeit the result is not statistically significant ($p = 0.12$).

Table 2. Mean Comparison of Likeability and Anthropomorphism Scores

	Likeability (*sd*)		Anthropomorphism (*sd*)	
Robot gender				
Female	5.27(1.36)	$p < 0.001$	4.87(0.81)	$p = 0.79$
Male	4.79(1.61)		4.86(0.83)	
Human gender				
Female	5.17(1.44)	$p = 0.12$	4.85(0.88)	$p = 0.56$
Male	5.03(1.50)		4.88(0.77)	

We further explored whether the same-gender effect exists for robot likeability. As shown in Table 2, the perceived likeability is significantly stronger ($p < 0.001$) for female robots (Mean = 5.27) than male robots (Mean = 4.79), indicating that people, in general, prefer female robots over male robots. As shown in Table 3, the ANOVA test revealed significant differences in the perceived likeability of different human-robot gender groups ($F(3, 1096) = 10.3, p < 0.001$). Tukey's test indicated that females prefer female robots over male ones ($p < 0.001$), and the same pattern can be observed for male participants ($p < 0.001$). In particular, females reported the highest likeability scores when observing female robots (5.36), while males reported the lowest when evaluating male robots (4.74). The results reject H2 but support H3. In other words, both male and female participants prefer female robots, contradicting the earlier research findings on the same-gender effect on robot likability.

Table 3. Likeability and Anthropomorphism Scores across Gender Match Groups

Categories—sample size	Likeability (*sd*)	Anthropomorphism (*sd*)
Human (F) & robot (F) – 275	5.36(1.33)	4.85(0.89)
Human (F) & robot (M) – 166	4.86(1.57)	4.85(0.87)
Human (M) & robot (F) – 402	5.22(1.38)	4.89(0.75)
Human (M) & robot (M) – 257	4.74(1.64)	4.87(0.81)

Note: *F* denotes Female; *M* indicates Male

The results indicate that male and female participants report no difference in their perceived anthropomorphism levels of the robots ($p > 0.05$), as shown in Table 2. A one-way ANOVA was conducted to examine the effect of different groups on the anthropomorphism. The results indicate no statistically significant difference among the groups ($F(3, 1096) = 0.149$, $p = 0.93$). Subsequent post-hoc comparisons using the Tukey HSD test revealed no significant pairwise differences in anthropomorphism between the different human-robot gender combinations (all $p > 0.05$). These findings suggest that the human-robot gender combinations do not significantly affect perceived robot anthropomorphism in the dataset; therefore, reject H4.

A fixed-effect multivariable linear regression was performed to explore the impact of robot anthropomorphism on robot likeability under different circumstances of human-robot gender combinations, as shown in Table 4. The model includes age, education, and emotion as control variables, and all the numeric variables are z-score transformed to minimize the risk of multicollinearity. The overall model was statistically significant, indicating a good model fit. The Generalized Variance Inflation Factors (GVIF) were computed to examine multicollinearity in the model. With a maximum GVIF value of 3.48, multicollinearity is thus unlikely an issue for the analysis (Alam et al. 2024).

The results reveal a positive and significant impact of anthropomorphism on robot likeability ($\beta = 0.158$, $p < 0.001$). Nonetheless, no significant moderating impact of human-robot gender combinations on the relationship between robot anthropomorphism and robot likeability was found. This indicates that H5 is rejected. In addition, age ($\beta = -0.125$, $p < 0.001$) was found to be negatively associated with robot likeability, whereas

Table 4. The Impacts of Robot Anthropomorphism on Robot Likeability

Predictors	Path Coefficients
Human (F) & robot (M)	-0.164^{***}
Human (M) & robot (F)	-0.095^{*}
Human (M) & robot (M)	-0.300^{***}
Anthropomorphism	0.158^{***}
Age	-0.125^{***}
Education	0.060^{**}
Emotion	0.609^{***}
Human (F) & robot (M) × anthropomorphism	$-0.032^{n.s.}$
Human (M) & robot (F) × anthropomorphism	$0.006^{n.s.}$
Human (M) & robot (M) × anthropomorphism	$0.066^{n.s.}$
$F(10, 1089) = 120.9$; adjust $R^2 = 52.18\%$	

Note: The reference category is Human (F) & Robot (F); *n.s* denotes not significant; * denotes $p < 0.05$; *** denotes $p < 0.001$

education ($\beta = 0.060$, $p < 0.01$) and education ($\beta = 0.609$, $p < 0.001$) were positively associated with robot likeability.

6 Conclusions and Implications

Our study contributes to the debate on the effect of robot gendering and human gender on robot perceptions. With a large sample size and a diverse selection of robot faces, the study provides empirical results with strong external validity. Specifically, contrary to our expectations, male respondents did not exhibit a more positive attitude toward robots than female respondents. Instead, females reported a higher likeability score for robots than males, albeit the difference is not statistically significant. In addition, female robots were preferred over male robots, as both male and female participants rated female robots more favorably than male robots. The result does not support the existence of the same-gender effect in terms of robot likeability.

Contrary to previous studies (e.g., Eyssel et al., 2012), our study did not find a significant difference between males and females in their tendency to anthropomorphize robots. This indicates that the participants were not more inclined to anthropomorphize robots of the same gender. Therefore, the same-gender effect does not hold in the context of robot anthropomorphism. Furthermore, the same-gender effect is only partially supported when considering its moderating influence on the relationship between robot anthropomorphism and robot likeability. Specifically, robot anthropomorphism appears to have a stronger influence on robot likeability for male participants observing male robots than other human-robot gender combinations.

Our study offers several implications for research and practice. Firstly, the study contributes to the discussion regarding the existence of same-gender or cross-gender effect of human-robot gender combinations. With a large number of survey responses on a wide range of different robot faces, we fail to find strong support for either the same-gender or cross-gender effect of human-robot gender preference. We did not discover evidence pertinent to the same-gender or cross-gender effects in the context of other hypotheses. This raises questions about whether same-gender or cross-gender preference truly exists. In this vein, we highlight that people, in general, prefer female robots, which represents the second theoretical contribution of this study. Thirdly, we found no difference in participants' ability to anthropomorphize robots of the same gender or the other gender.

For practitioners, our study indicates that designing robots as female can more easily elicit positive user attitudes, such as greater robot likeability. In addition, age negatively affects robot likeability, while education has a positive influence on it. Thus, designing service robots targeted at younger individuals with higher educational backgrounds could be an effective strategy for introducing these robots to the market.

Like past studies, the current study has several limitations. First, it is based on studying robot face photos rather than physical robots. Investigating the gendering effect in physical robots may yield interesting results. Second, participants' cultural backgrounds may influence their perceptions of male and female robots. The current study did not account for the cultural background of the experiment participants.

Acknowledgement. The authors gratefully acknowledge that the project is partly supported by the Finnish National Agency for Education (Project ID: AIRobinSers), the Jenny and Antti Wihuri Foundation (Project ID: Embracing the Future: Service Robots for Business Values and Social Welfare), and the Academy of Finland (Funding for mobility cooperation).

References

Alam, M.M., Rayhan, M.I., Mansur, M.: From the local disparities to national realities: mapping and multilevel modeling of catastrophic health expenditure in Bangladesh using HIES 2016. PLoS One. **19**(1), 1–24 (2024)

Borau, S., Otterbring, T., Laporte, S., Fosso Wamba, S.: The Most human bot: female gendering increases humanness perceptions of bots and acceptance of AI. Psychol. Mark. **38**(7), 1052–1068 (2021)

Bryant, D., Borenstein, J., Howard, A.: Why should we gender? The effect of robot gendering and occupational stereotypes on human trust and perceived competency. In: ACM/IEEE International Conference on Human-Robot Interaction, pp. 13–21. IEEE Computer Society (2020)

Bukowski, W.M., DeLay, D.: Studying the same-gender preference as a defining feature of cultural contexts. Front. Psychol. **11**, 1–6 (2020)

Carpenter, J., Davis, J.M., Erwin-Stewart, N., Lee, T.R., Bransford, J.D., Vye, N.: Gender representation and humanoid robots designed for domestic use. Int. J. Soc. Robot. **1**(1), 261–265 (2009)

Alexander, E., Caroline Bank, Yang, J.J., Hayes, B., Scassellati, B.: Asking for help from a gendered robot. In: Proceedings of the Annual Meeting of the Cognitive Science Society, pp. 2333–2338 (2014)

Eyssel, F., Kuchenbrandt, D., Bobinger, S., de Ruiter, L., Hegel, F.: If You Sound like me, you must be more human': on the interplay of robot and user features on human-robot acceptance and anthropomorphism. In: HRI'12, Boston, pp. 125–126 (2012)

Kislev, E.: The robot-gender divide: how and why men and women differ in their attitudes toward social robots. Soc. Sci. Comput. Rev. **41**(6), 2230–2248 (2023)

Mathur, M.B., Reichling, D.B.: Navigating a social world with robot partners: a quantitative cartography of the uncanny valley. Cognition. **146**, 22–32 (2016)

McDermott, H., Choudhury, N., Lewin-Runacres, M., Aemn, I., Moss, E.: Gender differences in understanding and acceptance of robot-assisted surgery. J. Robot. Surg. **14**(1), 227–232 (2020)

Mori, M.: The uncanny valley. Energy. **7**, 33–35 (1970)

Mori, M., AcDorman, K.F., Kageki, N.: The uncanny valley. IEEE Rob. Autom. Mag. **19**(2), 98–100 (2012)

Nomura, T.: Robots and gender. Gender Genome. **1**(1), 18–26 (2017)

Nunamaker, J., Derrick, D., Elkins, A., Burgoon, J., Patton, M.: Embodied conversational agent-based kiosk for automated interviewing. J. Manag. Inf. Syst. **28**(1), 17–48 (2011)

Robertson, J.: Gendering humanoid robots: robo-sexism in Japan. Body Soc. **16**(2), 1–36 (2010)

Siegel, M., Breazeal, C., Norton, M.I.: Persuasive robotics: the influence of robot gender on human behavior. In: 9 IEEE/RSJ International Conference on Intelligent Robots and Systems. IEEE, St. Louis, MO (2009)

Suzuki, T., Nomura, T.: Gender preferences for robots and gender equality orientation in communication situations. AI Soc. **39**(2), 739–748 (2024)

Thomas T., John R.T., Christopher J.S.: Choosing the best robot for the job: affinity bias in human-robot interaction. In: 12th International Conference on Social Robotics, pp. 490–501. Springer Nature (2020)

Wagner-Hartl, V., Schmid, R., Gleichauf, K.: The influence of task complexity on acceptance and trust in human-robot interaction—gender and age differences. Cogn. Comput. Internet Things. **43**(43), 118–126 (2022)

Zogaj, A., Mähner, P.M., Yang, L., Tscheulin, D.K.: It's a match! The effects of chatbot anthropomorphization and chatbot gender on consumer behavior. J. Bus. Res. **155**, 1–13 (2023)

A Systematic Literature Review on Human-AI Collaboration in the Information Systems Research

Chenglong Li[1,2], Xueman Li[1], and Ting Long[3](✉)

[1] School of Information Management, Central China Normal University, Wuhan 430079, China
[2] Data Governance and Intelligent Decision-Making Research Center, Central China Normal University, Wuhan 430079, China
[3] National Research Center of Cultural Industries, Central China Normal University, Wuhan 430079, China
ting.long@ccnu.edu.cn

Abstract. The function and role of AI in collaborating in future work scenarios has received a great deal of attention across industries, but there has been limited work on assessing the current state of research on human-AI collaboration and integrating research results. To fill this gap, we conducted a systematic review of 43 research papers on human-AI collaboration in the field of Information Systems. Our analysis focuses on conceptualization of human-AI collaboration, collaboration mechanism, human and AI characteristics in the literature. Based on the findings, we developed a conceptual framework that highlights the interrelationships between the four parts. Finally, we identify research gaps and propose future research directions for further exploration in this expanding research area.

Keywords: Human-AI Collaboration · Human-autonomy Team · Literature Review · Artificial Intelligence

1 Introduction

The rapid integration of artificial intelligence (AI) into organizational processes and decision-making systems has ushered in a new era of human-AI collaboration. AI broadly defined as algorithmic-based systems capable of performing cognitive tasks [1]. AI encompasses a wide range of intelligent technologies, such as chatbots, virtual agents, and autonomous robots [2]. While AI, like traditional technologies, can service as a tool to support tasks, or as a medium to facilitating human collaboration, its intelligent capacities set is apart [1]. AI can independently accomplish tasks and collaborate interdependently with humans, elevating it from a mere tool to a counterpart in the collaborative process [1]. Such changes in AI's role are reshaping the future of work by enabling innovative forms of human-AI collaboration, where it can function as a partner or teammate. Together, humans and AI can leverage their respective strengths to achieve shared goals, creating a synergistic relationship in which their combined contributions can exceed the sum of their individual capabilities [3]. Human-AI collaboration is not

Y. P. Tu and M. Chi (Eds.): WHICEB 2025, LNBIP 549, pp. 62–74, 2025.
https://doi.org/10.1007/978-3-031-94184-9_6

merely task completion but optimizing complementary strengths, driving efficiency, creativity, and innovation [4].

Additionally, AI's distinct characteristics, such as its invisibility, inscrutability, and changeability, present significant challenges to our understanding of how it operates and how it used in collaboration [1]. These complexities highlight the need for a deeper exploration into the mechanisms and outcomes of human-AI collaboration. Recognizing its transformative potential for workflows and organizational processes, scholars in the field of information systems (IS) have increasingly focused their attention on this critical phenomenon.

However, research on human-AI collaboration remains in its infancy. Theoretical frameworks in this domain are still underdeveloped, and systematic efforts to consolidate and integrate existing knowledge are still scarce. This fragmented understanding not only limits the academic discourse but also constrains practical advancements in leveraging human-AI collaboration effectively. Given its far-reaching implications for business innovation, workforce dynamics, and organizational progress, addressing these research gaps is imperative. Therefore, this study aims to conduct a literature review on human-AI collaboration in the field of information systems (IS). Specifically, it aims to answer the following questions:

Q1: How has the human-AI collaboration has been conceptualized, and how do humans and AI collaborate in the literature?
Q2: What aspects of AI side have been studied in the literature?
Q3: What aspects of human side have been studied in the literature?
Q4: What are the identified outcomes of human-AI collaboration in the literature?

The remainder of this paper is organized as follows: Sect. 2 outlines the research methodology, Sect. 3 presents the results, Sect. 4 identifies research gaps and proposes future research directions, and Sect. 5 concludes by summarizing the study's contributions and limitations.

2 Methodology

This study adopted a systematic literature review approach as proposed by [5] to identify research papers on human-AI collaboration, as illustrated in Fig. 1. Specifically, we utilized journals recommended by AIS community,[1] given their high-quality research in the IS field. We searched relevant papers in two ways: in May, 2024, we conducted a systematic search via Web of Science, focusing exclusively on the IS journals. Then, we performed manual searches on the official websites of each journal to ensure that no relevant articles were neglected. We used the following retrieval query to find the journal articles published in English, and no timeframe was used:

Topic = (human-AI OR human-agent OR human-machine OR human-autonomy OR intelligent agent OR human-robot) AND (collaboration OR cooperation OR team).*

We found 166 relevant articles. To ensure the quality and relevance of the selected papers, we applied rigorous inclusion and exclusion criteria (see Table 1). Furthermore,

[1] https://aisnet.org/page/SeniorScholarListofPremierJournals

a backward and forward search was also conducted, yielding two additional articles were found. Finally, 43 papers were included for the literature review. To systematically analyze the included studies, we created a detailed data extraction table in Microsoft Excel, which served as a framework for capturing essential information from each article. Specifically, we extracted data on the following categories: research focus, theoretical foundation, context, research methods, AI-related factors, human-related factors, collaboration mechanism, outcomes, and main findings. A content analysis approach was employed to code, analyze, and integrate the extracted information within each category [6]. To ensure reliability and consistency, all authors independently coded the data, then compared results and resolved discrepancies through further discussions.

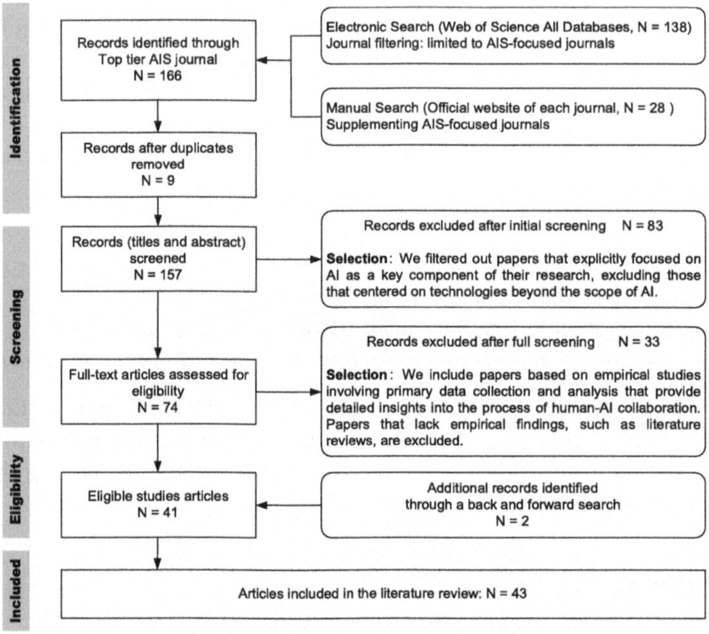

Fig. 1. Literature search and identification procedures

3 Results

3.1 Conceptualization of Human-AI Collaboration

The selected papers introduce various concepts, including human-AI collaboration, human-AI teams, human-autonomy teams, human-AI co-learning, and human-AI hybrid, among others. Table 2 presents the concepts, their definitions, and the differences between them. Other concepts, such as human-AI cooperation [7], human-autonomy interactions [8], are mentioned but lack clear definitions. Despite the varying definitions, these concepts share some key features. First, all definitions highlight the

Table 1. Inclusion and exclusion criteria

Inclusion criteria	Exclusion criteria
Papers must present full-text empirical studies that are grounded in original data collection and analysis	Papers that do not present empirical results, such as literature reviews, editorials, book reviews, education materials, and research notes
Papers must explicitly center on AI, clearly identifying AI as a key component of the study	Papers focusing on technologies outside the scope of AI, such as traditional technologies and non-cognitive technologies
Papers must examine the collaboration between humans and AI, providing detailed insights into how AI was used in collaboration	Articles that do not emphasize collaboration, such as those focusing solely on AI as a tool, without exploring its role in collaboration

collaborative process that involves both human and AI. Second, the collaborative efforts are directed toward common or shared goals. Third, in these definitions, AI can exhibit varying degrees of interdependencies with humans, from partial or complete.

However, there are also notable differences. For instance, human-autonomy teams emphasize the number of human and AI, involving at least one human and one AI, and can extend to more complex configurations. Additionally, hybrid service agent introduces the idea of combining AI and human agents within a single interface, but it does not fully specify how the two interact behind the scenes. These definitions fail to clearly delineate the distinct roles human and AI play in the collaborative process, leaving the specifics of their interactions and interdependencies ambiguous. The distinction between human and AI roles is unclear, creating gaps in understanding their collaborative mechanism.

3.2 The Mechanism of Human-AI Collaboration

The mechanism of human-AI collaboration refers to how humans and AI interact and collaborate to achieve shared goals. Although the reviewed papers do not provide a clear, unified definition of this mechanism, they do explore it through three main perspectives. The first is from the tool perspective, where AI is employed to augment human decision-making. For instance, in the context of recruitment, AI acts as a supportive tool to enhance human judgment, such as in job applicant selection, where AI aids in deciding who should receive a job offer, while in data collection and analysis, AI assists in improving the efficiency and accuracy [14].

The second lens is from the medium perspective, where AI acts as an intermediary to facilitate human-to-human interactions via fostering common ground by enabling knowledge sharing, enhancing communication, and bridging gaps between groups with diverse expertise and interests [1]. For example, AI serves as a mediator among coders in facilitating human collaboration in the context of code suggestion [15].

The third comes from the counterpart perspective, where AI operates as a partner or teammate working alongside humans to achieve a shared goal. In this setting, AI can assume various roles, such as supervisor, peer, or subordinate [16], or taking the leading position, colleague position, or subordinate in the team [17].

AI as a counterpart can encompass delegation, which is a task-assignment mechanism between humans and AI. Delegation operates in two primary ways: (1) AI to human, where AI decides which tasks it will handle itself and which it will delegate to human; (2) human to AI, where human decide which task to handle and which to assign to the AI [18]. Alternatively, delegation can be viewed through three levels of intervention:

Table 2. Definition and Distinction from Related Concepts

Conception	Definition	Differences
Human-AI collaboration	"*AI system and the user interact, share their prior knowledge, and ideally decide unanimously. The process aims to combine the complementary capabilities of the AI system and the human (the user), to achieve common goals more effectively*" [9]. It focuses on "*how humans work with AI systems, seeking to understand how AI-embedded sociotechnical systems should be designed, implemented, and managed to augment human work and extend human cognition*" [10]	Focus on blending capabilities and unanimous decisions.
Human-AI teams	"*AI teammates on human-AI team can make decisions and execute tasks autonomously from humans while also working interdependently with humans to accomplish overarching team goals more efficiently or effectively than human-only teams*" [3]	Focus on AI's autonomy in teams.
Human-autonomy teams	"*Involve at least one human working interdependently with at least one form of autonomy, where an autonomous agent represents a computational sub-system partially or completely self-governed with respect to team activity*" [11, 12]	Mention the number of humans and AI.

(*continued*)

Table 2. (*continued*)

Conception	Definition	Differences
Human-AI co-learning	"*A process in which collaborating partners adapt to each other and learn together over time. It is key that such learning does not happen separately, but through collaborative interaction that enable them to discover and learn about the task, themselves, and their team partners*" [4]	Focus on co-learning and adaptation.
Human-AI hybrid	"*Combination of AI agents and human agent that function as an integrated unit and serve users via a single interface*" [13]	Focus on integration via a single interface.

(1) automation (lowest level of intervention, where decision-making is fully delegation to AI), (2) adjustable automation (middle level of intervention, where both human and AI involve), and (3) augmentation (highest level of intervention, where humans play a dominate role) [19].

Partnership between human and AI can be evaluated based on five levels of AI input distribution: (1) 0% human input and 100% AI input, (2) 25% human input and 75% AI input, (3) equal input with 50% from both human and AI, (4) 75% human input and 25% AI input, and (5) 100% human input with 0% AI input [2].

Other factors shaping the human-AI relationship include (1) AI's activeness, where AI involve passively and actively, and (2) AI's cooperativeness, which is classified as cooperative, neutral, and selfish [20]. From an organizational level, the collaboration between humans and AI can be improved via the following interaction types: (1) negotiating interoperability (by fostering a clear understanding of each other's complementarities, prioritizing data requirements, and anticipating organizational constrains), (2) nurturing trust (by highlighting the benefits of AI and incrementing transparency), (3) mutual learning (by specializing resources, encouraging the socialization of learning, and cultivating a data-driven culture) [21].

Furthermore, experimentation and predictable unreliability have been identified as critical mechanisms in the collaborative process. Human can experiment with different AI scenarios, recognizing that while AI may exhibit predictable errors and unreliable in predictions, it remains useful for collaboration [10].

3.3 AI Related Factors

The AI side encompasses the designed characteristics and functionalities of AI that influence the human-AI collaboration. In the selected papers, various characteristics of AI, including its capabilities, AI transparency, AI tuning, AI type, and implementation context, have been reported. Specifically, AI capabilities emerged as a central focus. Some studies do not explicitly categorize AI's capabilities, but instead, compare AI capabilities with humans or computers to highlight their differences [22, 23]. Additionally, some studies identified several key dimensions of AI's capabilities. The first dimension is the *autonomy*, which refers to the extent to which AI can adapt their programmed level of autonomy for a defined task [24]. The autonomy has been generally divided into two categories: partial autonomy, where AI generates a decision that requires human approval before execution; and full autonomy, where AI independently executes a decision without prior human input [24]. Likewise, other research proposes a more nuanced three-tiered framework to describe autonomy: lower level, where human primarily manage the decision-making process; higher level, where AI manages the process entirely or almost entirely; and middle level, where AI augments human decision-making [14].

Another crucial capability is *intelligence*, which refers to the extent to which AI can learn, reason, and solve problem [25]. The intelligence is assessed by comparing different levels of AI's intellectual ability, such as high versus low levels [25].

The third capability is AI's *influence*, refers to the ability of an AI teammate to control, manipulate, and contribute to the shared resources and goals within a collaborative environment [26]. This influence is typically assessed based on two dimensions: level of influence (high versus low), and variability of influence (dynamic versus static) [26].

AI *tuning*, also known as algorithmic tuning, which refers to the adjustments of AI's parameters or the model to align the AI with desired outcomes [27], has been reported in literature. This characteristic of AI has also been found to influence the performance of human-AI collaboration [27].

AI *transparency* is another important studied characteristics of AI, focusing on reducing the information asymmetry between the human's mental model and the AI's decision model [9]. Research has shown AI transparency significantly influence trust in the human-AI collaboration and workability of unreliable AI [10].

AI's *social characteristics*, such as its framed social intent and behavior, have been examined. Social intent includes benevolence-based intent (self-sacrifice), where the AI prioritizes human safety over its own, and self-interest-based intent, where the AI prioritizes itself. Similarly, social behavior is categorized as benevolent behavior and self-interested behavior [8]. These social characteristics significantly influence human perceptions of trust, reliance intentions, and trust behaviors [8]. Etiquette has been found to increase trust and performance [28].

To measure the AI characteristics, in the reviewed studies, experimental methods emerged as the most commonly used approach. Experiments offer controlled environments that can systematically assess AI's characteristics, particularly, its capabilities. For instance, vignette-based experiments, which can present participants with constructed and realistic scenarios, have been used to compare human and AI capabilities [22] and to assess levels of autonomy [24]. Additionally, the wizard-of-Oz-experiment has been employed in several studies, allowing researchers to simulate AI by have a human experimenter covertly control the systems [4, 29]. For instance, this method has been used to control the robot behavior during the experiment [4, 16].

3.4 Human-Related Factors

Human side encompasses intrinsic characteristics, attributes, or predispositions before or during collaboration. In contrast, changes after collaboration are classified as outcomes in this review. In the reviewed studies, human perceptions are a focus, including individuals' perceptions regarding themselves, AI, task, and organizations. Specifically, *perceptions regarding themselves* come from various theories and can be summarized into key dimensions, including:

1. Self-capability, focusing on their own skills, knowledge, and competencies. This includes individuals' cognitive abilities, such as perceived cognitive ability from cognitive load theory [30], metaknowledge from a complementarity lens [18], knowledge imbalance [31]. From a self-expertise viewpoint, studies have examined individuals' own knowledge of a domain and AI technology, such as human expertise in a domain [27], prior experience with AI [29, 32], affinity for technology [32], familiarity with AI [14], and prior experience with a task (such as video game) [26].
2. Self-motivation. Drawing on motivation theory, individuals' motivation to perform well has been reported to affect human-AI collaboration, such as extrinsic motivation [32], and intrinsic motivation (such as need for cognition) [32].
3. Self-control, focusing on individuals' sense for control and responsibility during the collaborative process, such sense of control from a control lens [29], perceived decision control from a cognitive load theory [30], sense of responsibility from the attribution theory [16], and algorithm aversion [18].

Perceptions of AI also encompass various dimensions, including:

1. AI capability, focusing AI's ability and quality of information offered by AI. Such as perceived level of autonomy from the adaptive autonomy lens [24], perceived usefulness from technology acceptance model [27], perceived effectiveness and perceived authenticity from signaling theory [33], information accuracy from the perspective of trust calibration [32]. And perceived ability, perceived integrity, perceived benevolence from a trust perspective [22].
2. AI's humanlike features, such as perceived anthropomorphism [33], perceived warmth [3], perceived competence [3], and perceived personalization [29].
3. AI's status or role, such as perceived teammate identity [7].

Perceptions related to organizations have also been explored in the reviewed studies, such as perceived organizational AI readiness [25] and perceived power distance orientation [16]. Task-related perceptions have also been reported, such as perceived task complexity [30], task uncertainty and time horizon [19].

To measure human perceptions, self-reported survey and interviews are the predominant method used in literature [26, 33]. Even within experimental settings, during- or post-experiment interviews and surveys are frequently used to capture participants' reactions [22, 24].

3.5 Outcomes of Human-AI Collaboration

In the reviewed studies, various outcomes of human-AI collaboration have been reported, and can be classified into five main categories: human cognition, emotion, attitudes, behavior, and task related outcomes. Notably, the outcomes are dual in nature, while positive outcomes present, negative outcomes also emerge. First, regarding human cognition, positive cognition includes perceived utility of AI [27], perceived autonomy, perceived organizational support [23], perceived social influence [26], perceived receptivity to AI [3], perceived human-AI team viability [3], perceived justice [14], perceived control [14], and perceived self-efficacy [14]. Negative cognition includes perceived conflict [22], perceived risk [34], and perceived workload [7, 13].

Second, positive emotions include emotional preference for AI [17], emotional preference for intelligent interactive scenarios [17], and comfort with AI [24], while negative emotion includes psychological cost [23].

Third, positive human attitudes include trust in AI [7, 8, 22, 26, 30], trust in human-AI collaboration [9], process satisfaction [22], and job satisfaction [23].

Fourth, positive human behaviors include willingness to work with AI [22, 34], adoption [33], understanding of AI's recommendation [30], willingness to follow AI recommendations [31], reliance intention [8], communication style [13], dependence behavior [17], and innovation behavior [25]. Negative behaviors include compliance with AI recommendation [30] and conflict behavior [17].

Fifth, task-oriented outcomes include performance of human-AI collaboration [32, 34], efficiency [10, 15], time saving [10], classification accuracy [18], team performance [4], team efficiency [20], forecast accuracy [19], evaluations of co-created artifact [35], and evaluation of poetry [36].

Only a few studies reported outcome at an organizational level, that is company-directed reactions, measured by perceived fit, perceptions of the company's culture as supportive, and perceived innovation climate [14]. Figure 2 illustrates the framework summarizing key findings in literature.

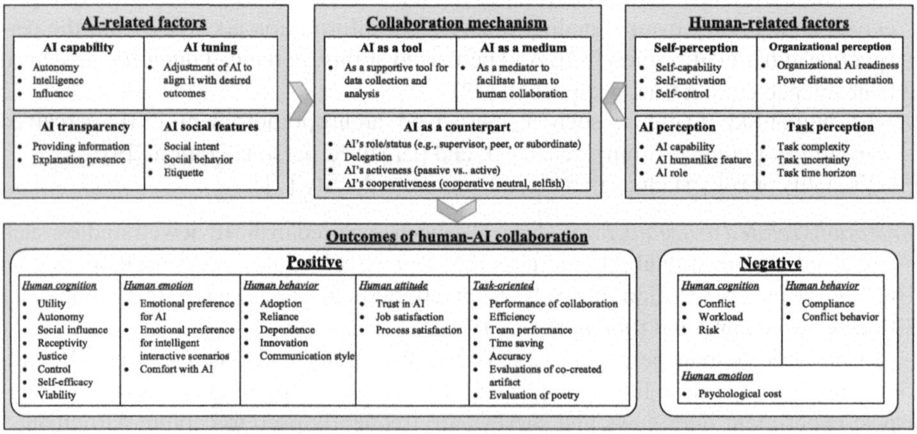

Fig. 2. The results of prior studies on human-AI collaboration

4 Research Gaps and Future Research Directions

First, regarding conceptualization of human-AI collaboration, the differences among various concepts may arise from variations in contexts, the nature and structure of collaboration between humans and AI. Therefore, future studies should explicitly define the roles of humans and AI within the collaborative settings, offering greater clarity on their roles and interdependencies. Additionally, future studies should address the configurations of collaboration, clearly outlining how humans and AI interact across different relationship structures, from simple one-to-one collaborations to more intricate many-to-many scenarios. This can help clarify how AI and humans interact at various levels and in different team structures.

Second, regarding the mechanism of human-AI collaboration, while prior studies have examined it from the perspectives of tool, medium, and counterpart, providing valuable insights, the overall understanding of how AI integrates into the collaborative process remains fragmented. Specifically, the roles, status, and capabilities of AI are often predefined through experiments, limiting the ability to capture the dynamic changes in these factors throughout the collaboration. Therefore, future research should consider employing ethnographic fieldwork or longitudinal studies to better capture the evolving dynamics of human-AI collaboration.

Third, while many AI characteristics have been examined, AI's specific features (e.g., invisibility, inscrutability, and changeability), as well as ethical issues (e.g., AI bias and privacy concerns), remain underexamined. These factors of AI may exhibit negative influences on human-AI collaboration by decreasing trust or performance. Thus, future studies should address these gaps by exploring how these factors of AI (such as invisibility and AI bias), shape the collaboration between humans and AI.

Likewise, negative human perceptions, such as perceived uncanniness toward AI have been ignored. Additionally, cultural and contextual factors have been neglected. Future research could explore how these negative perceptions and cultural dimensions (e.g., collectivism versus individualism), influence human-AI collaboration. Additionally, existing studies have primarily focused on static human perceptions, often relying on self-reported surveys or interviews. There is a need for longitudinal research to track how these perceptions evolve over time.

Finally, while many studies have focused on the positive outcomes of human-AI collaboration, only a few have explored the negative outcomes. Future studies should also focus on examining negative outcomes, as human-AI collaboration does not always guarantee positive results. Additionally, there is a limited body of research examining the outcomes at the organizational level. Future studies could investigate how human-AI collaboration influences organizational dynamics, such as changes in workflow processes, overall productivity, and organizational performance. Examining the long-term effects of human-AI collaboration on organizations could further enrich our understanding of its broader implications.

5 Conclusion

This literature review contributes to literature in the following ways. First, it provides a comprehensive analysis of the AI side, human side, mechanism of collaboration, and outcomes. This detailed investigation addresses critical components of human-AI collaboration, offering a clear and structured overview of how humans and AI function in their respective roles, how they interact, and the outcomes produced through their collaboration. Second, this review identifies key research gaps and proposes actionable directions for future studies. Specifically, it highlights the need for deeper exploration of conceptualization, collaboration mechanisms, longitudinal effects, and organizational and societal impacts. By doing so, this study not only synthesizes existing knowledge but also sets the stage for advancing our understanding of human-AI collaboration.

This study has several limitations. First, it focuses solely on peer-reviewed journal articles within IS field. While these journals represent high-quality research, this limitation excludes potentially valuable literature from other disciplines. Future studies should incorporate research from diverse fields to gain a more comprehensive understanding of the topic. Second, this study may not fully capture the latest developments in IS due to the rapidly evolving nature of the subject. Future research should consider adopting strategies for timely inclusion of relevant studies, such as developing a dynamic database for gathering relevant papers. Third, the scope of this review is confined to four main parts: the AI side, the human side, collaboration mechanism, and outcomes. Future research could explore additional factors, such as culture, to provide a more holistic understanding of human-AI collaboration.

References

1. Anthony, C., Bechky, B.A., Fayard, A.-L.: "Collaborating" with AI: taking a system view to explore the future of work. Organ. Sci. **34**(5), 1672–1694 (2023)
2. Haesevoets, T., De Cremer, D., Dierckx, K., Van Hiel, A.: Human-machine collaboration in managerial decision making. Comput. Hum. Behav. **119**, 1–11 (2021)
3. Harris-Watson, A.M., Larson, L.E., Lauharatanahirun, N., DeChurch, L.A., Contractor, N.S.: Social perception in human-AI teams: warmth and competence predict receptivity to AI teammates. Comput. Hum. Behav. **145**, 1–17 (2023)
4. Schoonderwoerd, T.A., Zoelen, E.M., Bosch, K., Neerincx, M.A.: Design patterns for human-AI co-learning: a wizard-of-Oz evaluation in an urban-search-and-rescue task. Int. J. Hum. Comput. Stud. **164**, 1–13 (2022)
5. Tranfield, D., Denyer, D., Smart, P.: Towards a methodology for developing evidence-informed management knowledge by means of systematic review. Br. J. Manag. **14**(3), 207–222 (2003)
6. Hsieh, H.-F., Shannon, S.E.: Three approaches to qualitative content analysis. Qual. Health Res. **15**(9), 1277–1288 (2005)
7. Zhang, G., Chong, L., Kotovsky, K., Cagan, J.: Trust in an AI versus a human teammate: the effects of teammate identity and performance on human-AI cooperation. Comput. Hum. Behav. **139**, 1–11 (2023)
8. Capiola, A., Lyons, J.B., Harris, K.N., Hamdan, I.A., Kailas, S., Sycara, K.: "Do what you say?" The combined effects of framed social intent and autonomous agent behavior on the trust process. Comput. Hum. Behav. **149**, 1–14 (2023)

9. Vössing, M., Kühl, N., Lind, M., Satzger, G.: Designing transparency for effective human-AI collaboration. Inf. Syst. Front. **24**(3), 877–895 (2022)
10. Bossen, C., Pine, K.H.: Batman and Robin in healthcare knowledge work: human-AI collaboration by clinical documentation integrity specialists. ACM Trans. Comput. Hum. Interact. **30**(2), 1–29 (2023)
11. Zhao, M., Eadeh, F.R., Nguyen, T.-N., Gupta, P., Admoni, H., Gonzalez, C., et al.: Teaching agents to understand teamwork: evaluating and predicting collective intelligence as a latent variable via hidden Markov models. Comput. Hum. Behav. **139**, 1–12 (2023)
12. Musick, G., O'Neill, T.A., Schelble, B.G., McNeese, N.J., Henke, J.B.: What happens when humans believe their teammate is an AI? An investigation into humans teaming with autonomy. Comput. Hum. Behav. **122**, 1–14 (2021)
13. Gnewuch, U., Morana, S., Hinz, O., Kellner, R., Maedche, A.: More than a bot? The impact of disclosing human involvement on customer interactions with hybrid service agents. Inf. Syst. Res. **35**(3), 936–955 (2024)
14. Gonzalez, M.F., Liu, W., Shirase, L., Tomczak, D.L., Lobbe, C.E., Justenhoven, R., et al.: Allying with AI? Reactions toward human-based, AI/ML-based, and augmented hiring processes. Comput. Hum. Behav. **130**, 1–16 (2022)
15. Gao, J., Choo, K.T.W., Cao, J., Lee, R.K.-W., Perrault, S.: CoAIcoder: examining the effectiveness of AI-assisted human-to-human collaboration in qualitative analysis. ACM Trans. Comput. Hum. Interact. **31**(1), 1–38 (2023)
16. Lei, X., Rau, P.-L.P.: Effect of relative status on responsibility attributions in human–robot collaboration: mediating role of sense of responsibility and moderating role of power distance orientation. Comput. Hum. Behav. **122**, 1–11 (2021)
17. Chen, A., Xiang, M., Wang, M., Lu, Y.: Harmony in intelligent hybrid teams: the influence of the intellectual ability of artificial intelligence on human members' reactions. Inf. Technol. People. **36**(7), 2826–2846 (2022)
18. Fügener, A., Grahl, J., Gupta, A., Ketter, W.: Cognitive challenges in human–artificial intelligence collaboration: investigating the path toward productive delegation. Inf. Syst. Res. **33**(2), 678–696 (2021)
19. Revilla, E., Saenz, M.J., Seifert, M., Ma, Y.: Human–artificial intelligence collaboration in prediction: a field experiment in the retail industry. J. Manag. Inf. Syst. **40**(4), 1071–1098 (2023)
20. Kang, M.: The effects of agent activeness and cooperativeness on team decision efficiency: a computational simulation study using team-soar. Int. J. Hum. Comput. Stud. **65**(6), 497–510 (2007)
21. Simón, C., Revilla, E., Jesús, S.M.: Integrating AI in organizations for value creation through human-AI teaming: a dynamic-capabilities approach. J. Bus. Res. **182**, 1–14 (2024)
22. Dennis, A.R., Lakhiwal, A., Sachdeva, A.: AI agents as team members: effects on satisfaction, conflict, trustworthiness, and willingness to work with. J. Manag. Inf. Syst. **40**(2), 307–337 (2023)
23. Ossadnik, J., Muehlfeld, K., Goerke, L.: Man or machine—or something in between? Social responses to voice assistants at work and their effects on job satisfaction. Comput. Hum. Behav. **149**, 1–16 (2023)
24. Hauptman, A.I., Schelble, B.G., McNeese, N.J., Madathil, K.C.: Adapt and overcome: perceptions of adaptive autonomous agents for human-AI teaming. Comput. Hum. Behav. **138**, 1–15 (2023)
25. Yin, M., Jiang, S., Niu, X.: Can AI really help? The double-edged sword effect of AI assistant on employees' innovation behavior. Comput. Hum. Behav. **150**, 1–12 (2024)
26. Flathmann, C., Schelble, B.G., Rosopa, P.J., McNeese, N.J., Mallick, R., Madathil, K.C.: Examining the impact of varying levels of AI teammate influence on human-AI teams. Int. J. Hum. Comput. Stud. **177**, 1–16 (2023)

27. Inkpen, K., Chappidi, S., Mallari, K., Nushi, B., Ramesh, D., Michelucci, P., et al.: Advancing human-AI complementarity: the impact of user expertise and algorithmic tuning on joint decision making. ACM Trans. Comput. Hum. Interact. **30**(5), 1–29 (2023)
28. Flathmann, C., McNeese, N.J., Schelble, B., Knijnenburg, B., Freeman, G.: Understanding the impact and design of AI teammate etiquette. Hum. Comput. Interact. **39**(5–6), 444–471 (2023)
29. Draxler, F., Werner, A., Lehmann, F., Hoppe, M., Schmidt, A., Buschek, D., et al.: The AI ghostwriter effect: when users do not perceive ownership of AI-generated text but self-declare as authors. ACM Trans. Comput. Hum. Interact. **31**(2), 1–40 (2024)
30. Westphal, M., Vössing, M., Satzger, G., Yom-Tov, G.B., Rafaeli, A.: Decision control and explanations in human-AI collaboration: improving user perceptions and compliance. Comput. Hum. Behav. **144**, 1–21 (2023)
31. Gomez, C., Unberath, M., Huang, C.-M.: Mitigating knowledge imbalance in AI-advised decision-making through collaborative user involvement. Int. J. Hum. Comput. Stud. **172**, 1–14 (2023)
32. Eisbach, S., Langer, M., Hertel, G.: Optimizing human-AI collaboration: effects of motivation and accuracy information in AI-supported decision-making. Comput. Hum. Behav. Artif. Hum. **1**(2), 1–12 (2023)
33. Li, Y., Li, Y., Chen, Q., Chang, Y.: Humans as teammates: the signal of human–AI teaming enhances consumer acceptance of chatbots. Int. J. Inf. Manag. **76**, 1–12 (2024)
34. Xiong, W., Wang, C., Ma, L.: Partner or subordinate? Sequential risky decision-making behaviors under human-machine collaboration contexts. Comput. Hum. Behav. **139**, 1–12 (2023)
35. Messer, U.: Co-creating art with generative artificial intelligence: implications for artworks and artists. Comput. Hum. Behav. Artif. Hum. **2**(1), 1–19 (2024)
36. Hitsuwari, J., Ueda, Y., Yun, W., Nomura, M.: Does human–AI collaboration lead to more creative art? Aesthetic evaluation of human-made and AI-generated haiku poetry. Comput. Hum. Behav. **139**, 1–10 (2023)

Form and Behavioral Anthropomorphism of Avatars: Influencing User Satisfaction through Cognitive, Affective, and Social Responses

Jiamin Chen and Yi Jiang(✉)

School of Economics and Management, China University of Geosciences(Wuhan), Wuhan, China

Abstract. This study explores how the form and behavioural anthropomorphism of avatars affect user satisfaction through cognitive, affective, and social responses. Whilst extant research has heretofore treated anthropomorphism in a unifying fashion, this study differentiates it into two distinct dimensions: form anthropomorphism and behavioural anthropomorphism. Utilising social response theory as a framework, the study hypothesises that perceived personalisation, entertainment, and informativeness mediate the relationship between these two types of anthropomorphism and user satisfaction. Additionally, the study explores the moderating effect of user openness. The Structural Equation Model (SEM) and the analyses of mediation and moderation demonstrate that both form and behavioural anthropomorphism have a positive effect on user satisfaction, with openness moderating the effect of form anthropomorphism. The findings contribute to the extant literature by clarifying the different impacts of form and behavioural anthropomorphism, emphasising the role of individual traits, and offering practical insights for avatar design in enhancing user satisfaction.

Keywords: Form Anthropomorphism · Behavioral Anthropomorphism · Cognitive Response · Affective Response · Social Response · User Satisfaction

1 Introduction

With the rapid development of Generative Artificial Intelligence (GAI), avatars have made significant improvements in imitating human behaviors and interactions. Anthropomorphism, as one of the core features of these avatars, has had a significant impact on user satisfaction, but existing studies tend to explore anthropomorphism as a holistic factor [1]. Such an approach ignores the different impacts of form anthropomorphism (e.g., appearance and body movements) and behavioral anthropomorphism (e.g., interactions and adaptive behaviors) on user perceptions.

Social response theory, which is sometimes referred to as the CASA paradigm (computers-as-social-actors) suggests that the anthropomorphic features of avatars will stimulate consumers' social perception, which is usually an automatic, spontaneous, and

Y. P. Tu and M. Chi (Eds.): WHICEB 2025, LNBIP 549, pp. 75–86, 2025.
https://doi.org/10.1007/978-3-031-94184-9_7

unconscious process that induces users to have different degrees of cognitive, affective, and social responses to avatars [2]. The anthropomorphic design of avatars has attracted much attention in both academia and practice and is mainly divided into form anthropomorphism (e.g., appearance, expression, body movement) and behavioral anthropomorphism (e.g., interactive naturalness, contextual adaptation) [3]. Since avatars have different functions and application scenarios, with some focusing more on appearance sophistication and others emphasizing interaction capabilities, it is particularly important to explore the different impacts of these two forms of anthropomorphism on user perceptions. Based on this, we propose the core research question:

Research Question. In what ways do form anthropomorphism and behavioral anthropomorphism of avatars, respectively, affect users' perceptions? How do these perceptions further contribute to user satisfaction?

This study takes the anthropomorphism of avatars as the core independent variable and splits it into two dimensions: form anthropomorphism and behavioral anthropomorphism [3]. From the perspective of social response theory, this study takes cognitive response, affective response, and social response as the analytical framework to explore the multi-level effects of different anthropomorphic forms on user satisfaction. Specifically, it is hypothesized that perceived personalization, perceived entertainment, and perceived informativeness mediate the relationship between form anthropomorphism behavioral anthropomorphism, and user satisfaction, respectively. In addition, the user's openness trait is introduced as a moderating variable, to further explore how individual differences affect the perceived effects of anthropomorphism types.

This study focuses on Structural Equation Modeling (SEM) and mediation and moderation effect tests to validate the mechanisms of different types of anthropomorphism of avatars on user satisfaction and their paths. The results show that both form anthropomorphism and behavioral anthropomorphism have significant effects on user satisfaction through perceived personalization, perceived entertainment, and perceived informativeness. At the same time, user openness significantly enhances the positive effect of form anthropomorphism on user satisfaction through perceived entertainment and perceived informativeness, however, under behavioral anthropomorphism, openness fails to significantly moderate the relationship with user satisfaction.

Our study contributes to the existing literature in three ways. First, from the perspective of avatar anthropomorphism segmentation, this study divides anthropomorphism into form and behavioral anthropomorphism and systematically explores how these two types of anthropomorphism affect user satisfaction through the cognitive, affective, and social response dimensions, respectively. In contrast, existing studies typically treat anthropomorphism as a holistic factor, overlooking the distinct impacts of each form on user perceptions. Second, this paper identifies the boundary condition that influences the different forms of anthropomorphism—the user's characteristics: openness. Finally, by subdividing the anthropomorphism of avatars into form and behavioral anthropomorphism, this study further enriches the understanding of the emotional and social dimensions of human-technology interactions in social response theory, providing new theoretical support and practical guidance for the application of the theory.

2 Theoretical Development and Hypotheses

2.1 Social Response Theory

Social response theory is one of the central theoretical frameworks guiding research on human interaction with avatars. First proposed by Nass et al. (1994), the theory seeks to explain how humans view computers and other AI systems as social actors, even though these systems do not possess the real social attributes of human beings [2]. The theory emphasizes that humans tend to respond cognitively, affectively, and socially to computers and virtual agents by adopting a social interaction approach [4]. Such responses are automatic and unconscious, and individuals are often unaware that they are applying social rules and behavioral patterns to non-human entities.

In this study, the variable for an affective response was perceived entertainment, the variable for a cognitive response was perceived informativeness and the variable for a social response was perceived personalization. This is due to the specificity and importance of these three variables in avatar interactions, which can more accurately capture users' multidimensional responses and are less commonly examined in existing research comprehensively.

2.2 Two Types of Anthropomorphism: Form and Behavioral

The anthropomorphization process of an avatar involves making the avatar closer to humans in appearance and behavior by simulating human appearance, language, behavior, and other characteristics, thus enhancing its interactive feelings with users [5]. As a digital and anthropomorphic virtual image, avatars have been widely used in many fields such as business, education, entertainment, and so on through the support of computer technology, especially playing an important role in the process of providing more humanized services. The anthropomorphism of avatars can be understood from two dimensions: form anthropomorphism and behavior anthropomorphism. Form anthropomorphism focuses on the appearance and movements of the avatar, while behavioral anthropomorphism is concerned with the adaptability and quality of interaction shown in the interaction process [6]. The introduction of anthropomorphism not only enhances the affinity of avatars but also provides the possibility for them to play important roles in social interactions.

2.2.1 Form Anthropomorphism

Form anthropomorphism of an avatar refers to the design of appearance and identity features so that they take on human-like visual effects and attributes. Such anthropomorphism can be achieved through a variety of design factors, including the spatial dimension of the avatar (e.g., 2D vs. 3D forms), the dynamic representation of the face and body (e.g., static vs. dynamic visual effects), and other features that enhance the perception of "humanity," such as gender, age, race, or name. Through these designs, the avatar can be presented in a more humanized form, thus enhancing the user's sense of intimacy and interactive experience [7].

The personalized aspects of the avatar, including elements like its name, gender, and appearance, contribute to its approachability and ability to satisfy user needs. Personalized avatars tend to evoke stronger emotional responses from users, increasing their emotional engagement and satisfaction [8]. This emotional connection is especially valuable in contexts such as emotional support or customer service. Furthermore, the avatar's form anthropomorphism also includes its appearance, movement, and interaction style, which significantly impact the user's experience. A more anthropomorphic avatar with engaging movements and expressions tends to provide greater entertainment, enhancing overall enjoyment and satisfaction. In addition, the form anthropomorphism affects how avatars communicate information. When avatars display behaviors and communication styles that mimic human interaction, users find the information clearer and more credible, improving their understanding and acceptance of the message. Thus, the form anthropomorphism of an avatar, through personalization, entertainment, and informativeness, plays a crucial role in enhancing user satisfaction. Based on this, we propose the hypothesis:

1a: Perceived personalization positively mediates the relationship between the form anthropomorphism of avatar and user satisfaction.
1b: Perceived entertainment positively mediates the relationship between the form anthropomorphism of avatar and user satisfaction.
1c: Perceived informativeness positively mediates the relationship between form anthropomorphization of avatar and user satisfaction.

2.2.2 Behavioral Anthropomorphism

Behavioral anthropomorphism enables avatars to provide personalized interactions that cater to users' needs, enhancing emotional engagement and trust [9]. When avatars respond based on user preferences or behaviors, users feel more attended to, which increases satisfaction. Perceived personalization, by deepening the emotional connection and social interaction, mediates the relationship between behavioral anthropomorphism and user satisfaction. Moreover, avatars that display humor, prompt responses, or personalized interactions tend to increase users' entertainment, which fosters emotional resonance and engagement. Perceived entertainment, as a mediator, strengthens the link between behavioral anthropomorphism and user satisfaction. Additionally, avatars that adapt their communication style to users' needs enhance the clarity and effectiveness of information delivery [10]. This improves perceived informativeness, which directly boosts user satisfaction, particularly in domains like customer service and education. Thus, perceived informativeness also mediates the relationship between behavioral anthropomorphism and user satisfaction.

H2a: Perceived personalization positively mediates the relationship between behavioral anthropomorphism of avatars and user satisfaction.
H2b: Perceived Entertainment plays a positive mediating role in the relationship between avatar behavioral anthropomorphism and user satisfaction.
H2c: Perceived informativeness positively mediates the relationship between behavioral anthropomorphism of avatars and user satisfaction.

2.3 The Moderating Role of Users' Characteristics

Openness is a key dimension of the Big Five personality and refers to the openness to new experiences, ideas, and concepts. Openness is closely related to an individual's acceptance of new experiences, ability to process complex information, and response to emotional and social interactions, so its role in avatar-user interactions cannot be ignored [11].

Research has shown that individuals with higher openness tend to be more receptive to novelty and change, which allows them to better perceive the personalized, entertaining, and informative features of anthropomorphic avatars when interacting with them. Specifically, when users have high openness, they are more receptive to and recognize the anthropomorphic features (e.g., emotional expression, interactive style, etc.) displayed by avatars, and thus the information conveyed by avatars is more easily accepted and their interactive experience is more enjoyable and attractive.

H3a: Users with high openness will experience a stronger positive impact of form anthropomorphism on the perceived personalization of the avatar.
H3b: Users with high openness will experience a stronger positive impact of form anthropomorphism on the perceived entertainment of the avatar.
H3c: Users with high openness will experience a stronger positive impact of form anthropomorphism on the perceived informativeness of the avatar.
H4a: Users with high openness will experience a stronger positive impact of behavioral anthropomorphism on the perceived personalization of the avatar.
H4b: Users with high openness will experience a stronger positive impact of behavioral anthropomorphism on the perceived entertainment of the avatar.
H4c: Users with high openness will experience a stronger positive impact of behavioral anthropomorphism on the perceived informativeness of the avatar.

The research model of this paper is shown in Fig. 1.

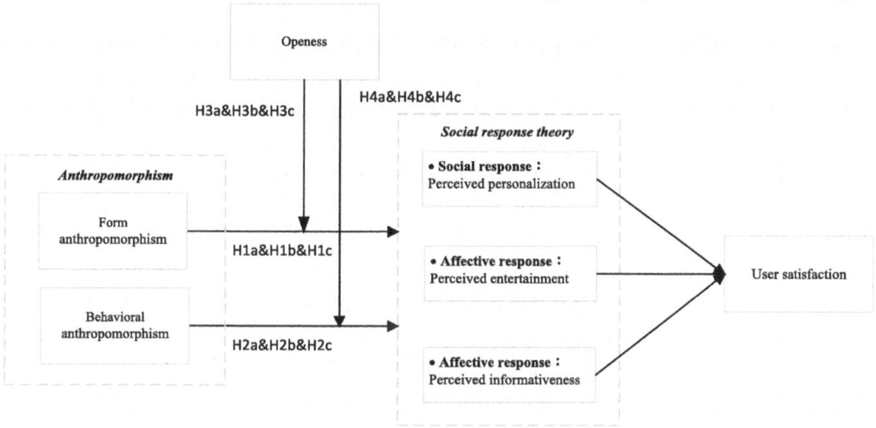

Fig. 1. Research model

3 Method

3.1 Construct Measurement

The questionnaire consists of three main sections: demographic characteristics, respondents' basic knowledge of avatars, and key variables influencing avatar user satisfaction. The first section collects demographic data such as gender, age, education, internet usage experience, and average daily use time to understand the sample's basic characteristics and assess the balance and representativeness of the distribution. The second section investigates respondents' usage of avatars, including whether they have used avatars and what types, providing insights into user familiarity and engagement with avatars. The third section is the key variable measurements including avatar user satisfaction, avatar anthropomorphism (both form and behavioral), and perceptions of personalization, informativeness, and entertainment. This part of the questionnaire items are measured using a seven-point Likert scale, the measurement items are shown in the table below.

3.2 Participants and Data Collection

A total of 586 questionnaires were collected in this study (through the Questionnaire Star platform), and after excluding the samples with too short response time and all options being the same as well as those who failed the polygraph questions, the valid sample was 346. Of the 346 respondents, 46.82% were male and 53.18% were female, with similar numbers of male and female respondents, 89.6% of the respondents were under 30 years of age, and 91.6% had received university or higher education, which is in line with this study's setting of the target group for the research.

4 Result

4.1 Reliability and Validity Analysis

The reliability coefficients of the question items of the variables in the questionnaire were calculated separately using SPSS 25, and the results are shown in Table 1. The Cronbach's α value of each variable was greater than 0.8, thus indicating that the consistency and stability of the scale design was good. Moreover, confirmatory factor analysis was used to evaluate the validity structure. The KMO value was reported as 0.961. This suggests that the items are suitable for factor analysis. Principal Component Analysis with a cumulative variance explained of 83.353%.

The factor loadings of all variables were above 0.5, while their combined reliability CR values were above the acceptable value of 0.70, indicating that the model has good convergent validity. In addition, the average extracted variance AVE values were all greater than 0.50 and the correlations among the variables were lower than the arithmetic square root of AVE, indicating that the model has good discriminant validity (see Table 2).

Table 1. Reliability and validity analysis

Constructs	Item	Loading	AVE	CR	Cronbach α
Form anthropomorphism (FA)	FA1	0.767	0.798	0.888	0.747
	FA2	0.816			
Behavioral athropomorphism (BA)	BA1	0.533	0.885	0.939	0.870
	BA2	0.810			
Perceived personalization (PP)	PP1	0.609	0.771	0.931	0.901
	PP2	0.650			
	PP3	0.662			
	PP4	0.683			
Perceived entertainment (PE)	PE1	0.737	0.826	0.965	0.951
	PE2	0.747			
	PE3	0.676			
	PE4	0.702			
Perceived informativeness (PI)	PI1	0.722	0.872	0.950	0.930
	PI2	0.715			
	PI3	0.733			
	PI4	0.736			
Openness (OP)	OP1	0.786	0.756	0.925	0.893
	OP2	0.818			
	OP3	0.794			
	OP4	0.840			
User satisfaction (US)	US1	0.725	0.854	0.967	0.957
	US2	0.675			
	US3	0.716			
	US4	0.728			
	US5	0.712			

4.2 Assessment of the Structural Model

To test the mechanism of avatar form and behavioral anthropomorphism on user satisfaction, we built a structural equation model based on PLS-SEM, which yielded a value of 0.038 (less than 0.08) for the model fitness indicator, SRMR, which proved that the fit was good. It can be seen from Fig. 2 that form anthropomorphism positively and significantly affects perceived personalization ($b = 0.357$, $p < 0.001$), perceived entertainment ($b = 0.449$, $p < 0.001$), and perceived informativeness ($b = 0.318$, $p < 0.001$). Meanwhile, perceived personalization ($b = 0.314$, $p < 0.001$) and perceived Entertainment ($b = 0.313$, $p < 0.001$), perceived Informativeness ($b = 0.340$, $p < 0.001$) had

Table 2. Table of differentiated validity

Constructs	FA	BA	PP	PE	PI	OP	US
FA	**0.798**						
BA	.672**	**0.885**					
PP	.631**	.652**	**0.771**				
PE	.638**	.583**	.769**	**0.826**			
PI	.553**	.559**	.786**	.777**	**0.872**		
OP	.443**	.449**	.504**	.501**	.525**	**0.756**	
US	.611**	.666**	.774**	.789**	.774**	.563**	**0.854**

Note: **$p < 0.01$; The values along the diagonal represent the square roots of the Average Variance Extracted (AVE) values. Off-diagonal values indicate the estimated correlations between constructs

a significant positive effect on user satisfaction, and Hypotheses H1a, H1b, and H1c were preliminarily verified when the independent variable was the dimension of form Anthropomorphism.

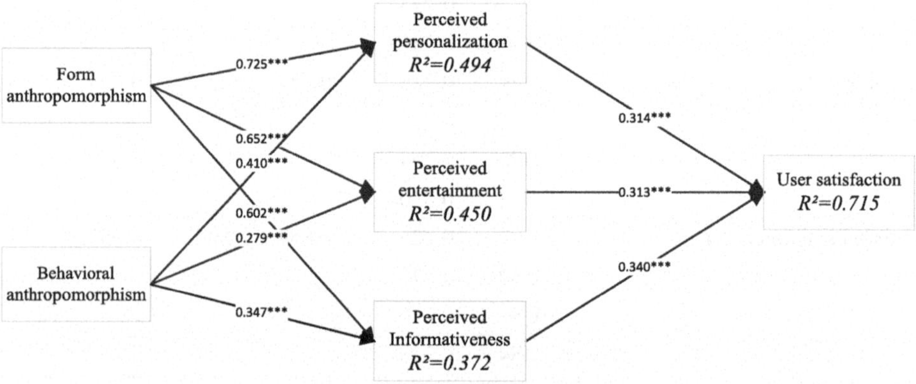

Fig. 2. Structural model results

Similarly, It can be seen from the figure below that behavioral anthropomorphism positively and significantly affects perceived personalization ($b = 0.410$, $p < 0.001$), perceived entertainment ($b = 0.279$, $p < 0.001$), and perceived informativeness ($b = 0.347$, $p < 0.001$). Hypotheses H2a, H2b, and H2c were also preliminarily verified when the independent variable was the dimension of behavioral anthropomorphism.

4.3 Mediation Effect Test

This paper uses Model4 of the Process add-in in SPSS developed by Hayes to test the mediating effects of perceived personalization, perceived entertainment, and perceived informativeness in the relationship between form and behavioral anthropomorphism and user satisfaction. Based on 5000 bootstrap samples, the mean estimated indirect effects of the mediating paths have been computed along with 95% confidence intervals for each estimate and the complete model coefficients have been given in Table 3 below.

Table 3. Mediation effects

Mediation pathway		Direct Effects			Indirect Effects		
		Effect	LLCI	ULCI	Effect	LLCI	ULCI
FA- PP-US	H1a	0.0877	0.4817	0.6352	0.1448	0.0709	0.2242
FA- PE-US	H1b	0.0877	0.4817	0.6352	0.1886	0.0978	0.2909
FA- PI-US	H1c	0.0877	0.4817	0.6352	0.1373	.0.0672	0.2082
BA- PP-US	H2a	0.1854	0.1224	0.2484	0.1027	0.0256	0.1844
BA- PE-US	H2b	0.1854	0.1224	0.2484	0.1617	0.0878	0.2480
BA- PI-US	H2c	0.1854	0.1224	0.2484	0.1262	0.0572	0.1924

From Table 3, it can be concluded that in the dimension of form anthropomorphism, the mediating effects of perceived personalization, perceived entertainment, and perceived informativeness faculty are significant and partially mediated. Hypothesis H1a, Hypothesis H1b, and Hypothesis H1c were validated.

At the same time, it can be concluded that in the dimension of behavioral anthropomorphism, the mediating effects of social presence, perceived entertainment, and perceived information faculty are also significant and partially mediated. Hypothesis H2a, Hypothesis H2b, and Hypothesis H2c were also validated. In addition, the indirect effect of form and behavioral anthropomorphism on user satisfaction through social presence, perceived entertainment, and perceived informativeness is not significantly different.

4.4 Moderating Effects Test

This paper uses Model 1 of the Process and examines it using the Bootstrap program with 5000 repetitive samples to investigate to what extent openness moderated the effects of form and behavioral anthropomorphism on perceived personalization, perceived entertainment, and perceived informativeness.

As shown in Table 4, the interaction term of form anthropomorphism with openness had a significant effect on perceived entertainment and perceived informativeness. Hypothesis H3b and Hypothesis H3c were all supported except Hypothesis H3a, which indicated that users with different openness had significant differences in perceived entertainment and perceived informativeness when using avatars. Figure 3 further illustrates this point.

The interaction term of behavioral anthropomorphism and openness does not have a significant effect on perceived personalization, perceived entertainment, and perceived information. Hypothesis H4a is not supported along with hypotheses H4b and H4c.

Table 4. Moderating effects

	Perceived personalization	Perceived entertainment		Perceived informativeness		
Constant	4.6577***	4.6600***	4.9167***	4.9497***	4.785***	4.9918***
FA	0.4758***		0.5058***		0.3489***	
BA		0.4576***		0.4245***		0.3305***
OP	0.3615***	0.3487***	0.3691***	0.4651***	0.4211***	0.5147***
FA × OP	0.0476		0.0571***		0.0503***	
BA ×OP		0.0417		0.0198		0.0420
R^2	0.4658	0.4845	0.4740	0.4124	0.4107	0.4137
Int LLCI	−0.0013	−0.0107	0.0066	−0.0390	0.0022	−0.010
Int ULCI	0.0964	0.0941	0.1076	0.0790	0.9840	0.0940

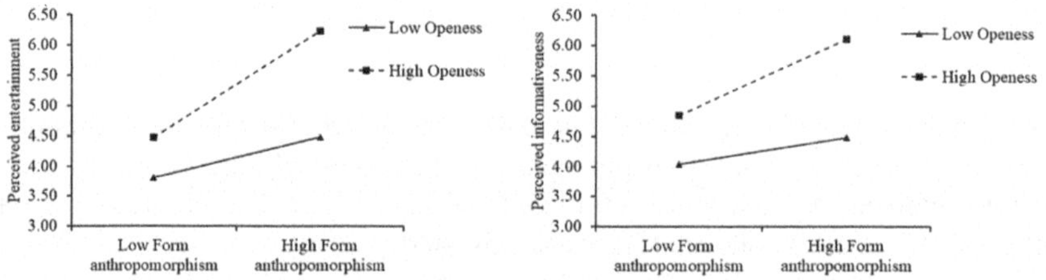

Fig. 3. Moderating Effect of Openness

5 Discussion and Conclusion

5.1 Conclusion

In this study, the effects of form anthropomorphism and behavioral anthropomorphism on user satisfaction were validated through the cognitive, affective, and social responses mediators. Specifically, form and behavioral anthropomorphism significantly increased user satisfaction through perceived personalization, entertainment, and informativeness. Although form and behavioral anthropomorphisms are expressed differently, they show similar mediating mechanisms in the path of influencing user satisfaction, suggesting that the core mechanisms still revolve around the stimulation of users' emotions and the enhancement of interactive experiences, whether in appearance design or behavioral interactions. In real avatar applications, the anthropomorphic approaches of form and behavior often do not operate independently, and they jointly influence users' perceptions and satisfaction in a complementary way, which explains why the paths of influence of the two exhibit similarity.

In addition, this study explored the moderating effect of openness features on anthropomorphization dimensions. The results showed that the interaction between anthropomorphism and users' openness traits had a significant effect on perceived entertainment and informativeness, whereas behavioral anthropomorphism failed to significantly modulate these perceived factors. This finding suggests that users' personality traits, especially openness, may play an important moderating role in interacting with virtual characters and influencing their responses to anthropomorphic designs. For form anthropomorphism, users with higher openness are more likely to derive entertainment and information from appearance and personalization, whereas behavioral anthropomorphism relies less on such personalized moderation and requires more immediate interaction and contextual factors to motivate user satisfaction.

5.2 Theoretical Implications

Our study contributes to the existing literature in three main ways. First, we differentiate between form and behavioral anthropomorphism and examine how each influences user satisfaction through cognitive, affective, and social responses. This segmentation offers a more precise understanding compared to previous research, which typically treats anthropomorphism as a single construct. By identifying these distinct types, we highlight their unique impacts on user perceptions and satisfaction, offering a more comprehensive framework for studying avatar interactions.

Second, we explore the moderating role of openness—a key personal characteristic—in the relationship between different forms of anthropomorphism and user perceptions. Our findings suggest that users with higher openness are more influenced by form anthropomorphism regarding perceived entertainment and informativeness. This insight adds to the growing body of research emphasizing the importance of individual differences in shaping users' interactions with anthropomorphic systems.

Finally, by categorizing anthropomorphism into form and behavioral dimensions, this study expands the application of social response theory, enhancing our understanding of emotional and social responses in human-technology interactions. We provide new theoretical insights and practical guidance for designing avatars and virtual assistants, showing that both forms of anthropomorphism contribute in different but complementary ways to user satisfaction.

5.3 Practical Implications

Based on the findings of this study, virtual character design should strike a balance between form and behavioral anthropomorphism. Although these two aspects differ in expression, both enhance user satisfaction by stimulating emotions and improving interactive experiences. In practical applications, form and behavioral anthropomorphism often complement each other, and designers should ensure these aspects work together to enhance the overall user experience.

Additionally, users' personality traits, particularly openness, play an important moderating role in interactions. For form anthropomorphism, users with higher openness traits are more likely to derive entertainment and informativeness from the avatar's appearance and personalization. Therefore, designers can customize the virtual character's appearance and interaction style based on users' personality differences to meet diverse user needs. In contrast, the effectiveness of behavioral anthropomorphism relies more on immediate interaction and contextual factors rather than solely on personalization traits. When designing behavioral interactions, considering immediate feedback and contextual variations can better stimulate user satisfaction.

Overall, virtual character design should account for individual personality differences, leveraging both form and behavioral anthropomorphism to enhance user engagement and satisfaction.

5.4 Limitations and Future Research

One limitation of this study is primary focuses on the general effects of form and behavioral anthropomorphism without exploring scenarios where there is a significant mismatch between the two. Future research could investigate the consequences of such discrepancies, particularly in experimental settings, to understand how users react when form and behavior are inconsistent in avatars. For instance, when an avatar has highly personalized visual features but lacks engaging or responsive behaviors (or vice versa), it could lead to confusion or dissatisfaction. Examining these inconsistencies could provide deeper insights into how different aspects of anthropomorphism interact and affect user satisfaction.

References

1. Söderlund, M., Oikarinen, E.-L.: Service encounters with virtual agents: an examination of perceived humanness as a source of customer satisfaction. Eur. J. Mark. **55**(13), 94–121 (2021)
2. Wang, L.C., et al.: Can a retail web site be social? J. Mark. **71**(3), 143–157 (2007)
3. Miao, F., et al.: An emerging theory of avatar marketing. J. Mark. **86**(1), 67–90 (2022)
4. Verhagen, T., et al.: Virtual customer service agents: using social presence and personalization to shape online service encounters. J. Comput.-Mediat. Commun. **19**(3), 529–545 (2014)
5. Blut, M., et al.: Understanding anthropomorphism in service provision: a meta-analysis of physical robots, chatbots, and other AI. J. Acad. Mark. Sci. **49**, 632–658 (2021)
6. De Visser, E.J., et al.: Almost human: anthropomorphism increases trust resilience in cognitive agents. J. Exp. Psychol. Appl. **22**(3), 331–349 (2016)
7. Janson, A.: How to leverage anthropomorphism for chatbot service interfaces: the interplay of communication style and personification. Comput. Hum. Behav. **149**, 107954 (2023)
8. Zhu, R., Yi, C.: Avatar design in Metaverse: the effect of avatar-user similarity in procedural and creative tasks. Internet Res. **34**(1), 39–57 (2024)
9. Barbier, L., Fointiat, V.: To be or not be human-like in virtual world. Front. Comput. Sci. **2**, 15 (2020)
10. Coble, K., Ratican, J., Hutson, J.: Beyond the pixelated mirror: understanding avatar identity and its impact on in-game advertising and consumer behavior. Meta. **4**(2) (2023)
11. Azhari, A., et al.: Viewing romantic and friendship interactions activate prefrontal regions in persons with high openness personality trait. Front. Psychol. **11**, 490 (2020)

Delegation or Satisfaction? Explaining AI Dependence in College Students' Learning

Yunqi Long, Nan Wang(✉), and Hao Zhang

Wuhan University, 299 Bayi Road, Wuhan 430072, China
nanwang@whu.edu.cn

Abstract. With the explosion of artificial intelligence (AI) technology, AI has gained widespread adoption and is increasingly integrated into educational practices. The prevalent trend of college students utilizing AI has given rise to dependency. This study innovatively integrates expectation-confirmation theory and agency theory to propose and empirically test two mechanisms explaining AI dependence among college students in their learning processes. Utilizing a survey methodology, we validate these two mechanisms. The results offer theoretical contributions and practical implications for understanding and managing AI dependence in educational settings.

Keywords: AI dependence · Delegation · Satisfaction · College students' leaning

1 Introduction

At present, artificial intelligence technology is widely adopted in various fields of social life. In the field of education, the application of AI has attracted wide discussion and attention. For teachers, AI can help them create courses, make lesson plans, and improve their work efficiency [1, 2]. For students, AI can increase opportunities for self-directed learning, such as creating positive learning experiences and enhancing interactivity in digital environments [1]. However, apart from bringing benefits in the education context, AI also causes some negative consequences. There are instances of students' incomplete use and excessive reliance on AI, which leads to the decline of learning skills and integrity [3]. According to a survey by China Youth News in 2023, more than 80% of college students use AI tools. Nearly 60% of college students believe that the use of AI tools poses risks, including over-dependence and academic fraud [4].

Regarding the AI reliance issue, previous studies have shown that over-reliance on AI may lead to the risk of thinking degradation and affect students' learning performance, among other things [5–7]. There is no doubt that dependence on AI has become a problem for students, especially college students. Besides, AI detection has a high misjudgment rate and is difficult to use to guide students rationally, which is a problem plaguing the education system [8]. Therefore, properly using and standardizing AI is of great significance to students, teachers, and educational institutions. In this regard, preventing and solving the problem of AI dependence is the most critical aspect in the use of

Y. P. Tu and M. Chi (Eds.): WHICEB 2025, LNBIP 549, pp. 87–98, 2025.
https://doi.org/10.1007/978-3-031-94184-9_8

AI. Thus, we can infer that it is important to first understand the phenomenon of AI dependence in college students' learning in order to better address the issue of AI reliance.

Previous studies have either explained AI dependence from individual factors, such as continuous usage intention, trust, and inertial thinking [9, 12], or focused on the cognition of AI, such as its assistance in learning and education [10, 11], or emphasized the risks arising from AI dependence, such as weakened decision-making ability and student's learning performance [3, 13]..

However, fewer studies have proposed mechanisms from the satisfaction and delegation perspective. Thus, building on the expectation confirmation theory and agency theory, this paper aims to validate two mechanisms to explain AI dependence on college students' learning. This paper guides students to correctly use AI, and contribute to the AI dependence literature.

2 Literature Review

2.1 AI Dependency

Dependence is defined as a behavior in itself [14, 15]. This signifies that dependency is not an emotional state or a sentiment, but rather a tangible behavior executed. It implies that dependency is observable through direct means [16].. Technical dependency is a high degree of dependence on specific technical tools and services, making them indispensable tools for accomplishing everyday tasks and achieving goals. When this dependence reaches a certain point, it can lead to the difficulty of operating without technology [17], a situation that needs to be avoided in education [18]. Nicolas et al. define dependency in an AI consultant environment as "the user following the recommended behavior of the system" [19]. Some studies suggest that AI dependence is defined as the overuse of AI techniques, leading to trends of dependence and addiction, which can have negative consequences [20–23].

Previous studies also discussed the consequences of AI dependence are multifaceted, such as affecting people's cognition and decision-making ability [26, 27], affecting people's mental health, bringing social problems and emotional distress, etc. [23, 24]. Krullaars et al. argue that AI dependence may undermine students' motivation and commitment to learning because they may rely too heavily on these systems to answer answers instead of actively participating in the learning experience [28]. The high study workload, micromanagement, time pressure and sense of constant surveillance due to the use of AI may cause stress and psychological discomfort [3]. In the educational context, AI tools assist learners by retrieving, answering, prompting, planning, summarizing, modifying, analyzing, and generating information, while AI and chat machines are neutral in nature, which is one of the reasons why the negative effects.

Further, previous studies explain AI dependence by identifying several antecedents, such as self-efficacy [18], trust in AI [24], lazy thinking, avoiding learning motivation, and positive experience [12]. Some studies have also shown that social motivation will increase dependence on AI, and people sometimes take AI tools as the object of emotional dependence and relieve negative emotions (such as loneliness, etc.) through dialogue with them, which will also promote dependence on AI [23, 25]. However, it is less investigated about the role of satisfaction and delegation intention in explaining AI dependence.

2.2 The Expectation Confirmation Theory

The expectation confirmation theory (ECT) was proposed by Oliver in 1980 [29]. The main concept is that consumers judge whether they are satisfied with a product or service based on the comparison between pre-purchase expectation and post-purchase performance, and satisfaction becomes a reference for the next purchase or use. This theory has also been applied to explain the willingness to technology continuous usage behavior. For example, ECT has been used to explain the use of technology in information systems [30] and has been used in the study of continuance intention to use mobile Apps [31]. This study believes that AI dependence is inevitably related to the continuous use of AI, which is an important part of dependency formation during continuous use, and also a manifestation of dependency formation. The research has shown that confirmation and satisfaction are critical in shaping users' intentions to continue using AI tools, highlighting the importance of meeting users' expectations to foster trust and ongoing engagement. This study extracts variables including performance expectation, and expectation confirmation, from the ECT model to explain AI dependency in student learning.

2.3 Agency Theory

Agency theory is the basic theory of agency which means that one person (the principal) delegates work to another person (the agent) [32–35]. Agency theory has been the subject of extensive research in the decades since its introduction and has applications in many disciplines [33, 36, 37]. Previous studies on agency theory focused on humans [33, 38, 39], both agents and principals are human beings. In recent years, more and more studies have been conducted on AI agents or technical agents, such as Alan R. Dennis et al.'s research on the influence of trust and control on software agents based on the agent theory [40]. Jeon studied the effect of the gender of AI agents on trust [41]. A research has shown that from the perspective of the agency theory, the human is the principal while the AI is the agent in the 'human-AI' relationship [3]. Similarly, the agent in this study is AI, and the principal is a group of college students. In AI dependence, letting AI complete the learning task on its behalf is the main manifestation of dependence. The concept of an AI agent is a kind of technical agent, similar to the software agent studied by Alan R. Dennis et al. [40], hence it is appropriate to use the agent theory to explain the content of this study.

3 Research Model and Hypothesis Development

3.1 Research Model

Based on the expectation confirmation theory and agency theory, this research model primarily encompasses two pathways leading to AI dependence: the satisfaction pathway and the delegation intention pathway [9, 42]. AI performance and self-expectation are extended from performance expectation and expectation confirmation, and the comparison between performance and expectation can highlight the comparison expectation degree of confirmation. Comparison expectation is the expectation of comparing the performance of college students with the performance of AI. Since this study takes college students as the object, it is necessary to fully consider the independent initiative of college students. Intention to delegate is derived from Stout et al. 's study on software agents [40]. In this study, it is believed that AI is dependent and the behavior of delegating tasks to AI is very similar to that of software agents. Therefore, it is appropriate to use this variable to describe college students' willingness to use AI instead of themselves to complete tasks. The model is constructed as follows (Fig. 1):

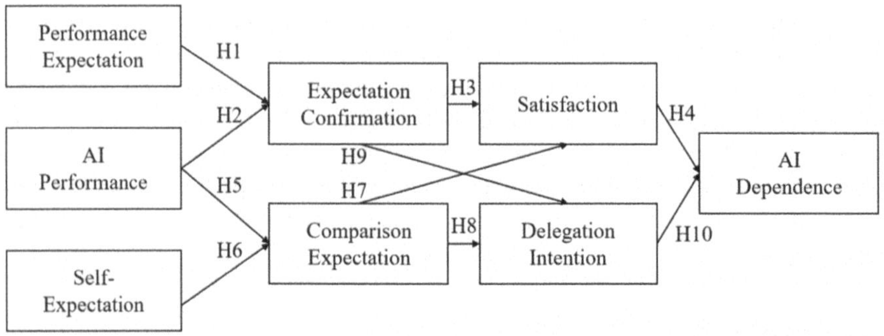

Fig. 1. Research model.

3.2 Performance Expectation, AI Performance, Expectation Confirmation, and Satisfaction

Based on the expectation confirmation theory, performance expectations are customer beliefs about product attributes or performance [43]. In this study, performance expectation is the college student's expectation of the effect that AI can bring. Thus, low expectations will lead to strong confirmation, while high expectations will be difficult to achieve [44–46]. AI performance is the actual performance during the use of AI. Validation relates to the process of comparing the user's prior expectations with the actual performance of the product [44]. Validation develops when a product is perceived to perform better than expected [29]. Thus, when an AI performs well above its expectations, it increases the expected confirmation. Therefore, two hypotheses are proposed:

H1: Performance expectation negatively affects expectation confirmation.
H2: AI performance positively affects expectation confirmation.

Satisfaction is a summary of the mental state associated with positive emotions [47]. When the expectation of a product is confirmed, users can generate satisfaction from their positive emotional state. Premkumar et al. found that expectation confirmation affects users' satisfaction with a product [45]. Yen and Lu show that confirmation of bidders in online auctions is positively correlated with satisfaction [48]. Thong, Hong, and Tam show that confirmation is a key prerequisite for user satisfaction [49]. It is thus concluded that when college students' expectations of AI are confirmed, it will have a positive impact on their satisfaction. Therefore, the hypothesis is proposed:

H3: Expectation confirmation positively affects satisfaction.

3.3 Satisfaction, and AI Dependence

Research has shown that satisfaction is a key prerequisite for an individual to re-purchase and reuse a product or service [50], and satisfaction is the strongest predictor of continued usage intentions [44]. Therefore, it is believed that the more satisfied with AI, the easier it is to form the behavior of repeated use of AI, and the easier it is to rely on AI. Therefore, the hypothesis is proposed:

H4: Satisfaction positively affects AI dependence.

3.4 Self-Expectation, Comparison Expectation, and Intention to Delegate

Self-expectations are extended from performance expectations, extending them from customers' beliefs about product attributes or performance to users' beliefs about their performance [43]. Comparison expectations are extended from expectation confirmation, which compares a user's performance expectations with experience [44], and comparative expectations, which compares a user's self-expected performance with AI performance. Research has shown that when performance is greater than expectations, it is conducive to the development of expectation confirmation [29]. Similarly, comparison expectations increase when AI performs better than self-expectations. When self-expectations are strong, and AI cannot perform better than expected, then comparative expectations decline. Therefore, the hypothesis is proposed:

H5: AI performance positively affects comparison expectations.
H6: Self-expectations negatively affect expectations.

According to Helson's adaptation level theory [51], it is postulated that an individual's satisfaction level is directly influenced by their baseline expectations. Specifically, when one holds a higher baseline level of expectations, their satisfaction tends to increase accordingly. Conversely, a lower baseline of expectations often leads to a decrease in satisfaction. In the context of artificial intelligence (AI) in learning, this theory can be applied to understand students' satisfaction with AI's performance. When students have high comparison expectations, meaning they strongly anticipate AI to perform better than they themselves could, this anticipation has the potential to elevate their satisfaction with the AI. Essentially, the stronger the belief that AI can outperform human capabilities, the more likely users are to be satisfied with the AI's performance. Thus, we proposed H7.

H7: Comparison expectation positively affects satisfaction.

Intention to delegate means the willingness to delegate decision-making to an agent. As proposed by Stout et al., in their research on software agents, as a dependent variable, agent intention directly reflects the user's agent willingness to delegate tasks to software [40]. In this study, agent intention refers to the intention of letting AI complete the learning task on behalf of the user. According to the social cognitive theory, individuals' emotions and behaviors are shaped and controlled by their cognitive abilities such as expectations and beliefs [52]. When the expectation is stronger, people think that AI's performance is better than their performance, and they are more inclined to let AI act as the agent for learning tasks. Similarly, when the expectation is more certain, people are more inclined to let AI act as the agent for learning tasks. It also has a positive shaping effect on agent motivation. Thus, H8 and H9 are proposed as below.

H8: Comparison expectation positively affects agent motivation.
H9: Expectations confirm a positive effect on the intention to delegate.

3.5 Intention to Delegate, and AI Dependence

When individuals delegate tasks to AI, which means they gain positive experiences, such as successful task completion and increased efficiency, reinforces their initial trust and perception of AI. Over time, as individuals continue to have positive experiences with AI, their reliance on AI for task execution increases. Thus, it is easy to infer that when the agent Delegate intention is strong and the belief of using the AI agent itself is strong, college students will be driven to use AI to complete the task instead of themselves, and maintain this behavior, thus promoting the formation of dependence. Therefore, we put forward H10.

H10: Delegate intention positively affects AI dependence.

4 Questionnaire Design and Data Collection

4.1 Questionnaire Design

The questionnaire involves two parts. The first part is to measure the demographic variables such as gender, age and education. Questionnaire will be ended if the participant has no previous AI usage experience for learning. The second part mainly measures the constructs in the research model and is mainly adopted from previous literature. Performance expectation, self-expectation and AI performance are adopted from Hamid et al. 's study [9]. Expectation confirmation, comparison expectation and satisfaction are adopted from Bhattacharjee's study [44]. Intention to delegate comes from Stout et al.'s study [40].AI dependence is taken from Ye et al. study [12].

4.2 Data Collection

The samples are college students. The Questionnaire was sent Through WeChat, QQ, rednote, and other network platforms, 431 questionnaires were collected, and 293 valid questionnaires were obtained after screening and elimination. Among them, in terms of gender, there were 117 males (39.9%) and 176 females (60.1%); in terms of age, 39 were under 18 years old (13.3%), 253 were between 18 and 25 years old (86.3%), and 1 was above 25 years old (0.3%); in terms of educational level, 255 were undergraduates (87%), and 38 had postgraduate degrees or above (13%).

5 Data Analysis

5.1 Measurement Model Analysis

To test the measurement model, SmartPLS 4 is adopted. Cronbach's Alpha (CA), composite reliability (CR), mean-variance extraction (AVE), and factor loading. The results show that the value of CA and CR of all variables is greater than 0.7, and the AVE values of all constructs are above 0.5, which has satisfactory reliability and convergence validity [53]. The measurement model analysis further shown that the loading of all measured items on their theoretical potential variables is greater than 0.7, showing a good convergence validity and discriminant validity [53]. Further, the square root of the AVE value of each construct is greater than their correlation with the other construct, confirming the discriminate validity [53].

5.2 Structural Model Analysis

With a reliable measurement model, we then use SmartPls4.1.0.9 to test the structural model, the results are shown in Fig. 2. First, performance expectation has a significant but negative effect on expectation confirmation, and H1 is not supported. AI performance ($\beta = 0.575$, $T = 12.750$, $p < 0.001$) had a significant positive impact on expectation confirmation, and had a significant positive impact ($\beta = 0.184$, $T = 5.784$, $p < 0.001$) on comparison expectation, indicating that H2 and H5 were confirmed. Self-expectation ($\beta = -0.729$, $T = 19.298$, $p < 0.001$) significantly negatively affected the comparison expectation, indicating that H6 was supported.

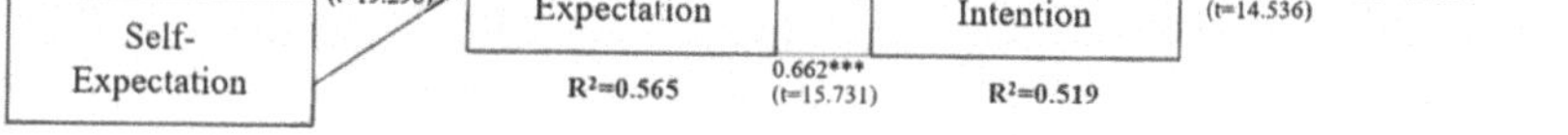

Fig. 2. Results of hypotheses testing.

Second, consistent with our propositions, Expectation confirmation ($\beta = 0.527$, $T = 13.170$, $p < 0.001$) had a significant positive impact on satisfaction, and a significant positive impact on the intention to delegate ($\beta = 0.177$, $T = 4.563$, $p < 0.001$), indicating that H3 and H9 were supported. Further, comparison expectation had a significant positive impact on satisfaction ($\beta = 0.313$, $T = 6.506$, $p < 0.001$) and also had a positive impact on delegate intention ($\beta = 0.662$, $T = 115.731$, $p < 0.001$).

Last, satisfaction ($\beta = 0.213$, $T = 4.342$, $p < 0.001$) significantly positively affected AI dependence, and intention to delegate ($\beta = 0.667$, $T = 14.536$, $p < 0.001$) also significantly positively affected AI dependence, indicating that H4 and H10 were established.

We future conduct the moderating analysis to examine the role of performance expectation in shaping the relationship between AI performance and expectation confirmation to explain the role of performance expectation. Our hypothesis posits that higher performance expectations from students negatively moderate the impact of AI performance on their expectation confirmation; in other words, when students anticipate superior AI performance, the actual performance has a relatively lesser influence on meeting or exceeding their expectations compared to when their expectations are lower. The results of the moderating analysis confirmed it ($\beta = -0.154$, $T = 3.825$, $p < 0.001$).

6 Discussion

6.1 Key Findings

Based on the Expectation-Confirmation Theory and Agency Theory, this study advances a theoretical model proposing two mechanisms—delegation and satisfaction—that influence AI dependence among college students in their learning contexts. The empirical results demonstrate that both satisfaction and delegation exert significant effects on the formation of AI dependence.

Furthermore, this study delves into the operationalization of these mechanisms. Regarding the satisfaction mechanism, we find that performance expectation and perceived AI performance positively influence expectation confirmation, which in turn affects satisfaction. For the delegation mechanism, we uncover that college students' self-expectation negatively correlates with comparison expectations. Concurrently, perceived AI performance positively impacts comparison expectations, which subsequently influence delegation intentions.

6.2 Theoretical Implications

This study has the following theoretical implications. First, this study innovatively integrates Expectation-Confirmation Theory and Agency Theory to propose two mechanisms—delegation and satisfaction—that offer a nuanced understanding of AI dependence in the learning contexts of college students. This integration is capable of providing a more comprehensive analysis of the behavioral motivations in complex educational scenarios. Second, beyond merely presenting these mechanisms, the paper delves deeper by elucidating the antecedents of delegation within this specific educational framework like AI performance and Self-expectation. Moreover, this research extends the applicability of both ECT and Agency Theory by applying them to an educational context, thereby broadening their theoretical reach.

6.3 Practical Implications

First, our findings reveal that satisfaction is one significant driver of AI dependence among college students. While AI expectations and AI performance positively influence satisfaction, to mitigate over-reliance on AI outcomes during the learning process, it is suggested to moderate students' perceptions of both AI performance and expectations. Second, our results further indicate that delegation plays a pivotal role in fostering AI dependence, and self-expectations amplify this effect. Therefore, fostering self-confidence and self-efficacy among students is crucial. Additionally, reducing the emphasis on AI performance can also help diminish delegation intentions, thereby promoting a more balanced reliance on AI in educational contexts. In summary, our study underscores the importance of carefully managing students' perceptions of AI performance and expectations, as well as fostering their self-confidence and self-efficacy, to ensure a healthy balance between human and AI collaboration in educational settings.

6.4 Limitations and Future Research

Firstly, it did not distinguish between levels of dependence on AI. Further research could explore whether the results vary among individuals with different levels of AI dependence. Secondly, this study did not account for the potential impacts of different types of learning tasks and personality differences on the results, which could be further discussed in future research. Furthermore, due to different cultural backgrounds, the effects of ECT theory in China may be different from those in other countries.. Lastly, this study utilized cross-sectional data to explain AI dependence. Future study could employ experimental designs to further validate the findings.

Acknowledgement. Grants from Comprehensive Reform Project for the Construction of Undergraduate Education Quality of Wuhan University in 2024 and Provincial Teaching Reform and Research Projects of Undergraduate Universities in Hubei Province (Project No. 2024010) supported this study.

References

1. Thomas, K.F.: Chiu: the impact of generative AI (GenAI) on practices, policies, and research direction in education: a case of ChatGPT and Midjourney. Interact. Learn. Environ. **32**(10), 1–17 (2023)
2. Ngao, A.I., Sang, G., Kihwele, J.E.: Understanding teacher educators' perceptions and practices about ICT integration in the teacher education program. Educ. Sci. **12**(8), 549 (2022)
3. Ivanov, S.: The dark side of artificial intelligence in higher education. Serv. Ind. J. **43**(15/16), 1055–1082 (2023)
4. Bi, R., Cheng, S., Li, Z.: More than 80% of the Surveyed College Students Have used AI Tools. China Youth News (2023) in Chinese
5. Zhai, C., Wibowo, S., Li, L.: Zhang Xin effects of over-reliance on AI dialogue systems on students' cognitive abilities: a systematic review. Smart Learn. Environ. **11**(1), 28 (2024)
6. Li, M.D., Little, B.P.: Appropriate reliance on artificial intelligence in radiology education. J. Am. Coll. Radiol. **20**(11), 1126–1130 (2023)
7. Kumar, S., Mahajan, S., Gadh, P., Jain, R., Jain, D.: Reliance of high school students on chat bots and its relationship with creativity. Educ. Res. (IJMCER). **6**(4), 286–290 (2024)

8. Yang, Y., Li, Y., Xiong, H.: Human and AI-generated marketing content comparison corpus, evaluation, and detection. In: Hadfi, R., Anthony, P., Sharma, A., Ito, T., Bai, Q. (eds.) PRICAI 2024: Trends in Artificial Intelligence. PRICAI 2024. LNCS, vol. 15282. Springer, Singapore (2024)
9. Shamszare, H., Choudhury, A.: The impact of performance expectancy, workload, risk, and satisfaction on trust in ChatGPT: cross-sectional survey analysis. JMIR Hum. Factors. **11**, 1–19 (2024)
10. Luckin, R., Cukurova, M.: Designing educational technologies in the age of AI: a learning sciences-driven approach. Br. J. Educ. Technol. **50**(6), 2824–2838 (2019)
11. Chen, L., Chen, P., Lin, Z.: Artificial intelligence in education: a review. IEEE Access. **8**, 75264–75278 (2020)
12. Ye, J.H., Zhang, M., Nong, W., Wang, L., Yang, X.: The relationship between inert thinking and ChatGPT dependence: an I-PACE model perspective. Educ. Inf. Technol. **1–25**, 3885–3909 (2024)
13. Adegbesan, A., Akingbola, A., Aremu, O., Adewole, O., Amamdikwa, J.C., Shagaya, U.: From scalpels to algorithms: the risk of dependence on artificial intelligence in surgery. J. Med. Surg. Publ. Health. **3**, 100140 (2024)
14. Dzindolet, M.T., Peterson, S.A., Pomranky, R.A., Pierce, L.G., Beck, H.P.: The role of trust in automation reliance. Int. J. Hum. Comp. Stud. **58**(6), 697–718 (2003)
15. Lee, J.D.: Katrina a see.: trust in automation: designing for appropriate reliance. Hum. Fact. **46**(1), 50–80 (2024)
16. Schemmer, M., Kühl, N., Benz, C., Bartos, A., Satzger, G.: Appropriate reliance on AI advice: conceptualization and the effect of explanations. In: 28th International Conference on Intelligent User Interfaces, vol. 23, pp. 1–13. ACM, Sydney, NSW/New York, NY (2023)
17. Davis, F.D.: Perceived usefulness, perceived ease of use, and user acceptance of information technology. MIS Q. **13**(3), 319–340 (1989)
18. Zhang, L., Xu, J.: The paradox of self-efficacy and technological dependence: unraveling generative AI's impact on university students' task completion. Internet High. Educ. **65**, 100978 (2025)
19. Scharowski, N., Perrig, S.A.C., von Felten, N., Brühlmann, F.: Trust and reliance in XAI–distinguishing between attitudinal and behavioral measures. arXiv preprint arXiv:2203.12318 (2022)
20. Wiederhold, B.K.: "Alexa, are you my mom?" The role of artificial intelligence in child development. Cyberpsychol. Behav. Soc. Net. **21**(8), 471–472 (2018)
21. Hu, B., Mao, Y., Kim, K.J.: How social anxiety leads to problematic use of conversational AI: the roles of loneliness, rumination, and mind perception. Comput. Hum. Behav. **145**, 107066 (2023)
22. Sandoval, E.B.: Addiction to social robots: a research proposal. In: In 2019 14th ACM/IEEE International Conference on Human-Robot Interaction (HRI), Daegu, Korea (South), pp. 526–527 (2019)
23. Laestadius, L., Bishop, A., Gonzalez, M., Illenčík, D., Campos-Castillo, C.: Too human and not human enough: a grounded theory analysis of mental health harms from emotional dependence on the social chatbot Replika. New Media Soc. **1**(3), 1–19 (2022)
24. Klingbeil, A., Grützner, C., Schreck, P.: Trust and reliance on AI—an experimental study on the extent and costs of overreliance on AI. Comput. Hum. Behav. **160**, 108352 (2024)
25. Patulny, R., Lazarevic, N., Smith, V.: "Once more, with feeling," said the robot: AI, the end of work, and the rise of emotional economies. Emot. Soc. **2**(1), 79–97 (2020)
26. Huang, S., Lai, X., Ke, L., Li, Y., Wang, H., Zhao, X., Wang, Y.: AI technology panic—is AI dependence bad for mental health? A cross-lagged panel model and the mediating roles of motivations for AI use among adolescents. Psychol. Res. Behav. Manag. **17**, 1087–1102 (2023)

27. Schoeffer, J., Jakubik, J., Voessing, M., Kuehl, N., Satzger, G.: On the interdependence of reliance behavior and accuracy in AI-assisted decision-making. Front. Artific. Intell. Appl. **368**, 46–49 (2023)
28. Krullaars, Z.H., Januardani, A., Zhou, L., Jonkers, E.: Exploring initial interactions: high school students and generative AI chatbots for relationship development. In: Mensch und Computer 2023-Workshopband, pp. 10–18420. Gesellschaft für Informatik eV (2023)
29. Oliver, R.L.: A cognitive model of the antecedents and consequences of satisfaction decisions. J. Mark. Res. **17**, 460–469 (1980)
30. Brown, S.A., Venkatesh, V., Goyal, S.: Expectation confirmation in technology use. Inf. Syst. Res. **23**(2), 474–487 (2012)
31. Tam, C., Santos, D., Oliveira, T.: Exploring the influential factors of continuance intention to use mobile apps: extending the expectation confirmation model. Inf. Syst. Front. **22**, 243–257 (2020)
32. Shapiro, S.P.: Agency theory. Annu. Rev. Sociol. **31**(1), 263–284 (2005)
33. Eisenhardt, K.M.: Agency theory: an assessment and review. Acad. Manag. Rev. **14**(1), 57–74 (1989)
34. Jensen, M., Meckling, W.: Theory of the firm: managerial behavior, agency costs, and ownership structure. J. Financ. Econ. **4**(3), 305–360 (1976)
35. Wilson, R.: The theory of syndicates. Econometrica. **36**(1), 119–132 (1968)
36. Pavlou, P.A., Liang, H., Xue, Y.: Understanding and mitigating uncertainty in online exchange relationships: a principal-agent perspective. MIS Q. **31**(1), 105–136 (2007)
37. Vaidyanathan, G., Devaraj, S., D'Arcy, J.: Does security impact E-procurement performance? Testing a model of direct and moderated effects. Decis. Sci. **43**(3), 437–458 (2012)
38. Bendor, J., Glazer, A., Hammond, T.: Theories of delegation. Annu. Rev. Polit. Sci. **4**(1), 235–269 (2001)
39. Leana, C.R.: Power relinquishment versus power sharing: theoretical clarification and empirical comparison of delegation and participation. J. Appl. Psychol. **72**(2), 228–233 (1987)
40. Stout, N., Dennis, A.R., Wells, T.M.: The buck stops there: the impact of perceived accountability and control on the intention to delegate to software agents. AIS Trans. Hum. Comp. Interac. **6**(1), 1–14 (2014)
41. Jeon, J.E.: The effect of AI agent gender on trust and grounding. J. Theor. Appl. Electron. Commer. Res. **19**(1), 692–704 (2024)
42. Zhang, S., Zhao, X., Zhou, T., Kim, J.H.: Do you have AI dependency? The roles of academic self-efficacy, academic stress, and performance expectations on problematic AI usage behavior. Int. J. Educ. Technol. High. Educ. **21**(1), 34 (2024)
43. Spreng, R.A., Mackenzie, S.B., Olshavsky, B.W.: A re-examination of the determinants of consumer satisfaction. J. Mark. **60**(3), 15–22 (1996)
44. Bhattacherjee, A.: Understanding information systems continuance: an expectation-confirmation model. MIS Q. **25**(3), 351–370 (2001)
45. Premkumar, G., Bhattacharjee, A.: Explaining information technology usage: a test of competing models. Omega-Int. J. Manag. Sci. **36**(1), 64–75 (2008)
46. Tsao, W.-Y.: Application of expectation confirmation theory to consumers' impulsive purchase behavior for products promoted by showgirls in exhibits. J. Promot. Manag. **19**(3), 283–298 (2013)
47. Oliver, R.L.: Measurement, and evaluation of satisfaction processes in retail settings. J. Retail. **57**(3), 25–48 (1981)
48. Yen, C.H., Lu, H.P.: Factors influencing online auction repurchase intention. Internet Res. **18**(1), 7–25 (2008)
49. Thong, J.Y., Hong, S.-J., Tam, K.Y.: The effects of post-adoption beliefs on the expectation-confirmation model for information technology continuance. Int. J. Hum. Comput. Stud. **64**(9), 799–810 (2006)

50. Mouakket, S.: Factors influencing continuance intention to use social network sites: the Facebook case. Comput. Hum. Behav. **53**, 102–110 (2015)
51. Helson, H.: Adaptation-Level Theory. Harper & Row, New York, NY (1964)
52. Bandura, A.: The explanatory and predictive scope of self-efficacy theory. J. Soc. Clin. Psychol. **4**(3), 359–373 (1986)
53. Hair, J.F., Ringle, C.M., Sarstedt, M.: PLS-SEM: indeed a silver bullet. J. Market. Theory Pract. **19**(2), 139–152 (2011)
54. Henseler, J., Ringle, C.M., Sarstedt, M.: A new criterion for assessing discriminant validity in variance-based structural equation modeling. J. Acad. Mark. Sci. **43**, 115–135 (2015)

Data Analytics and Digital Governance

The Impact of Clarification Announcements on Stock Price Crash Risk—Considering the Degree of Information Asymmetry and the Level of Digital Transformation

Jiani Liu(✉) and Mo Hai

Central University of Finance and Economics, Beijing 102206, China
Jianiliu2023@163.com

Abstract. This study explores how clarification announcements by listed companies on the Shanghai and Shenzhen A-share main board (2013–2023) mitigate stock price crash risk. Utilizing a two-way fixed effects model and mediation analysis, we demonstrate that addressing false rumors effectively reduces the risk of crashes, and conclusions are robust to PSM and variable substitution tests. The mechanism analysis indicates that these announcements reduce information asymmetry, thereby lowering crash risk. Heterogeneity analysis reveals that the impact is more significant in companies with higher digitalization levels. The findings suggest that timely clarification announcements can stabilize stock prices by alleviating information disparities, and that embracing digital transformation can enhance the effectiveness of such announcements in maintaining market stability.

Keywords: Clarification Announcements · Stock Price Crash Risk · Information Asymmetry · Digital Transformation

1 Introduction

The phenomenon of stock price crashes refers to the situation where the stock of a listed company is massively sold off in a short period of time, leading to a sharp decline in stock prices. During the stock market crash in 2015, the Shanghai Composite Index and the Shenzhen Component Index all experienced a drop of more than 8%, with many individual stocks hitting their daily limit down, and the phenomenon of plummeting stock prices not only caused investors to suffer huge economic losses but also plunged the entire capital market into turmoil. Existing research suggests that principal-agent problems and information asymmetry are the main causes of stock price crashes. The management of companies, considering their own interests, does not disclose negative news in a timely manner, and when bad news reaches a critical value and erupts, it triggers a stock price crash [1]. Based on this research, scholars have identified factors affecting stock price crash risk from both internal and external perspectives of a company. Internal factors include voluntary disclosure behavior, accounting conservatism [2], option incentives [1], and social responsibility disclosure [3]; external factors include media coverage [12],

Y. P. Tu and M. Chi (Eds.): WHICEB 2025, LNBIP 549, pp. 101–112, 2025.
https://doi.org/10.1007/978-3-031-94184-9_9

analysts' optimistic bias, investor sentiment [13] and investor attention [14]. However, from the internal perspective of the company, there is relatively little research on how listed companies' clarification announcements in response to false stock market rumors affect stock price crash risk.

Stock market rumors refer to messages disseminated in the stock market through public media about a listed company that are difficult to verify in terms of their authenticity and accuracy in a timely manner. The emergence of stock market rumors does harm to the stable development of the stock market. These rumors negatively affect investor decision-making, analyst forecasts, and abnormal stock returns [4]. Therefore, for rumors with significant impact, listed companies will issue clarification announcements to provide explanations. The China Securities Regulatory Commission (CSRC) issued the "Notice on Several Issues Concerning the Release of Clarification Announcements by Listed Companies" in 1996, requiring listed companies to promptly issue clarification announcements when encountering rumors that may affect the company's stock price, in order to correct investor misunderstandings. Current research on clarification announcements mainly focuses on their effectiveness in restoring the cumulative abnormal returns of stock prices. Existing studies have shown that the effectiveness of clarification announcements in restoring cumulative abnormal returns depends on the nature of the rumor, the method of clarification, and the characteristics of the company [5].

Based on current research, clarification announcements play a role in restoring stock price abnormal returns caused by stock market rumors and achieving stock price stability. This study aims to explore whether clarification announcements by listed companies can effectively reduce the risk of stock price crashes and the impact mechanism of information asymmetry in this process. Since the effect of clarification announcements is related to company characteristics, considering the differences in digital transformation among companies, this study investigates whether the clarification behavior of listed companies with different levels of digital transformation has different effects on suppressing the risk of stock price crashes. This paper uses data from A-share listed companies on the Shanghai and Shenzhen stock markets as the research sample and conducts empirical research through a two-way fixed effects model and a mediating effect test model, combined with various robustness and heterogeneity analysis methods. The main innovations of this paper are: (1) focusing on whether the clarification announcements made by listed companies in response to false stock market rumors will affect the risk of stock price crashes and the mediating role of information asymmetry; (2) selecting the degree of digitalization as a perspective for heterogeneity analysis, providing decision-making references for listed companies with different levels of digital development, and to some extent, studying the impact of digitalization on society and the economy.

2 Literature Review

2.1 Stock Price Crash Risk

The stock price crash risk of a listed company refers to the risk of a significant decline in stock prices over a short period of time. Principal-agent problems and information asymmetry are the main causes leading to stock price crashes in listed companies. Principal-agent problems arise from internal management agency issues such as political promotion and empire building, which conceal negative company information. When bad news can no longer be hidden and erupts, it causes a significant impact on stock prices. The information asymmetry between investors and companies prevents investors from fully understanding the true operating conditions of the company, which may lead to investors being deceived by false financial information, creating a bubble. When the truth is revealed, the bubble bursts, causing a downward impact on stock prices.

From an internal company perspective, improving accounting conservatism [2] can curb managerial opportunism, constrain managerial behavior, and reduce the risk of stock price crashes. Within the principal-agent framework, agents, motivated by aggressive tax avoidance and option incentives [1], have the motive to hide bad news, increasing the true understanding of the company's operating conditions for investors, reducing information transparency, and thereby increasing the risk of stock price crashes. Therefore, actions that reduce the degree of information asymmetry, such as improving the disclosure level of internal control information, increasing corporate social responsibility disclosure, and enhancing voluntary disclosure behavior, can significantly reduce the risk of stock price crashes.

From an external company perspective, the media, by frequently reporting on listed companies, significantly reduces the future stock price crash risk and plays a role in public supervision [12]. Analysts' optimistic tendencies and selective biases make it difficult to disclose negative company news to investors in a timely manner, increasing the degree of information asymmetry and leading to stock price crashes. High investor sentiment reduces stock liquidity, intensifying the risk of future stock price crashes [13], investor attention increases irrational investor sentiment and pricing errors, raising the risk of stock price crashes [14].

2.2 Stock Market Rumors and Clarification Announcements

Stock market rumors, which are unverified messages that significantly influence investor behavior, can be categorized into true and false based on their authenticity. These rumors have negative economic effects, impacting investor decisions, analyst forecasts, and causing abnormal stock returns. Clarification announcements are crucial for companies to address such rumors.

In recent years, research on clarification announcements has focused on their effectiveness in restoring abnormal stock returns caused by stock market rumors, and there is no consensus on the conclusions of these studies. Some scholars believe that clarification announcements for any type of rumor cannot quickly restore stock prices [4]. Other scholars argue that the effectiveness of clarification announcements varies depending on the nature of the rumor, the method of clarification, and the characteristics of the company. Companies with greater authority, higher investor recognition, and better social reputation, as well as companies with higher quality of information disclosure, have a more significant effect on clarifying false stock market rumors.

In summary, current research has identified that both internal and external factors of companies can influence stock price crash risk, and stock rumors leads to abnormal returns. Clarification announcements play a role in normalizing returns and stabilizing prices. Few research has analyzed the relationship between them. So this paper uses data from A-share companies listed on the Shanghai and Shenzhen markets from 2013 to 2023 to examine the impact of such announcements on crash risk and the underlying mechanisms. It also explores how digital transformation, which varies among companies, affects the efficacy of these announcements in mitigating crash risk.

3 Hypotheses

In China's stock market, which is dominated by retail investors, these investors are at a disadvantage in terms of information acquisition and processing. They may treat false news released by the media as reliable signals for trading, causing asset values to deviate from their true values and leading to excessive stock price reactions.

According to the signal transmission theory [6], company management, as the party with more information, has the motive to convey information about the company's operations to those at an information disadvantage, such as investors, especially in highly competitive market conditions. Therefore, when false rumors about listed companies circulate in the stock market, these companies will promptly issue clarification announcements with rich information content to counteract the negative impacts of these rumors, thereby influencing investor decision-making. As a signal, clarification announcements can reduce investors' uncertainty about the company's future prospects, stabilize investor confidence and sentiment, reduce panic selling, and thereby lower the risk of stock price crashes. Thus, we propose Hypothesis 1:

H1: Listed companies' issuance of clarification announcements in response to false stock market rumors will reduce the risk of stock price crashes.

Clarification announcements, as an emergency form of information disclosure by listed companies, are a common strategy to reduce the impact of stock market rumors. On one hand, listed companies can use clarification announcements to detail the inaccuracies of false rumors, providing investors with timely and accurate information, reducing uncertainty, and increasing the number of informed traders. This motivates investors to search online more actively for relevant information [7], effectively alleviating the degree of information asymmetry and suppressing the risk of stock price crashes.

On the other hand, clarification announcements made in response to false stock market rumors may also be accompanied by disclosures of other company-related business plans and operational developments, enhancing the informational richness of the stock price, reducing the degree of information asymmetry, and decreasing the risk of stock price crashes. A significant reduction in the degree of information asymmetry substantially suppresses the risk of sharp declines in individual stocks. As information asymmetry is alleviated, investors can understand the actual operating conditions of the company and make corresponding decisions, allowing stock prices to truly reflect the company's actual operating conditions, reducing stock price deviations, and lowering the risk of stock price crashes. Therefore, we propose Hypothesis 2:

H2: Listed companies' issuance of clarification announcements in response to false stock market rumors alleviates the risk of stock price crashes by reducing the degree of information asymmetry.

4 Research Design

4.1 Data Resource

This study utilizes data from A-share companies listed on the main boards of the Shanghai and Shenzhen stock markets between 2013 and 2023. The research sample includes data on whether companies issued clarification announcements regarding false stock market rumors, stock price crash risk indicators, control variables, and the degree of digital transformation for heterogeneity analysis, all sourced from the CSMAR database. To ensure data accuracy, the following processing steps were taken: (1) Exclusion of companies designated as ST and *ST; (2) Exclusion of financial industry companies due to their unique financial and operational characteristics; (3) Winsorization of continuous variables at the top and bottom 1% to mitigate the impact of extreme values. A total of 26,915 data points were collected, and the empirical analysis was conducted using Stata 16.0.

4.2 Variable Description

4.2.1 Dependent Variable: Stock Price Crash Risk

The proxy variable for stock price crash risk, the negative conditional skewness (NCSKEW), is constructed according to the literature [8]. The higher the NCSKEW, the greater the risk of stock price crashes. In formula (1), $R_{i,\,t}$ represents the return of stock i in week t considering reinvestment of cash dividends, $R_{m,\,t}$ represents the weekly return of the circulating market with equal weighting in week t, $R_{m,\,t-1}$ is the lagged market return for the previous week, $\varepsilon_{i,\,t}$ is the residual of formula (1), and n represents the number of trading weeks for the stock.

$$R_{i,t} = \alpha_i + \beta_1 R_{m,t-2} + \beta_2 R_{m,t-1} + \beta_3 R_{m,t} + \beta_4 R_{m,t+1} + \beta_5 R_{m,t+2} + \varepsilon_{i,t} \tag{1}$$

$$W_{i,t} = \ln\left(1 + \varepsilon_{i,t}\right) \tag{2}$$

$$NCSKEW_{i,t} = -\frac{\left[n(n-1)^{3/2} \sum W_{i,t}^3\right]}{\left[(n-1)(n-2)\left(\Sigma W_{i,t}^2\right)^{3/2}\right]} \tag{3}$$

4.2.2 Independent Variable: Clarification Announcements

The CSMAR database includes a section for company announcements, clarifying IPOs, significant events, and risk warnings. Official announcements are more influential on stock prices due to their persuasiveness and information content compared to social media posts. By reading each clarification announcement, we collected those confirming the rumors as false and excluded those repeatedly clarified or supplemented the same false stock market rumor. The independent variable is whether listed companies have issued clarifications for false stock market rumors each year.

4.2.3 Mediator Variable: Degree of Information Asymmetry

Research report attention is used as a measure of information asymmetry, representing the annual count of reports analyzing a company. Analysts, with their expertise, gather and process information to understand companies' operations, enriching stock price information and market efficiency. These reports help investors access company information, easing information processing and reducing asymmetry. Companies with more report attention have better disclosure, leading to less information asymmetry.

4.2.4 Control Variables

According to the literature, the following variables are selected as control variables: total assets (Size), company age (Age), leverage (Lev), return on assets (ROA), return on equity (ROE), book-to-market ratio (BM), audit quality (BIG4), revenue growth rate (Growth), and the concentration of equity (TOP1). For specific variable details, please refer to Table 1.

Table 1. Variable Symbols and Definitions

Variable Code	Variable Name	Variable Description
NCKSEW	Stock price crash risk	Negative skewness coefficient
Clarification	Clarification announcements	Whether listed companies issued clarification announcements regarding false stock market rumors
Report attention	Attention from research reports	Proxy variable for the degree of information asymmetry
Size	Total assets of the company	Natural logarithm of total assets
ROA	Return on assets	Net profit/Total assets
BM	Book-to-market ratio	Shareholders' equity / market value of the company
Lev	Debt-to-asset ratio	Total liabilities/Total assets
Growth	Company growth	Growth rate of operating income
Age	Company age	Natural logarithm of company age + 1
BIG4	Audit quality	Whether audited by one of the big four accounting firms
ROE	Return on equity	Net profit/shareholders' equity
TOP1	Degree of shareholding concentration	Proportion of shares held by the largest shareholder

4.3 Research Model

4.3.1 Main Effect Model

To investigate whether companies' clarification announcements regarding false stock market rumors can reduce the risk of stock price crash, a two-way fixed effects regression model by industry and year is constructed to test Hypothesis 1 (H1), as shown in Equation (4). In this model, the dependent variable is the stock price crash risk, denoted as $NCSKEW_{i,\,t}$.The independent variable, $Clarification_{i,\,t}$ indicates whether the public company i has issued a clarification announcement regarding false stock market rumors in year t. $Control_{i,\,t}$ represents the control variables, $year_{i,\,t}$ and $industry_{i,\,t}$ are dummy variables for year and industry. If β_1 is significantly negative, it suggests that listed companies' clarification announcements regarding false stock market rumors can significantly reduce the risk of stock price crash, thus supporting Hypothesis 1.

$$NCSKEW_{i,t} = \beta_0 + \beta_1 Clarification_{i,t} + \sum \beta_n Control_{i,t} + year_{i,t} + industry_{i,t} + \varepsilon_{i,t} \tag{4}$$

4.3.2 Mediation Effect Model

Using the three-step method to test mediation effects of information asymmetry. The testing steps are as follows: In Model (5), if β_1 is significantly positive, it indicates that listed companies' issuance of clarification announcements regarding false stock market rumors can increase the attention from research reports, thereby reducing the degree of information asymmetry. In Model (6), if β_1 is significantly negative, it suggests that the higher the report attention, the lower the degree of information asymmetry, and consequently, the lower the risk of stock price crash. In Model (7), if both β_1 and β_2 are significantly negative, it demonstrates that the clarification of rumors can suppress the risk of stock price crash by reducing the degree of information asymmetry.

$$Report\ Attention_{i,t} = \beta_0 + \beta_1 Clarification_{i,t} + \sum \beta_n\ Control_{i,t} + year_{i,t} + industry_{i,t} + \varepsilon_{i,t} \tag{5}$$

$$NCSKEW_{i,t} = \beta_0 + \beta_1 ReportAttention + \sum \beta_n Control_{i,t} + year_{i,t} + industry_{i,t} + \varepsilon_{i,t} \tag{6}$$

$$NCSKEW_{i,t} = \beta_0 + \beta_1 Clarification_{i,t} + \beta_2 ReportAttention_{i,t} + \sum \beta_n Control_{i,t} + year_{i,t} + industry_{i,t} + \varepsilon_{i,t} \tag{7}$$

5 Empirical Results and Analysis

5.1 Benchmark Regression Results

The regression results from Table 2 indicate that the coefficient between Clarification and NCSKEW is −0.074, which is significantly negative at the 1% level. This suggests that listed companies' release of clarification announcements regarding stock rumors can significantly reduce the risk of stock price crash, thus Hypothesis 1 (H1) is supported.

Table 2. Benchmark regression results

VARIABLES	NCSKEW
Clarification	−0.074***
	(−2.80)
Constant	−3.171***
	(−24.06)
Observations	26,915
R-squared	0.094
Controls	YES
Industry FE	YES
Year FE	YES

The symbols ***, **, * respectively indicate significance at the 1%, 5%, and 10% levels, with the values in parentheses representing the t-values.

5.2 Robustness Test

5.2.1 Propensity Score Matching (PSM)

This paper employs the Propensity Score Matching (PSM) method to address potential endogeneity issues. There are differences in the operational conditions between companies that clarify false stock market rumors and those that do not. These differences might be the cause of the variation in stock price crash risk. Therefore, a 1:1 nearest neighbor matching method was applied to pair each listed company that issued a clarification with a control company that did not issue a clarification but was highly similar in terms of company characteristics. After passing the PSM balance test, a benchmark regression was conducted again. Table 3 reports the results of the benchmark regression after PSM. There were 2628 samples in the matched group. The regression coefficient between Clarification and NCSKEW was −0.083, which is significantly negative at the 5% level. This indicates that listed companies' clarification of false stock market rumors can effectively reduce the risk of stock price crash, further validating Hypothesis 1 (H1) and demonstrating the robustness of the conclusions drawn in this paper.

5.2.2 Replace the Dependent Variable

Using the fluctuation ratio of returns DUVOL to represent the risk of stock price crash. The higher the DUVOL, the greater the risk of a stock price crash. The calculation formula for DUVOL is shown in Equation (8), where n_{up} represents the number of weeks that stock i 's daily idiosyncratic return $W_{i,\,t}$ exceeds the annual average return.

$$DUVOL_{i,t} = \ln\left(\frac{(n_{up}-1)\,\Sigma_{down} W_{i,t}^{2}}{(n_{down}-1)\,\Sigma_{up} W_{i,t}^{2}}\right)\#(8) \tag{8}$$

Table 4 presents the results of the benchmark regression after replacing the dependent variable. It is evident that the regression coefficient between Clarification and the stock

Table 3. Benchmark regression after PSM

VARIABLES	NCSKEW
Clarification	−0.083**
	(−2.13)
Constant	−2.984***
	(−7.20)
Observations	2628
R-squared	0.117
Controls	YES
Industry FE	YES
Year FE	YES

price crash risk DUVOL is −0.047, which is significantly negative at the 5% level. This suggests that listed companies' clarification of false stock market rumors can effectively reduce the risk of stock price crashes, Hypothesis 1 (H1) is still supported.

Table 4. Benchmark regression after replacing the dependent variable

VARIABLES	DUVOL
Clarification	−0.047**
	(−2.03)
Constant	−1.131***
	(−9.66)
Observations	26,915
R-squared	0.082
Controls	YES
Industry FE	YES
Year FE	YES

5.3 Mediation Effect Analysis

The results of the mediation effect test on the degree of information asymmetry are shown in Table 5. From columns (2) and (4), it is evident that the clarifications issued by public companies have a significant effect in reducing the risk of stock price crashes. In column (1), the regression coefficient between Clarification and Report Attention is 1.316, which is significantly positive at the 5% level, indicating that the clarification of rumors by listed companies can effectively increase the report attention and reduce the degree of information asymmetry. In column (3), when both the mediating variable and the independent variable are included in the model, the regression coefficient between Report Attention and NCSKEW is −0.002, which is significantly negative at the 1% level, and the regression coefficient between Clarification and NCSKEW is −0.065, which is significantly negative at the 5% level. This suggests that the clarification of false stock market rumors by listed companies mitigates the risk of stock price crashes by reducing the degree of information asymmetry. Column (5) presents the mediation effect test with the dependent variable replaced by DUVOL, leading to the same conclusion that the degree of information asymmetry plays a partial mediating role, supporting Hypothesis 2 (H2).

Table 5. Results of the Mediation Effect Test

VARIABLES	(1)	(2)	(3)	(4)	(5)
	Report Attention	NCSKEW	NCSKEW	DUVOL	DUVOL
Clarification	1.316**	−0.074***	−0.065**	−0.047**	−0.041*
	(2.50)	(−2.80)	(−2.50)	(−2.03)	(−1.74)
Report attention			−0.002***		−0.002***
			(−5.07)		(−6.32)
Constant	−137.941***	−3.171***	−3.868***	−1.131***	−1.865***
	(−57.09)	(−24.06)	(−30.39)	(−9.66)	(−16.50)
Observations	26,915	26,915	26,915	26,915	26,915
R-squared	0.318	0.094	0.101	0.082	0.088
Controls	YES	YES	YES	YES	YES
Industry FE	YES	YES	YES	YES	YES
Year FE	YES	YES	YES	YES	YES

5.4 Heterogeneity Analysis

This paper will further investigate whether there is a significant difference in the effect of rumor clarification on the suppression of stock price crash risk among listed companies with different levels of digital transformation. The digital transformation of listed companies involves the use of modern technologies such as artificial intelligence, blockchain, cloud computing, and big data to deeply optimize and upgrade the company's technical architecture and production processes [10]. Companies with a high level of digital transformation can improve corporate decision-making efficiency and enhance their social responsibility performance through efficient digital operations [11], establishing reputational capital among investors. When facing false rumors circulating in the stock market, they can issue effective clarification announcements in a timely manner. Compared to companies with a lower level of digital transformation, they are more significantly effective in suppressing the risk of stock price crashes.

In this study, the extent of digital transformation will be assessed by the frequency of occurrence of digital-related terms in the annual reports of listed companies. The companies will be categorized into two groups: high digital transformation and low digital transformation, based on whether their level of digital transformation exceeds the median. From columns (1) and (2) of Table 6, it is observed that in listed companies with a high level of digital transformation, the regression coefficient between Clarification and NCSKEW is significantly negative at the 1% level. In the sample of companies with a low level of digital transformation, the regression coefficient between Clarification and NCSKEW is negative but not significant. When the dependent variable is replaced with DUVOL in columns (3) and (4), the same results are obtained. Therefore, the conclusion is drawn that the effect of issuing clarification announcements regarding false stock market rumors is more pronounced in listed companies with a higher degree of digital transformation in terms of mitigating the risk of stock price crashes.

Table 6. Heterogeneity Analysis

	(1)	(2)	(3)	(4)
	Higher	Lower	Higher	Lower
VARIABLES	NCSKEW	NCSKEW	DUVOL	DUVOL
Clarification	−0.116***	−0.029	−0.076**	−0.017
	(−2.95)	(−0.82)	(−2.17)	(−0.55)
Constant	−3.714***	−3.313***	−1.824***	−1.311***
	(−19.77)	(−16.59)	(−10.89)	(−7.42)
Observations	13,316	13,599	13,316	13,599
R-squared	0.110	0.099	0.094	0.090
Controls	YES	YES	YES	YES
Industry FE	YES	YES	YES	YES
Year FE	YES	YES	YES	YES

6 Conclusion

This study analyzes A-share companies listed on the Shanghai and Shenzhen main boards from 2013 to 2023. It uses a two-way fixed effects model and mediation analysis to assess the impact of companies' clarification announcements on false stock rumors and stock price crash risk. Key findings include: (1) Such announcements can effectively suppress the risk of stock price crashes, the result that holds true after conducting several different robustness checks; (2) Mechanism analysis reveals that such effect can be alleviated by the degree of information asymmetry; (3) Heterogeneity analysis finds that the inhibitory effect is more significant in more digitally transformed companies.

Based on the research findings, the following policy recommendations are proposed: First, listed companies should promptly issue corresponding clarification announcements when faced with false rumors circulating in the stock market, detailing the inaccuracies to suppress the risk of stock price crashes and promote the stable growth of the stock market. Second, information asymmetry is a significant cause affecting the risk of stock price crashes, and clarification announcements are just one way to mitigate this asymmetry. Therefore, listed companies should actively address information asymmetry issues both internally and externally, strengthen the proactive disclosure of business information, and ensure that stock prices truly reflect their fundamental value, thereby reducing the risk of stock price crashes. Third, digital transformation profoundly impacts society and the economy, so listed companies should deepen their digital transformation strategies, enhance management efficiency through digital operations, and strengthen their reputational capital. This way, when the company faces false rumors, clarification announcements can more effectively counteract the risk of stock price crashes.

References

1. Kim, J.B., Li, Y., Zhang, L.: Cfos versus ceos: equity incentives and crashes. J. Fin. Econ. **101**(3), 713–730 (2011)
2. Kim, J.B., Zhang, L.: Accounting conservatism and stock price crash risk: firm-level evidence. Contemp. Account. Res. **33**(1), 412–441 (2016)
3. Tian, L.H., Wang, K.D.: The "camouflaging effect" of corporate social responsibility disclosure and the crash risk of listed companies: a DID-PSM analysis from the Chinese stock market. J. Manage. World. **11**, 146–157 (2017). https://doi.org/10.19744/j.cnki.11-1235/f.2017.11.011. in Chinese
4. Zhao, J.M., He, X., Wu, F.Y.: Rumor research in the Chinese stock market: the spread and refutation of rumors and their impact on stock prices. J. Manage. World. **11**, 38–51 (2010). https://doi.org/10.19744/j.cnki.11-1235/f.2010.11.005. in Chinese
5. Liu, C.L., Zhang, N.: Study on the effectiveness of public company's rumor denial announcements: evidence from Chinese stock market. J. Manage. Sci. China. **15**(5), 42–54 (2012) in Chinese
6. Spence, M.A.: Market Signalling: The Informational Structure of Job Markets and Related Phenomena. (1974)
7. He, F., Feng, Y., Hao, J.: Information disclosure source, investors' searching and stock price crash risk. Econ. Lett. **210**, 110202 (2022)
8. Chen, J., Hong, H., Stein, J.C.: Forecasting crashes: trading volume, past returns and conditional skewness in stock prices. J. Financ. Econ. **61**(3), 345–381 (2001)
9. Meng, Q.B., Li, X.Y., Wang, H.C.: The impact of corporate rumors, clarification announcements, and informed trading: evidence from China's short-selling market. J. Manage. Sci. China. **23**(6), 90–109 (2020) in Chinese
10. Qi, Y.D., Xiao, X.: Corporate rumors, clarification announcements, and informed trading: evidence from China's short-selling market. Journal of. Manage. World. **6**, 135–152+250 (2020). https://doi.org/10.19744/j.cnki.11-1235/f.2020.0091. in Chinese
11. Luo, J.-H., Wu, Y.-L.: Digital operation level and real earnings management. J. Manage. Sci. **34**(4), 3–18 (2021). https://doi.org/10.3969/j.issn.1672-0334.2021.04.001. in Chinese in Chinese
12. Luo, J.-H., Du, X.-Q.: Media coverage, institutional environment, and stock price crash risk. Account. Res. **9**, 53–59+97 (2014) in Chinese
13. Baker, M., Wurgler, J.: Investor sentiment in the stock market. J. Econ. Perspect. **21**(2), 129–151 (2007)
14. Chen, J., Tang, G., Yao, J., Zhou, G.: Investor attention and stock returns. J. Financ. Quant. Anal. **57**(2), 455–484 (2022)

User Search Assistance in Information Retrieval: Building a Classification System and Predicting User Needs

Yiming Zhao[1,2,3,4], Zhan Chen[2,3,5], Fan Zhang[2], Jiani Wu[6], Yanming Chen[7], Qiuqi Xie[7], and Shuaiju Yu[8](✉)

[1] Center for Studies of Information Resources, Wuhan University, 430072 Wuhan, China
[2] School of Information Management, Wuhan University, Wuhan 430072, China
[3] Big Data Institute, Wuhan University, Wuhan 430072, China
[4] Wuhan Institute of Data Intelligence, Wuhan 430072, China
[5] National Demonstration Center for Experimental Library and Information Science Education, Wuhan University, Wuhan 430072, China
[6] Wuhan Children's Library, Wuhan 430014, China
[7] Hubei Standardization and Quality Institute, Wuhan 430061, China
[8] Business School, University of Shanghai for Science and Technology, Shanghai 200093, China
shuaijuyu@163.com

Abstract. This study establishes a comprehensive classification system for user search assistance needs through extensive research on existing studies and in-depth interviews with search users. Subsequently, based on the proposed auxiliary demand classification, three machine learning algorithms and a deep learning algorithm are applied to construct a classification prediction model, which implements a classification prediction method from user search behavior characteristics to user search auxiliary demand. The experimental results show that the random forest model exhibits the best performance in the prediction problem, and its average prediction accuracy and AUC index for the six categories of search assistance auxiliary needs are close to 0.9.

Keywords: Information Retrieval · Intelligent Search Assistance · Auxiliary Needs Classification System · Ancillary Needs Classification Forecasts · Deep Learning

1 Introduction

With the rapid development of network big data and the continuous improvement and maturity of information retrieval technologies, information retrieval systems have become indispensable tools in daily life and academic research. However, users often encounter various difficulties when using information retrieval systems, such as information overload, mismatch between retrieval results and requirements, improper construction of query formulas, etc. [1]. These difficulties not only reduce users' information

Y. P. Tu and M. Chi (Eds.): WHICEB 2025, LNBIP 549, pp. 113–125, 2025.
https://doi.org/10.1007/978-3-031-94184-9_10

retrieval efficiency but also affect their retrieval experience. Therefore, how to identify the difficulties encountered by users in the information retrieval process and provide reasonable intelligent assistance to improve the efficiency and experience of users' information retrieval has become an important topic that urgently needs to be solved in the field of information retrieval in recent years.

To achieve accurate intelligent assistance for information retrieval, two parts of functions need to be realized: first, it is necessary to identify the search state of the user during the search process and their search assistance needs, and then provide targeted recommendations and auxiliary content according to different search assistance needs.

Although current research has provided certain explanations for the classification of search states from different perspectives such as difficulties [2], intentions [3], and cognition [4], there is still no complete and authoritative classification system for users' search assistance needs. The current research on the classification and prediction of search states generally has poor performance and has not yet formed a prediction model solution with high accuracy.

Based on this, this study proposed the following research questions.

- How to construct a classification system for search assistance needs?
- How to predict search assistance needs based on user behavior features?

2 User Search Assistance Needs Classification Framework

2.1 Literature Research

Existing research maps users' search assistance needs from other dimensions like search difficulty and satisfaction to guide search assistance strategies [2, 5, 6]. However, this mapping is unclear and non-intuitive. For instance, in the search difficulty dimension, the difficulty classification framework can't match search difficulty with assistive needs one- to- one, with many complex situations. Also, the clustering analysis boundary of search difficulty is vague, and the prediction model is only moderately effective, leading to inaccurate judgment of search assistance needs. Therefore, this study proposes a new approach: treating search assistance needs as special search state dimensions for direct classification and prediction, thus eliminating complex mapping conversions and improving judgment accuracy.

Regarding search auxiliary requirements classification, existing studies focus on single search state dimensions, so the coverage of auxiliary requirements is insufficient. But they have high consistency in defining and describing the same type of auxiliary requirements. Through literature research, types of auxiliary requirements such as query-based recommendation, search result processing, and search opinions and guidance have been initially summarized.

2.2 User Interviews

Based on literature research, semi-structured in-depth interviews are used to supplement the classification of auxiliary needs and verify its rationality. This method, common in qualitative research, uses open-ended guiding questions and flexible ways of asking. It can effectively capture key details during interviews, leading to a more in-depth understanding.

(1) The Interview Outline

Combined with the results of the previous literature research, a preliminary outline of the interview was determined, and a formal interview outline was obtained after the initial trial interviews were conducted and amended, as shown in Table 1.

Table 1. Outline of user interviews

Interview topics	Interview questions
Basic information about the interviewee	Gender, age, education and occupation of the respondents
	Interview notes, recording notes, information privacy notes
Main issues	What information retrieval system do you normally use the most, how often do you use it, and what kind of information do you mainly use to retrieve (academic needs/life needs)? How do you feel about your information retrieval skills?
	Have you encountered any difficulties or obstacles in using information retrieval systems? Difficulties or obstacles here also include problems with the user experience and search efficiency
	How do you typically address these search difficulties or obstacles you encounter?
	Have you tried using such big language models like ChatGPT for information retrieval, and can it solve these search difficulties or barriers you just mentioned?
	For the search difficulties and obstacles you encountered, what kind of intelligent assistive functions would you like the information retrieval system to provide you to improve the efficiency and experience of searching?
	Do you have anything to add about the difficulties in information retrieval engineering and the need for intelligent assistive functions?

(2) The Interview Process

A total of 20 interviewees were selected for the interview study, following the principle of theoretical sampling, taking into account convenience and comprehensiveness, and covering different ages, different fields, and different levels of information literacy, so as to ensure the maximization of the coverage of concepts and categories.

In terms of the interview method, offline face-to-face conversations or online voice calls were used according to the actual situation of the interviewees, and all the interviews were audio-recorded. At the end of the interviews, information is extracted from the interview records and coded to be converted into user search-assisted demand classification.

2.3 User Search Assistance Needs Classification

(1) Open Coding

The results of the relevant literature and user interviews were open coded to extract as comprehensively as possible the concepts related to the user's search assistance needs involved in them, and for the same concepts, they were coded only once. The results of open coding are shown in Table 2.

(2) Spindle Coding

The purpose of axial coding is to explore the hierarchical relationships among the concept of assistance needs derived from open coding, conduct clustering and integration, define the boundaries of similar concepts and make appropriate mergers. Meanwhile, it filters out assistance needs that have no practical research value in the study of intelligent search assistance systems, such as the inability to retrieve foreign web page results and paid resources.

The axial coding process is guided by three experts to ensure that the final classification framework of assistance needs is complete and independent. It can not only cover all relevant concepts in open coding, but also ensure that there is no overlapping of concepts among different categories. From the results of open coding, it can be seen that users' search assistance needs mainly occur in three stages of multi-round queries.

Specifically, the spindle coding culminates in the user search-assisted requirements categorization framework and its conceptual descriptions as shown in Table 3.

3 Simulation Experiments

3.1 Information Retrieval User Experiment System Development

In order to collect users' search data more completely on the basis of not destroying users' original search experience, the development of the experimental system adopts the form of Chrome browser plug-in, realizes the data collection script for the most commonly used search engine in China, Baidu (https://www.baidu.com/), and listens to the user's query input data, search result data, user behavior data and user feedback data in the page. The user behavior data includes user input, mouse clicks, page scrolling, browsing, etc., and the user feedback data includes the user's auxiliary demand feedback needed for this study. The opening portal of data listening is Baidu search page, the detail page opened from the search page and the deeper page opened from the detail page will be associated with this search to ensure that the user's complete search path can be captured, and the complete search data will be saved and exported to the user's browser locally in the Json format after the search session is over.

Table 2. Open coding of user search assistance needs

ID	Auxiliary requirements primitive statements	Core concept
1	I don't know how to describe my information needs, I don't know what to look up, and I need some query-based recommendations	Inability to describe information needs, query-based recommendations
2	The search result I get is not what I want, I feel that the query style I constructed is inaccurate, I hope the system can help me to modify the query style	Query-based inaccuracies, query-based modifications
3	But I feel like it's incomplete, but then again I don't know what other relevant information is out there, and I need some query-based recommendations on related topics	Related topic recommendation
4	There are so many search results, I don't know which ones are useful, I would like help filtering some useful results	Information overload, search result filtering
5	My question is simple, but there are too many search results, the content is too long, I have to read through it to find the answer, can you output the answer I want directly without other irrelevant content	Information overload, summary of answers
6	I need authoritative and official information, but I feel that many of the results are reprinted, even with advertisements, and I can't tell if they are authoritative and true and reliable.	Search result quality judgment, search result filtering
7	I just need to understand a certain concept, but some of the search results are too long and too complicated, some of the technical implementation, mathematical principles and what not I don't really care, I hope it can give me an overview of the content, so that I can quickly understand on the line	Resulting content is too long and content is summarized and generalized
8	I'm completely unfamiliar with the field and I don't even know how to go about searching for this problem. I may need someone to guide me step by step on how to proceed, like what to search for first and then what to search for, like a class to give me a learning path	Lack of subject knowledge, search guidance, search path recommendations

(*continued*)

Table 2. (*continued*)

ID	Auxiliary requirements primitive statements	Core concept
9	This is a new field for me, and I don't understand a lot of the concepts, so I'm struggling to read some of the articles and need to keep looking up some of the concepts. It would be nice if the search engine could just give me some layman's explanations or additions to the concepts, or actually I'm reading in the wrong order, I should search for some basic questions or read some basic articles first, but I can't realize that on my own	Lack of subject knowledge, additional knowledge, search opinions, search path recommendations
10	I feel like the data I want can't be answered in a search engine, and I may have to go to some data platforms, but I don't know where such data platforms are, and search engines can't search for them	Search opinions, search strategies, search platform recommendations
11	When I look up some questions, it's hard to find the original question, sometimes I can find some similar questions, but it's always a pain in the ass to understand the similar questions once before solving my own. I want to get the answer I want directly, so I sometimes ask ChatGPT directly now.	Integrated information processing questions, ChatGPT answer generation
12	There are some search results that you have to pay or log in to see when you click on them, and it annoys me to see this, can you filter these results out, or is there any way to see the answers without these steps	Paid access to resources

3.2 User Experimentation and Data Acquisition

Based on the information retrieval user experiment system developed above, user experiments were conducted. In terms of the design of experimental tasks, this study designed three search experimental tasks of receptive, evaluative, and creative [1], as shown in Table 4, based on the theory of search learning patterns, which are all of a certain level of complexity so that the search sessions in the experimental data can generally contain multiple consecutive complex or simple queries. The study recruited 30 experimenters of different ages, domains, and levels of information literacy, and asked them to install the experimental system extensions in the Google Chrome browser on their personal computers and complete the search tasks. All experimental data were counted at the end of the experiment, yielding a total of 90 search session data, 480 query records, and 751 search result page data.

Table 3. Framework for classifying user search assistance needs

Principal dimension	ID	Sub-dimension	Supporting needs descriptions and manifestations of difficulties
Query -based recommendations	1	Query -based refactoring recommendations	Inability to accurately describe the information need, inaccurate query style construction resulting in not getting the desired search results. Lack of subject matter knowledge and lack of clarity on what exactly to look for
	2	Related topic recommendations	Have completed the current query and would like to know some relevant information, but it is not clear what is relevant. Lacks subject matter knowledge and is not clear on what exactly to look for
Search result processing	3	Search result filtering recommendation	Not knowing which of the search results are reliable, useful and authoritative. Search results contain a lot of bad or useless information. It takes more time to sift through the useful information
	4	Summary of the content of the search results	For factual questions, want direct answers without having to read the entire page to find the answer or summarize the generalization. Unsure of the usefulness of a search result, need to read the whole text to be sure, but this is too time consuming. Information overload, feeling that you are getting too many search results and need a short general summary
Search strategy assistance	5	Search path recommendation	Lack of subject matter knowledge, do not know how to complete complex search tasks, need some expert search advice or guidance to complete the search. The search task is too large, covering multiple sub-tasks, and it is difficult to get all the information you want through a generalized query style, and you want to get a split search path to guide you to complete the sub-tasks step by step to get better retrieval results
	6	Answer generation, search opinion generation	Direct valid answers are not found in the search results, and the information may need to be synthesized before it can be used. (for example, the answer to a similar question is found, but there is no direct answer to the original question). For some incomprehensible knowledge in specialized fields, it is hoped that some popular explanations or supplementary content can be obtained to assist understanding. For some open-ended exploratory tasks, some synthesized and comprehensive views or opinions are desired

(continued)

Table 3. (*continued*)

Principal dimension	ID	Sub-dimension	Supporting needs descriptions and manifestations of difficulties
No assistance required	0	–	–

Table 4. User experiment task design

Type of task	Description of the task
Receptive	In this task, you need to acquire knowledge about the weather phenomenon of tornadoes, including their formation, characteristics, classification, and potential impact on human activities
Evaluative	In this task, you need to learn about the life of Sun Tzu and his book, the art of war, and give your opinion of Sun Tzu as a historical figure
Creative	In this task, you need to acquire knowledge about the symptoms, causes, prevention and treatment of altitude sickness, and develop a plan to deal with altitude sickness for people who are traveling or climbing high mountains

3.3 Model Feature Selection and Data Preprocessing

In terms of model feature selection, we mainly refer to the feature system of user search state classification prediction model in existing research [4], covering query-style features and user search result page behavioral features. Considering the different search assistance needs caused by user differences [7], temporal features (the relationship between the current query feature value and the average feature value of other queries in the current session) and user features (the relationship between the current query feature value and the average feature value of the user's historical query) are added to the feature set. In addition, based on the search assistance strategies obtained from existing research and user interviews, relevant variables such as retrieval task complexity and query type (factual/exploratory) are added to the feature set. The final complete feature set contains 196 features. After filtering temporal features and user features with repetitive meanings, the query-based includes query_session_index, query_length, que-ry_terms, query_terms_add, query_terms_delete, last_query_terms_sim, query_time, query_input_time, query_input_speed, query_complexity, query_type, query_relation, user_session_query_num_avg, user_session_query_num_avg_ratio. The retrieval res-ult page includes SERP_index, SERP_page_index, query_SERP_num, SERP_time, S-ERP_active_time. The user behavior includes query_open_link_num, query_open_lin-k_rank_avg, query_open_link_rank_max, SERP_open_link_num, SERP_open_deep_link_num, SERP_open_link_dwell_avg, SERP_open_link_dwell_total, SERP_mous-e_move_num, SERP_mouse_move_time, SERP_mouse_move_proportion, SERP_m-ouse_scroll_num, SERP_mouse_scroll_dist.

The experimental system generates user search data in JSON format, which needs to be converted to CSV for use in machine learning models. To predict user search assistance needs in real-time, the data is sliced into 20-second intervals, with feature values calculated based on a feature system. The search feedback time is filtered to restore the search state. Some features, like query type, were manually labeled by evaluators. A total of 2702 data points were obtained, and the distribution of assistance needs is shown in Fig. 1.

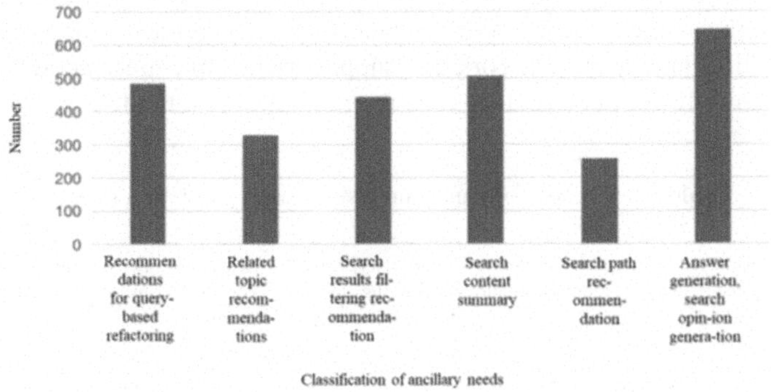

Fig. 1. Statistical distribution of ancillary needs classification

3.4 Classification Forecasting Model Construction

In this study, three machine learning algorithms (Decision Tree, Random Forest, and Support Vector Machine) and one neural network algorithm (Fully Connected Feedforward Neural Network) are used to construct a classification prediction model for search assistance needs.

In terms of model construction, since the target variables are six types of user search assistance needs and the machine learning classification model cannot output multiple results at the same time, the six types of needs are uniquely coded into six binary variables, and binary classification models are constructed separately. The deep learning model realizes simultaneous multi-label prediction by adjusting the last layer of the neural network to output a 6-dimensional vector with sigmoid activation function.

For model optimization, the machine learning model uses grid search to adjust parameters, such as the maximum depth and the minimum number of samples of leaf nodes for random forests and decision trees, and the C and kernel parameters for support vector machines [8–10]. Deep learning models, on the other hand, optimize the parameters by adjusting the network structure, learning rate, batch size, number of iterations, and optimize the parameters with the Adam optimizer.

For model evaluation, considering the imbalance in the number of positive and negative labels in the dataset, in addition to the accuracy rate, the AUC metric is used, which is not affected by category imbalance and is calculated based on the ROC curve. The dataset is processed by 50% cross validation to ensure the stability and reliability of the evaluation results.

The implementation and evaluation of the algorithmic model is based on Python, and the scikit-learn library is used to construct the machine learning model, and the pyTorch library is used to construct the deep learning neural network.

3.5 Model Performance Analysis

After parameter adjustment and optimization, each model achieves the best performance in the corresponding prediction task. The results of the quantitative evaluation with AUC and accuracy are shown in Tables 5 and 6, which show that among the four models, the Random Forest model has the best performance, with the AUC and accuracy indexes close to 0.9 in the average results of different auxiliary categories, which is a significant prediction ability. The neural network and support vector machine models are the next best, with slightly lower performance than the random forest model.

Table 5. AUC performance analysis of each prediction model

Predictive models	Recommendations for query-based refactoring	Related topic recommendations	Search results filtering recommendation	Search content summary	Search path recommendation	Answer generation, search opinion generation
Decision trees	0.699	0.749	0.835	0.813	0.922	0.651
Random forests	0.866	0.870	0.920	0.912	0.927	0.822
Support vector machines	0.835	0.844	0.799	0.879	0.922	0.797
Neural network	0.837	0.873	0.864	0.901	0.918	0.842

Table 6. Accuracy performance analysis of each prediction model

Predictive models	Recommendations for query-based refactoring	Related topic recommendations	Search results filtering recommendation	Search content summary	Search path recommendation	Answer generation, search opinion generation
Decision trees	0.790	0.731	0.834	0.847	0.801	0.715
Random forests	0.833	0.890	0.898	0.950	0.947	0.823
Support vector machines	0.801	0.875	0.836	0.902	0.910	0.828
Neural network	0.853	0.886	0.866	0.917	0.935	0.844

The random forest model is further analyzed by focusing on the top 25 features in terms of importance (see Table 7). Although there are differences in the importance ranking of features in different auxiliary category prediction models, user features ("user_" prefix, reflecting the relationship between user history and the current search session)

Table 7. Ranking of feature importance of random forest models on each prediction task (top 25)

ID	Recommendations for query-based refactoring	Related topic recommendations	Search results filtering recommendation	Search content summary	Search path recommendation	Answer generation, search opinion generation
1	last_query_terms_sim	user_query_SERP_num_avg	SERP_mouse_move_time	user_SERP_mouse_scroll_dist_avg	last_query_length_ratio	SERP_mouse_move_time
2	user_SERP_active_time_avg	last_query_terms_sim	query_SERP_mouse_move_num_avg	user_SERP_mouse_scroll_num_avg	last_query_terms_ratio	user_query_SERP_dwell_avg_avg
3	session_SERP_mouse_move_num_avg	user_query_SERP_num_ratio	SERP_mouse_move_num	SERP_mouse_move_num	last_query_time	user_SERP_active_time_avg
...	...	...	...	...	...	...
23	user_SERP_mouse_move_proportion_ratio	user_SERP_mouse_move_time_avg	session_query_input_time_ratio	session_SERP_time_avg	session_SERP_mouse_move_num_ratio	query_complexity
24	session_SERP_mouse_scroll_dist_avg	user_query_time_avg	session_query_input_time_avg	user_SERP_active_time_ratio	query_type	session_SERP_mouse_move_time_ratio
25	session_SERP_mouse_move_time_avg	user_query_SERP_dwell_avg_avg	query_complexity	user_SERP_open_link_dwell_total_ratio	last_query_terms	user_SERP_mouse_move_num_ratio

account for about 43%, accounting for a larger proportion in the ranking; followed by temporal features ("session_" prefix, reflecting the relationship between user history and the current query in the current session), accounting for about 20%. This shows that in auxiliary demand prediction, single query behavioral features can hardly fully reflect user auxiliary demand, and combining with historical behavioral data can better reflect its implied meaning.

In addition, the feature variables (retrieval task complexity, query style type, and query refactoring pattern) related to existing search assistance strategies in this study also have high importance in the prediction model. The query refactoring pattern feature is prominent in two types of assisted demand prediction tasks, query refactoring recommendation and related topic recommendation; retrieval task complexity and query style type have high importance in the remaining four types of assisted demand prediction tasks, which further confirms the effectiveness of the current research on search-assisted strategies.

4 Conclusion

This study aims to provide search users with intelligent search assistance to solve the various difficulties they encounter in the search process, so as to optimize their search efficiency and search experience. Through extensive research on existing studies and in-depth interviews with search users, this study constructs a comprehensive categorization system of users' search assistance needs, which provides a new and innovative perspective for the study of users' search status in information retrieval. On this basis, this study conducted extensive user experiments to collect real user search behavior data and feedback on search assistance needs. Using these experimental data, this study constructed four models, namely, decision tree, random forest, support vector machine and neural network, to realize a classification prediction method from user search behavior characteristics to user search assistance needs. After a comparative analysis of the model effects, it is found that the random forest model shows the best performance in the prediction problem. There are potential limitations in this study. Firstly, the study only includes 20 interviewees for qualitative research and 30 participants for data collection, which may not fully represent the search needs of diverse user groups, affecting the generalization ability of the model. In addition, the neural network model used in the study is a fully connected feedforward neural network. More advanced architectures such as Transformers or LSTM can be considered in future studies to potentially improve prediction performance.

Acknowledgements. This research was supported by the National Key Research and Development Program for Young Scientists of China (NO.2024YFB3310100), the National Natural Science Foundation of China (NO.72274146), the S&T Plan Projects of the State Administration for Market Regulation (NO.2023MK088) and the Fundamental Research Funds for the Central Universities.

References

1. Lee, H.J., Lee, J., Makara, K.A., et al.: Does higher education foster critical and creative learners? An exploration of two universities in South Korea and the USA[J]. Higher Educ. Res. Dev. **34**(1), 131–146 (2015)
2. Wang, B., Liu, J.: Extracting the implicit search states from explicit behavioral signals in complex search tasks[J]. Proc. Assoc. Inf. Sci. Technol. **58**(1), 854–856 (2021)
3. Liu, J., Sarkar, S., Shah, C.: Identifying and predicting the states of complex search tasks[C]. In: Proceedings of the 2020 Conference on Human Information Interaction and Retrieval, pp. 193–202 (2020)
4. Liu, J., Yu, R.: State-aware meta-evaluation of evaluation metrics in interactive information retrieval[C]. In: Proceedings of the 30th ACM International Conference on Information & Knowledge Management, pp. 3258–3262 (2021)
5. Kim, Y., Hassan, A., White, R.W., et al.: Modeling dwell time to predict click-level satisfaction[C]. In: Proceedings of the 7th ACM International Conference on Web Search and Data Mining, pp. 193–202 (2014)
6. Fukazawa, Y., Karapetsas, E., Zhu, D., et al.: Exploratory activity search[J]. Int. J. Knowl. Based Intell. Eng. Syst. **19**(1), 15–25 (2015)
7. Crescenzi, A., Capra, R., Arguello, J.: Time limits, information search and the use of search assistance[C]. In: Proceedings of the 2017 Conference on Conference Human Information Interaction and Retrieval, pp. 349–352 (2017)
8. Breiman, L.: Random forests[J]. Mach. Learn. **45**, 5–32 (2001)
9. Breiman, L.: Classification and Regression Trees[M]. Routledge (2017)
10. Vapnik, V.N., Chervonenkis, A.Y.: On the uniform convergence of relative frequencies of events to their probabilities[M]. In: Measures of Complexity: Festschrift for Alexey Chervonenkis. Springer International, Cham

Post-disaster Emergency Supplies Distribution Optimization: A Deep Reinforcement Learning Approach

Shimin Gao, Jian Wang(✉), Hui Li, and Xi Wang

School of Information, Central University of Finance and Economics, Beijing, China
wanderingful@126.com

Abstract. After the sudden disaster occurred, the damage to communication infrastructure and road capacity can lead to an explosive increase in demand for emergency supplies, and the demands for different types of emergency supplies can vary depending on the period. Due to the poor communication between the affected area and the external environment, the demand generation pattern will be unpredictable. To address this challenge, we propose a novel anticipatory routing, acceptance, and postponement policy for the Multi-period Dynamic Vehicle Routing Problem with Stochastic Requests (MDVRPSR). We first provide a detailed description of the unique features of MDVRPSR, followed by the formulation of a mathematical model using Markov Decision Process (MDP). Our model is designed to respond to stochastic requests within a multi-period dynamic framework, offering a comprehensive perspective on the decision state, reward setting, transition process, and objective function. Subsequently, we employ Deep Reinforcement Learning (DRL) to optimize the routing policy. Experiments demonstrate that the DRL-based policy improves the effectiveness of emergency supplies distribution in dynamic and uncertain scenarios.

Keywords: Emergency Supplies Distribution · Dynamic Vehicle Routing · Stochastic Requests · Deep Reinforcement Learning

1 Introduction

In recent years, natural disasters such as earthquakes, floods, and snowstorms have occurred with increasing frequency. These disasters not only pose a significant threat to human lives but also cause severe damage to social and economic development. For example, the 2008 Wenchuan earthquake in China, with a magnitude of 8.0, affected 46 million people and resulted in direct economic losses totaling 845 billion yuan [1]. Similarly, the 2024 Noto earthquake in Japan, with a magnitude of 7.5, led to more than 240 fatalities and 60,000 damaged buildings [2]. After disasters occur, post-disaster emergency supply distribution network must be rapidly deployed to avoid a massive humanitarian crisis. However, the poor communication conditions in disaster-stricken areas, coupled with damaged road networks, present numerous challenges to the distribution process [3]. Furthermore, the demand for various types of emergency supplies

Y. P. Tu and M. Chi (Eds.): WHICEB 2025, LNBIP 549, pp. 126–138, 2025.
https://doi.org/10.1007/978-3-031-94184-9_11

fluctuates during the rescue operation, which complicates the emergency distribution process [4].

According to the definition provided by Shen et al., the emergency supplies distribution problem can be modeled as a vehicle routing problem (VRP), where multiple vehicles depart from warehouses to serve a series of requests [5]. If the request information could be known in advance, this problem could be formulated as a Deterministic and Static Vehicle Routing Problem (DSVRP). But considering the challenging conditions in the disaster area, additional stochastic requests may arise while vehicles running, and the demand for different supplies may also change over time as the disaster evolves [4]. With these stochastic features, we consider the problem a Multi-period Dynamic Vehicle Routing Problem with Stochastic Request (MDVRPSR), which is closer to real-world scenarios but far more complex than DSVRP in terms of finding an optimal solution. Since Deep Reinforcement Learning (DRL) have been successfully applied to decision-making problems like autonomous driving [6], we apply DRL to the MDVRPSR to develop an optimal decision policy for efficient emergency supply delivery.

The contributions of our study are as follows: (1) We propose an evaluation model for the MDVRPSR, which incorporates: (i) multi-variety supplies with distinct characteristics in post-disaster rescue operations, (ii) the multi-period nature of emergency distribution and vehicle routing, and (iii) stochastic requests encountered during vehicle operations. (2) We apply DRL to find optimal policy and make comparison with rule-based benchmark policies. Through experimental evaluation, we demonstrate that the DRL-based policy generates efficient routing strategies, enabling vehicles to deliver a larger quantity of supplies in emergency distribution scenarios.

2 Problem Overview

In this section, we first provide a description of the problem we focus on. Then, we introduce the relevant studies and discuss their limitations. Finally, we outline our research questions.

2.1 Problem Description

The Multi-period Dynamic Vehicle Routing Problem with Stochastic Requests (MDVRPSR) considered in this paper involves the allocation and distribution of emergency supplies, accounting for stochastic requests over multiple periods and involving various types of goods. The problem entails distributing supplies and routing vehicles from multiple distribution warehouses to several affected areas with uncertain demand.

In the aftermath of a disaster, the demand for emergency supplies in the affected areas is highly variable. As shown in Fig. 1, supplies can be categorized into two types: Type A Supplies (One-time Demand) and Type B Supplies (Periodic Demand). A key modeling assumption is that any unfulfilled demand for Type A supplies is split and postponed to subsequent delivery periods [7]. In contrast, any unmet demand for Type B supplies does not carry over to the next period. Due to the different characteristics of the two types of supplies, vehicles must adopt distinct routing priorities when responding to stochastically generated requests over multiple periods. This increases the complexity of finding optimal routing solutions.

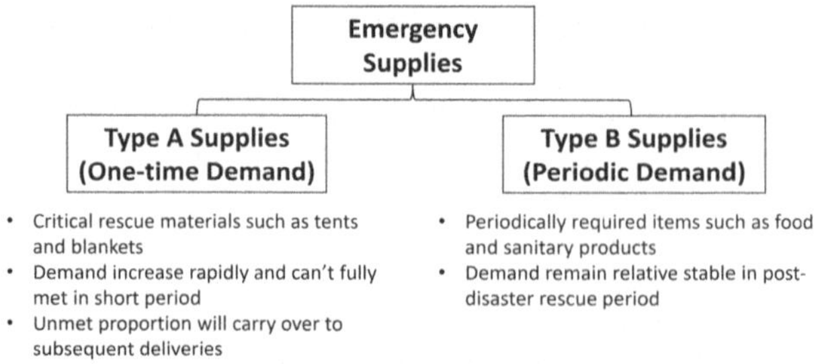

Fig. 1. Two types of supplies in MDVRPSR

2.2 Related Works

Both domestic and international researchers have extensively studied emergency logistics optimization. Early research on emergency logistics and supply distribution primarily focused on demand timeliness and road capacity, with an emphasis on optimizing travel time or other single-objective metrics. Wang et al. proposed a mixed-integer linear programming space-time network model to optimize Vehicle Routing for Emergency Material Distribution (VREMD), considering scenarios with time-varying supply and demand for emergency materials [8]. Fontem et al. explored the static open-routing distribution problem on a network composed of rescue warehouse nodes and material demand nodes, aiming to minimize distribution costs [3]. Wang et al. demonstrated that the time required to distribute relief materials after a disaster significantly impacts the survival rate of affected individuals. To address this, they developed an optimal routing model designed to minimize the combined travel time of all distribution vehicles [9]. Sabouhi et al. analyzed the scheduling and routing optimization of emergency vehicles under the scenario where shelters and vehicles have limited capacity [10].

Recently, numerous studies have focused on using Reinforcement Learning (RL) to solve dynamic vehicle routing problems. Ulmer et al. employed value function approximation to address the dynamic multi-period vehicle routing problem [11]. Chen et al. applied Deep Q-learning to the same-day delivery problem, utilizing both vehicles and drones [12]. Zhou et al. used reinforcement learning to improve policies generated from supervised learning, ultimately finding optimal solutions for vehicle routing problems with stochastic demand [13]. These studies demonstrate that using RL to solve dynamic vehicle routing problems is feasible, and applying Deep Reinforcement Learning (DRL) to solve the Multi-period Dynamic Vehicle Routing Problem with Stochastic Requests (MDVRPSR) remains a promising area for future research.

These studies primarily focus on the timeliness of distribution and associated costs during post-disaster relief operations. However, they overlook the multi-period effects and the multi-variety nature of supplies in large-scale disasters, which can significantly influence emergency supply distribution. Furthermore, while DRL has been applied to dynamic vehicle routing problems [13], its use in complex scenarios involving stochastic factors, multi-period planning, and multi-variety goods remains limited.

2.3 Research Questions

Based on the above limitations, we address our research questions as follows: (1) What is the impact of incorporating multi-period and multi-variety supplies on the efficiency of emergency distribution? (2) How can the supply distribution process be optimized using a DRL-based policy? In the following section, we will introduce our proposed evaluation model based on these research questions.

3 The Proposed Model

In this section, we first give a detailed statement of MDVRPSR and then use Markov Decision Process to formulate an evaluation model. We also provide an example figure to illustrate the decision point and the state transition procedure of the problem.

3.1 Problem Statement

We consider a finite number of periods $\Delta = \{\delta_1, \ldots, \delta_{\max}\}$. Each period contains a sequence of points of time $T = \{t_0, t_1, \ldots, t_{max}\}$ with time unit $t = t_n - t_{n-1}$. The emergency supplies are carried by a fleet of i homogeneous vehicles $V = \{v_1, \ldots, v_i\}$ from j warehouses $W = \{w_1, \ldots, w_j\}$ to a set of requests R. Each vehicle has a maximum load capacity Q_{max}, and each warehouse or request involves two types of supplies, $\gamma \in \{A, B\}$, as described earlier. All warehouses and requests are located on a synthetic grid network and the distance between them is given by Manhattan distance (Table 1).

On start time t_0 of every period, the vehicles departure from a warehouse and start delivering supplies to a set of early requests R_e known in advance. During and over the periods, new requests from the set of late requests R_l arrive stochastically over time. The overall set of requests is $R = R_e \cup R_l$, and each request $r \in R$ is defined by a vector $\left(l_r, \delta_r, t_r, q_r^{\gamma}\right)$ containing the location l_r, the request period $\delta_r \in \Delta$, the request arriving time $t_r \in T$, and the quantity of type γ supplies q_r^{γ}. Their arriving times and locations follow a temporal and spatial probability distribution [14, 15]. Notably, these late requests remain unknown before their arriving time. When a vehicle arrives at a warehouse or request point, it incurs a setup time t_s and an unloading time t_u.

The dispatcher needs to make decisions upon receiving new requests, selecting a subset of requests to accept for the current period and postponing the remaining requests to the next period. When a request is accepted for the current period, the dispatcher must assign an available vehicle to serve it and incorporate the request into the vehicle's route. After the decision is made, the vehicle proceeds to serve the next customer on the route, and the dispatcher observes any new incoming requests.

3.2 Markov Decision Process

In this section, we present the evaluation model based on Markov Decision Process (MDP), which describes the MDVRPSR as a sequence of states S_k connected by decisions x_k with reward $R(S_k, x_k)$ and transitions based on a stochastic procedure ω_k. In the following, we formally define the components of the MDP for the MDVRPSR and provide an illustrative example to facilitate understanding (Table 2).

Table 1. Notation of Problem Statement

Notation	Description
$\Delta = \{\delta_1, \ldots, \delta_{max}\}$	Problem periods
$T = \{t_0, t_1, \ldots, t_{max}\}$	Points of times with time unit $\bar{t}$
$V = \{v_1, \ldots, v_i\}$	Vehicles
$w = \{w_1, \ldots, w_j\}$	Warehouses
Q_{max}	Vehicle capacity
$\gamma \in \{A, B\}$	Types of supplies
$r = \left(l_r, \delta_r, t_r, q_r^{\gamma}\right)$	Vector of single request
l_r	Request location
q_r^{γ}	The demand of type γ supplies of request r
R_e	Early requests that are known in advance
R_l	Late requests that generated stochastically
$R = R_e \cup R_l$	Set of requests
t_s	Loading time at the warehouse
t_u	Unloading time at request locations
ϵ	Vehicles reload threshold

A route-based MDP is a generalization of an MDP and incorporates a routing plan in decision space and state space. That means that a route-based MDP models the development of routing-updates over the decision process. We draw on the route-based MDP because it aligns our routing heuristic to the MDP terminology. Figure 2 below illustrates an example of our route-based MDP procedure. The upper subfigures represent the evolution of disaster area in the current period δ_k, while the bottom plots show the same procedure of next period δ_{k+1}.

Decision Point and State. A decision point k occurs when new requests arrive and are pending for decisions, meanwhile the decision state S_k is given by the vector

$$S_k = \left(\delta_k, t_k, V_k, W_k, R_k^{\delta}, R_k^{\delta+1}, \theta_k, R_k^{new}\right) \tag{1}$$

A decision state S_k contains the current period δ_k, the point of time t_k, the status V_k of all vehicles $v_i \in V$, the status W_k of all warehouses $w_j \in W$, the set of customers R_k^{δ} to serve in current period, the set of customers $R_k^{\delta+1}$ that will be served in the following period, the vehicles' routing plans in the current period θ_k^{δ}, and the new arrived requests R_k^{new}. The vehicles' status includes their current locations and load of two types of supplies, while the warehouses' status contains their stocks. Each request $r \in R_k^{\delta} \cup R_k^{\delta+1} \cup R_k^{new}$ is defined by a vector $\left(l_r, \delta_r, t_r, q_r^{\gamma}\right)$, described in Sect. 3.1.

A routing plan θ_k consists of multiple vehicles' routing sequences $C_{(v_i,k)}$ covering all requests to be served in the current period. Each vehicle's sequence begins either at its current location or at a warehouse, based on whether the vehicle has already departed

Table 2. Notation of the Markov Decision Process

Notation	Description
k	Decision point No.
$\delta_k \in \Delta$	Period in decision point k
$t_k \in T$	Time in decision point k
S_k	Decision state in decision point k
S_k^x	Post-decision state following S_k and x_k
ω_k	Stochastic transition from S_k^x to S_{k+1}
$x_k \in \pi(S_k)$	Decision based on policy π
$R_k^\delta, R_k^{\delta+1}$	Set of requests to serve in decision point k of current and next period
R_k^{new}, R_k^{acc}	New requests and accepted requests at decision point k
θ_k^x	New routing plans for decision x_k in current period
θ_k	Routing plan in current period
$C_{(v_i,k)}$	Routing sequences of vehicle v_i in decision point k
$R(S_k, x_k, v_i)$	Reward of vehicle v_i from x_k in S_k
τ_γ	The penalty factors for delivery delay of type γ supplies
$q_{v_i}^\gamma$	The load of type γ supplies of vehicle v_i

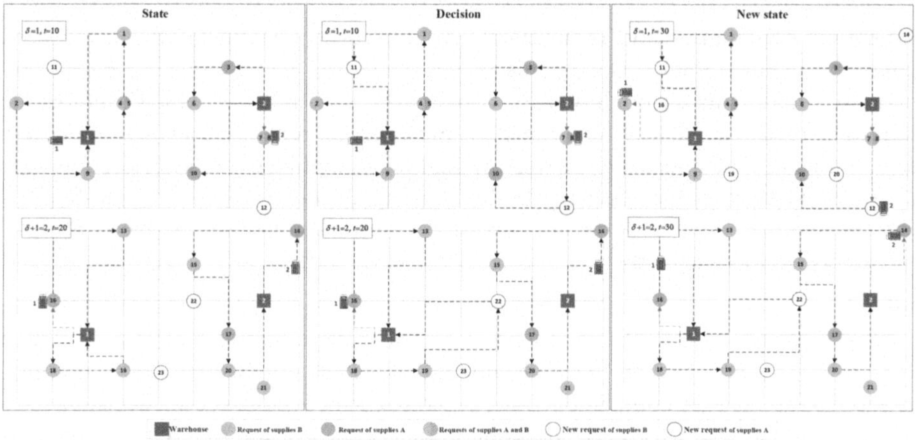

Fig. 2. An example illustration of MDP

from the warehouse. Vehicles serve a series of requests in one sequence and eventually return to a warehouse to reload supplies. A typical routing plan and its sequences is illustrated as follows:

$$\theta_k = \bigcup_{v_i} C_{(v_i,k)} = \bigcup_{v_i} (l_k, r_1, \ldots, r_n, w_1) + (w_1, r_{n+1}, \ldots, r_{n+m}, w_2) + \ldots \quad (2)$$

Decisions and Rewards. In every decision point k, decision x_k will be generated by agent based on state S_k. The decision contains the subset R_k^{acc} of R_k^{new} to accept in this period or postpone to the next period and the vehicles assigned for serving each request in R_k^{acc}. Furthermore, a decision will determine the update of route plans θ_k^x incorporating R_k^{acc}. The decision is feasible if the running time limitations of the vehicle exist and if the capacity limitations of the vehicle and warehouse still exist. The combination of a state S_k and a decision x_k leads to a known post-decision state:

$$S_k^x = \left(\delta_k, t_k, W_k, V_k, R_k^{\delta,x}, R_k^{\delta+1,x}, \theta_k^x, \varnothing\right) \tag{3}$$

where $R_k^{\delta,x} = R_k^{\delta} \cup R_k^{acc}$and $R_k^{\delta+1,x} = R_k^{\delta+1} \cup \left(R_k^{new} - R_k^{acc}\right)$. For example, in the upper subplots of Fig. 2, decision x_k involves accepting request 12 for vehicle 2 and request 11 for vehicle 1. Following this decision, the system transitions to a post-decision state, as illustrated in the middle subplot.

We define the reward $R(S_k, x_k)$ based on the return obtained when the vehicle completes the accepted requests R_k^{acc}. When a request is served by a vehicle, the immediate return is determined by both the quantity of supplies delivered and the ratio of the request's completion time, $t - t_r$, to the global average completion time $\overline{t_c}$. In addition, the two types of supplies are associated with distinct penalty factors τ_γ, which reflect their respective levels of urgency. Based on these settings, the reward is defined as follows:

$$R(S_k, x_k) = \sum_{r \in R_k^{acc}} \sum_{\gamma} \tau_\gamma \left(1 - \frac{t - t_r}{\overline{t_c}}\right) * \min\left(q_r^\gamma, q_{v_i}^\gamma\right) \tag{4}$$

Exogenous Information and Transitions. After the decision is made, vehicles proceed along their planned routes. During this process, new late requests may stochastically arrive. We model this uncertainty using a stochastic transition ω_k, which captures the realization of exogenous information (i.e., the random generation of new requests). The combination of post-decision state S_k^x and ω_k determines the next decision state S_{k+1}. As illustrated in the upper-right subplot in Fig. 2, after the post-decision state, the vehicles continue move until the next decision point, when new late requests $R_{k+1}^{new} = \{r_{14}, r_{16}, r_{19}, r_{20}\}$ generated.

Objective Function. The objective for our dynamic decision problems is to obtain an optimal decision policy $\pi^* \in \Pi$ leading to the highest cumulative rewards, which is equivalent to maximizing the total amount of supplies delivered while minimizing the overall request completion time. A policy π is a sequence of decision rules $\left(X_0^\pi, X_1^\pi, \ldots, X_k^\pi, \ldots\right)$ for every decision point. Each decision rule X_k^π specifies the decision $x \in X(S_k)$ to select when the process occupies decision state S_k. An optimal policy minimizes the sum of expected rewards as follows:

$$\pi^* = \arg\max_{\pi \in \Pi} \mathbb{E}\left[\sum_{k} \sum_{v_i \in V} R\left(S_k, X_k^\pi\right) | S_0\right] \tag{5}$$

4 Solution Approach

After establishing the evaluation model of MDVRPSR, we applied Deep Reinforcement Learning (DRL) to identify the optimal policy that generates efficient vehicle routing solutions.

4.1 DRL Policy

We utilize the Proximal Policy Optimization (PPO) algorithm to create the policy optimization framework. PPO is a model-free, on-policy reinforcement learning algorithm that improves the stability and reliability of policy updates. It strikes a balance between exploration and exploitation by limiting how much the policy can change at each step, leading to more consistent learning and better overall performance.

Setup. As shown in Fig. 3, we use multi-layer perceptron for both the actor and critic networks. The input layer receives a feature vector representing the environment's state, which is processed through two hidden layers, each comprising 256 neurons and employing ReLU activation. The actor network's output layer generates a probability distribution over possible actions (i.e., the policy), while the critic network estimates the value of current state. As described in Sect. 3.2, the output of the actor network is a two-dimensional probability vector. The first dimension encodes the decision of whether to accept or postpone a request, while the second dimension represents the vehicle dispatching decision using one-hot encoding.

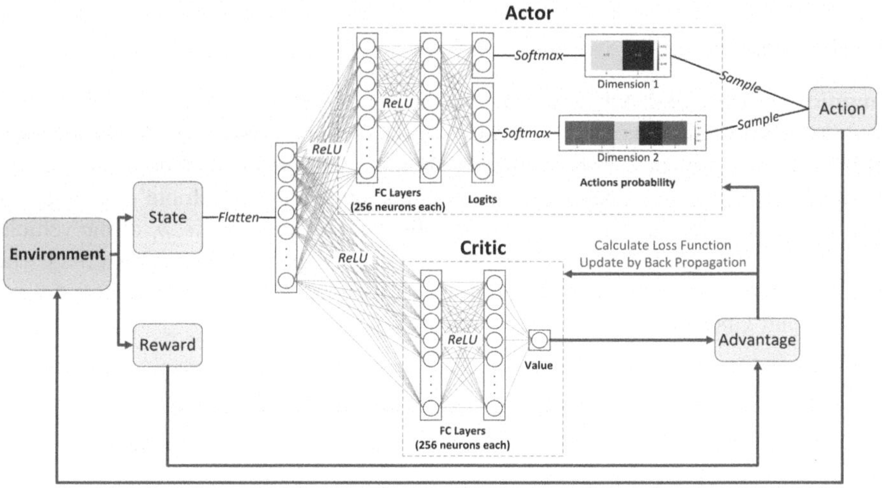

Fig. 3. DRL-based Policy Network Structure

Training. The training procedure of PPO alternates between interacting with the environment and updating the policy based on the collected experience. We set the algorithm's batch size to 64 and use 4 parallel threads for policy updates. The learning rate is set to

$\alpha = 0.5 \times 10^{-4}$ to ensure a stable training process. The discount factor, which controls the trade-off between future and immediate rewards, is set to 0.99.

4.2 Routing Heuristic

Once a decision is made by DRL policy at decision point k, the accepted request for this trip is added to the selected vehicle's delivery route. To strike a balance between travel cost and computational efficiency, we adopt the Cheapest Insertion Heuristic proposed by Ulmer et al. [11] to update the routes of individual vehicles. Figure 4 illustrates the detailed process of route updating based on this heuristic.

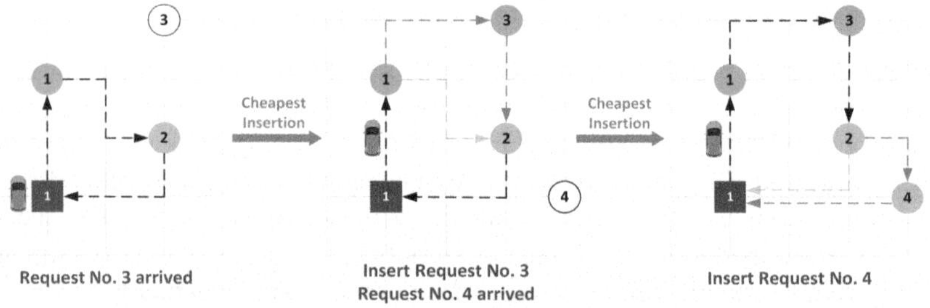

Fig. 4. Illustration of Cheapest Insertion Heuristic

4.3 Methodology

Dynamic Vehicle Load Adjustment. As the vehicle accepts and serves requests, it will dynamically adjust its loading strategy based on upcoming requests to maximize supply delivery efficiency. Each vehicle v_i holds a parameter p_i, which indicates the maximum loading percentage of Type A supplies relative to the vehicle's capacity. The remaining capacity is filled with Type B supplies, which occupy $1 - p_i$ of the vehicle's total capacity. The parameter p_i is updated at decision point k and takes effect when the vehicle arrives at warehouse W_m and starts reloading. The update formula for p_i at decision point k is given by:

$$p_i = \frac{\sum_{r \in \theta_k^{\delta,x}} q_r^A}{\sum_{r \in \theta_k^{\delta,x}} \sum_\gamma q_r^\gamma} \tag{6}$$

Where q_r^A is the quantity of Type A supplies for request r, and $\sum_\gamma q_r^\gamma$ is the total quantity of supplies for request r.

Reload Strategy. When a vehicle starts delivering supplies according to its set route, it follows a rule-based strategy to control when it should replenish its supply load. This strategy uses a threshold value ϵ, which defines the minimum supply level required before initiating replenishment. When the total load $\sum_\gamma q_k^{v_i\gamma}$ of vehicle v_i drops below this threshold, it will add the nearest optimal warehouse as its next destination. The selected warehouse will be the one closest to both the vehicle's current location and the next request on the route.

5 Experiment

In this section, we present the experiment for MDVRPSR. We begin by outlining the simulation settings and introducing the benchmark policies and evaluation metrics. Then, we present our preliminary results based on a series of one hundred independent runs. All experiments are conducted on a laptop equipped with Intel Core Ultra 9185H CPU (2.50 GHz), 32GB RAM and Windows 10 OS.

5.1 Simulation Settings

The simulation is conducted on a 20 × 15 grid, where each edge represents 20 min of vehicle travel time. The environment includes three warehouses and seven vehicles. We assume that each warehouse has sufficient supplies. Each vehicle has a maximum capacity $Q_{max} = 600$ units and initialized loading percentage $p_i = 0.5$ at start, with both unloading time (t_u) and loading time (t_s) set to 20 min.

The maximum number of periods is set to $\delta_{max} = 7$ days, with each period lasting $t_{max} = 1440$ min. Initially, ten early requests are generated, followed by 283 late requests that are stochastically generated over the course of the simulation. To assess the robustness of the policy in highly complex environments, the generation of late requests is modeled using a spatially uniform distribution [14] and a temporally Poisson-distributed arrival process [15]. The supply demand for each request follows a normal distribution. The initial average demand is set to 100 units (with a variance of 30) for Type A supplies and 75 units (with a variance of 10) for Type B supplies. To simulate the saturation process of demand for Type A supplies, the average demand is gradually reduced over time by applying a per-period discount factor of 0.75.

5.2 Benchmark Policies and Evaluation Metrics

We compare our DRL policy with three rule-based benchmark policies: (1) Selects actions randomly at each decision point, serving as a baseline to evaluate the feasibility of other policies. (2) Greedy Policy: Accepts all late requests at each decision point and assigns them to the nearest available vehicle, aiming to minimize the overall travel cost. (3) Heuristic Policy: For each request, selects the vehicle with the highest supply fulfillment ratio, aiming to reduce the split count of Type A supplies.

To compare the performance of different policies, we adopt the cumulative reward at the model level as a primary evaluation metric. Additionally, to assess the effectiveness of the policies in post-disaster relief scenarios, we incorporate three domain-specific metrics related to emergency supply distribution: (1) The ratio of the total amount of supplies delivered by vehicles to the total demand generated. (2) The total number of completed requests. Given that both the maximum number of periods and the total simulation time are fixed, the above two metrics reflect the effectiveness of the policy in dispatching vehicles. (3) The count of splits for Type A supplies during simulation, which indicates the policy's responsiveness to urgent Type A demands.

5.3 Preliminary Results

As shown in Fig. 5a, the DRL policy achieves a significantly higher cumulative reward compared to the benchmark policies. Figure 5 b and c further demonstrate that the DRL policy results in a higher delivery ratio for both types of supplies, indicating more efficient vehicle scheduling. In Fig. 6a, the difference in the number of completed requests between the DRL policy and the benchmark policies supports the above argument. Then we compare the split count over multiple periods of Type A supply in Fig. 6b. The results show that the DRL policy maintains a relatively low split count compared to the Greedy policy and approaches the performance of the Heuristic policy. This indicates that the DRL policy is capable of effectively responding to urgent and high-priority requests.

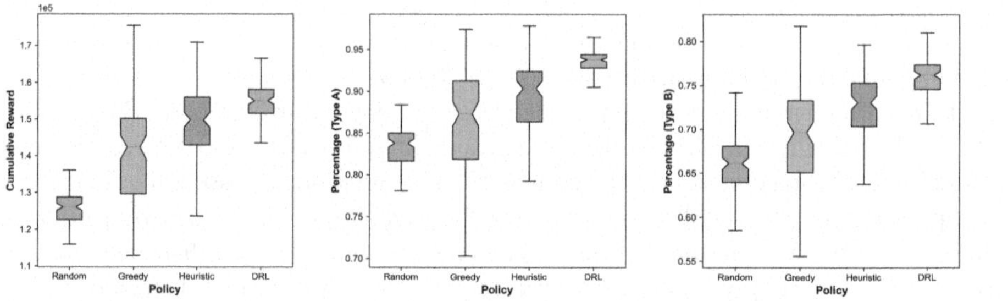

(a) Cumulative Reward (b) Delivery Ratio of Type A Supp. (c) Delivery Ratio of Type B Supp.

Fig. 5. Cumulative Reward and Supplies Delivery Ratio

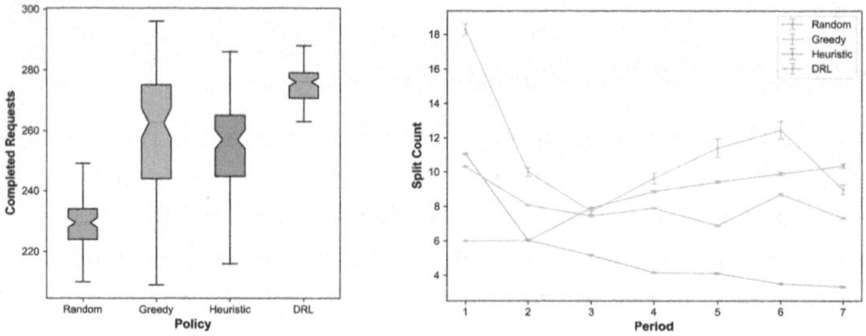

(a) Total Completed Requests (b) Split Count over Multiple Periods

Fig. 6. Total Number of Completed Requests and Split Count

6 Conclusion

In this paper, we address the problem of post-disaster emergency supply distribution and formulated as the MDVRPSR. Then we propose a solution for the routing policy based on DRL. The simulation results show that the DRL-based policy effectively and robustly schedules and routes vehicles, delivering more supplies than benchmark policies. This highlights the DRL-based approach's advantages in both efficiency and robustness in managing the complexity of multi-variety supply distribution.

There are several directions for our future work. Our simulation experiments may deviate from real-world disaster scenarios, so we could enhance the study by incorporating real-world data to improve the model's applicability. Moreover, the pre-training and "black-box" characteristics of deep learning could become the barrier of DRL-based approach's application. In the future, we will focus on further enhancing the robustness of the DRL approach under complex conditions. Additionally, we aim to explore its potential for integration into real-world emergency logistics scheduling systems by considering the characteristics of various types of disasters.

Acknowledgements. This work was supported by the Beijing Social Science Foundation 24GLC056; the National Natural Science Foundation of China under Grants 72104261; Central University of Finance and Economics under the Program for Innovation Research.

References

1. Yang, S., Chen, L.: Post-disaster rescue: a case study of Wenchuan earthquake. J. Southeast Univ. (Philosophy & Social Science). **01**, 94-99+147-148 (2018) (in Chinese)
2. Suppasri, A., Kitamura, M., Alexander, D., Seto, S., Imamura, F.: The 2024 Noto peninsula earthquake: preliminary observations and lessons to be learned. Int. J. Dis. Risk Reduct. **104611** (2024)
3. Fontem, B., Melouk, S.H., Keskin, B.B., Bajwa, N.: A decomposition-based heuristic for stochastic emergency routing problems. Expert Syst. Appl. **59**, 47–59 (2016)
4. Feng, C., Xiang, Y., Xue, K., Feng, R.: Multi-period multi-commodity emergency material distribution multi-objective optimization model. Chin. J. Manage. Sci. **25**(4), 124–132 (2017) (in Chinese)
5. Shen, J., Liu, K., Ma, C., Zhao, Y., Shi, C.: Bibliometric analysis and system review of vehicle routing optimization for emergency material distribution. J. Traff. Transp. Eng. (English edition). **9**(6), 893–911 (2022)
6. Kiran, B.R., Sobh, I., Talpaert, V., Mannion, P., Al Sallab, A.A., Yogamani, S., Pérez, P.: Deep reinforcement learning for autonomous driving: a survey. IEEE Trans. Intell. Transp. Syst. **23**(6), 4909–4926 (2021)
7. Huang, M., Hao, Y., Wang, Y., Hu, X., Li, L.: Split-order consolidation optimization for online supermarkets: process analysis and optimization models. Front. Eng. Manag. **10**(3), 499–516 (2023)
8. Wang, L., Song, J., Shi, L.: Dynamic emergency logistics planning: models and heuristic algorithm. Optim. Lett. **9**, 1533–1552 (2015)
9. Wang, X., Choi, T.-M., Liu, H., Yue, X.: A novel hybrid ant colony optimization algorithm for emergency transportation problems during post-disaster scenarios. IEEE Trans Syst Man Cybern Syst. **48**(4), 545–556 (2016)

10. Sabouhi, F., Bozorgi-Amiri, A., Moshref-Javadi, M., Heydari, M.: An integrated routing and scheduling model for evacuation and commodity distribution in large-scale disaster relief operations: a case study. Ann. Oper. Res. **283**, 643–677 (2019)
11. Ulmer, M.W., Soeffker, N., Mattfeld, D.C.: Value function approximation for dynamic multi-period vehicle routing. Eur. J. Oper. Res. **269**(3), 883–899 (2018)
12. Chen, X., Ulmer, M.W., Thomas, B.W.: Deep Q-learning for same-day delivery with vehicles and drones. Eur. J. Oper. Res. **298**(3), 939–952 (2022)
13. Zhou, C., Ma, J., Douge, L., Chew, E.P., Lee, L.H.: Reinforcement learning-based approach for dynamic vehicle routing problem with stochastic demand. Comput. Ind. Eng. **182**, 109443 (2023)
14. Akbari, V., Çatay, B., Sadati, İ.: Route optimization of battery electric vehicles using dynamic charging on electrified roads. Sustain. Cities Soc. **109**, 105532 (2024)
15. Zhang, J., Luo, K., Florio, A.M., Van Woensel, T.: Solving large-scale dynamic vehicle routing problems with stochastic requests. Eur. J. Oper. Res. **306**(2), 596–614 (2023)

Data Intelligence and Social Computing on Digital Platforms

How the Content Consistency Within the Consumer Feedback Information on E-commerce Affects Sales

Feng Xiaodong[1(✉)], Huang Yuhang[1], and Li Chenhui[2]

[1] School of Information Management, Sun Yat-Sen University, Guangzhou, China
fengxd5@mail.sysu.edu.cn

[2] School of Economics and Management, Harbin Institute of Technology, Harbin, China

Abstract. Consumer feedback in e-commerce platforms is an important source of information that determines subsequent consumer purchasing decisions. The consistency of content among feedback information by different consumers and its impact on sales has received little attention. Based on the theory of cue consistency, this study constructs a model for the impact of content consistency between different consumers' feedback information on the sales, including the consistency of review texts, images, and answers, and explores the moderating effect of product prices. Based on large-scale real data from *JD.hk*, text mining and image analysis tools with the help of deep learning techniques are utilized to measure multiple content consistency features and theoretical models are examined through econometric models. Results indicate that the content consistency of review text, image, and answers all positively affect sales, which are positively moderated by product prices. The research findings expand the theoretical perspective of the relationship between online consumer feedback and sales, and provide practical insights for the operation and management of online merchants.

Keywords: E-commerce · Online Review · Commercial Q&A · Cue consistency · Deep Learning

1 Introduction

In e-commerce platforms, to obtain consumers' evaluations of products and services, improve the online reputation of merchants, and eliminate consumers' uncertainty about products and services, almost all e-commerce platforms provide information feedback functions for consumers. Consumer online feedback information, such as online reviews plays a key role in affecting merchants' reputation and thus future sales [1, 2]. Considerable scholarly attention has been paid to examining the impact of online word-of-mouth on product sales or consumer purchasing decisions. In summary, these studies explore influencing factors from the meta attributes of online reviews (such as rating and volume) [3], as well as review content [4], multimedia cues (such as images and videos) [5, 6], and reviewer characteristics [1]. These studies have mainly extracted extensive features from online reviews.

Y. P. Tu and M. Chi (Eds.): WHICEB 2025, LNBIP 549, pp. 141–152, 2025.
https://doi.org/10.1007/978-3-031-94184-9_12

When consumers make online decisions, they usually reply to multiple feedback information, such as text and images. In the previous studies, the aggregation from a set of multiple reviews mainly comes from the overall naïve aggregation of the single features of each individual review, such as the counts, average, variance, or proportion of some numeric feature values or discrete variables referring to some appearance [5]. Among them, the variance in review ratings or valence is used to measure consistency or differences between different reviews [7], but the consistency of product attributes obtained from review content is rarely discussed. It is noted that some recent research on the topic of online review helpfulness begins focusing on the consistency between review content and ratings, including individual rating and average rating [8], top reviews and all reviews [9], or review text and images [10]. Nevertheless, they usually discuss the consistency between information from different sources but have paid less attention to the content consistency or differences between multiple reviews from different consumers, and how it affects the potential consumers' decision or sales. Obviously, the consistency or differences in the content between different reviews about the same product would influence how consumers perceive confidence about the quality of the products and the sales.

Also, the existing studies mostly focus on the text content of the review, and the influence of multiple types of consumer feedback information is rarely discussed. With the continuous development of e-commerce platforms, images in reviews have gradually become another important form of consumer feedback [10]. As the practice of photo sharing gains traction among both consumers and businesses, it becomes essential to deepen our comprehension of the influence of images in online reviews. However, they mainly used simple meta features such as the appearance/numbers of images/video [5, 6]. Also, the Q&A feature of products has also become a way for consumers to interact with each other [11]. Consumers who have purchased products or experienced services could provide feedback information by answering specific questions posted by platforms or other consumers, which has gradually been favored and adopted by various platforms. Some works also begin to examine how images in reviews or Q&A features would influence consumer purchase behavior or product sales, which adopt survey-based methodology or simply measure statistics of questions or answers [11]. However, the effect of the valuable content features from review images or questions -answers is not well documented.

Accordingly, to fulfill this research gap, investigating how the content consistency between different forms of online feedback information would affect sales becomes the first research objective of this study. Specifically, under the unifying framework of cue consistency, we will try to explore the content consistency between different review texts, review images, and product answers to the same question about the products respectively. Furthermore, when consumers rely on online reviews to make decisions to purchase products, product prices are among the crucial information cues for them to evaluate the product quality, where the moderating role of the product price proves to be a critical signaling factor affecting consumer behaviors in many marketing and information systems studies [12]. Thus, we are also interested in investigating how product prices moderate the main effects of cue consistency on sales.

Therefore, based on the cue consistency theory, this article constructs a theoretical model of the impact of content consistency over different online feedback information on sales, including review text consistency, image consistency, and answer consistency, and explores the moderating effect of product prices. Based on a large-scale real online review and Q&A data of 3589 products collected from *JD.hk*, a popular e-commerce platform in China, text mining and image analysis tools are employed to measure consistency features, and the theoretical model is examined through econometric models.

2 Related Works

In this section, we review literature closely related to our study. Specifically, we survey research in information systems and related areas that explore the economic impact of online feedback information and the role of cue consistency.

2.1 Online Feedback Information and Consumer's Purchase Decisions

Various forms of online feedback information, also known as user-generated content (UGC), are available on different e-commerce platforms. Traditionally, online reviews serve as the primary form of UGC, offering personal experiences and feelings regarding purchased products or services. The prevailing understanding of online reviews is that they can mitigate information asymmetry between consumers and online retailers, building trust, and thereby influencing consumers' purchasing decisions [2]. The impact of online reviews on aggregated consumer purchase decisions, specifically product sales, has been extensively documented. The early studies usually pay attention to the volume of reviews and the review rating, and the following studies focus on the extensive textual features of the reviews [3], such as the informative/imaginative text in the review [1] and comparative review types [4]; other meta features such as review popularity and reviewer expertise would also have an impact on consumers' purchase intention [1].

In addition to the effects of product reviews on e-commerce platforms, the UGC or eWOM on external social media can also serve as a predictor for the movie box office [13]. Furthermore, scholars have increasingly focused on studying the impact of multimedia content or Q&A on consumers' purchase decisions or sales [2, 6, 11]. For example, the number of answers to each question and the question word count are positively correlated to product sales [11].

2.2 Cue Consistency of Online Reviews

When consumers make purchasing decisions based on online reviews or other online feedback information, they typically need to aggregate diverse review information by different consumers across various time periods, considering both text and image forms, as well as additional online feedback, such as Q&A. Thus, how to aggregate multiple information is a necessity when discussing the impacts of online feedback on consumer purchase decisions or product sales. The early studies on this topic proposed using the variance of review rating and discussing its direct or moderating effects on purchase decisions [7]. In addition, recent studies began to pay attention to the difference or consistency between different sources of online information and its impact on perceived review usefulness, subsequent reviews, or purchase decisions. For example, the mutual information between the rating distribution of top reviews and that of all reviews can mitigate information overload and increase consumer satisfaction measured by the dispersion of subsequent review ratings [9]; the consistency between an individual review rating and the accumulated rating, review text and its rating, and the review title and content text would positively determine the review helpfulness [8, 14]; the object consistency between images and text in reviews improves review helpfulness for search products [10].

In summary, extensive research has explored the impact of various features with online reviews and other information on consumers' purchase decisions or product sales. However, little focus has been directed toward the different content of online feedback provided by different consumers, specifically the consistency of information content, and its influence on consumer purchasing decisions. This gap in research forms the core focus that this study aims to address.

3 Theoretical Foundation and Hypothesis Development

To answer the research questions mentioned above, the study adopted the cue consistency theory as the theoretical foundation to build our hypotheses. Based on the Cue Consistency Theory, this work uses the content consistency characteristics of product review text, product review images, and product answer text as the core explanatory variables to study the impact of online feedback information on consumer decision-making in e-commerce platforms and the moderating effects of product prices, as shown in Fig. 1.

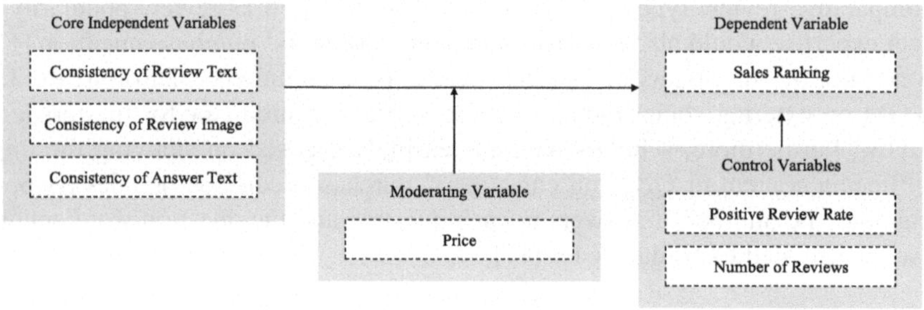

Fig. 1. Research model

3.1 The Content Consistency of Online Feedback Information

When consumers browse online feedback provided by other consumers to make online purchase decisions, they rely on various information cues to assess the quality of the product or service they intend to pay for. Different theories can be applied in this context. According to attribution theory, consumers will speculate on the motives behind a consumer's writing based on various existing information cues. They will infer whether the consumer wrote the online review for reasons related to the product's performance or for reasons unrelated to the product. Previous research has often used the variance of overall product ratings to quantify the dispersion of eWOM and then analyze the impact in different domains on product sales [7]. Conflicting findings have emerged regarding the effect of eWOM dispersion. Some researchers argue that people tend to be risk-averse, and differentiated information has a negative impact on purchasing decisions [15]. Other researchers believe that inconsistent WOM can stimulate consumer curiosity and enhance the desire to make a purchase [16], and contradictory WOM, to a certain extent, paradoxically possesses greater persuasive power [17].

The degree of consistency between different information cues is referred to as information consistency [14]. Consistency in information from multiple sources enhances the perceived credibility of the information by the information receiver and reduces perceived uncertainty about the information. According to the evidence discussed before, consumers tend to utilize a linear averaging method to analyze consistent cues. Furthermore, signaling theory holds that conflicting signals may confuse the receiver and the confidence would be reduced, leading to lower communication efficiency, while consistent signals can alleviate this efficiency trap and enhance signal persuasiveness as they are more reliable and more beneficial for decision-making [18]. Empirical studies found the positive effects of consistency between the first photo in the hotel description and the headline on booking intentions [6].

In the context of online shopping, platforms offer various forms of consumer feedback information from different consumers as external cues, including multiple individual reviews in text and images and Q&A sections as new features. For example, the review text typically outlines the consumer's evaluation of various attributes of the product, while review images may focus on different aspects. Additionally, answers to the same question about the product may vary or show inconsistencies. One would therefore expect that when the textual or visual content of different reviews can mutually mirror each other, the well impression of the product by consumers tends to be enhanced, the decision uncertainty could be reduced, and consequently the willingness to make a purchase will be increased. Similarly, multiple different answers to the same question will increase consumers' uncertainty about the product and reduce their purchase intention, while the answer with the same direction will make consumers more confident in the characteristics of the product, and then positively affect their purchase decision. Therefore, we hypothesize that:

H1: *The content consistency of online feedback information is positively correlated to product sales.*

Referring to the different forms of feedback information, we have the following three sub-hypothesis:

H1a: *The content consistency of text of different reviews is positively correlated to the product sales.*
H1b: *The content consistency of images of different reviews is positively correlated to the product sales.*

H1c: *The content consistency of answers to the same questions is positively correlated to product sales.*

3.2 The Moderating Role of Product Prices

Consumers have different decision-making processes when purchasing low-priced and high-priced products when facing the same type of product. Compared to lower-priced goods, consumers will pay more money and have greater decision-making risks when purchasing higher-priced goods. Perceived risk, referring to the evaluation of the consequences of purchasing errors and the likelihood of such errors occurring by consumers, is an important factor that affects consumer decision-making behavior. The higher the perceived risk of decision-making, the more cautious consumers will be. The concept of perceived risk plays a pivotal role in consumer decision-making. It encompasses the consumer's evaluation of the potential adverse outcomes of a purchase and the likelihood of such outcomes. Compared to low-risk decisions not involving money, high-risk decisions involving money were more affected when perceived risk changed. Another study found when buying new products, consumers are precepting high risks, and low review variance would result in more adoption [7]. This indicates that consumers are more cautious when facing products with higher prices, as high-priced products usually imply a high risk of buying [19], and they will refer to more external cues to support their consumption decisions.

Therefore, we assume that when consumers purchase high-priced goods, external cues with high consistency have a greater impact on consumer decision-making than buying low-priced goods, as the following hypothesis.

H2: *The effect of content consistency of online feedback information on product sales will be larger for higher-priced products than lower-priced ones.*

Referring to the different forms of online feedback information, we have three sub-hypotheses:

H2a: *The effect of content consistency of text of different reviews on product sales will be larger for higher-priced products than lower-priced ones.*
H2b: *The effect of content consistency of images of different reviews on product sales will be larger for higher-priced products than lower-priced ones.*
H2c: *The effect of content consistency of answers to the same questions on product sales will be larger for higher-priced products than for lower-priced ones.*

4 Research Design

4.1 Data Collection and Pre-Processing

We selected the JD.hk (https://www.jd.hk/) as the data source because it is one of the largest e-commerce platforms with a vast user base. We used Python to crawl data from JD.hk, covering 3589 products across 12 categories. For each product, we collected reviews, and Q&A from the first five pages; if a product's reviews and Q&A did not span five pages, we retrieved all available content. In total, we collected 212,366 product reviews and 150,051 answers to 22,203 questions. The product data includes rankings, total price, positive review rate, number of reviews, number of positive reviews, number of negative reviews, and other relevant details. The review data include ratings, content, images, and timestamps. For the Q&A, we collected question content, question time, answer content, and answer time. During preprocessing, we first removed links, '@', usernames, and special characters from the reviews and answers, and dropped meaningless stopwords. Next, we used the Jieba library in Python for word segmentation. We manually labeled the quantity of each product to calculate its unit price. We then normalized the prices within each category (Z-score normalization) due to significant price differences across product categories.

4.2 Research Variables and Operationalization

4.2.1 Dependent Variable

Sales. JD.hk does not provide exact sales figures for products. Referring to the literature on online product sales [5], we measure sales using product sales rankings. Specifically, when crawling product information, we sort the products within each category in descending order of sales, and a lower sales rank indicates higher sales.

4.2.2 Independent Variable

Consistency of Review Text (Con_Review). We use the LDA model to obtain the topic distribution of review texts and use cosine similarity to calculate the consistency of review texts, and wen normalize it within the same category using Z-score. It is also noted that we determined the optimal number of topics for the LDA model using perplexity (lower is better) and we selected 16 topics for the review texts.

Consistency of Answer Text (Con_Answer). We used the same way to compute the cosine similarity of topic distribution of each answer, and using the same approach as above, the final number of topics for the answer texts was determined to be 17.

Consistency of Review Image (Con_image). We use the image subject detection API from Baidu AI[1] to obtain multiple subject keywords and their confidence scores for a given review image. We then calculated the consistency of review images by the cosine similarity of the subject belonging vectors and also normalized it using a z-score.

4.2.3 Moderating Variable

Prices. Since the prices vary significantly across categories, and in order to eliminate the interference of this factor, we normalize product prices within each category using a z-score.

4.2.4 Control Variables

Previous studies have found that the proportion of positive reviews and the number of reviews can influence the consumer decision-making process [3, 20]. Therefore, we include the positive review rate and the number of reviews as control variables, with both variables being normalized.

[1] API functional Introduction Website: https://ai.baidu.com/tech/imagerecognition/object_detect

The complete variable definitions are provided in Table 1, where the mean and Std. are before the normalization.

Table 1. Definition of Variables

Group	Name	Definition	Mean	Std.
Dependent variable	*Sales*	[1:+∞): Product's sales rank under its category	194.59	155.70
Independent variables	*Con_Review*	[0:1]: Cosine similarity of the topic distribution of review text	0.250	0.121
	Con_Image	[0:1]: Cosine similarity of the topic distribution of comment images	0.520	0.310
	Con_Answer	[0:1]: Cosine similarity of the topic distribution of the answer text	0.052	0.111
Moderating variable	*Price*	(0:+ ∞): Price of product	652.71	2603
Control variables	*Pro_Positive*	[0:1]: The proportion of positive reviews relative to the total number of reviews	0.966	0.064
	Vol_Reviews	[0: + ∞): Number of all reviews for a product	101,097	530,699

5 Research Result

5.1 Correlation Analysis

Firstly, we analyzed the Pearson correlation coefficients between the variables, as shown in Table 2. As indicated in Table 2, all three core independent variables exhibit a negative correlation with the dependent variable, suggesting that the consistency of the review text, review image, and answer text positively influences product sales. Among these, the consistency of the answer text shows the strongest correlation with the dependent variable (PCCs = −0.366), followed by the consistency of the review image (PCCs = −0.172,), while the consistency of the review text has the weakest correlation with the dependent variable (PCCs = −0.055). The consistency of the review text is strongly positively correlated with the consistency of the review image (PCCs = 0.432). This is mainly because the textual and visual elements of the same reviews complement each other, leading to a strong correlation between them. Additionally, the consistency of the review text is positively correlated with answer text consistency (PCCs = 0.193), and the consistency of the review image is positively correlated with the consistency of answer text (PCCs = 0.225), though these correlations are relatively weak.

Table 2. Correlation between Variables

id		1	2	3	4	5	6	7
1	*Sales*	1.000						
2	*Pro_Positive*	0.010	1.000					
3	*Vol_Reviews*	−0.261 ***	0.053 ***	1.000				
4	*Price*	0.014	−0.014	−0.133 ***	1.000			
5	*Con_Review*	−0.055 ***	−0.056 ***	0.035 **	−0.165 ***	1.000		
6	*Con_Image*	−0.172 ***	0.019	0.111***	−0.162 ***	0.432 ***	1.000	
7	*Con_Answer*	−0.366 ***	0.026	0.359***	−0.191 ***	0.193 ***	0.225 ***	1.000

Note: *: significance <0.1; **: significance <0.05; ***: significance <0.01

5.2 Regression Analysis

The regression results for the models are presented in Table 3.

Table 3. Regression analysis results (base model)

Variables		Model 1	Model 2	Model 3	Model 4	Model 5
	R-squared	0.033	0.071	0.090	0.154	0.164
Control variables	*Pro_Positive*	0.225	0.191	0.231	0.234*	0.276**
	Vol_Reviews	−1.716 ***	−1.470 ***	−1.389 ***	−0.847 ***	−0.813 ***
Independent variables	*Con_Review*		−0.045 ***			0.059 ***
	Con_Image			−0.146 ***		−0.115 ***
	Con_Answer				−0.313 ***	−0.300 ***

Note: The dependent variable (sales rank) is presented in descending order, with a higher sales rank indicating lower sales.*: significance <0.1; **: significance <0.05; ***: significance <0.01

As shown in Table 3, in Models 2–4, the coefficients for the *Con_Review*, *Con_Image,* and *Con_Answer* are all significantly negative, indicating that H1a, H1b, and H1c are all supported, implying that the consistency of review text/images/answers positively influences sales. It is noteworthy that in Model 5, the regression coefficients for the three core explanatory variables are 0.059 ($p < 0.01$), −0.115 ($p < 0.01$), and −0.300

($p < 0.01$). The regression coefficient for the consistency of the review text changes to a positive value, likely due to multicollinearity between the consistency of the review text and the consistency of the review image (with a correlation coefficient of 0.432, as shown in Table 2).

5.3 Moderating Effects of Price

To test H2, we treat price as a moderating variable and examine the interaction terms between price and the three core explanatory variables using multiple linear regression. The regression results for the models are presented in Table 4.

Table 4. Regression analysis results (moderating effect)

Variables		Model 6	Model 7	Model 8	Model 9
	R-squared	0.073	0.092	0.159	0.174
Control variables	*Pro_Positive*	0.163	0.228	0.227*	0.231*
	Vol_Reviews	−1.492 ***	−1.423 ***	−0.880 ***	−0.840 ***
Independent variables	*Con_Review*	−0.043 ***			0.062 ***
	Con_Image		−0.150 ***		−0.120 ***
	Con_Answer			−0.342 ***	−0.324 ***
Moderating variable	*Price*	−0.037 **	−0.049 ***	−0.085 ***	−0.097 ***
	*Price*Con_Review*	−0.034 ***			−0.050 ***
	*Price*Con_Image*		−0.017		−0.008
	*Price*Con_Answer*			−0.048*	−0.022

*: significance <0.1; **: significance <0.05; ***: significance <0.01

As shown in Table 4, in Models 6–8, the interaction terms between price and *Con_Review*and *Con_Answer* all have a significant negative coefficient. Also, the coefficients are in the same direction as that of the corresponding independent variables, suggesting that price has a positive moderating effect, which supports H2a and H2c. However, the moderating effect on *Con_Image* is not significant. In Model 9, all core independent variables and their interaction terms with price are included. The regression coefficients for the independent variables are consistent with those presented in Table 3. In this model, all interaction terms between price and the independent variables have negative regression coefficients. However, due to multicollinearity between variables, some interaction terms have non-significant coefficients. Thus, results in Models 6 to 8 demonstrate the positive moderating effects of product prices.

6 Conclusion and Discussion

6.1 Main Findings

This study reveals that the consistency of review text, image, and the consistency of answer text all positively influence product sales, and that the consistency of review text and the consistency of review image have a strong correlation. Firstly, the review text with consistent directionality positively influences sales. As the primary source of external cues for consumers, consistent review text helps avoid confusion when browsing reviews, thus enhancing the decision-making process by providing more reliable information. Secondly, the consistency of review images also exerts a positive influence on sales. Compared to text, consumers tend to remember images more easily. Consistent review images create a sense of realism and persuasiveness, further influencing consumer decisions. Thirdly, the consistency of the answer text positively impacts consumer decision-making. When multiple answers to a given question are consistent, they can significantly boost consumer confidence in their decision-making. We also found that product price positively moderates the effect of the information consistency on consumer purchase. When consumers face high-priced products, they perceive higher levels of risk and, consequently, seek more external cues to support their decisions, such as reading more product reviews and Q&A content. As a result, inconsistencies in directional cues within product reviews and Q&A sections become more influential in shaping consumer decisions.

6.2 Implications

Based on the observed findings and insights, we propose the following practical recommendations for e-commerce platforms.

First, prioritizing product review and Q&A, an emerging feedback channel known for relevance and authenticity, aiding consumer decisions. Many e-commerce sites, like JD.hk, undervalue this, placing reviews at the end of product pages without easy navigation. Additionally, Q&A sections often have repetitive questions. E-commerce platforms can use some techniques to direct users to existing answers.

Second, optimizing product review presentations to boost reliability. While reviews provide valuable insights, vast numbers cause information overload, leading to consumer anxiety and decision delay. E-commerce platforms should use technology to highlight high-quality, authentic reviews. Additionally, fake reviews undermine review credibility, especially for lesser-known brands, hindering sales. Platforms can enforce policies to regulate and penalize such reviews, keeping feedback integrity.

This study is not without limitations. First, the model uses the sale ranking as the outcome variable, which may not fully reflect the sales outcomes and the data of the real sales can improve the robustness of the study. Second, extending the empirical studies to various platforms can increase the generality of the findings. In addition, the investigation of other variables such as product category and consumer demographics should be included in the calculation of the moderating effect as a way of obtaining a more comprehensive picture of consumer decision-making.

References

1. Zhang, D., Niu, B.: Leveraging online reviews for hotel demand forecasting: a deep learning approach. Inf. Process. Manag. **61**(1), 103527 (2024)
2. Chen, G., Huang, L., Xiao, S., et al.: Attending to customer attention: a novel deep learning method for leveraging multimodal online reviews to enhance sales prediction. Inf. Syst. Res. **35**(2), 829–849 (2024)
3. Ye, Q., Law, R., Bin, G., et al.: The influence of user-generated content on traveler behavior: an empirical investigation on the effects of e-word-of-mouth to hotel online bookings. Comput. Hum. Behav. **27**(2), 634–639 (2011)
4. Li, Y., Min Zhang, G., Wang, A., et al.: The effect of different types of comparative reviews on product sales. Decis. Support. Syst. **184**, 114287 (2024)
5. Yin, H., Zheng, S., Yeoh, W., et al.: How online review richness impacts sales: an attribute substitution perspective. J. Assoc. Inf. Sci. Technol. **72**(7), 901–917 (2021)
6. Lim, J., Jang, J.: Does photo presentation matter for increasing booking intention? J. Hosp. Market. Manag. **31**(8), 1009–1025 (2022)
7. Yuanyuan, W., Liu, T., Teng, L., et al.: The impact of online review variance of new products on consumer adoption intentions. J. Bus. Res. **136**, 209 (2021)
8. Aghakhani, N., Onook, O., Gregg, D.G., et al.: Online review consistency matters: an elaboration likelihood model perspective. Inf. Syst. Front. **23**(5), 1287–1301 (2021)
9. Jabr, W., Rahman, M.S.: Online reviews and information overload: the role of selective, parsimonious, and concordant top reviews. MIS Q. **46**(3), 517 (2022)
10. Yang, Y., Wang, Y., Zhao, J.: Effect of user-generated image on review helpfulness: perspectives from object detection. Electron. Commer. Res. Appl. **57**, 101232 (2023)
11. Khern-am-nuai, W., Ghasemkhani, H., Qiao, D., et al.: The impact of Online Q&As on product sales: the case of Amazon answer. Inf. Syst. Res. **35**(2), 747–765 (2024)
12. Chengcheng, X., Zheng, X., Yang, F.: Examining the effects of negative emotions on review helpfulness: the moderating role of product price. Comput. Hum. Behav. **139**, 107501 (2023)
13. Bogaert, M., Ballings, M., Van den Poel, D., et al.: Box office sales and social media: a cross-platform comparison of predictive ability and mechanisms. Decis. Support. Syst. **147**, 113517 (2021)
14. Li, Q., Park, J., Kim, J.: Impact of information consistency in online reviews on consumer behavior in the e-commerce industry: a text mining approach. Data Technol. Applic. **58**(1), 132–149 (2024)
15. Tang, T., Fang, E., Wang, F.: Is neutral really neutral? The effects of neutral user-generated content on product sales. J. Mark. **78**(4), 41–58 (2014)
16. He, S.X., Bond, S.D.: Why is the crowd divided? Attribution for dispersion in online word of mouth. J. Consum. Res. **41**(6), 1509–1527 (2015)
17. Reich, T., Tormala, Z.L.: When contradictions foster persuasion: an attributional perspective. J. Exp. Soc. Psychol. **49**(3), 426–439 (2013)
18. Fischer, E., Reuber, R.: The good, the bad, and the unfamiliar: the challenges of reputation formation facing new firms. Entrep. Theory Pract. **31**(1), 53–75 (2007)
19. Homburg, C., Lauer, K., Vomberg, A.: The multichannel pricing dilemma: do consumers accept higher offline than online prices? Int. J. Res. Mark. **36**(4), 597–612 (2019)
20. Park, D.-H., Lee, J., Han, I.: The effect of on-line consumer reviews on consumer purchasing intention: the moderating role of involvement. Int. J. Electron. Commer. **11**(4), 125–148 (2007)

From Single Platform Crisis to Innocent Platform: The Impact of Ctrip's Price Discrimination on Tongcheng Platform

Jing Yang[1], Kang Yang[1], Qiuying Gu[1], Ningnan Zhou[2](✉), Yucheng Zhang[2], and Xiang Shu[1]

[1] School of Business Administration, Nanjing University of Finance and Economics, Nanjing 210046, China
[2] Nanjing University of Finance and Economics Hongshan College, Nanjing 211300, China
15951754427@163.com

Abstract. In the complex and competitive digital economy, a platform's crisis has far-reaching consequences. This study uses Ctrip's price discrimination as an example to explore its negative impact on Tongcheng Online Travel Platform from the users' perspective. Based on Situational Crisis Communication Theory and Accessibility-Diagnosticity theory, the research investigates the relationship between the similarity between the Ctrip platform and the Tongcheng platform and the intention to boycott the Tongcheng platform, with emotional reputation and cognitive reputation as mediating variables. The study also integrates crisis history as a moderating variable. Data from 382 valid survey out of 500 participants, mostly users who frequently use the Tongcheng travel platform, were analyzed. The study demonstrates that the similarity between the Ctrip platform and the Tongcheng platform indirectly affects the intention to boycott the Tongcheng platform through the mediating roles of the Tongcheng platform's emotional reputation and cognitive reputation, while the crisis history of the Tongcheng platform positively moderates this mediating process.

Keywords: Ctrip Online Travel Platform · Similarity · Emotional Reputation · Cognitive Reputation

1 Introduction

In the era of the booming platform economy, online travel platforms have emerged as indispensable channels for modern travelers to plan and book their journeys. They provide users with rich information on travel products and services, including hotels, air tickets, travel routes, scenic spots tickets, etc. As a leading enterprise in the industry, Ctrip, an online travel platform, has occupied a prominent position in the online travel market by offering a wide range of travel booking services to its large user base. However, the exposure of Ctrip's price discrimination incident has not only attracted the attention and heated discussions of a large number of users, but also had a negative impact on other platforms, for example Tongcheng platform, in the same industry.

Y. P. Tu and M. Chi (Eds.): WHICEB 2025, LNBIP 549, pp. 153–162, 2025.
https://doi.org/10.1007/978-3-031-94184-9_13

Platform scholars generally believe that stakeholder trust in such platforms is crucial for their success [1]. Crises can significantly impact the way in which platforms interact with key users, damaging stakeholder relationships and thereby affecting the platforms' reputation [2]. Previous studies have inadequately explored the impact of crises on other platforms [3]. Based on the big data analysis of users' browsing and consumption habits, the Ctrip platform offers different prices to different users for the same product and service. In fact, other travel platforms will also be negatively affected. Even if they may not have similar problems, it can still make users reluctant to use their services.

The research incorporates Situational Crisis Communication Theory (SCCT) and Accessibility-Diagnosticity theory into an empirical model, which is validated using statistical methods. This approach provides a comprehensive framework for understanding the complex dynamics between crisis platforms and innocent platforms during crisis events. The study's contributions include revealing the impact of the crisis platform on innocent platform, enhancing the understanding of platform-related crisis events, and exploring the impact of similarity between the innocent platform and the crisis platform during a crisis on users' intention to boycott an innocent platform. The study finds that similarity affects this process through emotional reputation and cognitive reputation, while the crisis history of innocent platforms plays a moderating role in this process. It emphasizes the importance of inter-platform relationships and the historical factors of platforms themselves in understanding and dealing with platform crises, providing a key theoretical basis for platform managers to formulate crisis-response strategies.

2 Literature Review

2.1 Situation Crisis Communication Theory

In the digital age, the diffusion mechanisms of platform crises are increasingly complex, primarily due to the rapid spread of information enabled by social media and the interconnected nature of online platforms. This complexity is further amplified by the diverse ways users interact with content, making it harder to predict and manage how crises might escalate. The Situation Crisis Communication Theory (SCCT) offers a valuable analytical framework for understanding this phenomenon. This theory emphasizes stakeholders' attribution and responses in crisis situations. It assesses the potential crisis responsibility through identifying crisis types and notes that the initial crisis responsibility, crisis history, and platform's relationship history directly impact the crisis diffusion scope across platforms [4]. For example, in the case of Kickstarter's union scandal, when the platform was accused of systemic management flaws, users tended to see this crisis as an industry issue, thus affecting similar platforms [5]. This cross-platform impact is evident in the Situation Crisis Communication Theory framework. Preventable crises are more likely than accidental ones to trigger chain reactions through user cognitive associations [6]. For instance, Meta's (formerly known as Facebook) 2021 algorithmic bias disclosure, a preventable crisis, not only led to user doubts about Meta but also caused sustained questioning of recommendation mechanisms on platforms like TikTok and Twitter. This skepticism, fueled by anti-monopoly sentiments, created a cross-platform trust collapse [7]. This effect weakens user trust in individual platforms and may trigger an industry trust crisis, affecting the healthy development of platform economies.

Therefore, platforms must prioritize crisis management, using effective communication strategies and transparent operations to ease user concerns and prevent uncontrolled crisis spread.

2.2 Accessibility-Diagnosticity Theory

Accessibility-Diagnosticity theory further uncovers the cognitive mechanisms behind cross-platform impacts. It delves into how individuals explain event causes and their behavioral influences from a cognitive psychology perspective. Users assess crisis responsibility across three attributional dimensions: accessibility, diagnosticity, and relative accessibility [8]. These factors significantly strengthen negative associations with similar platforms [9]. For example, when a platform is exposed for algorithmic bias, users explain the event based on their attribution tendencies. If they see it as an inherent flaw in the platform's business model rather than a random technical error or individual oversight, they may assume other platforms with similar algorithms or models have the same risks [10]. This assumption is subjective and based on attribution bias, not objective analysis. In such cases, users' trust in similar platforms can plummet, triggering cross-platform trust crises. Attribution bias is especially pronounced at the group level. For instance, when shared economy platforms frequently have safety incidents, users often attribute them to industry wide regulatory failures rather than isolated platform issues. This collective attribution bias intensifies negative perceptions and distrust of the entire industry, making users resist other shared economy platforms even if they haven't had similar safety problems. Such cross-platform attribution biases and negative associations not only affect user behavior but also pose significant challenges to platform reputation and industry health.

3 Theoretical Framework and Hypotheses

3.1 Perceived Similarity, Cognitive Reputation, Emotional Reputation and Intention to Boycott

Perceived similarity is defined as a subjective assessment of the degree of similarity between two objects, based on an individual's knowledge, experience, and judgement [11]. This concept can be used as a psychological measurement indicator to evaluate the extent of similarity between two or more objects in specific aspects.

According to Accessibility-Diagnosticity theory, when the similarity between two platforms is higher, users receive information about an innocent platform from negative information about another platform's crisis [12]. That is, the information about the crisis is diagnosable for innocent platforms. In this case, the memory nodes about the crisis platform and the innocent platforms are activated at the same time in the users' mind, which creates a cognitive bias. Then, users infer from the information about the crisis platform that the innocent platforms are equally problematic, which generates intention to boycott.

H1: The similarity between the innocent platform and the crisis platform will have a positive impact on users' intention to boycott.

Platform reputation, derived from SCCT, refers to the overall assessment made by users. This assessment is based on the platform's past behaviors and compares it with user expectations. This study uses a user-based measure of platform reputation to consider users' overall assessment of the platform. Based on previous research, this study divides reputation into cognitive and affective dimensions: the affective dimension involves emotional evaluations such as trust, cordiality and admiration, while the cognitive dimension assesses the platform's commercial competence, professionalism and brand image [13].

According to SCCT and Accessibility-Diagnosticity theory, users' attitudes and behavioral intentions towards the innocent platforms change when a crisis occurs. Similarity may weaken emotional ties, and lead to negative reputation perceptions, and increase the intention to boycott. High similarity also makes users more reliant on crisis information, makes them doubt the ability of the innocent platforms, reduces reputation evaluation, and may ultimately lead to a boycott. Therefore, we propose the following hypothesis:

H2a: The similarity between the innocent platform and the crisis platform has a negative impact on users' emotional reputation for the innocent platform.
H2b: The similarity between the innocent platform and the crisis platform has a negative impact on users' cognitive reputation for the innocent platform.

In SCCT, the reputational damage caused by a crisis has an impact on the interactions between the platform and its users. The more negative the platform's reputation, the more pronounced the users' behavioral intentions to boycott the platform. After a crisis, both the emotional and cognitive reputational dimensions of the platform are negatively affected. The appeal of the platform's reputation to users is weakened, and its competitiveness is questioned. As a result, unfavorable judgements and low confidence in the platform are generated.

H3a: The emotional reputation of the innocent platform will negatively affect users' intention to boycott it.
H3b: The cognitive reputation of the innocent platform will negatively affect users' intention to boycott it.

Individual behavior changes are often triggered by external events. When a crisis occurs, the more similar the crisis platform and the innocent platform are, the more valuable the information users obtain from the crisis platform is, and the more this information will help users judge the innocent platform. The memory nodes in users' minds about the similarity between the crisis platform and the innocent platform will be easily activated. Perceptual transfer will take place between the two platforms, and the crisis information will have a higher diagnostic value for the innocent platform. Users will perceive the possibility of a similar crisis occurring in the innocent platform and develop a negative reputation perception of the innocent platform, thus reducing the evaluation of the innocent platform and ultimately resulting in a boycott intention. Based on SCCT theory, the similarity will affect users' emotional reputation and cognitive reputation of the innocent platform, and then produce a boycott intention.

H4a: The emotional reputation of innocent platform mediates the positive impact between its similarity to crisis platform and the intention to boycott the innocent platform.

H4b: The cognitive reputation of innocent platform mediates the positive impact between its similarity to crisis platform and the intention to boycott the innocent platform.

Crisis history refers to an individual's perception of whether an entity has experienced a crisis in the past or in recent years [6]. Because information is easily accessible, stakeholders can instantly use the internet to search for all information about an entity from its inception. Therefore, entity that have experienced crises must include crisis history in their crisis management strategy [14]. Crisis history is usually used to evaluate an entity's crisis-handling performance, and this study focuses on users' perception of whether innocent platforms similar to crisis platforms have experienced or frequently experienced similar crises in the past. This study defines it as the crisis history of innocent platforms. Frequent crises will gradually lead platforms to lose the trust of users and even affect the entire industry. Platforms with a positive crisis history may survive the current crisis, but if they do not handle it well, a positive crisis history will still damage their reputation. On the other hand, a negative crisis history will make the platform's situation worse.

In the context of crisis communication theory, crisis history is considered one of the three major factors that form a reputation threat in a crisis situation. Crisis history will indirectly threaten reputation by strengthening the attribution of crisis responsibility. That is, compared with platforms without a crisis history, platforms that have experienced similar crises in the past will bear greater crisis responsibility and suffer more damage to their reputation.

H5a: The crisis history of the innocent platform will moderate the impact of similarity on emotional reputation. The stronger the perception of the crisis history of the innocent platform, the greater the negative impact of similarity on emotional reputation.
H5b: The crisis history of the innocent platform will moderate the impact of similarity on cognitive reputation. The stronger the perception of the crisis history of the innocent platform, the greater the negative impact of similarity on cognitive reputation (Fig. 1).

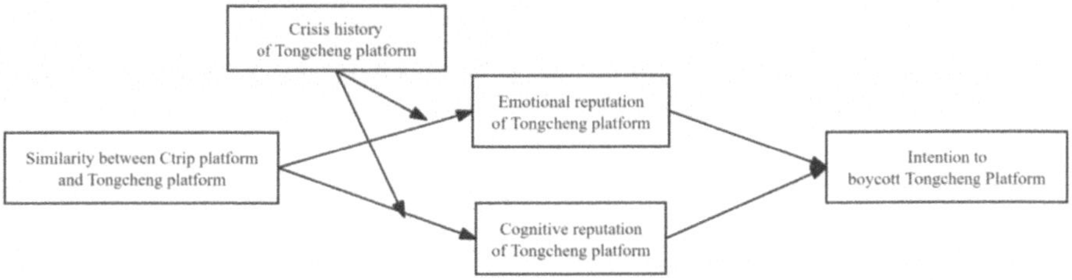

Fig. 1. Hypothetical model

4 Data Analysis and Results

4.1 Data Collection

This study focuses on travel platform users and collects the necessary data by distributing questionnaires through a combination of online and offline approaches. In total, 500 questionnaires were distributed. After careful screening to eliminate invalid ones, 382 valid questionnaires were acquired. The criteria for invalid questionnaires are as follows: choosing the same option for all questions, clearly stating that the respondent has never used any travel platform, or taking less than 120 seconds to complete the questionnaire.

The demographic and descriptive statistical information includes age, educational background, monthly income, and the frequency of travel platform usage. Among the 382 travel platform users surveyed, the age distribution is relatively diverse. Those aged 18–25 account for 25. 1%, those aged 26–35 account for 38.7%, those aged 36–45 account for 22.5%, and those over 45 account for 13.7%. In terms of the frequency of Tongcheng online travel platform usage within one year, it is classified into several categories, namely 0 times (10.8%), 1–3 times (42.6%), 3–5 times (20.4%), and more than 5 times (26.2%).

4.2 Measurement Tools

In this study, the similarity between platforms was modified based on the scale developed by Pappu and Cornwell (2014), which includes 3 items [15]. The emotional and cognitive reputation scales of the innocent platform by users adopted the scales developed by Manfred (2004), both of which contain 3 items [16]. The resistance intention of users towards the innocent platform adopted the scale developed by Li et al. (2019), which contains 4 items [17]. The scale for measuring the relationship history of the innocent platform adopted the scale developed by Eaddy (2018), which contains 4 items [14].

5 Method

The method used in this study is confirmatory factor analysis (CFA), which is used to evaluate the reliability and validity of the model (Table 1).

Table 1. KMO and Bartlett tests

KMO sampling suitability quantity		0.758
Bartlett sphericity test	Approximate chi square	421.747
	Freedom	10
	Significance	0.000

The KMO statistic value is greater than 0.5, and the Bartlett sphericity test result is less than 0.05, which is suitable for factor analysis (Table 2).

Table 2. Bootstrap analysis of the direct effects among variables

Route	Effect value	S.E.	95% confidence interval
Similarity → Intention to boycott	0.480	0.048	[0.387,0.574]
Similarity → Emotional reputation	−0.538	0.069	[−0.675, −0.402]
Emotional reputation → Intention to boycott			
Emotional reputation → Intention to boycott	−0.246	0.033	[−0.311, −0. 182]
Similarity → Cognitive reputation	−0.609	0.063	[−0.732, −0.486]
Cognitive reputation → intention to boycott	−0.249	0.037	[−0.321, −0. 177]

Note: * $P < 0.05$, ** $P < 0.01$, *** $P < 0.001$

The results show that in the path of similarity→emotional reputation→intention to boycott, the direct effect value of similarity on intention to boycott is 0.480, and the 95% confidence interval is [0.387, 0.574]. The confidence interval does not contain zero, the main effect reaches a significant level, thus supporting H1. The direct effect value of similarity on emotional reputation is −0.538, and the 95% confidence interval is [−0.675, −0.402]. As zero is excluded from the confidence interval, the negative effect is significant, thus supporting H2a. In the path of similarity→cognitive reputation→intention to boycott, the direct effect value of similarity on cognitive reputation is −0.609, and the 95% confidence interval is [−0.732, −0.486]. As zero is excluded from the confidence interval, the negative effect is significant, thus supporting H2b.

The direct effect value of emotional reputation on intention to boycott is −0.246, and the 95% confidence interval is [−0.311, −0.182]. As zero is excluded from the confidence interval, the negative effect is significant, thus supporting H3a. The direct effect value of cognitive reputation on intention to boycott is −0.249, and the 95% confidence interval is [−0.321, −0.177]. As zero is excluded from the confidence interval, the negative effect is significant, thus supporting H3b (Table 3).

The mediating effect value of similarity through emotional reputation to intention to boycott is 0.102, with a 95% confidence interval of [0.058, 0.156], which does not include zero. The mediating effect value of similarity through cognitive reputation to intention to boycott is 0.104, with a 95% confidence interval of [0.055, 0.162], which does not include zero. These results indicate that emotional reputation and cognitive reputation play a significant mediating role between similarity and intention to boycott. Therefore, hypotheses H4a and H4b are supported. The confidence interval of the difference between the two mediating effects is [−0.732, −0.486], which does not include zero, indicating that there is no significant difference between the two mediating effects.

H5a and H5b respectively assume that the crisis history of the innocent platform will positively moderate the relationship between the similarity of the innocent platform and the crisis platform and the influence of users on the emotional reputation and cognitive reputation of the innocent platform. In Table 4, the results of M3 show that the interaction

Table 3. Analysis of the Parallel Mediation Effects of Emotional Reputation and Cognitive Reputation

Route	Effect value	S.E.	95% confidence interval	Proportion of total effect
Total indirect effect	0.205	0.034	[0.143,0.277]	34%
Indirect effect 1				
Similarity → Emotional reputation → Intention to boycott	0.102	0.052	[0.058,0. 156]	17%
Indirect effect 2				
Similarity → Cognitive reputation → Intention to boycott	0.104	0.027	[0.055,0. 162]	17%
Comparing indirect effect(Ind1-Ind2)	−0.002	0.040	[−0.732, −0.486]	

Note: * P < 0.05, ** P < 0.01, *** P < 0.001

between similarity and crisis history has a significant negative impact on emotional reputation ($\beta = -0.138$, $p < 0.001$), and the results of M6 also show that the interaction between similarity and crisis history has a significant negative impact ($\beta = -0.168$, $p < 0.001$). This shows that the crisis history significantly moderates the negative impact of similarity on emotional reputation and cognitive reputation. Therefore, H5a and H5b are supported.

Table 4. Analysis Results

Variable	Emotional reputation				Cognitive reputation	
	Model 1	Model 2	Model 3	Model 4	Model 5	Model 6
Gender	0.032	0.031	0.022	0.060	0.063	0.051
Age	−0.072	−0.068	−0.059	0.035	0.022	0.034
Educational background	−0.155***	−0.153***	−0.127**	−0.184**	−0.189	−0.158
Monthly income	0.062	0.062	0.057	0.007	0.002	−0.004
Frequency of use	−0.100**	−0.099	−0.104*	−0.098**	−0.102	−0.108
Similarity	−0.369***	−0.371***	−0.375***	−0.457**	−0.447**	−0.451***
Crisis history		0.024	0.010		−0.089*	−0.106
Similarity *Crisis history			−0.138**			−0.168***
R^2	0.182	0.183	0.201	0.235	0.243	0.269
Adjusted R^2	0.169	0.168	0.184	0.223	0.228	0.254
F	4.177***	5.744***	8.378***	3.455***	3.775***	13.611***

Note: * P < 0.05, ** P < 0.01, *** P < 0.001

6 Conclusions

Based on a survey of 382 users of online travel platforms, this study reaches several significant conclusions. First, when there is similarity between the innocent platform and the crisis platform, it significantly boosts users' intention to boycott the innocent platform. This is because users tend to transfer negative information about the crisis platform to the innocent platform. Second, further analysis reveals that this intention to boycott the innocent platform stems from users' perception of the similarity between the innocent platform and the crisis platform. This perception impacts the innocent platform in two ways: emotional and cognitive reputation. The negative impact on these reputation aspects leads to users' intention to boycott. Third, the innocent platform's crisis history strengthens the impact of similarity on its emotional and cognitive reputation. If the innocent platform has experienced crises before, users more easily link past and current issues, increasing crisis-responsibility attribution. This means platforms with past similar crises face greater reputation loss and stronger users' intention to boycott.

Theoretically, this study makes several significant contributions. First, by investigating the negative impact on innocent platforms, it provides novel methods for platforms to identify and warn of potential associated risks. This enables them to detect possible crises early due to similarity with other platforms and take preventive measures. Second, it innovatively explores the influence mechanism of similarity between innocent and crisis platforms on users' intention to boycott the innocent platform. The study finds that similarity is a crucial factor in crisis spread across platforms, revealing a new cross-platform crisis spread path and offering empirical support for platform crisis communication and management theories. Third, based on situational crisis communication theory and the Accessibility-Diagnosticity theory, it constructs and verifies a theoretical model for non-crisis subjects from the micro perspective of individual users' reputation perception. This model helps understand users' behavioral intentions in crisis situations, expands the boundaries of situational crisis communication theory, and opens up new research directions.

While this study has achieved some results in exploring platform crisis impacts, it also has limitations. First, the research scope is narrow, focusing only on online travel platforms and the negative impact on a single innocent platform. This limits the universality of the results, as different platforms may face different crisis situations and user reactions. Future research could expand the sample to include more online travel platforms and platforms from other industries for more representative and universal findings. Additionally, by choosing innocent platforms within the same industry, there might be a single perspective issue. In reality, crises can affect not only within but also outside the industry. Future research could explore the negative impacts across industries to better understand the cross-industry crisis spread mechanism. For example, it could study whether a crisis in one industry's platform triggers a chain reaction in related or unrelated industry platforms and the specific paths and extent of such cross-industry impacts.

Acknowledgement. This research was supported by the Jiangsu Province Postgraduate Research Innovation Project(Y-KXW24001), Nanjing University of Finance & Economics Hongshan College Young Faculty Research Capacity Enhancement Program.

References

1. Klarin, A., Suseno, Y.: A state-of-the-art review of the sharing economy: Scientometric mapping of the scholarship. J. Bus. Res. **126**, 250–262 (2021)
2. Siebold, N., Oelrich, S., Roche, O.P.: "I am your partner, am I not?" An inquiry into stakeholder inclusion in platform organizations in times of crisis. J. Bus. Res. **160**, 113776 (2023)
3. Gu, M., et al.: Social media user behavior and emotions during crisis events. Int. J. Environ. Res. Public Health. **19**(9), 5197 (2022)
4. Coombs, W.T.: Protecting organization reputations during a crisis: the development and application of situational crisis communication theory. Corp. Reput. Rev. **10**, 163–176 (2007)
5. Hong, S., Kim, J.J., Vana, P.: When Crisis Hits the Platform Economy: The Effects on Supply, Demand, and Spillovers. Prasad, When Crisis Hits the Platform Economy: The Effects on Supply, Demand, and Spillovers (2023)
6. Coombs, W.T., Holladay, S.J.: Helping crisis managers protect reputational assets: initial tests of the situational crisis communication theory. Manag. Commun. Q. **16**(2), 165–186 (2002)
7. Meintjes, C., Botha, Y.: Rebranding as a crisis response strategy: a stakeholder perspective. Corp. Reput. Rev., 1–17 (2024)
8. Feldman, J.M., Lynch, J.G.: Self-generated validity and other effects of measurement on belief, attitude, intention, and behavior. J. Appl. Psychol. **73**(3), 421–435 (1988)
9. Zimand-Sheiner, D., Levy, S., Eckhaus, E.: Exploring negative spillover effects on stakeholders: a case study on social media talk about crisis in the food industry using data mining. Sustain. For. **13**(19), 10845 (2021)
10. Potocka-Sionek, N., Aloisi, A.: The spillover effect of algorithmic management and how (not) to tame it. In: The Elgar Co.mpanion to Regulating Platform Work, pp. 253–271. Edward Elgar Publishing (2025)
11. Yu, T., Sengul, M., Lester, R.H.: Misery loves company: the spread of negative impacts resulting from an organizational crisis. Acad. Manag. Rev. **33**(2), 452–471 (2008)
12. Janakiraman, R., Sismeiro, C., Dutta, S.: Perception spillovers across competing brands: a disaggregate model of how and when. J. Mark. Res. **46**(4), 467–481 (2009)
13. Uzunca, B., Sharapov, D., Tee, R.: Governance rigidity, industry evolution, and value capture in platform ecosystems. Res. Policy. **51**(7), 104560 (2022)
14. Eaddy, L.L.: Unearthing the facets of crisis history in crisis communication: a conceptual framework and introduction of the crisis history salience scale. Int. J. Bus. Commun. **60**(4), 1177–1196 (2023)
15. Pappu, R., Cornwell, T.B.: Corporate sponsorship as an image platform: understanding the roles of relationship fit and sponsor–sponsee similarity. J. Acad. Mark. Sci. **42**, 490–510 (2014)
16. Schwaiger, M.: Components and parameters of corporate reputation—an empirical study. Schmalenbach Bus. Rev. **56**, 46–71 (2004)
17. Li, J., et al.: An empirical study of the Volkswagen recall crisis in China: customer's risk perceptions and behavior responses based on an information flow. Hum. Ecol. Risk Assess. Int. J. **25**(6), 1488–1507 (2019)

Information Foraging Behaviors in Fitness Livestreaming on TikTok

Jing Qin and Nan Zhang(✉)

Harbin Institute of Technology, No.92, Xidazhi Street, Harbin, Heilongjiang, P.R. China
andyzhang@hit.edu.cn

Abstract. Fitness livestreaming rooms on TikTok have become a new type of gym for the public. Competition in the fitness livestreaming industry is becoming increasingly fierce. The reason why users select a certain livestreaming room remains ambiguous. Existing research has shown that information cues in live streams have a significant impact on user behavior. Users explore fitness livestreaming room on TikTok in an exploratory manner. Therefore, according to information foraging theory based on explaining exploratory search, this study constructs a model to investigate the impact of information cues in fitness livestreaming on user engagement behavior. Specifically, the study partitions live stream spaces into streamer patch and bullet comment patch. Aligning with human attention's goal-driven selectivity, the information resources in each patch are categorized as fitness-related cues, social-related cues. and repeated cues named flooding comment which are irrelevant with goals but have notable stimulus. By analyzing the streamer's conversation content, bullet comment, and real-time back-end data from one fitness livestreaming, the study estimates the research model using multivariable linear regression model. The results indicate that the fitness and social information of the streamer's conversation content, embedded in the bullet comment have positive impact on user engagement behavior, while flooding comment has a negative impact. For individuals with fitness goals, bullet comments have greater influence on user decisions than the streamer. The results of this study provide some practical inspiration for the development of fitness streamers and platforms.

Keywords: Fitness Livestreaming · Information Foraging Theory · Engagement Behavior · Video Analysis

1 Introduction

With the prevalence of livestreaming across various industries, fitness livestreaming has emerged as a new option for online fitness. According to statistics from TikTok, there were over 60,000 registered fitness streamers in 2022. Recently, fitness livestreaming covers more types, like aerobics, dance, yoga, Tai Chi. With a diverse range of options available to users, in order to enhance user retention, it is meaningful for streamers and platforms to figure out the mechanism influencing user engagement in a certain livestreaming room.

Y. P. Tu and M. Chi (Eds.): WHICEB 2025, LNBIP 549, pp. 163–174, 2025.
https://doi.org/10.1007/978-3-031-94184-9_14

Existing research in livestreaming suggests that informational cues play a significant role in influencing user engagement behaviors such as viewing, interacting, and giving rewards. Persuasive models such as the Elaboration Likelihood Model (ELM) are commonly used in e-commerce livestreaming to explore their relationship [1]. However, unlike in shopping scenarios, the ambivalence towards fitness inherent in human nature weakens the intensity of attitudes, making the relationship between attitudes and behaviors uncertain [2]. Therefore, analyzing the impact of information cues on user behavior in a fitness livestreaming context is unsuitable for employing persuasive models.

Users on TikTok discover target livestreaming rooms through exploratory search, involving browsing, evaluating, and integrating numerous information cues They ultimately conclude search and choose a particular livestreaming room. Therefore, user engagement is based on the perceived value of the information cues, aligning with their needs. Information Foraging Theory (IFT) provides a framework for the adaptive interaction between an information seeker and information provision, explaining how individuals search for information in a given environment [3]. Similar to online shopping, where consumers often lack specific shopping goals or sufficient product information before making a purchase [4]. Currently, research on the influence of information cues in fitness livestreaming based on IFT is lacking.

To fill the research gap, this study aims to address one core question: How do information cues in fitness livestreaming affect user engagement behavior?

2 Theoretical Background and Proposed Research Model

2.1 Information Foraging Theory

Information foraging theory (IFT)theorizes that individuals engage in information foraging behaviors to achieve a designated objective [3]. These behaviors include following the information scent and using a personal information diet to find the necessary information within or between information patches. Foragers assess the value of the patch based on information scent within the patch combined with their personal information diet. The perceived value influences search behavior, such as deciding whether to stay in the current patch or move on to the next one.

IFT comprises three core concepts: information patch, information scent, and information diet.

Information patch refers to a physical or conceptual space for information [5]. Each patch can contain smaller patches. For example, shopping websites contain nested yet relatively independent patches, such as shopping carts and favorites .

Information scent refers to the information cue that helps an information forager determine the potential value [5]. Information cues must be able to "capture the user's attention," which is influenced by two factors: one is the individual goal orientation. Due to the goal-driven nature of selective attention to information, individuals can be categorized as: relationship-oriented (with the primary goal of establishing and maintaining intimate relationships) and task-oriented (with the primary goal of completing a specific task) in livestreaming interaction [6]. Therefore, information cues can be divided into two types within the first category. The other category is by being a salient stimulus feature, unconstrained by goal orientation, like flooding comments [7].

Information diet refers to a strategy adopted by information foragers to select, combine, and sort target information [5].

The information foraging theory suggests that foragers assess the value of patches based on information cues. In order to maximize value, users will create their own information diets. The value of patches determines whether to continue search behavior. When users explore fitness livestreaming rooms on TikTok in an exploratory manner, they stop search upon obtaining satisfactory outcomes, demonstrated by their decision to enter a specific livestreaming room and stay in this current patch. Therefore, exploring the influence of information cues on user engagement behavior from the perspective of IFT is justified.

2.2 Research Model and Hypothesis Development

Based on information foraging theory, we propose our research model. The definitions of the three core constructs of IFT in this study are summarized in Table 1. According to the content theme, there are two information patches in the fitness livestreaming: streamer patch and bullet comment patch. In the streamer patch, due to individual goal orientation, its scent is composed of steamers' conversation contents, which are divided into fitness-related sentences and social-related sentences. In the bullet comment patch, similar to the streamer patch, its scent includes fitness-related comments, social-related comments. Additionally, it also includes repeated comments named flooding comment, which are irrelevant with individual goals but have notable stimulus. The most common flooding comment is the password to grab lucky bag. Users integrate information from both patches to assess the value of the livestreaming room, thus deciding whether to select one livestreaming room and trigger subsequent engagement behaviors such as entry and like.

Table 1. Contextualization of IFT Constructs.

IFT Construct	Contextualization in the Fitness Livestreaming Room
Information patch	Each room can be regarded as one large patch. According to the content theme, it can be divided into streamer patch for the conversation content and bullet comment patch for discussions of content
Information scent	Task-oriented users focus on fitness-related cues. Relationship-oriented users focus on social-related cues. Also, there are repeated cues named flooding comment in bullet comment patch
Information diet	The information derived from streamer patch and bullet comment patch collectively influences users' overall evaluation of the room value

In summary, the composition of information patch and information scent in fitness livestreaming room is shown in Fig. 1. The research model is depicted in Fig. 2.

Prior research has demonstrated that in the context of fitness livestreaming, high quality fitness content provided by streamers enhances user stickiness through perceived

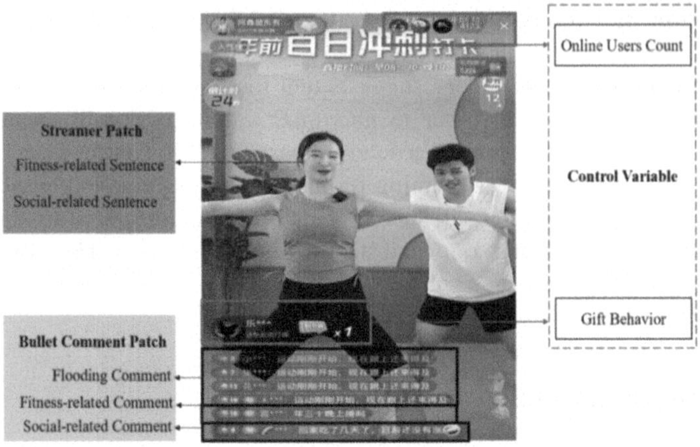

Fig. 1. Fitness Livestreaming Room Screen.

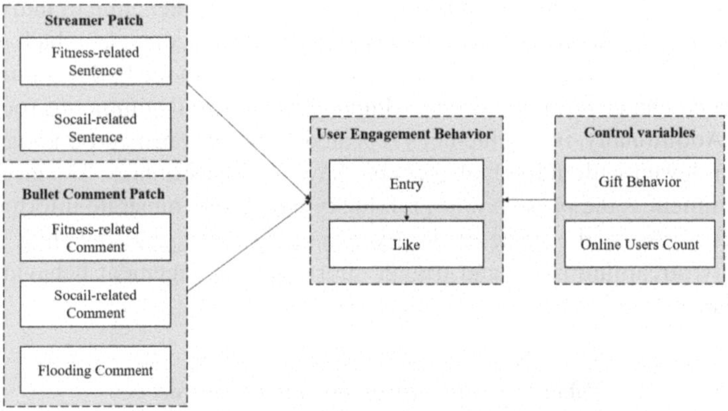

Fig. 2. Research Model.

usefulness [8]. For fitness streamer, in addition to proficient and patient exercise explanations, the emotional energy accumulated during social interactions is also a significant driver for sustained user engagement [9].

H1: In the streamer patch, fitness-related sentences positively influence user engagement behavior.
H2: In the streamer patch, social-related sentences positively influence user engagement behavior.

Existing literature on bullet comment has explored superficial features such as quantity and efficacy [10]. Regarding content, studies have focused on its relevance and reliability [11], yet discussions on its typological attributes are lacking. In e-commerce live streaming, the relevance of bullet comment content to the products can boost user purchase intention.

H3: In the bullet comment patch, fitness-related comments positively influence user engagement behavior.

Users who lack fitness experience pay more attention to the livestreaming environment in order to complete exercise target [8]. According to statistics, fitness livestreaming users are generally female with average athletic ability, and social-related comments can create relaxed and interesting atmosphere.

H4: In the bullet comment patch, social-related comments positively influence user engagement behavior.

As for the flooding comments, since human attention resources are limited, repetitive comments with same content substantially increase users' time costs in extracting useful information. As the value is the ratio of benefits to costs. Users may perceive lower value in this livestreaming room, leading to departure.

H5: In the bullet comment patch, flooding comments negatively influence user engagement behavior.

3 Research Design and Methodology

3.1 Data Collection and Preprocessing

This research focuses on the online platform TikTok as the research context, which has emerged as a hub for fitness livestreaming. This research selected a non-celebrity streamer room (TikTok ID: A Xin Aerobic Exercise) with 5.859 million followers belonging to the top-tier streamers. The dataset comprises both recorded livestreaming videos and real-time livestreaming data.

Firstly, we record a livestreaming video of this streamer lasting 4108 seconds using OBS Studio, while simultaneously collecting real-time backend data via the WebSocket protocol, including second-level bullet comment content, number of entries, number of likes, online users, and gift behaviors.

Next, we conduct data preprocessing, including cleaning, transformation, and integration. In the data cleaning stage, we eliminated time points where no bullet comment appeared. In the data transformation stage, we transcribe the streamer's conversation content into text data on a sentence basis using speech recognition technology. By measuring the streamer's speech rate and combining it with the number of words, we determine the time points for the end of each sentence. In the data integration stage, as the bullet comment data is obtained from the backend with timestamps accurate to milliseconds, we associate the streamer patch and bullet comment patch based on the bullet comment time in seconds. Considering that user feedback on the streamer requires time, when the end time of a sentence falls between two bullet comment time points, we attribute this sentence to the latter time point.

Finally, the dataset comprises backend data for 721-time points, covering 1327 streamer sentences and 2101 bullet comments.

3.2 Variables and Measures

Dependent Variables. The dependent variables are user engagement behaviors, including number of entry and number of like. About entry behavior, it serves as a representation of selecting one livestreaming room. Number of entry refers to the count of individuals entering the livestreaming room at a certain second, extracted from the backend data. About like behavior, this action occurs after users enter the livestreaming room, signifying a higher level of engagement and reflecting user's approval. Unlike other rewarding actions such as "joining the fan club" or "gift", like has no cost barrier, resulting in a larger volume of data that is beneficial for behavioral analysis. The number of like at a certain second can be scrapped from backend data.

Independent Variables. In the streamer patch, task-oriented information cues as fitness-related sentence and relationship-oriented information cues as social-related sentence are measured by the number of fitness-themed and social-themed texts at a certain second, requiring thematic analysis of text data. In the measurement of social-related comments and fitness-related comments, when conducting topic analysis on text data, the operation process is basically the same as the streamer conversation content except that the stop word dictionary need modify. The flooding comment is measured by the repetition frequency at a certain second.

During text thematic analysis, taking bullet comment text as an example, in the text preprocessing stage, after removing flooding bullet comment, we perform Jieba word segmentation and stop-word removal on the remaining data. Then, we transform text data into term frequency matrix by CountVectorizer, employ LDA model from scikit-learn to fit the data, obtain the corresponding words for each topic and transform the data to determine the topic of each bullet comment message.

We determine the optimal number of topics by calculating the perplexity of the LDA model at different numbers of topics. Through observing the perplexity curve, a turning point appeared at two topics, with a relatively gradual change in the decreasing trend from 2 to 3. Additionally, PyLDAvis visualize the results of the LDA topic model with two topics, showing evenly distributed bubbles representing the topics without overlapping (Figs. 3 and 4).

In the streamer's speech thematic analysis, the optimal number of topics output is 3, with the third category related to product sales, which is unrelated to fitness and thus categorized under social theme.

Control Variables. Online users count, serving as basic information about livestreaming, may induce herd behavior among viewers, thereby reducing their focus on the content. Furthermore, due to the TikTok platform's tendency to prioritize and recommend livestreaming with higher online count and popularity. The online users count should be included as control variable.

Additionally, in the bullet comment patch, gift behavior will suddenly appear above the text, which is very conspicuous compared to the text and may distract users from the bullet text, which should be considered as control variable. The measurement of gift behavior involves quantifying the frequency of gift occurrences at a certain second.

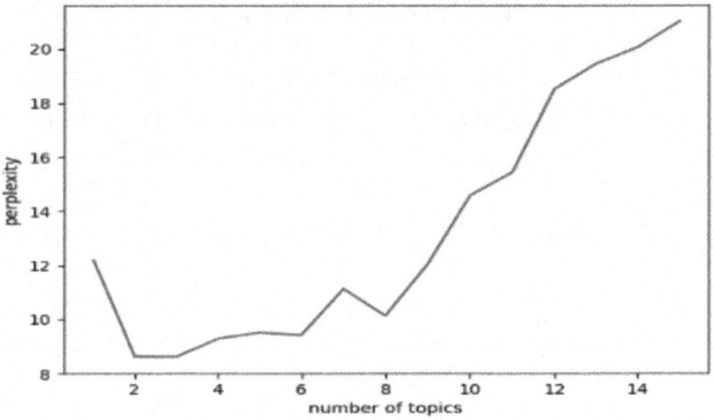

Fig. 3. Perplexity Plot.

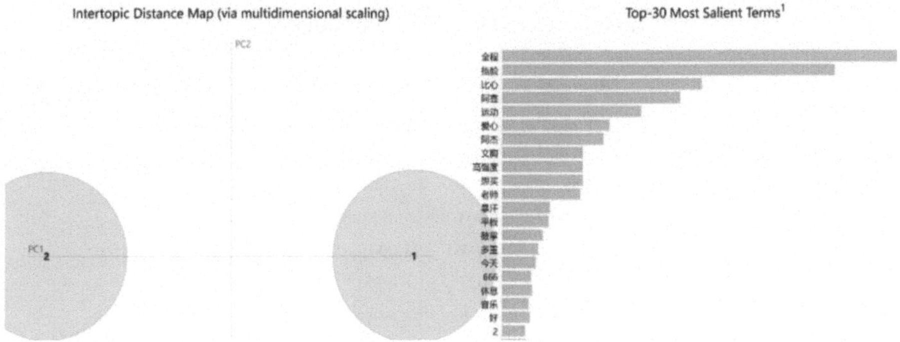

Fig. 4. Bubble Plot.

3.3 Estimation Models

Formula (1) is used to test the impact of information cues on user engagement behavior of entering livestreaming room. Formula (2) explores the further engagement behavior of like after entry.

$$\mathrm{EntryNum_i} = \beta_0 + \beta_1\mathrm{SS_{i1}} + \beta_2\mathrm{FS_{i2}} + \beta_3\mathrm{SC_{i3}} + \beta_4\mathrm{FC_{i4}} + \beta_5\mathrm{FlC_{i5}} + \beta_6\mathrm{Gift_i} + \beta_7\mathrm{Online_i} + \varepsilon_i \quad (1)$$

$$\mathrm{LikeNum_i} = \beta_0 + \beta_1\mathrm{SS_{i1}} + \beta_2\mathrm{FS_{i2}} + \beta_3\mathrm{SC_{i3}} + \beta_4\mathrm{FC_{i4}} + \beta_5\mathrm{FlC_{i5}} + \beta_6\mathrm{Gift_i} + \beta_7\mathrm{Online_i} + \beta_8\mathrm{EntryNum_{i6}} + \varepsilon_i \quad (2)$$

4 Results

4.1 Data Analysis and Results

Before the regression analysis, we perform descriptive statistics and correlation analysis. The results are presented in Tables 2 and 3, respectively. The results of multivariate regression models are reported in Table 4.

Table 2. Descriptive statistics.

Variables	Variables abbreviation	Mean	SD	Min	Max
Number of entry	EntryNum	7.50	7.29	0	44
Number of like	LikeNum	6517.52	5762.313	640	22,536
Social-related sentence	SS	0.94	1.662	0	17
Fitness-related sentence	FS	0.80	1.435	0	11
Social-related comment	SC	2.05	3.152	0	27
Fitness-related comment	FC	0.86	3.152	0	25
Flooding comment	FlC	1.11	1.847	0	23
Gift behavior	Gift	1.64	2.823	0	24
Online users count	Online	3520.05	400.917	2101	3939

Table 3. Correlation matrix of variable.

Variables	1	2	3	4	5	6	7	8	9
1	1.000								
2	0.437^{***}	1.000							
3	0.162^{***}	0.279^{***}	1.000						
4	0.253^{***}	0.196^{***}	-0.100^{**}	1.000					
5	0.078^{*}	0.037^{*}	0.075^{*}	−0.065	1.000				
6	0.096^{**}	0.270^{***}	-0.175^{***}	0.023	-0.351^{***}	1.000			
7	-0.428^{*}	-0.396^{***}	-0.318^{***}	-0.206^{*}	-0.086^{*}	0.404^{***}	1.000		
8	0.279^{***}	-0.055^{*}	-0.089^{*}	0.048	0.151^{***}	−0.030	−0.068	1.000	
9	-0.222^{***}	-0.087^{*}	-0.169^{***}	-0.088^{*}	-0.399^{***}	0.421^{***}	0.343^{***}	−0.052	1.000

Notes: 1: Number of Entry; 2: Number of Like; 3: Social-related Sentence; 4: Fitness-related Sentence; 5: Social-related Comment; 6: Fitness-related Comment; 7: Flooding Comment; 8: Gift Behavior; 9: Online Users Count. * $p < 0.05$, ** $p < 0.01$, *** $p < 0.001$

In Model 1, regarding factors influencing user choice to select and enter livestreaming room, with EntryNum as the dependent variable, the independent variables SS, FS, SC, FC, FlC, and the control variables Gift and Online are all statistically significant ($p < 0.001$). Within streamer cues, both social-related sentence ($\beta = 0.150$, $p < 0.001$) and fitness-related sentence ($\beta = 0.156$, $p < 0.001$) have positive and significant effects with similar magnitudes. This suggests that both fitness functionality and social entertainment aspects of streamer conversation content are what users consider, and their influence is comparable. Therefore, H1 and H2 are supported. Concerning bullet comments, fitness-related comment ($\beta = 0.241$, $p < 0.001$) is shown to have more positive effect compared to social-related comment ($\beta = 0.078$, $p < 0.001$). This implies that users are more inclined to seek feedback and shares about exercise from other users. Social-related comments also have positive influence ($\beta = 0.078$, $p < 0.001$). Social related

Table 4. Results of the main models' estimations.

Variables	Model 1	Model 2
	EntryNum	LikeNum
Independent variables		
SS	0.150*** (0.139)	0.165*** (6.006)
FS	0.156*** (0.163)	0.070*** (2.524)
SC	0.078* (0.072)	0.070*** (2.602)
FC	0.241*** (0.146)	0.373*** (11.041)
FIC	−0.365*** (0.158)	−0.304*** (−8.406)
Control variables		
Gift	0.299*** (0.081)	−0.175*** (−6.170)
Online	−0.134*** (0.001)	−0.178*** (−6.397)
Entrynum	–	0.409*** (12.790)
Constant	13.964*** (2.131)	12748.005*** (8.616)
Adjusted R^2	0.324	0.508
F-statistic	50.348***	93.804***
N	721	721

Notes: * $p < 0.05$, ** $p < 0.01$, *** $p < 0.001$

comments can alleviate the pain of exercise. The flooding comments have notably negative impact ($\beta = -0.365$, $p < 0.001$). Identical comments appear frequently, leading to user disengagement. Therefore, H3, H4, H5 are supported.

Within the control variables, the beta coefficient for Gift is significantly positive ($\beta = 0.299$, $p < 0.001$). Gift serves as valuable feedback for streamers, users seek references from others about the livestreaming effectiveness. Thus, gift, more than text comments, signals higher acknowledgment of room value, exerting more notable positive impact. Moreover, the negative correlation ($\beta = -0.134$, $p < 0.001$) between online user count and number of entry indicates that more viewers are leaving than entering, reflecting unsustainable user engagement in this livestreaming room.

In Model 2, with LikeNum as the dependent variable, EntryNum from Model 1 is also included as an independent variable to examine factors influencing like behavior. The standardized coefficient for EntryNum is 0.409, higher than any variable, indicating that EntryNum has significant impact on LikeNum. Other independent variables SS, FS, SC, FC, FlC, and the control variables Gift and Online still remain statistically significant ($p < 0.001$). The impact of bullet comment patch is similar to Model 1. But for the streamer, although beta coefficients of social-related sentence ($\beta = 0.373$, $p < 0.001$) and fitness-related sentence ($\beta = 0.070$, $p < 0.001$) are both positive, unlike in Model 1, where the values of the two beta coefficients were almost equivalent, social-related sentence demonstrate notably stronger impact than fitness-related sentence on like behavior. In the controlled variables, the beta coefficient for Gift shifts from positive to negative ($\beta = -0.175$, $p < 0.001$), indicating potential conflict between two behaviors occurring simultaneously.

4.2 Robustness Check

To examine the robustness of the empirical test results, we adjusted our regression model to see if our result still holds. Our dependent variables EntryNum and LikeNum are numerical variables. Therefore, we have adopted the negative binomial regression for estimation [12]. Negative binomial regression is a type of generalized linear model that is commonly used for count variables. It effectively addresses the problem of over-dispersion and bias in estimating standard errors [13]. By using negative binomial regression, we can better analyze the relationships between these variables and account for the greater variance observed in count data. The regression results are shown in Table 5 (Model 3, Model 4), which are consistent with the results using linear regression in Table 4 (Model 1, Model 2).

Table 5. Estimation results of alternative regression model.

Variables	Model 3	Model 4
	EntryNum	LikeNum
Independent variables		
SS	0.089^{***} (0.139)	0.102^{***} (0.027)
FS	0.088^{**} (0.163)	0.036^{*} (0.285)
SC	0.021^{*} (0.015)	0.029^{*} (0.013)
FC	0.092^{***} (0.028)	0.285^{***} (0.039)
FlC	-0.198^{***} (0.029)	-0.249^{***} (0.029)
Control variables		
Gift	0.081^{***} (0.015)	-0.044^{***} (0.014)
Online	-0.915^{**} (0.339)	-0.225^{*} (0.328)

(continued)

Table 5. (*continued*)

Variables	Model 3	Model 4
	EntryNum	LikeNum
Entrynum	–	0.049^{**} (0.007)
Constant	9.155^{***} (2.769)	7.796^{***} (0.397)
Log likelihood	−2133.843	−6914.823
Likelihood ratio χ^2	171.304^{***}	276.468^{***}
N	721	721

Notes: * $p < 0.05$, ** $p < 0.01$, *** $p < 0.001$

5 Discussions and Conclusions

In this study on fitness livestreaming, it was revealed that user engagement depends on the combined impact of the streamer and bullet comments, all of information cues from two categories are significant. Furthermore, apart from flooding comments which have negative influence, both fitness and social information cues are positive. For users with fitness goals select livestreaming room, the influence of other users' reaction, including fitness-related bullet comment and gifting behavior, is more effective compared to the content delivered by streamer. Therefore, for fitness streamer, it is necessary to pay attention to user exercise experience shown in the bullet comments and make prompt adjustments. Additionally, during the workout sessions, it is crucial to strike a balance between instructional rigidity and entertainment value. Not to simply explain movements and shout slogans but to blend training with enjoyment. Both aspects are equally crucial in users' decision to engage with one fitness livestreaming room.

When it comes to like behavior, it predominantly manifests among new users entering livestreaming room. Streamers may find success in prefacing like requests with a phrase of "New friends, please show your support with a like." Interestingly, social interactive words from streamer seem to receive more likes from users compared to streamer's physical exertions. Furthermore, special attention should be directed towards managing the bullet comment, particularly control the display of flooding comments, including lucky bag passwords or comment sent by livestreaming assistants aiming to create hot atmosphere. Although the repeated exposure brought by flooding comments can strengthen impression and have such brainwashing effect, the current finding suggests that they are not conducive to user engagement. When presented on the user's screen, their proportion should be restricted.

This study makes theoretical and practical contributions on fitness livestreaming. Firstly, previous studies on fitness livestreaming focus on its development status from the field of journalism and communication. There is a lack of comprehensive exploration into the impact of various types of information in fitness livestreaming. Secondly, this study takes a new perspective, applying information foraging theory to analyze the influence of information cues on user engagement in fitness livestreaming. It provides practical strategies to enhance user retention rates and offers recommendations for the platform's development. Thirdly, this study introduces a novel approach by crowling real-time backend data, speech recognition, and text recognition to measure variables, complementing traditional survey-based research methods in livestreaming studies.

The limitations of this study offer insights for future research. Further research could explore the specific mechanisms of each information cue, integrating laboratory experiments or surveys. Additionally, concerning streamers' information cues, our study solely focused on audio, neglecting visual cues such as facial expression, which is crucial and easily captured in social interaction. Subsequent research could encompass more comprehensive evaluation of information cues.

Acknowledgement. This research was supported by the National Natural Science Foundation of China [72371083, 72121001].

References

1. Luo, X., Cheah, J.H., Hollebeek, L.D.: Boosting customers' impulsive buying tendency in live-streaming commerce: the role of customer engagement and deal proneness. J. Retail. Consum. Serv. **77**, 103644 (2024)
2. Rothman, N.B., Pratt, M.G., Rees, L.: Understanding the dual nature of ambivalence: why and when ambivalence leads to good and bad outcomes. Acad. Manag. Ann. **11**(1), 33–72 (2017)
3. Pirolli, P., Card, S.: Information foraging. Psychol. Rev. **106**(4), 643–675 (1999)
4. Li, X., Hitt, L.M., Zhang, Z.J.: Product reviews and competition in markets for repeat purchase products. J. Manag. Inf. Syst. **27**(4), 9–41 (2011)
5. Li, M., Tan, C.H., Wei, K.K.: Sequentiality of product review information provision. MIS Q. **41**(3), 867–8A7 (2017)
6. Wang, X., Lin, X., Gonzales, A.: The impacts of social media on job satisfaction: task-oriented use and relationship-oriented use. Int. J. Huma. Comput. Interact. **40**(14), 3732–3747 (2024)
7. Yantis, S.: Stimulus-driven attentional capture. Curr. Dir. Psychol. Sci. **2**(5), 156–161 (1993)
8. Cheng, Y., Wu, Y.: Empirical research on the influence of " central-peripheral " dual route factors on user stickiness in fitness live streaming : based on ELM perspective. J. Capit. Inst. Phys. Educ. **35**(6), 626–638 (2023) (in Chinese)
9. Lim, J.S., Choe, M.J., Zhang, J.: The role of wishful identification, emotional engagement, and parasocial relationships in repeated viewing of live-streaming games: a social cognitive theory perspective. Comput. Hum. Behav. **108**, 106327 (2020)
10. Zhou, J., Zhou, J., Ding, Y., Wang, H.: The magic of danmaku: a social interaction perspective of gift sending on live streaming platforms. Electron. Commer. Res. Appl. **34**, 100815 (2019)
11. Zeng, Q., Guo, Q., Zhuang, W.: Do real-time reviews matter? Examining how bullet screen influences consumers' purchase intention in live streaming commerce. Inf. Syst. Front. **25**(5), 2051–2067 (2023)
12. Yang, X., Liu, Y., Dong, J., Li, S.: Impact of streamers' characteristics on sales performance of search and experience products: evidence from Douyin. J. Retail. Consum. Serv. **70**, 103155 (2023)
13. Zhuang, W., Zeng, Q., Zhang, Y., Liu, C., Fan, W.: What makes user-generated content more helpful on social media platforms? Insights from creator interactivity perspective. Inf. Process. Manag. **60**(2), 103201 (2023)

Supporting Truths and Challenging Lies: Enhancing Fake News Detection via Comment Self-Selection

Yingchao Fu, Guoyin Jiang(✉), Ruoqi Cao, and Linxin Zhu

University of Electronic Science and Technology of China, Chengdu 611731, China
jiangguoyin@uestc.edu.cn

Abstract. With the ongoing advancement of digitalization and mobile internet, the spread of fake news on social media has become increasingly pervasive. However, existing approaches often fail to effectively model the interactions between comments and multimodal tweet content, primarily focusing on single-dimensional comment filtering and neglecting other critical factors in refuting false information. In this study, we propose a multimodal comment self-selection model (CSSFND) for fake news detection. This model identifies comments that effectively support or refute the veracity of a tweet based on true and false attention scores, thereby providing valid support for true information and strong rebuttals for false claims. Unlike fake news detection methods that rely solely on pre-trained models, our approach integrates the collective intelligence of users while leveraging the internal knowledge of these models. We conduct comprehensive comparative experiments on two real-world social media datasets and validate the effectiveness of the comment self-selection module through ablation studies, achieving near state-of-the-art results on both datasets.

Keywords: Fake News Detection · Comment Self-Selection · Multimodal Learning

1 Introduction

In the digital era, social media has emerged as a primary platform for acquiring information, exchanging ideas, and expanding social networks. With billions of users sharing content, these platforms create a vast network that facilitates rapid information dissemination. However, this environment also presents opportunities for the spread of fake news. As a result, fake news detection has garnered significant attention and has become a top priority in recent years.

There has been a growing emphasis on the interpretability of detection results, particularly in studies that extract high-confidence information from claim-related textual content (e.g., articles, comments) to support judgments [1, 2]. Although these prior studies have proven relatively effective, they are primarily limited to high-confidence evidence and lack multi-dimensional perspectives necessary for supporting true information or refuting false claims. While some research has explored additional aspects of

Y. P. Tu and M. Chi (Eds.): WHICEB 2025, LNBIP 549, pp. 175–185, 2025.
https://doi.org/10.1007/978-3-031-94184-9_15

related content, such as emotional consistency [3], these efforts remain confined to single-dimensional support. Furthermore, these methods typically rely on single-modality text data, which restricts their ability to fully capture contextual information in multimodal social media environments, thereby exposing significant limitations.

To overcome the aforementioned limitations, we propose an interpretable fake news detection framework based on comment self-selection. This framework consists of two main components: (1) Comment Filtering based on true-false attention scores, which identifies the most valuable comments for judgment through multimodal interactions; and (2) Prompt-Based Integrated Inference, which utilizes the reasoning capabilities of large language models (LLMs) to automatically determine judgment-supporting dimensions for the filtered comments and generate interpretable reasoning processes for fake news detection.

Specifically, we introduce a comment self-selection module that categorizes comments into supporting and refuting groups, aiming to identify robust evidence for true information and strong counterarguments for false claims. By filtering comments using true and false attention scores, we prioritize those that are most critical for accurate classification. To enhance interpretability and explore how comments support judgment (e.g., credible evidence, emotional consistency, linguistic logic), we design a prompt-based integrated reasoning network inspired by the advanced reasoning capabilities of LLMs. This network automatically generates and refines reasoning processes for selected comments, providing clear justifications for their roles in the judgment. Furthermore, it enables the LLM to utilize its extensive internal knowledge to revise preliminary judgments and deliver final decisions.

Our contributions are summarized as follows:

First, we propose CSSFND, a multimodal fake news detection model that effectively leverages the collective intelligence of social media users alongside the extensive knowledge of LLMs.
Second, our framework avoids early-stage reliance on a single predefined dimension for comment filtering. Instead, it employs the reasoning capabilities of LLMs to retrospectively uncover the reasoning processes supported by comments, ensuring comprehensive utilization of comment information.
Third, the CSSFND achieves state-of-the-art performance on two widely used social media fake news detection datasets. Ablation experiments demonstrate the effectiveness of each module.

2 Related Works

2.1 Unimodal Fake News Detection

Fake news often exhibits linguistic inconsistencies, emotional tones, and biased stances, making linguistic features like semantics, emotion, style, and argument structure valuable for detection. For instance, Zhang et al. [3] introduced dual emotion (publisher and social emotion) and demonstrated its effectiveness, particularly through the emotion gap. Trueman et al. [4] proposed a C-BiLSTM model enhanced with an attention mechanism, which combines the strengths of CNN and BiLSTM, to capture local, global, and temporal sentence meanings. Additionally, Lee and Ram [5] developed a computational framework based on Toulmin's argumentation model to analyze claim-evidence relationships, enhancing false information detection.

In parallel, the rise of LLMs has also opened new avenues for text-based fake news detection. However, they often underperforms compared to fine-tuned small language models (SLMs) [6]. To address this, Hu et al. [6] proposed an adaptive rationale guidance network (ARG), enabling SLMs to selectively integrate LLMs' multi-perspective rationales, positioning LLMs as advisors rather than primary actors. In addition, other studies have leveraged LLMs as final integrators to enhance model interpretability [1]. However, these studies rely solely on single-modal information, overlooking cross-modal features and the inherent inter-modal correlations in raw data.

2.2 Multimodal Fake News Detection

Recently, with the improved effectiveness of cross-modal feature extraction and fusion, some methods have leveraged cross-modal interaction patterns to detect fake news, achieving remarkable performance [7, 8]. Research on multimodal fake news detection in social media has primarily focused on textual and visual information. For example, Wei et al. [9] proposed the CMC framework, which enhances the alignment and interaction between textual and visual modalities through contrastive learning. CAFE [10] utilizes attention mechanisms to dynamically fuse multi-modal features, capturing fine-grained correlations between modalities. Further advancing this field, Tong et al. [7] proposed a multi-modal, multi-domain fake news detection model that incorporates domain embeddings and attention mechanisms within a progressive hierarchical extraction network, facilitating domain-adaptive knowledge extraction. Building on these advancements, our study employs the BLIP-2 [11] model to extract and fuse multimodal features, enhancing semantic capture capabilities and further interacting with user comments for improved detection performance.

2.3 Comment Based Fake News Detection

Extracting credible evidence from comments has become an effective method for verifying fake news, focusing on aspects such as emotional consistency, logical coherence, and other relevant factors. Zhang et al. [3] proposed Dual Emotion Features, utilizing the emotion gap between publishers and audiences to verify news veracity. Wu et al. [2] developed a Decision Tree-based Co-Attention model (DTCA) to discover evidence for explainable claim verification. These approaches collectively demonstrate the value of leveraging user comments and multi-perspective evidence for fake news detection.

However, they tend to focus on extracting effective comments from a single dimension, overlooking broader factors that could support truthful news and refute fake news. Our model addresses this by calculating true and false attention scores to filter valuable comments and leveraging LLMs' prompt-based reasoning to integrate them into the reasoning process. This approach enhances interpretability by allowing the LLM to analyze comments from perspectives such as credibility, logical coherence, and emotional consistency, while facilitating the self-reinforcement of effective comments, while facilitating the self-reinforcement of effective comments.

3 Problem Statement

Each input in multimodal social media news is represented as $N = [T, I, C] \in D$, where T denotes the tweet text, $I = \{i_k\}_{i=1}^{|I|}$ represents a set of images attached to the tweet, $C = \{c_l\}_{l=1}^{|C|}$ represents a set of user comments, and D is the dataset. CSSFND aims to predict the veracity $y^* \in \{true, false\}$ of a given tweet by the interaction between C and $[T, I]$, while employing LLMs to generate a reasoning process of how comments supporting the judgement.

4 Methodology

In this section, we introduce CSSFND, a fake news detection framework that selects valuable comments through multimodal interactions between tweet content (text and images) and comments, and leverages LLMs to generate interpretable reasoning processes. The model structure is illustrated in Fig. 1, comprising three key components: a multi-view feature extraction module (§4.1), a comment self-selection module (§4.2), and a prompt-based module for generating explainable reasoning processes using large vision-language model (LVLM) and LLM (§4.3).

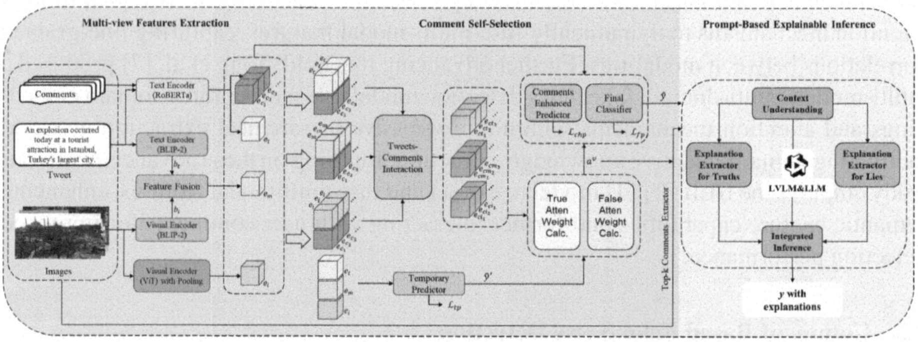

Fig. 1. An overview of the proposed comment self-selection for fake news detection (CSSFND) framework.

4.1 Multi-View Features Extraction

We use multiple pre-trained models to encode text and images separately, generating single-modal embeddings. For multimodal embeddings, we leverage BLIP-2, a pre-trained model with effective text-image interaction, to extract and fuse text and image embeddings, enabling richer multimodal representation.

Text Feature Extraction. Given a tweet T, we extract its textual representation using a pre-trained RoBERTa model [12] and an MLP, generating an aligned text embedding $e_t \in \mathbb{R}^{1 \times h}$. We also use BLIP-2's text encoder to extract an aligned vector $b_t \in \mathbb{R}^{1 \times h}$ for fusion with image features. For a comment c_l, we similarly generate an aligned embedding $e_{c_l} \in \mathbb{R}^{1 \times h}$ using RoBERTa and an MLP.

Image Feature Extraction. For the multiple images associated with a tweet, we extract features for each image using a ViT encoder [13] and an MLP, aggregating their embeddings via average pooling to obtain an overall representation $e_i \in \mathbb{R}^{1 \times h}$. We also use BLIP-2's visual encoder to obtain a matrix of aligned image features $b_i \in \mathbb{R}^{|I| \times h}$.

Multimodal Feature Extraction. To capture the true semantic relationship between a tweet and its images and understand the comprehensive semantic features, deep interaction and fusion between text and images are required. However, RoBERTa and ViT encoders, trained on different datasets, exhibit a significant cross-modal semantic gap, making their encoded vectors difficult to fuse effectively. To address this challenge, we use BLIP-2's text and image representations for fusion. BLIP-2, trained on large-scale image-text datasets with a two-stage pre-training process, bridges the modality gap and improves multimodal task performance [11]. For deep fusion, we employ multi-head cross-attention to extract image content relevant to the tweet. Formally, the multi-head attention can be formulated as:

$$Q_i = QW_i^Q, K_i = KW_i^K, V_i = VW_i^V \tag{1}$$

$$head_i = Attention(Q_i, K_i, V_i) = softmax\left(\frac{Q_i K_i^T}{\sqrt{D}}\right) V_i \tag{2}$$

$$O' = MultiHead(Q, K, V) = [head_1; head_2; \ldots; head_d] W^o \tag{3}$$

where $Q = b_m$, $K = V = b_i$ denote using the tweet vector as the query and the image matrix as the key and value. $W_i^Q \in \mathbb{R}^{h \times D}$, $W_i^K \in \mathbb{R}^{h \times D}$, $W_i^V \in \mathbb{R}^{h \times D}$ and $W^o \in \mathbb{R}^{h \times h}$ are trainable parameters, where $D = h/d$.

The outputs of the multi-head attention are then fed into a feed-forward network (FFN) to enhance the representation of nonlinear features:

$$O = FFN(O') = Activation(O' W_1 + b_1) W_2 + b_2 \tag{4}$$

where $Activation(\bullet)$ is an activation function, W_1, W_2, b_1 and b_2 are the learnable parameters.

Subsequently, the text embedding and the extracted image embedding are connected via a residual connection to obtain the multimodal feature representation e_m:

$$e_m = e_t + O \tag{5}$$

4.2 Comment Self-Selection Based on True-False Attention Scores

At this stage, our goal is to filter the most valuable comments by enabling semantic interaction between comments and the tweet representation from the initial stage. To achieve this, we propose a comment self-selection network. This network first generates a temporary prediction label $\hat{y}'$ for the tweet's veracity based on its multi-view raw representation. Then, depending on the temporary label, it automatically selects either the true attention score or the false attention score to filter comments, thereby supporting the temporary judgement.

Temporary Classification Prediction. Understanding the temporary label is essential for automatically adopting different attention scores to filter comments. We first construct a temporary prediction task, which requires judging the tweet's veracity based on multi-view representations from the initial stage. Specifically, we concatenate the three-view tweet representations and feed them into an MLP-based binary classifier:

$$\hat{y}' = softmax\Big(MLP\Big([e_t, e_m, e_i], \theta^{(p)}\Big)\Big), \mathcal{L}_{tp} = CE\big(\hat{y}', y\big) \tag{6}$$

where $\theta^{(p)} \in \mathbb{R}^{3h \times 2}$ are the learnable parameters of the MLP. y and $\hat{y}'$ the ground-truth label of the tweet's veracity and its predicted label, respectively. The loss $\mathcal{L}_{tp}$ is a cross-entropy loss: $CE\big(\hat{y}', y\big) = -ylog\hat{y}' - (1-y)\log\big(1-\hat{y}'\big)$.

Tweets-Comments Interaction. Before calculating the true/false attention scores, semantic interaction between multi-view tweet representations and comment representations is required to ensure the model fully captures tweet-comment relationships. We first use dot product similarity to evaluate the relevance between them. Negative dot products indicate opposite semantics between tweets and comments, yet still highlight the importance of such comments. Therefore, we take the absolute value of the dot product results. Finally, we compute the attention weights for each comment relative to the multi-view tweet representations, reflecting their importance in supporting or refuting the tweet's veracity:We then fuse multi-view tweet and comment representations using an MLP, and weight the results using the relevance weights, thereby obtaining tweet representations enriched with comment information:where $\theta^{(ct)}$, $\theta^{(cm)}$, $\theta^{(ci)} \in \mathbb{R}^{2h \times h}$ are the learnable parameters of these MLPs.

Calculation of True and False Attention Weights. Based on the temporary prediction, the model uses true attention scores to filter supporting comments if the tweet is judged as true, or false attention scores to filter refuting comments if the tweet is judged as false. Specifically, the multi-view representations fused with comment information are input to an MLP-based module to compute attention scores and normalize them to obtain true and false attention weights:

$$a^{v} = softmax\Big(\Big[MLP\Big(\Big[e_{ct}^{(l)}, e_{cm}^{(l)}, e_{ci}^{(l)}\Big], \theta^{(v)}\Big)\Big]_{l=1}^{|C|}\Big) \tag{13}$$

where $v \in \{-, +\}$ depends on the result of the temporary prediction. a^{-} and a^{+} denote the false and true weights, respectively, while θ^{-} and $\theta^{+} \in \mathbb{R}^{3h \times 1}$ represent the learnable parameters for computing the true and false attention scores, respectively.

Prediction. The primary goal of this module is to rank and filter comments with significant value for supporting the temporary judgement using true and false attention weights. We fuse the tweet representation with weighted comment representations and predict based on the temporary label, ensuring the selected comments maximally support the judgement. Formally, the prediction process can be formulated as:

$$e_{wct} = MLP\Big([e_t, e_c], \theta^{(wct)}\Big) \tag{15}$$

$$e_{wcm} = MLP\Big([e_m, e_c], \theta^{(wcm)}\Big) \tag{16}$$

$$e_{wci} = MLP\Big([e_i, e_c], \theta^{(wci)}\Big) \tag{17}$$

$$\hat{u} = softmax\Big(MLP\Big([e_{wct}, e_{wcm}, e_{wci}], \theta^{(p)}\Big)\Big), \mathcal{L}_{chp} = CE\big(\hat{u}, \hat{y}'\big) \tag{18}$$

where e_c is the comment representation weighted by the true/false attention weights, while e_{wct}, e_{wcm} and e_{wci} are vectors from fusing comments with textual, cross-modal, and image-based tweet representations. The parameters $\theta^{(wct)}$, $\theta^{(wcm)}$ and $\theta^{(wci)}$ are learnable. This predictor shares the same parameters with the temporary prediction module, indicating that the selected comments reinforce the temporary judgement based on the original tweet representations.

Finally, the fusion vectors e_{wct}, e_{wcm} and e_{wci} are also utilized to predict the tweets' veracity for the final judgement:

$$\hat{y} = softmax\Big(MLP\Big([e_{wct}, e_{wcm}, e_{wci}], \theta^{(fp)}\Big)\Big), \mathcal{L}_{fp} = CE(\hat{y}, y) \tag{19}$$

The total loss function is the weighted sum of the loss terms mentioned above:

$$\mathcal{L} = \mathcal{L}_{fp} + \beta_1 \mathcal{L}_{tp} + (1 - \beta_1)\mathcal{L}_{chp} \tag{20}$$

where β_1 is a hyperparameter. Note that the comment self-selection module adaptively focuses the final judgement on samples where the temporary judgement is incorrect. Specifically, if the temporary judgement is wrong, it filters comments to reinforce this error, which will increase the loss of the final judgement.

4.3 Prompt-Based Explainable Inference

To explore how the selected comments support the judgement, we designed an expert network based on LVLM and LLM. Leveraging the powerful image understanding capabilities of LVLM and the reasoning capabilities of LLM, this network integrates comments to provide an interpretable reasoning process and the final judgement.

Evidence Extraction and Integrated Inference. The network first uses an LVLM-based image understanding expert to identify tweet-image relationships and generate image descriptions. Based on the prior prediction $\hat{y}$, it selects an LLM-based supportive or refuting reasoning expert to explain why comments support or refute the tweet from multiple perspectives. The LLMs are prompted to comprehensively evaluate comment-tweet relationships. Finally, the tweet, image descriptions, reasoning processes, and prior predictions are sent to the judgement expert. To effectively leverage the vast internal knowledge of LLMs and avoid incorrect self-reinforcement, we prompt the judgement expert to reflect on these inputs and making a comprehensive judgement.[1]

[1] Because of space limitations, the prompts and the work flow for LVLM and LLM are available upon request from the authors.

5 Experiments

5.1 Experimental Settings

Datasets. Our model is evaluated on two fake news detection datasets: Weibo [14] and Weibo-21 [15]. The Weibo dataset contains 9,528 multimodal tweets collected from the Weibo platform between May 2012 and January 2016. It includes true news from authoritative sources (e.g., Xinhua News Agency) and false news verified by Weibo's rumor debunking system. We adopt the same data partitioning method as [16] to obtain the training, validation and testing sets. To ensure dataset quality, we follow the preprocessing steps from previous studies [14, 16], first removing duplicates (using locality-sensitive hashing) and low-quality images, then extracting tweets related to emerging events using single-pass clustering. Additionally, the dataset was expanded to include comments for each tweet. Weibo-21 is a more recent dataset containing 9,128 tweets collected from Sina Weibo between December 2014 and March 2021. We partition this dataset following the methods used in [15], and preprocess the data using the same steps as in [7].

Baseline. To conduct a comprehensive evaluation of our proposed model, we compare it with several multimodal fake news detection approaches.

EANN [16]: A multimodal fake news detection model based on generative adversarial networks (GANs), capable of learning event-invariant representations, making it suitable for newly emerging and time-sensitive events.
SpotFake [17]: Utilizes a pre-trained BERT model for text and the VGG-19 model for images to extract and fuse multimodal features for fake news detection.
CAFE [10]: Adaptively aggregates unimodal features and cross-modal correlations through cross-modal ambiguity learning.
CMC [9]: Improves fake news detection by capturing cross-modal feature correlations through cross-modal distillation.
BMR [8]: A multimodal fake news detection method that employs an improved Multi-gate Mixture-of-Experts network (iMMoE) to aggregate multi-view features while ensuring cross-modal consistency through weighted integration.
MMDFND [7]: Integrates domain embeddings and attention mechanisms into a Progressive Layered Extraction network for multi-domain multimodal fake news detection, enabling adaptive extraction of domain-specific knowledge.

Implementation Details. In the text encoding section, the maximum input length for text is set to 320 tokens. Textual data is encoded using RoBERT-base and BLIP-2 models. For the image encoding part, the input images are resized to 224×224 pixels and encoded using pre-trained ViT and BLIP-2 models, respectively. The top-k filtered comments are limited to a maximum number of 5. As for the LVLM and LLM in §4.3, Qwen2-VL and Qwen-Max are utilized, respectively. The evaluation metrics for the models include Accuracy, Precision, Recall, and F1 Score. The experiments are conducted with a batch size of 32, employing the Adam optimizer, where the learning rate is set to 5e-5 with linear warmup. The models are trained over 50 epochs with early stopping implemented to prevent overfitting.

5.2 Overall Performance

The comparison results between CSSFND and various baseline multimodal fake news detection methods are shown in Table 1. The results indicate that CSSFND achieves performance comparable to the current state-of-the-art (SOTA) models on the Weibo dataset and significantly outperforms all baseline methods on the Weibo-21 dataset. The improved performance stems from: (1) CSSFND leverages user comments to provide additional knowledge, which helps support or refute the veracity of tweets. (2) From an optimization perspective, CSSFND adaptively increases attention to misjudged samples, enabling the learning of deeper patterns. (3) CSSFND achieves semantically consistent multimodal feature fusion through the BLIP-2 encoder. (4) By leveraging the reasoning capabilities of LLMs, CSSFND provides explanations for post-filtered comments, avoiding information loss caused by pre-filtering comments.

Table 1. Comparison between CSSFND and the latest multimodal methods.

Datasets	Methods	Accuracy	Fake			Real		
			Precision	Recall	F1 score	Precision	Recall	F1 score
Weibo	EANN	0.827	0.847	0.812	0.829	0.807	0.843	0.825
	SpotFake	0.892	0.902	0.964	0.932	0.847	0.656	0.739
	CAFE	0.840	0.855	0.83	0.842	0.825	0.851	0.837
	CMC	0.893	0.940	0.869	0.899	0.876	0.945	0.907
	BMR	0.918	0.882	**0.948**	0.914	**0.942**	0.870	0.904
	MMDFND	**0.934**	–	–	**0.936**	–	–	**0.932**
	CSSFND	0.927	**0.948**	0.909	0.928	0.907	**94.64**	0.926
Weibo21	EANN	0.870	0.902	0.825	0.862	0.841	0.912	0.875
	SpotFake	0.851	0.953	0.733	0.828	0.786	0.964	0.866
	CAFE	0.882	0.857	0.915	0.885	0.907	0.844	0.876
	CMC	0.897	–	–	0.903	–	–	0.912
	BMR	0.929	0.908	0.947	0.927	0.946	0.906	0.925
	MMDFND	0.939	–	–	0.940	–	–	0.939
	CSSFND	**0.991**	**0.993**	**0.988**	**0.991**	**0.989**	**0.994**	**0.991**

5.3 Ablation Studies

We evaluate each CSSFND component by removing them individually: (1) **w/o MFE**: Remove the multi-view feature extraction module, using only plain text for feature extraction. (2) **w/o CSS**: Remove the comment self-selection module, relying solely on tweet information for judgement. (3) **w/o PEI**: Remove the prompt-based explainable inference module. Ablation results (Table 2) show that CSSFND performs poorly with a single modality, highlighting the importance of multimodal fusion and comment interaction. Performance also degrades without comments, proving their effectiveness in enhancing judgement.

Table 2. Ablation study on the network design of CSSFND.

Datasets	Methods	Accuracy	F1 score	
			Fake News	Real News
Weibo	**CSSFND**	**0.927**	**0.928**	**0.926**
	-w/o MFE	0.897	0.902	0.892
	-w/o CSS	0.919	0.921	0.918
	-w/o PEI	0.924	0.925	0.923
Weibo21	**CSSFND**	**0.991**	**0.991**	**0.991**
	-w/o MFE	0.987	0.988	0.987
	-w/o CSS	0.911	0.901	0.919
	-w/o PEI	0.990	0.990	0.991

6 Conclusion

We propose CSSFND, an interpretable fake news detection framework based on comment self-selection. CSSFND integrates user comments and LLMs' reasoning capabilities to combine external and internal knowledge for multimodal detection. It filters valuable comments via true and false attention scores and achieves interpretability through an LLM network. Experiments on two widely used social media datasets demonstrate that CSSFND achieves near state-of-the-art performance. Ablation studies further validate the effectiveness of each module.

Acknowledgement. This work was partially supported by the National Social Science Foundation of China [grant number: 22&ZD128], the National Natural Science Foundation of China [grant number: 72071031], the Sichuan Philosophy and Social Science Key Research Base [grant number: SC23DCMB017], and the National Natural Science Foundation of Sichuan [grant number: 2024NSFSC0265].

References

1. Wang, B., et al.: Explainable fake news detection with large language model via defense among competing wisdom. In: Proceedings of the ACM Web Conference 2024, pp. 2452–2463. Association for Computing Machinery, Singapore (2024)

2. Wu, L., Yuan, R., Zhao, Y., Liang, H., Nazir, A.: DTCA: Decision tree-based co-attention networks for explainable claim verification. In: Proceedings of the 58th Annual Meeting of the Association for Computational Linguistics, pp. 1024–1035. Association for Computational Linguistics (2020)
3. Zhang, X., Cao, J., Li, X., Sheng, Q., Zhong, L., Shu, K.: Mining dual emotion for fake news detection. In: Proceedings of the Web Conference 2021, pp. 3465–3476. Association for Computing Machinery, Ljubljana (2021)
4. Trueman, T.E., et al.: Attention-based C-BiLSTM for fake news detection. Appl. Soft Comput. **110**, 107600 (2021)
5. Lee, K., Ram, S.: Explainable deep learning for false information identification: an argumentation theory approach. Inf. Syst. Res. **35**(2), 890–907 (2023)
6. Hu, B., et al.: Bad actor, good advisor: Exploring the role of large language models in fake news detection. In: Proceedings of the AAAI Conference on Artificial Intelligence, pp. 22105–22113. AAAI Press, Vancouver (2024)
7. Tong, Y., Lu, W., Zhao, Z., Lai, S., Shi, T.: MMDFND: Multi-modal multi-domain fake news detection. In: Proceedings of the 32nd ACM International Conference on Multimedia, pp. 1178–1186. Association for Computing Machinery, Melbourne, VIC (2024)
8. Ying, Q., Hu, X., Zhou, Y., Qian, Z., Zeng, D., Ge, S.: Bootstrapping multi-view representations for fake news detection. In: Proceedings of the AAAI Conference on Artificial Intelligence, pp. 5384–5392. AAAI Press, Washington, DC (2023)
9. Wei, Z., Pan, H., Qiao, L., Niu, X., Dong, P., Li, D.: Cross-modal knowledge distillation in multi-modal fake news detection. In: ICASSP 2022–2022 IEEE International Conference on Acoustics, Speech and Signal Processing (ICASSP), pp. 4733–4737, Singapore (2022)
10. Chen, Y., et al.: Cross-modal ambiguity learning for multimodal fake news detection. In: WWW '22: Proceedings of the ACM Web Conference 2022, pp. 2897–2905. Association for Computing Machinery, Virtual Event (2022)
11. Li, J., Li, D., Savarese, S., Hoi, S.: BLIP-2: Bootstrapping language-image pre-training with frozen image encoders and large language models. In: Proceedings of the 40th International Conference on Machine Learning, pp. 19730–19742. JMLR.org, Honolulu (2023)
12. Liu, Y., et al.: RoBERTa: a robustly optimized BERT pretraining approach. arXiv, (2019)
13. Dosovitskiy, A., et al.: An image is worth 16x16 words: Transformers for image recognition at scale. In: ICLR 2021 The Ninth International Conference on Learning Representations. Virtual Only Conference (2021)
14. Jin, Z., Cao, J., Guo, H., Zhang, Y., Luo, J.: Multimodal fusion with recurrent neural networks for rumor detection on microblogs. In: Proceedings of the 25th ACM international conference on Multimedia, pp. 795–816. Association for Computing Machinery, Mountain View, CA (2017)
15. Nan, Q., Cao, J., Zhu, Y., Wang, Y., Li, J.: MDFEND: Multi-domain fake news detection. In: Proceedings of the 30th ACM International Conference on Information & Knowledge Management, pp. 3343–3347. Association for Computing Machinery, Virtual Event, QLD (2021)
16. Wang, Y., et al.: EANN: Event adversarial neural networks for multi-modal fake news detection. In: Proceedings of the 24th ACM SIGKDD International Conference on Knowledge Discovery & Data Mining, pp. 849–857. Association for Computing Machinery, London (2018)
17. Singhal, S., Shah, R.R., Chakraborty, T., Kumaraguru, P., Satoh, S.: SpotFake: A multi-modal framework for fake news detection. In: 2019 IEEE Fifth International Conference on Multimedia Big Data (BigMM), pp. 39–47. IEEE, Singapore (2019)

A Study of Factors Influencing Users' Continuance Intention of Digital Platform

Jin Li, Yan Chen, Xiao Ren Mei(✉), and Qing Xia(✉)

School of Management, Guangdong University of Education, Guangzhou, Guangdong, China
411522102@qq.com, 93117109@qq.com

Abstract. Studying the factors affecting users' continuance intention on Meituan Youxuan platform is of vital importance to Meituan Youxuan platform operators, which helps to accurately grasp users' behavior. Based on the Information System Continuous Use Model (ECM-ISC), this paper incorporates the two factors of trust and habit into the model to deeply explore their impact on users' continuance intention. SPSS 26 and Amos 24 were used to conduct an empirical study on 220 valid questionnaires. The results show that: (1) expectation confirmation, perceived usefulness and trust have a significant positive impact on user satisfaction; (2) perceived usefulness, satisfaction, trust and habits all have a significant positive effect on users' Continuance Intention. Based on this, according to the five aspects of expectation confirmation, perceived usefulness, satisfaction, trust and habits, specific suggestions are put forward for Meituan Youxuan platform operators to further enhance user loyalty.

Keywords: Digital Platform · ECM-ISC model · Continuance Intention

1 Introduction

Community group buying has been developed since 2014. After a long period of development, it has become one of the important ways for residents to purchase daily necessities. With the increasing diversification of residents' needs, if the Meituan Youxuan platform operator wants to continue to obtain the dividends of the community group buying track, it still depends on the continuous use and loyalty of users.

This paper systematically combine the relevant research on the influencing factors of the continuance intention of community group buying users using the psychological model. On the ECM-ISC model, trust and usage habits are added. From the perspective of users, a theoretical model for studying the continuance intention of users of the Meituan Youxuan e-commerce platform is constructed, and the model is tested through empirical analysis.

Y. P. Tu and M. Chi (Eds.): WHICEB 2025, LNBIP 549, pp. 187–198, 2025.
https://doi.org/10.1007/978-3-031-94184-9_16

2 Literature Review

2.1 Continuance Intention (CI)

The concept of "continuance intention" was originated from the discussion of behavioral intention and was later cited in the field of information system research. Bhattacherjee first defined it, pointing out that "continuance intention" refers to the personal willingness of users to continue using the information system in the future after experiencing it [1]. This paper defines the continuance intention as the subjective tendency and willingness of users to continue to choose the Meituan Youxuan platform after using it for the first time.

2.2 Expectation Confirmation (EC)

Expectation confirmation comes from the Expectation Confirmation Theory (ECT), which was first proposed by Oliver in 1980 and used to study consumer behavior. In this theory, expectation confirmation is defined as the difference between the expected performance generated by consumers before using a product or service and the perceived performance after using [2]. In 2001, Bhattacherjee described expectation confirmation as the degree to which users compare their expectations before use with the feelings they actually get from use [1]. Based on the conceptual definitions of the two scholars, this paper defines expectation confirmation as the gap between users' expectations of using the Meituan Youxuan platform and their actual experience after using the Meituan Youxuan platform for community group buying.

2.3 Perceived Usefulness (PU)

Perceived usefulness comes from the Technology Acceptance Model (TAM), which was first proposed by Davis et al. in 1989. It refers to the degree to which a person believes that using a particular system will improve his or her work performance [3]. Based on this, this paper defines perceived usefulness as the degree to which users can feel that their life and shopping efficiency has improved after using the digital platform like Meituan.

2.4 Satisfaction (CS)

Xiao Xue et al. pointed out that satisfaction is a positive or negative emotional response of users to a product or service [4]. Li Qingwei et al. defined user satisfaction as an emotional state generated after a user uses a platform after a short or long-term experience [5]. Based on this, satisfaction in this paper refers to an emotional state generated after the users utilize the Meituan Youxuan platform after a short or long-term experience.

2.5 Trust (TR)

Trust was first proposed by Moorman et al. in 1992 and is defined as an individual's willingness to trust and rely on a trading partner [6]. In 2004, Pavlou et al. proposed that trust is the degree to which users can rely on a platform after a transaction because it can meet their needs [7]. Based on this, trust is defined in this article as the degree to which users believe that the Meituan Youxuan platform can meet their needs and generate dependence after using the Meituan Youxuan platform.

2.6 Habit (HA)

Habit Theory is originated from the field of psychology. It was proposed by James in the 1990s and defined as the spontaneous psychological activity of an individual based on past behavioral experience [8]. In 2007, in the context of studying information systems, Limayem believed that habit refers to the degree to which people actively use information systems after learning [9]. Based on this, this article defines habit as the automatic and unconscious behavior of users continuing to use the Meituan Youxuan platform in a certain specific situation through continuous learning.

2.7 Hypothesis

When exploring the willingness of users of academic WeChat public accounts to continue using, Tan Chunhui et al. concluded that expected confirmation has a significant positive effect on perceived usefulness [10]. Based on this, the following hypothesis is proposed:

H1: Expected confirmation positively affects users' perceived usefulness of the Meituan Youxuan platform.

Jin Xin et al. conducted an empirical analysis on the factors affecting the continuance intention of users of knowledge payment platforms and found that expected confirmation significantly affects user satisfaction [11]. Based on this, the following hypothesis is proposed:

H2: Expected confirmation positively affects users' satisfaction with the Meituan Youxuan platform.

Zhang Piaoxin et al. combined the ECM and ISSM models to study the willingness to continue using social software, and found through empirical evidence that perceived usefulness has a positive impact on satisfaction [12]. Based on this, the following hypothesis is proposed:

H3: Perceived usefulness has a positive impact on user satisfaction with the Meituan Youxuan platform.

Song Huiling et al. found in an empirical study on the willingness of users to continue using knowledge question and answer communities that perceived usefulness directly and significantly positively affects users' willingness to continue using [13]. Based on this, the following hypothesis is proposed:

H4: Perceived usefulness positively affects users' willingness to continue using the Meituan Youxuan platform.

Luo Mengli et al. found through empirical analysis that satisfaction has a significant positive impact on users' willingness to continue using science-based WeChat public accounts in their study of users' willingness to continue using them [14]. Based on this, the following hypothesis is proposed:

H5: Satisfaction positively affects users' willingness to continue using the Meituan Youxuan platform.

Lin Yanru et al. found through a study of factors affecting knowledge user satisfaction based on ECT theory that trust positively affects knowledge-based paid users' satisfaction [15]. Based on this, the following hypothesis is proposed:

H6: Trust has a positive impact on user satisfaction with the Meituan Youxuan platform.

Huang Sihao et al. studied the continued purchase intention of consumers on social e-commerce platforms and found that trust has a positive impact on users' continued purchase intention [16].

H7: Trust has a positive impact on users' continuance intention of the Meituan Youxuan platform.

Gefen et al. introduced the variable of habit into the TAM model by studying the repeated behavior of users on the same shopping website. Through empirical analysis, it was found that continuance intention is also affected by habit [17]. Based on this, the following hypothesis is proposed:

H8: Habits positively affect users' continuance intention of the Meituan Youxuan platform.

2.8 Theoretical Model

In 2001, Bhattacherjee combined the Technology Acceptance Model (TAM) and the Expectation Confirmation Theory (ECT) when studying the electronic banking system, and first proposed the Expectation-Confirmation Model of IS Continuance (ECM-ISC). Bhattacherjee believes that when users use information systems, they not only rely on the results after one use, but also the satisfaction formed after the first use, which leads to the users' continued use.

After the model was proposed, many scholars have widely covered it in various fields of research. Usually, considering the diversity of research objects, the ECM-ISC model will be expanded to a certain extent and other variables will be introduced. In this research, we add trust and two habit indicators to the model to monitor the user behavior multidimensionally. Based on the above research hypotheses, the research model of this paper is proposed, as shown in Fig. 1.

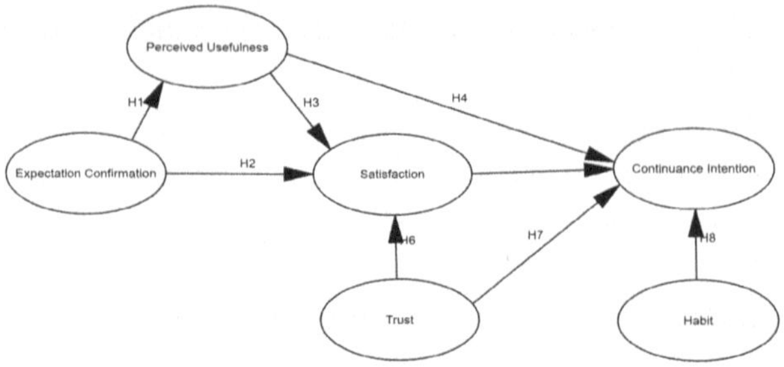

Fig. 1. Theoretical model of continuance intention of Meituan's preferred platform

3 Methodology

3.1 Questionnaire Design

The scale of this paper is determined by reasonable adjustment and optimization based on the mature scales of various variables of previous scholars and the characteristics of the Meituan Youxuan platform. The questionnaire mainly includes variables of influencing factors and continuance intention variables. The variables of influencing factor include perceived usefulness, expectation confirmation, satisfaction, trust and usage habits. Each variable is measured using the Likert five-level scale. The items of perceived usefulness and their theoretical sources mainly refer to the four-item scale developed by Davis [4], the items of expectation confirmation and their theoretical sources mainly refer to the scale of Bhattacherjee, the items of satisfaction and their theoretical sources mainly refer to the scales of Bhattacherjee, Oliver [2] and Qin Suxiang et al. [18], the items of trust and their theoretical sources mainly refer to the scales of Lee et al. [19] and Pan Lan et al. [20], the items of usage habits and their theoretical sources mainly refer to the scales of Landis et al. [21] and Deng Wenjuan et al. [22], and the items of continuance intention and their theoretical sources mainly refer to the scale of Bhattacherjee.

3.2 Questionnaire Distribution, Collection, and Data Analysis

The data were collected mainly from users who had used the Meituan Youxuan platform. This paper mainly created the questionnaire on the Wenjuanxing website and sent it to WeChat Moments, various WeChat groups of community group buying, QQ groups, Weibo, Xiaohongshu and other social software, and asked users who had used the Meituan Youxuan platform to forward it. This survey collected 250 questionnaires. After eliminating invalid questionnaires, 220 valid questionnaires were retained, with an efficiency of 88%.

4 Results

4.1 Reliability and Validity Testing

This paper uses confirmatory factor analysis to test the scale reliability and validity. Cronbach's α coefficient and combined reliability (C.R.) are used to test the scale reliability, and convergent validity (AVE) and discriminant validity are used to test the scale validity.

When α is greater than 0.7, the reliability of the scale is good. The Cronbach's α coefficients of perceived usefulness, expectation confirmation, satisfaction, trust, usage habits and continuance intention in this article are 0.91, 0.773, 0.892, 0.863, 0.843 and 0.907, respectively, all greater than 0.7, indicating that the sample data has good reliability. AMOS software was used for analysis. Only two indicators in the table had factor loading coefficients slightly less than 0.7, while the others all met the requirement of factor loading coefficients greater than 0.7. The combined reliability (CR) was between 0.70 and 0.92, both reaching the minimum standard of 0.7. The average variance extracted (AVE value) was greater than 0.5, indicating that each dimension in the model in this paper had good convergent validity (Table 1).

Table 1. Reliability and Validity Test

Variable	Question	Unstandardized coefficient	Standard error	Z-Value	P-Value	Standardized coefficient	Cronbach's α	CR	AVE
Perceived usefulness	PU1	1				0.778	0.91	0.913	0.725
	PU2	1.138	0.078	14.539	***	0.88			
	PU3	1.055	0.082	12.907	***	0.801			
	PU4	1.239	0.079	15.598	***	0.938			
Expectation confirmation	EC1	1				0.696	0.773	0.785	0.554
	EC2	1.068	0.128	8.334	***	0.645			
	EC3	1.306	0.141	9.288	***	0.872			
Satisfaction	CS1	1				0.845	0.892	0.893	0.735
	CS2	0.968	0.064	15.14	***	0.859			
	CS3	0.994	0.065	15.308	***	0.868			
Trust	TR1	1				0.766	0.863	0.866	0.685
	TR2	1.091	0.088	12.379	***	0.831			
	TR3	1.104	0.086	12.854	***	0.881			
Habit	HABIT1	1				0.811	0.843	0.849	0.654
	HABIT2	0.875	0.08	10.984	***	0.715			
	HABIT3	1.063	0.082	12.975	***	0.891			
Continuance intention	CI1	1				0.891	0.907	0.908	0.767
	CI2	0.984	0.06	16.265	***	0.838			
	CI3	1.009	0.056	18.002	***	0.897			

Table 2 is a discriminant validity table. The correlation coefficients between each variable and other variable in this paper are all less than the square root of AVE, indicating that the dimensions in this model have good discriminant validity, and the measurement indicators can reflect the differences between the latent variables. Therefore, the measurement model has discriminant validity.

Table 2. Discriminant Validity Test

Variable	Continuance Intention	Habit	Trust	Satisfaction	Expectation Confirmation	Perceived Usefulness
Continuance intention(CI)	**0.876**					
Habit(HA)	0.417	**0.809**				
Trust(TR)	0.478	0.478	**0.828**			
Satisfaction(SA)	0.488	0.428	0.513	**0.857**		
Expectation confirmation(EC)	0.462	0.325	0.369	0.44	**0.744**	
Perceived usefulness(PU)	0.448	0.409	0.462	0.542	0.394	**0.851**

4.2 Model Fit Test of the Research Model

Model fit refers to the degree of consistency between the constructed theoretical model and the sample model. This paper uses the maximum likelihood method in AMOS software to estimate the parameters of the structural equation model. The obtained fit indexes are shown in Table 3. According to Bentler's evaluation criteria, $\chi 2/df = 1.203$, less than 3; RMSEA is 0.03, less than 0.080; GFI, AGFI, IFI, CFI and TLI are all greater than 0.900. All datas show that the research model has a good fit.

Table 3. Model fitting test

Fit index	$\chi 2$ /df	SRMR	RMSEA	GFI	AGFI	IFI	CFI
Reference value	<3.000	<0.080	>0.900	>0.900	>0.900	>0.900	>0.900
Test value	1.203	0.03	0.927	0.901	0.989	0.989	0.986

4.3 Hypothesis Testing

The hypothesized paths were tested using AMOS software, as shown in Table 4. At the significance level of path coefficient $P < 0.05$, the constructed paths all passed the significance test. This paper proposes a total of 8 hypotheses, H1, H2, H3, H4, H5, H6, H7, and H8 are established.

Table 4. Model Path Test Results

Hypothesis	Path	Unstandardized coefficient	Standard error	Z value	P value	Standardized coefficient	Result
H1	EC → PU	0.533	0.099	5.378	***	0.441	Supported
H2	EC → SA	0.264	0.102	2.574	0.01	0.22	Supported
H3	PU → SA	0.329	0.073	4.493	***	0.331	Supported
H4	PU → CI	0.197	0.081	2.443	0.015	0.182	Supported
H5	CS → CI	0.246	0.093	2.644	0.008	0.226	Supported
H6	TR → SA	0.286	0.072	3.956	***	0.294	Supported
H7	TR → CI	0.234	0.09	2.593	0.01	0.221	Supported
H8	HA → CI	0.167	0.081	2.062	0.039	0.16	Supported

4.4 Mediation Effect Test

This paper uses the Bootstrap method to test the mediating effect of perceived usefulness between expectation confirmation and satisfaction. The Bootstrap sample size is set to 1000, and the confidence level is set to 95%. When the upper and lower limits of the bias-corrected and percentile indicators do not contain 0, it is considered that the mediating effect exists at the 95% confidence level. The results of the mediating effect analysis of perceived usefulness between expectation confirmation and satisfaction are shown in Table 5. At the 95% confidence level, perceived usefulness has a mediating effect between expectation confirmation and satisfaction.

Table 5. Mediation Effect Test

Path	Point estimation	Standard Error	Z Value	Bootstrapping,1000 times,95% CI			
				Bias-corrected	Percentile		
				Lower	Upper	Lower	Upper
Indirect effect							
EC → PU → SA	0.216	0.063	3.429	0.118	0.39	0.11	0.351
Direct effect							
EC → SA	0.337	0.106	3.179	0.144	0.564	0.143	0.562
Total effect							
EC → SA	0.553	0.111	4.982	0.349	0.785	0.343	0.78

The results of the mediating effect analysis of satisfaction between trust and continuance intention are shown in Table 6. At the 95% confidence level, satisfaction has a mediating effect between trust and continuance intention.

Table 6. Mediation Effect Test

Path	Point estimation	Standard Error	Z Value	Bootstrapping,1000 times,95% CI			
				Bias-corrected	Percentile		
				Lower	Upper	Lower	Upper
Indirect effect							
TR → SA → CI	0.185	0.055	3.364	0.096	0.328	0.088	0.315
Direct effect							
TR → CI	0.337	0.103	3.272	0.141	0.536	0.144	0.547
Total effect							
TR → CI	0.523	0.097	5.392	0.345	0.737	0.337	0.732

The results of the mediating effect analysis of satisfaction between perceived usefulness and continuance intention are shown in Table 7. At the 95% confidence level, satisfaction has a mediating effect between perceived usefulness and continuance intention.

Table 7. Mediation Effect Test

Path	Point estimation	Standard Error	Z Value	Bootstrapping,1000 times,95% CI			
				Bias-corrected		Percentile	
				Lower	**Upper**	**Lower**	**Upper**
Indirect effect							
PU → SA → CI	0.21	0.066	3.182	0.101	0.374	0.093	0.357
Direct effect							
PU → CI	0.291	0.11	2.645	0.088	0.513	0.092	0.522
Total effect							
PU → CI	0.5	0.098	5.102	0.32	0.703	0.33	0.706

4.5 Chain Mediation Effect Test

At the 95% confidence level, the data was sampled 1000 times, and the results are shown in Table 8. When the 95% confidence interval does not contain the number 0, the mediation effect is significant. Perceived usefulness and satisfaction play a partial mediating role between expectation confirmation and continuance intention. Expectation confirmation can affect continuance intention through perceived usefulness, and the mediation effect accounts for 9.64% of the total effect; it can also affect continuance intention through satisfaction, and the mediation effect accounts for 15.01% of the total effect. In addition, it can also affect users' continuance intention through perceived usefulness and satisfaction, and the indirect effect accounts for 42.02% of the total effect.

Table 8. Boostrap analysis table for chain mediation effect test

Effect Type	Path	Standardized indirect effect size	Bootstrapping, 1000 times, 95% CI		Effect size
			Upper	**Lower**	
Mediation effect	EC → PU → CI	0.11	0.019	0.244	17.38%
	EC → CS → CI	0.095	0.026	0.216	15.01%
	EC → PU → CS → CI	0.061	0.019	0.141	9.64%
Total median effect		0.266	0.149	0.428	42.02%
Total effect		0.633			

Perceived usefulness and satisfaction both play a mediating role in the effect of expectation confirmation on continuance intention.

5 Conclusions

5.1 Main Research Conclusions

Expectation Confirmation and Perceived Usefulness and Satisfaction.
The research results show that in the process of user purchases on the Meituan Youxuan platform, expectation confirmation will positively affect both perceived usefulness and user satisfaction. Perceived usefulness has mediation effect on expectation confirmation and satisfaction.

Perceived Usefulness and Satisfaction, Continuance Intention.
The results of this paper show that perceived usefulness has a significant positive impact on both satisfaction and continuance intention. Satisfaction has a mediation effect on perceived usefulness and continuance intention. Perceived usefulness and satisfaction have chain mediating effect on expectation confirmation and continuance intention. Users' confirmation expectations can influence their continued use intention through perceived usefulness and satisfaction.

Satisfaction and Continuance Intention.
Satisfaction plays a significant positive role in the user's continuance intention. That is to say, when users make group purchases on the Meituan Youxuan platform, their

satisfaction with the platform will be directly related to whether they are willing to continue to use the platform.

Trust and Satisfaction, Continuance Intention.
In this article, trust has a significant positive impact on both user satisfaction and continuance intention. The improvement in satisfaction will prompt users to continue to use the Meituan Youxuan platform. Satisfaction acts as a mediator between trust and users' continuance intention.

Usage Habits and Continuance Intention.
According to the research results of this article, usage habits positively affect users' continuance intention. For users, if they can naturally open the Meituan Youxuan platform when they want to shop through the community group buying platform, then the users will have a high loyalty to the Meituan Youxuan platform and a strong willingness to continue using it.

Overall, users' continuance intention is driven by multiple factors such as expectation confirmation, perceived usefulness, satisfaction, trust, and user habits. According to research data, the optimization of these factors is conducive to improve continuance intention. From the perspective of digital platform merchants, through the phased dynamic balance and collaborative strengthening of the five influencing factors, we design a habit development path, accurately manage user expectations, strengthen core values and scenario-based applications, establish a closed-loop feedback mechanism to improve satisfaction, and establish a trust system in layers, thereby achieving the improvement of continuance intention and establishing a long-term and healthy user relationship.

5.2 Research Deficiencies and Prospects

Although this paper has conducted a preliminary study on the factors affecting the continuance intention of users of the Meituan Youxuan e-commerce platform, the research content still needs to be further improved:

- We can further introduce variables such as perceived risk and perceived value on the basis of the existing information system continuous use model to make the research model more comprehensive in the future.
- Future research should expand the sample size and collect more valid data to improve the accuracy of data analysis and make the research conclusions more convincing.

Acknowledgement. This research was supported by the Industry-University-Research Innovation Foundation of China under Grant 2023YC008.

References

1. Bhattacherjee, A.: Understanding information systems continuance: an expectation-confirmation model. MIS Q. **25**(3), 351–370 (2001)

2. Oliver, R.L.: A cognitive model of the antecedents and consequences of satisfaction decisions. J. Mark. Res. **17**(4), 460–469 (1980)
3. Davis, F.D.: Perceived usefulness, perceived ease of use, and user acceptance of information technology. MIS Q. **13**(3), 319–340 (1989)
4. Xiao, X., Xing, C., Shen, N.: Research on the influence of perceived value on user satisfaction and continued participation willingness of university library reading clubs. Library. **2023**(7), 89–98 (2023)
5. Li, Q., Liao, M., Zhao, X.: Research on the influencing factors of user satisfaction of audiobook platforms from the perspective of information ecology. Modern Intell. **43**(11), 168–177 (2023)
6. Moorman, C., Zaltman, G., Deshpande, R.: Relationships between providers and users of market research: the dynamics of trust within and between organizations. J. Mark. Res. **29**(3), 314–329 (1992)
7. Pavlou, P.A., Gefen, D.: Building effective online marketplaces with institution-based trust. Inf. Syst. Res. **15**(1), 37–59 (2004)
8. James, W.: The Principle of Psychology, pp. 63–79. Henry Holt and Company, New York (1890)
9. Limayem, M., Hirt, S.G., Cheung, C.M.K.: How habit limits the predictive power of intention: the case of information systems continuance. MIS Q. **31**(4), 705–737 (2007)
10. Tan, C., Yi, Y., Li, L.: Research on the factors affecting the continuance intention of academic WeChat public account users. Modern. Intelligence. **41**(1), 50–59+77 (2021)
11. Jin, X., Zhu, L.: Analysis of the factors affecting the continuance intention of knowledge payment platform users. Media. **2020**(14), 73–76 (2020)
12. Zhang, P., Zhu, Z., Liu, C.: Research on the influencing factors of the willingness to continue using social software. Manag. Modern. **39**(6), 61–64 (2019). https://doi.org/10.19634/j.cnki.11-1403/c.2019.06.013
13. Song, H., Shuai, C., Li, W.: An empirical study on users' willingness to continue using knowledge question and answer communities. J. Inform. Resour. Manag. **9**(4), 68–81 (2019). https://doi.org/10.13365/j.jirm.2019.04.068
14. Luo, M., Chen, J.: An empirical analysis of the users' willingness to continue using popular science WeChat public accounts. Popul. Sci. Res. **18**(2), 64–73+82+113–114 (2023)
15. Lin, Y., Yu, F., Hou, S.: Research on the factors affecting the satisfaction of knowledge payment users based on ECT theory. New Cent. Lib. **2020**(1), 25–29 (2020). https://doi.org/10.16810/j.cnki.1672-514X.2020.01.005
16. Huang, S., Xiao, J., Jin, Y.: Consumer continuous purchase on social e-commerce platform based on S-O-R theory. Soft Sci. **34**(6), 115–121 (2020)
17. Gefen, D.: TAM or just plain habit: a look at experienced online shoppers. J. Organ. End User Comput. (JOEUC). **15**(3), 1–13 (2003)
18. Qin, S., Song, Q.: Research on the influencing factors of continuous use intention of Pinduoduo platform based on ECM-ISC model. Market Forum. **2021**(12), 62–68 (2021)
19. Lee, M.K.O., Turban, E.: A trust model for consumer internet shopping. Int. J. Electron. Commer. **6**(1), 75–91 (2001)
20. Pan, L., Lin, B., Fang, M., et al.: Study on the willingness to continue using tourism apps under the background of smart tourism. Tourism Tribune. **31**(11), 65–73 (2016)
21. Landis, D., Triandis, H.C., Adamopoulos, J.: Habit and behavioral intentions as predictors of social behavior. J. Soc. Psychol. **106**(2), 227–238 (1978)
22. Deng, W., Yu, G.: Factors affecting consumers' continued use of community group buying. J. South-Central Univ. National. **42**(12), 144–152 (2022)

How Does the Design Combination of Badges Affect Users' Continuous Knowledge Contribution? An Empirical Study Based on Question-and-Answer Communities

Jun Yin, Shuya Huang(✉), and Wei Zhang

Department of Economics and Management, Jiangsu University of Science and Technology, Zhenjiang, China
18252742699@163.com

Abstract. Badges are commonly used as a gamification tool in Question-and-Answer communities to encourage knowledge sharing. However, the impact of badge design on motivation has been insufficiently explored. This study addresses this gap by optimizing badge design to maximize its motivational effect. Using reinforcement theory, an incentive model is developed and validated with panel data from user log records in a Q&A community. The results show that both the total value and the number of badges significantly enhance user knowledge contributions. Additionally, a U-shaped relationship is found between the time interval of badge issuance and user behavior, which is further amplified when badge attributes are aligned with user actions. These findings provide valuable theoretical insights and practical guidelines for improving badge design to effectively motivate users in Q&A communities.

Keywords: Question and Answer Communities · Badge Design · Reinforcement Theory · Gamification

1 Introduction

With the advancement of internet technology, knowledge acquisition has transcended the temporal and spatial constraints of traditional methods, making Question-and-Answer (Q&A) communities pivotal platforms for personalized knowledge sharing. By January 2023, China's Zhihu had over 400 million registered users, while global platforms like Quora attracted 300 million monthly active users [1]. However, such communities face persistent challenges, including low user engagement (e.g., only 25% of Zhihu users are active [2]) and free-riding [3] behavior. User-generated content, particularly knowledge contributions, is critical to community sustainability, yet it demands significant time and effort. Effective incentive mechanisms are thus essential to sustain participation [4].

Badges enhance user participation by addressing intrinsic motivations (e.g., pride, belonging). Stack Overflow's "Newcomer" badge encourages novices, and Baidu's "Best

Y. P. Tu and M. Chi (Eds.): WHICEB 2025, LNBIP 549, pp. 199–211, 2025.
https://doi.org/10.1007/978-3-031-94184-9_17

Answer" badge rewards high-quality contributions. However, prior research oversimplifies badge design, ignoring static attributes (fixed traits like visual design [5], behavioral criteria) and dynamic attributes (emergent traits like scarcity [6], award timing [7]). Two approaches exist: level-linked badges (simple but low-quality) and behavior-triggered badges (complex but precise). This study focuses on behavior-triggered badges to avoid gamification pitfalls. Existing work examines static or dynamic attributes separately, but their synergistic effects are underexplored. For example, static attributes (e.g., "Expert" badge criteria) set behavioral goals, while dynamic attributes (e.g., rarity) modulate incentive intensity. How they interact to shape sustained knowledge contributions is a critical gap addressed here.

To address these gaps, this study uses a Chinese knowledge-based Q&A community as the research object, given its scale, representativeness, and mature badge system. Based on reinforcement theory, a research model is proposed, and panel data derived from user log records are used to test the hypotheses. The subsequent sections will elaborate on the methodology and findings.

2 Literature Review

2.1 Gamification and Knowledge Contribution in Q&A Communities

In Q&A communities, knowledge acquisition relies on collaborative interactions: users post questions based on personal needs and receive tailored answers, distinct from passive content-sharing platforms. Unlike traditional knowledge communities, Q&A participation requires both comprehension and active contribution. Motivation—particularly intrinsic motivation (self-efficacy, enjoyment, altruism)—plays a pivotal role in driving contributions. Cho [8] highlights that intrinsic incentives (e.g., altruism) are twice as effective as extrinsic motivators (e.g., monetary rewards), which may undermine long-term engagement despite short-term gains.

Gamification mechanisms enhance extrinsic motivation (e.g., rewards) while internalizing it through achievement visualization or task completion, creating dual behavioral pathways [4]. In Q&A communities, elements like badges, points, and levels [9] apply game mechanics to non-game contexts, fostering engagement. Studies show that gamified rewards bridge intrinsic and extrinsic motivations: Luyao [10] found contributions are driven by both, but dominated by internal drives. Huseyin [4] further highlights that extrinsic rewards not only directly boost contributions but also accelerate their transformation into intrinsic motivation, sustaining long-term engagement.

Current research on gamification in Q&A communities is limited, often examining gamification structures broadly rather than exploring the unique mechanisms of elements like badges. This systemic approach marginalizes badge-specific studies, hindering understanding of how badges influence knowledge contribution. Without in-depth analysis, it remains unclear how badge attributes shape users' psychological perceptions and behavioral decisions, their interaction with intrinsic and extrinsic motivations, and contextual motivational differences.

This study examines how badges in gamification impact user knowledge contribution behavior, aiming to reveal their unique role in motivating contributions. The results will provide Q&A community operators with targeted incentive strategies to enhance user contributions and optimize community knowledge.

2.2 Review of Badge Design Attributes

Badges, a common gamification element in the PBL framework, have two main functions: representing achievements and guiding behavior [11]. One type is linked to user levels, awarded when points reach a threshold, serving as a visual progress indicator. The other type is granted based on specific user behavior and status conditions, offering more diversity and design complexity.

This study of badge design focuses on two main categories: static and dynamic attributes. Static attributes, fixed at design, include classification dimensions such as reward types, visibility, and activity requirements. Hamari [12] and Sheffler [5] found visible badges boost user motivation, while Kyewski [13]'s education study revealed self-visible badges better incentivized students, highlighting unresolved contextual factors. Researchers like Park [11] and Facey [14] further categorized badges by activity type, difficulty, and visual design, but classifications remain inconsistent across fields. Dynamic attributes, emerging from user interactions, include badge value (decreasing as more users obtain them, per Immorlica [15] and Easley [6]), value distribution (Anderson [11] found multiple badges with equal value more effective than a single high-value badge), and timing (Bhattacharyya [7] noted delayed badge acquisition reduces incentive effects). These findings underscore the complexity of badge design's impact on user behavior, with unresolved questions about contextual influences and unified frameworks.

However, existing research has limitations. Most studies examine static or dynamic badge attributes in isolation, neglecting their synergistic effects. Building on prior work, this study focuses on continuous knowledge contribution behavior in Q&A communities and uses an empirical approach to investigate the interactive effects among dynamic badge attributes.

2.3 Reinforcement Theory

Skinner's reinforcement theory, a key motivational theory, guides behavior control and change, with wide applications in education and management. It posits that behavior is shaped by its consequences: positive outcomes reinforce behavior, while negative ones deter it. Positive reinforcers encourage desired behaviors, and negative reinforcers discourage undesired ones. The effectiveness depends on timing, frequency, and perceived importance. Badge dynamics, like reward intervals and static properties like rank and appearance, are related to these factors. Too short intervals may cause user adaptation and weak incentives; too long may weaken the link between contributions and badge acquisition. Only a moderate interval optimizes motivation. High-level badges motivate users to improve both the quality and quantity of their knowledge contributions, while unique designs further emphasize their importance.

Different reinforcement schedules are used in badge design: continuous reinforcement attracts new users (e.g., first question and answer rewards), while interval reinforcement maintains long-term engagement (e.g., regular rewards for active users). By combining badge dynamics and static attributes and designing an effective incentive mechanism based on reinforcement theory, continuous knowledge contribution behavior can be influenced, Q&A community vitality can be enhanced, and knowledge sharing quality can be improved.

Therefore, this study uses reinforcement theory to build an empirical model to explore how the dynamic and static attributes of badges affect users' continuous knowledge contribution behavior.

3 Model Construction and Research Hypothesis

3.1 Research Model

The study proposes a badge design incentive model (Fig. 1) that shows how dynamic attributes promote continuous knowledge contribution in Q&A communities. Total badge value and number of badges positively correlate with sustained contribution, while badge issuance time interval has an inverted U-shaped relationship. Additionally, contributive design within static badge attributes amplifies the positive effects of dynamic attributes. Theoretical underpinnings are elaborated in subsequent analyses.

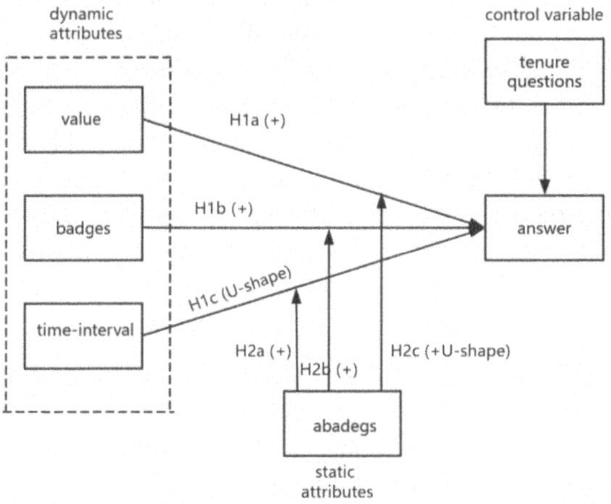

Fig. 1. Research Model

3.2 The Motivational Effect of Dynamic Attributes of Badges

In the studied Q&A community, badges are digital with no tangible value or privilege links. Initially, a badge has no objective value, but once in the community, differences in accessibility and acquisition rates create value. High-value badges indicate users' knowledge levels, boosting their confidence in contributing. They also symbolize social recognition and honor, fulfilling users' respect needs. From reinforcement theory, badges act as reinforcers, making users aware that knowledge contribution is rewarded, thus encouraging repeated behavior. Higher reinforcer value generally means stronger positive feedback, leading us to hypothesize that:

H1a: The total value of badges has a positive motivational effect on users' continuous knowledge contribution behavior.
H1b: The number of badges has a positive motivational effect on users' continuous knowledge contribution behavior.

Previous research shows that badges have short-term impacts on motivation and behavior, with diminishing effects over time [7]. Repeated use of badges can reduce their effectiveness due to satiation. Short intervals between badge acquisitions weaken their impact, as frequent rewards may make users undervalue them. Long intervals, however, can make users forget the connection between their behavior and rewards, weakening the association due to lack of timely feedback. Only balanced intervals between badge awards can maximize their motivational effect on knowledge contribution. Thus, we hypothesize:

H1c: There is a U-shaped relationship between the time interval of badge awarding and users' knowledge-contribution behavior.

3.3 The Moderating Role of Static Attributes

Most users don't participate just to get badges. When they receive a badge, they first notice its dynamic attributes, then static ones. We focus on answering behavior in the community. Badges for answering and other behaviors exist, and past research shows different badges have a motivational spillover effect. When a badge's static attributes target answering behavior, reinforcement theory suggests users better recognize the link between the incentive and their behavior, enhancing the badge's role as a reinforcer. From the goal-setting theory perspective, if users are motivated by obtaining a specific badge, achieving it brings greater satisfaction, driving continuous knowledge contribution [9]. Total badge value reflects scarcity and social recognition, while quantity captures cumulative reinforcement. Thus, we hypothesize:

H2a: Contribution-oriented badges enhance the positive motivational effect of the total value of badges on knowledge contribution behavior.
H2b: Contribution-oriented badges enhance the positive motivational effect of the number of badges on knowledge contribution behavior.

When the motivational effect of badges is enhanced, even if the marginal diminishing effect still exists, the strengthened motivation means that users will continue to be influenced by repeated badge acquisitions in the short term. Moreover, when the time interval between badge acquisitions is too long, the enhanced motivational effect of the badges will still exert a stronger pull on users. Therefore, when badges reward corresponding behaviors, the U-shaped relationship between time interval and knowledge contribution behavior is intensified. Thus, we hypothesize:

H2c: Contribution-oriented badges enhance the U-shaped relationship between the time interval of badge awards and knowledge contribution behavior.

4 Research Methods

4.1 Research Settings

This study analyzes data from a popular Chinese tech Q&A community launched in 2012. It has over 10 million users and features a unique badge system with public records. We collected data from June 1, 2016 to June 15, 2023 using Python's Selenium package. Data before June 2016 were excluded due to a site restructuring and badge mechanism relaunch. We ultimately gathered 122,964 answers and 19,769 articles from 2,843 users.

4.2 Variables

Table 1 summarizes information about the main variables and control variables.

1. Dependent Variable: In Q&A communities, user activities include asking questions, answering questions, and subsidiary activities like commenting and liking. This paper focuses on answering behavior, which is considered the most valuable. Unlike question-asking, answering requires extra incentives. Therefore, this study uses the number of answers users post per week as the dependent variable to evaluate the impact of badge design on knowledge-contribution behavior.
2. Independent Variables: The main independent variables are total badge value, number of badges, time interval between badges, and contribution-type badge count. Badge value is determined by 1/Qbadgest,j, where Qbadgest,j is the number of people obtaining badge j at time t. Total badge value is the sum of values of badges obtained by time t.:

$$\text{value}_t = \sum 1/\text{Qbadgest}, \text{j} \tag{1}$$

Badge count refers to badges earned by a user within time t, contribution-based badges indicate specifically those earned in this period, and time interval measures the duration between t and the last badge acquisition.

3. Control Variables: This study controls for user tenure and the number of prior questions posted to ensure accuracy. User tenure indicates participation duration and experience, removing time-related bias. The number of prior questions is controlled because it can affect subsequent answering behavior. Based on reciprocity psychology, users who ask more questions initially may be more likely to answer later. Including this variable helps exclude the impact of reciprocal behavior and more accurately reflects the relationship between badge design and user knowledge contribution.

4.3 Models and Estimation

Before model construction, diagnostic tests were conducted. A Hausman test rejected the null hypothesis at the 1% significance level (Table 2). Descriptive statistics are in Table 3, the correlation matrix in Table 4 shows no significant correlations among variables. Therefore, a fixed-effects panel model is used to control for unobserved individual heterogeneity and ensure valid estimates. This model is suitable for dynamic panel data

Table 1. Variable Description

Variable type	Variable	Description
Primary variable	answer	The number of answers submitted by users to the community in the t + 1 period
	value	The sum of the value of the badges earned by the user during the t period
	badges	The number of badges earned by the user in time period t
	Time interval	The time interval between time t and the last time the user received the badge
	abadegs	The number of contribution badges earned by the user in the time period t
Control variable	tenure	The time period during which the user has been active in the community
	questions	The number of issues posted by users in the t time period, like the community

and captures time-series characteristics well, allowing analysis of the dynamic impact of badge design on user behavior. The specific model is as follows:

$$\begin{aligned} answer_{it+1} &= \beta_{i0} + \tau_{it} + \beta_1 value_{it} + \beta_2 badges_{it} + \beta_3 interval_{it} + \beta_4 interal_{it}^2 \\ &+ \beta_3 value_{it} \times abadges_{it} + \beta_6 badges_{it} \times abadges_{it} + \beta_7 \text{interval}_{it} \times abadges_{it} \\ &+ \beta_8 \text{interval}_{it}^2 \times abadges + \beta_9 tenure_{it} + \beta_{10} question_{it} + \rho answer_{it} + \varepsilon_{it+1} \end{aligned} \quad (2)$$

Here, $\text{answer}_{\text{it+1}}$ represents the count of answers posted by participant $_{\text{i}}$ at time $_{\text{t+1}}$; value_{it} 、 $\text{badges}_{\text{it}}$ 、 $\text{interval}_{\text{it}}$ and $\text{badges}_{\text{it}}$ denote the total value of badges, the number of badges, the time interval, and the number of contribution-type badges of participant i at time t respectively; $\text{tenure}_{\text{it}}$ and $\text{question}_{\text{it}}$ represent the control variables of tenure and the number of questions asked;β_{i0} and τ_{it} represent the individual effect and time effect of the user.ρ is the coefficient of the lag term of the explained variable.

Table 2. Hausman test

	Coef
Chi-square test value	83.119
P-value	0

5 Results

Table 5 shows the panel regression results on knowledge contribution. Model 1 includes the main independent variables and fixed effects: badge value (value), number of badges (badges), time interval between badge acquisitions (time_interval), its square

Table 3. Descriptive Statistics

	(1)	(2)	(3)	(4)
Variable	Mean value	Variance	Minimum value	Maximum value
badges	0.148	0.465	0	20
answer	0.240	1.895	0	240
tenure	1,221	757.9	0	4390
question	0.135	0.657	0	37
time_interval	1	6.025	0	302
value	0.000176	0.0114	0	3.559
is_answer	0.00659	0.0873	0	5

Table 4. Correlation Coefficient Test

	1	2	3	4	5	6	7
answer	1						
value	0.054***	1					
badges	0.140***	0.170***	1				
time_interval	0.030***	0.035***	0.366***	1			
abadges	0.303***	0.040***	0.279***	0.076***	1		
tenure	−0.040***	0.011***	0.054***	0.032***	−0.033***	1	
question	0.051***	0.002*	0.097***	0.027***	0.043***	−0.100***	1

(time_interval2), and number of contribution-oriented badges (abadges). Model 2 adds control variables to Model 1: user tenure (tenure) and number of questions posted (question). Model 3 includes interaction terms of the moderating variable with the main independent variables. Model 4 adds the same control variables as in Model 2 to Model 3.

In Models 1 and 2, badge total value ($\beta 1 = 0.081$–0.082, $p < 0.05$) and quantity ($\beta 2 = 0.022$, $p < 0.01$) have significant positive effects on user knowledge contribution, supporting Hypotheses H1a and H1b. The time interval has a significant negative linear effect ($\beta 3 = -0.015$, $p < 0.01$) and a positive quadratic term ($\beta 4 = 0.027$–0.028, $p < 0.01$), confirming a U-shaped relationship and validating H1c, suggesting an optimal interval maximizes badge incentives.

When incorporating contribution-oriented badges and their interaction terms, Models 3 and 4 reveal significantly positive interactions between these badges and both total value ($\beta 5 = 13.947$–14.052, $p < 0.05$) and quantity measures ($\beta 6 = 1.752$–1.792, $p < 0.01$), supporting H2a-b. Notably, the interaction between badge quantity

Table 5. Impact of Badge Design on Knowledge Contribution

model	(1)	(2)	(3)	(4)
variable				
value	0.081**	0.082**	0.057**	0.058**
	(0.035)	(0.035)	(0.026)	(0.026)
badges	0.022***	0.022***	0.023***	0.023***
	(0.002)	(0.002)	(0.002)	(0.002)
time_interval	−0.015***	−0.015***	−0.010***	−0.010***
	(0.002)	(0.002)	(0.003)	(0.003)
time_interval^2	0.027***	0.028***	0.021***	0.021***
	(0.005)	(0.005)	(0.007)	(0.007)
abadges	1.056***	1.048***	0.596***	0.576***
	(0.096)	(0.096)	(0.139)	(0.139)
abadges × value			13.947**	14.052**
			(6.991)	(6.961)
abadegs × badges			1.752***	1.792***
			(0.672)	(0.668)
abadegs × time_interval			−1.953	−1.890
			(1.972)	(1.967)
abadegs × time_interval^2			2.896	2.816
			(3.676)	(3.670)
tenure		−0.001***		−0.002***
		(0.000)		(0.000)
question		0.013***		0.014***
		(0.001)		(0.001)
Observations	512,482	512,482	512,482	512,482
R-squared	0.097	0.099	0.107	0.110
Number of user_id	2806	2806	2806	2806

*** $p<0.01$, ** $p<0.05$, * $p<0.1$

and squared time interval ($\beta 8 = 2.816$) strengthens the U-shaped dynamics, confirming H2c. These findings indicate that contribution-oriented badges amplify motivation effects while optimizing the temporal pattern of incentive impacts.

To address endogeneity, we applied GMM and PSM. The GMM results showed key variables (badge value, quantity, time interval) remained significant, with the interaction term abadges × value having a stronger positive effect. PSM confirmed users with contribution-oriented badges (Treat4) exhibited higher answering activity. Both methods validate the motivational impact of aligned badge design. Results are in Tables 6 and 7.

Table 6. Dynamic Panel Regression Results (GMM)

	(1)	(2)	(3)	(4)
	Answer	Answer	Answer	Answer
L.value	0.094***	0.095***	0.062***	0.062***
	(0.034)	(0.034)	(0.023)	(0.023)
L.badges	0.015***	0.015***	0.016***	0.015***
	(0.002)	(0.002)	(0.002)	(0.002)
L.time_interval	−0.010***	−0.010***	−0.009***	−0.009***
	(0.002)	(0.002)	(0.002)	(0.002)
L.time_interval^2	0.020***	0.020***	0.018***	0.019***
	(0.005)	(0.005)	(0.006)	(0.006)
L.abadges	0.546***	0.540***	0.599***	0.583***
	(0.056)	(0.056)	(0.080)	(0.080)
tenure		−0.001***		−0.001***
		(0.000)		(0.000)
question		0.018***		0.019***
		(0.001)		(0.001)
L.abadges × value			18.583**	18.675**
			(8.326)	(8.294)
L.abadegs × badges			0.566*	0.533
			(0.340)	(0.342)
L.abadegs × time_interva			−1.931	−1.864
			(1.458)	(1.457)
L.abadegs × time_interval^2			3.203	3.111
			(2.679)	(2.680)
_cons	0.001***	0.001***	0.001***	0.001***
	(0.000)	(0.000)	(0.000)	(0.000)
N	509,676	509,676	509,676	509,676
Adj. R^2	0.031	0.034	0.039	0.042

Table 7. Propensity Score Matching (PSM) Analysis

	(1)	(2)	(3)	(4)
	Answer	Answer	Answer	Answer
Treat1	0.003***			
	(0.000)			
Treat2		0.002***		
		(0.000)		
Treat3			−0.004***	
			(0.000)	
Treat4				0.009***
				(0.002)
value		0.105***	0.079**	0.052
		(0.035)	(0.035)	(0.158)
badges	0.031***		0.026***	0.263***
	(0.005)		(0.005)	(0.038)
time_interval	−0.015***	−0.019***		−0.099***
	(0.002)	(0.002)		(0.015)
time_interval^2	0.031***	0.037***		0.147***
	(0.005)	(0.005)		(0.023)
abadges	0.031***		0.026***	0.263***
	(0.005)		(0.005)	(0.038)
tenure	−0.006***	−0.006***	−0.006***	−0.004
	(0.000)	(0.000)	(0.000)	(0.003)
question	0.005**	0.003	0.005**	0.093***
	(0.002)	(0.002)	(0.002)	(0.014)
_cons	0.006***	0.006***	0.006***	0.015***
	(0.000)	(0.000)	(0.000)	(0.001)
N	121,066	121,066	121,066	6278
Adj. R^2	0.105	0.104	0.105	0.104

6 Conclusion

6.1 Theoretical Significance

From a theoretical standpoint, his study uses reinforcement theory to analyze how dynamic and static attributes in badge design work together, overcoming previous limitations. Results show that badge value and quantity significantly enhance user contributions. There is a U-shaped relationship between badge issuance intervals and user behavior, indicating nonlinear incentives. Contribution-oriented badges boost motivation and optimize time intervals. These findings expand reinforcement theory's application, support badge design models empirically, fill the gamification research gap, and advance the theory of gamified user motivation.

6.2 Practical Significance

From a practical standpoint, this study offers insights for Q&A community managers on motivating continuous knowledge contributions. At the badge design stage, balancing badge difficulty levels to evenly distribute badge values is recommended. This ensures users feel the value of their badges is maximized, prevents frequent badge acquisition or discouragement from high difficulty, and maintains a balanced interval between badge acquisitions. Community managers can introduce new badges to reward unrecognized contributors, avoiding frustration. Lastly, to stimulate more knowledge contributions, more badges corresponding to such behaviors should be allocated.

6.3 Limitations and Future Directions

This study on badge design has limitations. First, it only examined one static attribute (activity-type) due to constraints. Future research should explore more design combinations. Second, this study didn't differentiate users by type or traits, which affect badge motivation. Future studies could include user characteristics in the model. Lastly, the optimal time interval and stimulation point for badge awards were not defined. Future research could use machine learning to create a model that identifies the optimal point, considering user traits and general badge effects. This would help community managers adjust awards more effectively.

Acknowledgement. This work was supported by Jiangsu Higher Education Reform Research Project, Talent Training Mode Reform of Big Data and Credit Management From the Perspective of "Industry Embedment" (No. 2021JSJG227) and Research on Panoramic Decision Value Discovery Method Based on Manufacturing Enterprise Information System Using Multi-source Data National Natural Science Foundation of China (71972090).

References

1. Wei, F., & Gao, Y.. Research on the Value evaluation of knowledge-paying Enterprises from the perspective of Business Model: A case study of Zhihu [J]. Inner Mongolia Science and Technology and Economy. 57–63 (2024)
2. Imtiaz, Z., Umer, M., Ahmad, M., Ullah, S., Choi, G.S., Mehmood, A.: Duplicate questions pair detection using Siamese MaLSTM. IEEE Access. **8**, 21932–21942 (2020)
3. Amaral, I.O.J., do, Kang, M.: Gamification effects on users' motivation to contribute knowledge in a Portuguese Q&A community. Aslib J. Inf. Manag. **73**, 578–599 (2021)
4. Cavusoglu, H., Li, Z., Kim, S.H.: How do virtual badges incentivize voluntary contributions to online communities? Inf. Manag. **58**, 103483 (2021)
5. Sheffler, Z.J., Liu, D., Curley, S.P.: Ingredients for successful badges: evidence from a field experiment in bike commuting. Eur. J. Inf. Syst. **29**, 688–703 (2020)

6. Easley, D., Ghosh, A.: Incentives, gamification, and game theory: an economic approach to badge design. ACM Trans. Econ. Comput. **4**, 1–26 (2016)
7. Bhattacharyya, S., Banerjee, S., Bose, I., Kankanhalli, A.: Temporal effects of repeated recognition and lack of recognition on online community contributions. J. Manag. Inf. Syst. **37**, 536–562 (2020)
8. Cho, I., Park, H., Kim, J.K.: The relationship between motivation and information sharing about products and services on Facebook. Behav. Inf. Technol. **34**, 858–868 (2015)
9. Chen, L., Baird, A., Straub, D.: The impact of hierarchical privilege levels and non-hierarchical incentives on continued contribution in online Q&A communities: a motivational model of gamification goals. Decis. Support. Syst. **153**, 113667 (2022)
10. Lu, Y., Mao, X., Zhou, M., Zhang, Y., Li, Z., Wang, T., Yin, G., Wang, H.: Motivation under gamification: an empirical study of developers' motivations and contributions in stack overflow. IEEE Trans. Softw. Eng. **48**, 4947–4963 (2022)
11. Park, S., Kim, S.: A badge design framework for a gamified learning environment: cases analysis and literature review for badge design. JMIR Serious Games. **7**, e14342 (2019)
12. Hamari, J.: Transforming homo economicus into homo ludens: a field experiment on gamification in a utilitarian peer-to-peer trading service. Electron. Commer. Res. Appl. **12**, 236–245 (2013)
13. Kyewski, E., Krämer, N.C.: To gamify or not to gamify? An experimental field study of the influence of badges on motivation, activity, and performance in an online learning course. Comput. Educ. **118**, 25–37 (2018)
14. Facey-Shaw, L., Specht, M., Van Rosmalen, P., Borner, D., Bartley-Bryan, J.: Educational functions and design of badge systems: a conceptual literature review. IEEE Trans. Learn. Technol. **11**, 536–544 (2018)
15. Immorlica, N., Stoddard, G., Syrgkanis, V.: Social status and badge design. In: Proceedings of the 24th International Conference on World Wide Web, pp. 473–483. International World Wide Web Conferences Steering Committee, Florence (2015)

Prediction of Influence for Scientific Popularization Videos on Bilibili Based on Multimodal Features

Lang Duan(✉), Pengyu Lu(✉), and Meizhu Zheng(✉)

School of Management, Harbin Institute of Technology, Heilongjiang, China
987540560@qq.com, lupengyu@hit.edu.cn, zmz_harbin@hotmail.com

Abstract. Bilibili's scientific popularization sub-sectors under the knowledge category provides an excellent learning platform for a broad audience. However, some science popularization videos on the platform suffer from low popularity. Research on how to identify scientifically influential videos remains underexplored. Against this backdrop, this research defines a video influence calculation method based on entropy weight, tailored to Bilibili's specific characteristics, and constructs a Multimodal CNN-Transformer model (MMCT) that integrates text, social, audio, image, and content modalities to predict the influence of scientific popularization videos on Bilibili. Experiments are conducted on video influence regression prediction using crawled Bilibili video data, and the model's effectiveness is validated through ablation studies. Furthermore, benchmarks are set to verify the effectiveness of the multimodal feature fusion in video influence classification. The results indicate that MMCT achieves an SRCC of 0.7895, improving by 0.0566 compared to the baseline model, while MSE decreases by 0.4022 compared to the baseline model. This study contributes to Bilibili's ability to identify highly influential popular science videos, thereby enhancing the platform's commercial value and competitiveness while promoting the effective and high-quality dissemination of popular science knowledge on Bilibili.

Keywords: Video Influence Prediction · Multimodal Features · Convolutional Neural Network · Transformer

1 Introduction

The technological conveniences brought by the information age have profoundly changed the way we learn and work. According to the 52nd "Statistical Report on Internet Development in China" published by the China Internet Network Information Center, by June 2023, the number of internet users in China reached 1.079 billion, with an internet penetration rate of 76.4%. In today's rapidly developing internet landscape, learning through watching educational videos online has become an efficient and convenient way to acquire knowledge. Meanwhile, online social video platforms have created virtual learning communities for users, where they can share related knowledge videos, engage with corresponding content, and provide feedback through comments, collections, likes, and other interactive features, thus facilitating the spread of videos.

Y. P. Tu and M. Chi (Eds.): WHICEB 2025, LNBIP 549, pp. 212–223, 2025.
https://doi.org/10.1007/978-3-031-94184-9_18

Among the numerous online social video platforms, Bilibili holds a crucial position. Bilibili attracts a large number of Generation Z users, characterized by a substantial user base, youthfulness, and strong engagement. The knowledge section alone includes eight areas: Science Popularization, Campus Learning, Social Sciences, Law and Psychology, Career and Workplace, Humanities and History, Design and Creativity, Finance and Business, and Wild Skills Association. Among these, science popularization videos aim to spread scientific knowledge through video formats, contributing positively to enhancing national scientific literacy in an era where online learning is becoming increasingly popular.

However, some science popularization videos suffer from low popularity, making it difficult for them to fully realize their potential. In order to enhance the platform's commercial value and competitiveness and promote the effective and high-quality dissemination of popular science knowledge, further research is needed on how platforms can identify science popularization videos with strong influence.

To identify highly influential science popularization videos, this study constructs a Multimodal CNN-Transformer model (MMCT), which includes five feature extraction modules: text modality, social modality, audio modality, image modality, and content modality. These modules perform parallel feature extraction and fusion on Bilibili science popularization video data. The fused features are then input into a Transformer to output an influence score. For the crawled Bilibili science popularization video data, an empirical study is conducted using a custom video influence calculation method to predict video influence. Experimental results show that the model achieves significant performance improvements over baseline models, demonstrating its effectiveness.

2 Related Works

2.1 Video Influence Prediction

In terms of video influence prediction, existing studies have shown that both the characteristics of video creators and various intrinsic video features can be used to predict influence or popularity. For example, Hengmin Zhu et al. [1] developed a popularity prediction model based on network representation learning, integrating text, network, and image features to offer a new perspective on multimodal fusion. Minhwa Cho et al. [2] employed an attention mechanism to enhance feature fusion for short video popularity prediction. Shijie et al. [3] designed an estimation method to calculate video capture probability by investigating user interests and social relationships. Peiguang Jing et al. [4] addressed data missingness and dimensionality differences among raw features using modality correlation, thereby obtaining a more comprehensive feature representation. Pradeep K T et al. [5] implemented a semi-supervised machine learning method, classifying videos into low, medium, and high popularity categories by identifying suitable popular videos in a given area with a cache-based push method to enhance user experience quality.

2.2 Features Extraction for Different Modalities

As a carrier of diverse information, videos encompass multiple modalities, such as text, audio, and images. Extracting and processing these features from videos has been a prominent area of focus in machine learning and deep learning.

Text Features Extraction.
Models such as word embeddings and deep learning-based feature extraction models are widely used. Davoodi A et al. [6] employed a word embedding approach to convert alert labels into real-valued vectors for grouping and visualizing relevant alerts. Wanli Zhang et al. [7] introduced a topic inference method via an encoder, integrating external semantic knowledge into topic modeling, where topics are represented in a mixed von Mises-Fisher distribution within the word embedding space in a generator network. Bangzhi Yin et al. [8] used graph convolutional neural networks (GCNs) to capture complex relationships between words in sentences. Dashuai Li et al. [9] utilized CNN networks and max-pooling layers to extract local word-level vector features, effectively addressing semantic issues such as double negatives and comparative negations in English text. Huang Yuan et al. [10] proposed a dual-channel A-BiLSTM model optimized with CNN for text classification, using an attention mechanism to focus on parts of the text contributing most to classification. Alnowaiser et al. [11] applied CNN features and ensemble learning models for scientific citation analysis, providing theoretical value for qualitative citation assessment.

Audio Features Extraction.
Mel-frequency cepstral coefficients (MFCCs), which capture both time-domain and frequency-domain characteristics, are widely applied. Jia'an Zhang et al. [12] addressed low accuracy in blade fault diagnosis by proposing a wind turbine blade fault diagnosis method based on an improved MFCC algorithm. Xiyang Huang et al. [13] introduced a bidirectional long short-term memory (BiLSTM) network combined with convolutional neural networks (CNNs), integrating MFCCs and their differential spectra to enhance speech emotion recognition performance. Jiping Sun et al. [14] extracted MFCC-based spectrograms from collected sounds to improve accuracy in detecting gas and coal dust explosions in coal mines.

Image Features Extraction.
Tianto et al. [15] used ResNet18 for lung cancer classification. Verma et al. [16] introduced ResNeXt and NF-ResNet for transformer tracking. Xing et al. [17] proposed a novel model named Gate Convolution SENet ResNet (GCSR-Net), which enhanced the ability for image classification. Tanone et al. [18] extracted image features by using ViT-CB to detect brain tumor. Liu et al. [19] managed image restoration effectively by using Cross-ViT. Dwika Hefni Al-Fahsi et al. [20] has proposed a high- performance medical image segmentation model based on CNN.

3 The Proposed Model

The model proposed in this study, MMCT, employs a mid-fusion approach. After parallel extraction of features from five modalities, the features are fused and then fed into the Transformer to output influence scores. The structure is illustrated in Fig. 1.

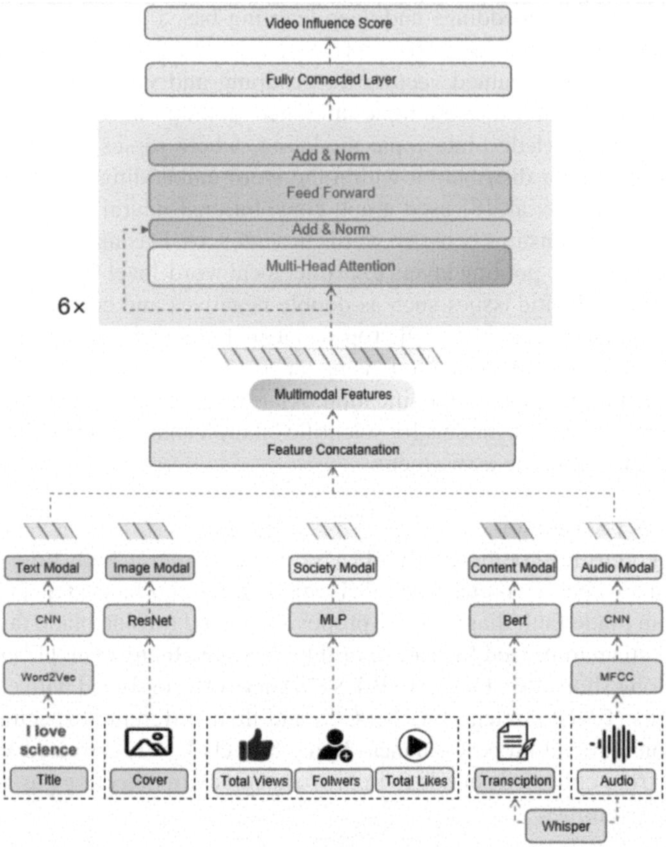

Fig. 1. Model Structure

3.1 Text Modal Module

In this study, we designed a text feature extraction module shown in Fig. 2, which is based on 100-dimensional Word2Vec and a CNN and specifically tailored to efficiently capture the core contextual information and keywords. The core design elements are as follows.

Diversity of convolutional kernel sizes: We employed convolutional kernels of varying sizes, specifically 3 × 100, 4 × 100, and 5 × 100, to adapt to 100-dimensional

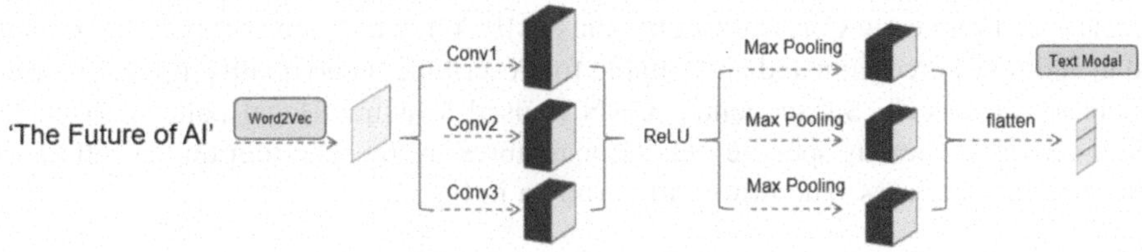

Fig. 2. Text Feature Extracting

word embeddings and to extract 3-gram, 4-gram, and 5-gram fragment features from the video titles. Keywords and their combinations in titles often appear within short-range contextual relationships. By using kernels of different sizes, the model can effectively capture local features at various granularities, thereby enhancing its sensitivity to critical information.

Multi-channel feature extraction: The output of each convolutional kernel is treated as an independent channel. After convolution, a maximum pooling operation is applied to extract the most prominent features from each channel. This design not only significantly reduces the feature dimensionality but also preserves the most representative n-gram information from the title.

Feature integration and representation: After convolution and pooling, the feature vectors extracted by different convolutional kernels are concatenated to form a global feature representation of the video title. This approach enables the model to integrate contextual information at varying granularities, providing high-quality textual features for subsequent multimodal fusion.

3.2 Society Modal Module

This study extracts social features from the total views, total likes, and fans of the uploader, reflecting the potential impact of the uploader's social influence on the video. The three numerical variables are first standardized, and then features are extracted using a Multi-Layer Perceptron (MLP). Let the input social features be $X = [x_1, x_2, x_3]$. the formula for the first fully connected layer is shown in Eq. (1), where $W_1 \in \mathbb{R}^{h_1 * d}$ is the weight matrix, $b_1 \in \mathbb{R}^{h1}$ is the bias term, and h_1 is the number of neurons in the first layer.

$$h_1 = ReLU(W_1 X + b_1) \tag{1}$$

The output layer formula is shown in Eq. (2), where $W_0 \in \mathbb{R}^{1*h_n}$ is the weight matrix of the output layer, h_n represents the number of neurons in the layer preceding the output layer, $b_0 \in \mathbb{R}$ is the bias term, and $\hat{y}$ is the final output of the model.

$$\hat{y} = W_0 h_n + b_0 \tag{2}$$

3.3 Audio Modal Module

The quality of audio can affect the audience's evaluation, and the quality is often reflected through the stability and clarity of local frequency components. Therefore, this study extracts Mel-Frequency Cepstral Coefficients (MFCC), which are designed to simulate human auditory perception and are suitable for describing audio quality, pitch, emotion, and clarity of speech. Subsequently, CNN is used to extract local patterns from the MFCC features, such as specific details or textures in the spectrogram, to reflect the audio modality features. The flowchart is shown in Fig. 3.

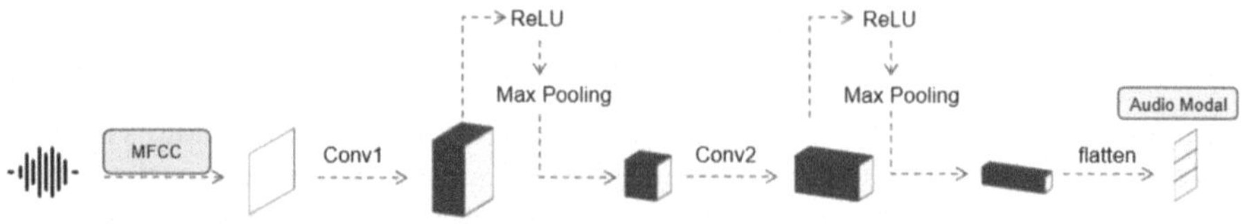

Fig. 3. Audio Feature Extracting

In the first convolutional layer, we employed convolutional kernels with a size of 3×3. By maintaining a small receptive field, the layer can capture short-term variation features, such as rapid pitch changes or transient energy fluctuations in speech.

In the second convolutional layer, by expanding the receptive field to 5×5, the model is allowed to aggregate contextual information over a larger range, capturing continuous tonal changes and mid-term audio background characteristics.

3.4 Image Modal Module

Figure 4 demonstrates the visual contrast between a well-designed cover and a standard one. Undoubtedly, well-crafted covers tend to be more favored by viewers. In this study, the video cover is input into a pre-trained ResNet model to extract the image modality features for the video, which performs well in extracting detailed textures, color combinations, the contours and structures of the main objects, as well as the arrangement of text on the cover.

Fig. 4. A Well-crafted Cover VS A Standard Cover

3.5 Content Modal Module

In this study, OpenAI's Whisper model is used for audio transcription, followed by the use of a pre-trained BERT model to extract semantic information, which serves as the content feature of the video. Science popularization videos typically contain detailed scientific explanations. After transcription, the model can extract content related to explanations and reasoning, thereby inferring the professionalism and depth of the video in the field of science, as well as its clarity and conciseness. At the same time, the BERT model can effectively capture the temporal features in the transcribed text. BERT, through its bidirectional context encoding mechanism, can effectively capture these temporal relationships and extract semantic information, helping the model understand the scientific discussions, experimental processes, and conclusions in the video.

3.6 Transformer Module

After the parallel extraction of text, social, audio, image, and content modality features, this study fuses the five modality features and uses them as input to a Transformer model, ultimately yielding the influence score. Specifically, the content modality features are extracted through BERT, which retains the inherent temporal structure of the video transcript via token-level embeddings and positional encoding. Although simple concatenation is adopted for feature fusion, the Transformer's self-attention mechanism can still partially capture the sequential dependencies within the content modality—for example, identifying how the appearance order of key scientific terms in the transcript correlates with audience engagement patterns.

The local features extracted by the CNN help the model understand the key information within the multimodal features, while the Transformer further integrates, aligns, and establishes global relationships across modalities. Notably, the interaction between modalities is enhanced through the following mechanisms:

Temporal-Social Alignment: The sequential text features from BERT (e.g., gradual explanation of complex concepts) dynamically interact with static social features to model how content delivery rhythms affect viewer retention.
Cross-Modal Attention: The self-attention layers allow content tokens to attend to relevant audio frames (e.g., emphasis in speech corresponding to key transcript segments) and image regions (e.g., cover visuals reinforcing the title's claim).
Positional Context Preservation: Despite feature concatenation, the positional encoding inherited from BERT and the Transformer's own positional awareness help maintain temporal coherence in content modality, enabling the model to recognize critical time windows (e.g., hook phrases in the first 30 seconds).

4 Experiment

4.1 Dataset

The data required for this study can be divided into four dimensions, as shown in Table 1.

This study conducts web scraping in multiple steps while adhering to Bilibili's regulations and requirements. After data cleaning based on video release time and video duration, a total of 5,356 valid data entries were obtained.

Table 1. Summary of Required Data

Dimension Name	Corresponding Indicators
Influence data	View count, favorite count, coin count, like count, share count, comment count, Danmaku count
Uploader data	Follower count, Total views, Total likes
Video data	Title text, audio, cover
Time data	Video release time, video duration

4.2 Influence Scoring

Referring to the definition of video influence by Jin Xinyi et al. [21], This study defines a video influence formula, as shown in Eq. (3). In this formula, X_i (where i = 1,2,3,4,5,6,7) corresponds to the seven influence data indicators mentioned above, and b_i (where i = 1,2,3,4,5,6,7) represents the weights calculated using the entropy weight method based on the values of these seven video influence indicators.

$$W_0 = b_1 \ln(x_1 + 1) + b_2 \ln(x_2 + 1) + b_3 \ln(x_3 + 1) + b_4 \ln(x_4 + 1) + b_5 \ln(x_5 + 1) + b_6 \ln(x_6 + 1) + b_7 \ln(x_7 + 1) \quad (3)$$

Based on Eq. (3), this study obtains the corresponding weight values for the seven video influence indicators, as shown in Table 2.

Table 2. Entropy Weight Size of Each Indicator

Indicator Name	Entropy Weight Size
Play count	0.1537117
Damuku count	0.14872481
Comment count	0.15939296
Favorite count	0.13918312
Coin count	0.12156301
Like count	0.15238883
Share count	0.12503557

After calculating the entropy weights, Each video is assigned an influence score based on the influence scoring formula.

4.3 Parameter Settings

The relevant parameters for this experiment are shown in Table 3.

Table 3. Parameter Settings Table

Parameter Name	Parameter Values
Word embedding dimension	100
Number of MFCCs	13
Batch training samples	32
Learning rate	0.001
Training set proportion	70%
Optimizer	Adam
Loss function	MSELoss

4.4 Evaluation Metrics

In this study, two commonly used evaluation metrics were employed to assess the performance of the multimodal video influence prediction model: Mean Squared Error (MSE) and Spearman Rank Correlation Coefficient (SRCC). The formulas for these metrics are shown in Eqs. 4 and 5, respectively.

$$\text{MSE} = \frac{1}{N}\sum_{i=1}^{N}(y_i - \hat{y}_i)^2 \tag{4}$$

where y_i is the true influence score of the i-th sample, $\hat{y}_i$ is the predicted score for the sample by the model, and N is the total number of samples.

$$\text{SRCC} = 1 - \frac{6\sum d_i^2}{N\left(N^2 - 1\right)} \tag{5}$$

4.5 Baseline Models

This study uses MTAF and Mutimodal CNN(MMC) as the baseline Models to validate the effectiveness of the proposed model.

MTAF [22] extracts multimodal features separately and designs a multimodal and temporal attention mechanism layer to combine features from multiple sources, demonstrating excellent performance in the influence prediction task of promotional micro-videos.

Compared to MMCT, MMC extracts and integrates the five modality features in the same way, but instead of inputting the fused features into a Transformer, it directly outputs the results through a fully connected layer.

4.6 Experimental Results and Analysis

The experimental results of all models are shown in Table 4.

Table 4. Experimental Results

Model	MSE	SRCC
MMCT	**1.5049**	**0.7895**
MMC	2.2231	0.6211
MTAF	1.9067	0.7339

The results show that MMCT outperforms the two baseline models, demonstrating the effectiveness of the model. Meanwhile, the results indicate that the design that combines CNN and Transformer optimizes the model's capability in modeling local features, global relationships, and temporal dynamics, making it well-suited for handling complex multimodal data structures and long-range dependencies. This design is particularly effective for tasks like scientific popularization videos, which involve knowledge transfer, emotional expression, and visual appeal.

4.7 Ablation Experiments

The experimental results of all models are shown in Table 5, where T, S, A, I, and C represent the text, social, audio, image, and content modalities, respectively.

Table 5. Ablation Experiments Results

Modalities	MSE	SRCC
T+S+A+I+C	**1.5049**	**0.7895**
T+S+C+I	1.6887	0.7732
T+S+A+C	1.7232	0.7701
S+A+C+I	1.7681	0.7694
T+A+C+I	2.0238	0.7357
T+S+A+I	2.7116	0.6562

This study conducted ablation experiments, comparing the performance of the model when one modality was removed versus when all modalities were retained. The experimental results indicate that the model's performance decreases regardless of which modality is removed, with the largest performance drop occurring when the content modality is removed. This suggests that content modality features have a significant impact on video influence. Furthermore, the results indicate that the fusion of multimodal features allows for the full utilization of different information sources from each modality, enhancing the model's ability to perform a comprehensive evaluation of video influence.

5 Conclusions

This study proposes the MMCT model for predicting the influence of scientific popularization videos on Bilibili. MMCT integrates text, social, audio, image, and content modality features, combining CNN and Transformer models, and outperforms the baseline models on the dataset. In the ablation experiments, removing any modality leads to a decrease in model performance, with the content modality having the greatest impact. The experimental results demonstrate that multimodal features are beneficial for video influence prediction tasks, and the combination of CNN and Transformer allows the model to leverage the strengths of both, extracting both local and global complex features.

References

1. Zhu Hengmin, X., Ning, W.J., Chao, S.: Research on popularity prediction of short videos based on network representation learning. J. Inf. Sci. **09**, 1105–1115 (2024)
2. Cho, M., Jeong, D., Park, E.: AMPS: Predicting popularity of short-form videos using multi-modal attention mechanisms in social media marketing environments [J]. J. Retail. Consumer Serv., 78103778 (2024)
3. Shijie, J., Yan, C., Xiaoyan, S., et al.: A social-aware video sharing solution using demand prediction of epidemic-based propagation in wireless networks [J]. Multimedia Syst. **29**(6), 3505–3520 (2023). https://doi.org/10.1007/S00530-023-01167-X
4. Peiguang, J., Xuqing, Y., Liu, Y., et al.: Short video popularity prediction based on bidirectional deep encoding network [J]. Laser & Optoelectron. Prog. **59**(08), 300–308 (2022)
5. Pradeep, K.T., Ankit, M., Rohit, K.G., et al.: Popularity prediction of video content over cloud-based CDN using end user interest [J]. Int. J. Softw. Innov. (IJSI). **10**(1), 1–13 (2022). https://doi.org/10.4018/1JS1.301227
6. Davoodi, A., Dabbagh, A.W.A.: Hierarchical grouping and visualization of correlated alarms using time-augmented word embedding[J]. Contr. Eng. Pract., 154106130 (2025). https://doi.org/10.1016/J.CONENGPRAC.2024.106130
7. Wanli, Z., An, T., Wenqiao, L.: Remote supervision method for long-tail relation extraction based on constraint graph [J]. Modern Electron. Technol. **47**(21), 91–96 (2024). https://doi.org/10.16652/j.issn.1004-373x.2024.21.014
8. Yin Bangzhi, X., Jian, T.C.: Text sentiment analysis based on graph neural network and representation learning [J]. J. Nanjing Normal Univ. (Natural Science Edition). **47**(03), 97–103 (2024)
9. Dashuai, L., Chengyin, Y.: Short text classification method based on label-aware attention [J]. Softw. Guide. **23**(09), 110–115 (2024)
10. Yuan, H., Xiaohong, D., Weijian, H., et al.: Text classification based on A-BiLSTM and CNN [J]. Comput. Eng. Design. **45**(05), 1428–1434 (2024)
11. Alnowaiser, K.: Scientific text citation analysis using CNN features and ensemble learning model [J]. PloS one. **19**(5), e0302304 (2024)
12. Jia'an, Z., Jiahui, T., Tiecheng, W., et al.: Fault diagnosis method for wind turbine blades based on an improved MFCC algorithm [J]. Acta Energ. Sola. Sin. **45**(01), 285–290 (2024). https://doi.org/10.19912/j.0254-0096.tynxb.2022-1523
13. Huang Xiyang, D., Qingzhi, L.H., et al.: Speech emotion recognition algorithm based on MFCC feature fusion [J]. J. Shaanxi Univ. Technol. (Natural Science Edition). **39**(04), 17–25 (2023)

14. Jiping, S., Yu, X., Wang, Y.: Coal mine methane and coal dust explosion identification method based on spectrogram and SVM [J]. Coal Sci. Technol.
15. Tianto, E., Chandaka Samudera, A., Adeta, F., Nadia, N.: Lung cancer classification using modified ResNet architecture. In: 2024 8th International Conference on Information Technology, Information Systems and Electrical Engineering, ICITISEE 2024, pp. 280–285 (2024). https://doi.org/10.1109/ICITISEE63424.2024.10730161
16. Verma, S., Singla, R., Verma, O.P., Sharma, R., Gupta, H., Sharma, T., Muthanna, A.: Enhancing transformer tracking using NF-ResNet and ResNeXT backbones. In: Machine Intelligence for Research and Innovations. MAiTRI 2023 Lecture Notes in Networks and Systems, vol. 831, pp. 217–226. Springer, Singapore (2024). https://doi.org/10.1007/978-981-99-8135-9_19
17. Xing, S., Tang, H.: Combining gated SENet with ResNet backbone for image classification. In: Proceedings of the 36th Chinese Control and Decision Conference, CCDC, vol. 2024, pp. 5927–5931 (2024). https://doi.org/10.1109/CCDC62350.2024.10588317
18. Tanone, R., Li, L.-H., Saifullah, S.: ViT-CB: integrating hybrid vision transformer and CatBoost to enhanced brain tumor detection with SHAP. Biomed. Signal Proces. Contr. **100**, 107027 (2025). https://doi.org/10.1016/j.bspc.2024.107027
19. Liu, H., Li, L.: Image restoration employing cross-ViT combined generative adversarial networks. In: Proceedings of SPIE - The International Society for Optical Engineering, p. 13250 (2024). https://doi.org/10.1117/12.3038514
20. Dwika Hefni Al-Fahsi, R., Naghim Fauzaini Prawirosoenoto, A., Adi Nugroho, H., Ardiyanto, I.: GIVTED-net: GhostNet-Mobile involution ViT encoder-decoder network for lightweight medical image segmentation. IEEE Access. **12**, 81281–81292 (2024). https://doi.org/10.1109/ACCESS.2024.3411870
21. Xinyi, J., Guoyan, W.: Analysis of the communication power of popular science short videos on Douyin [J]. Popul. Sci. Res. **16**(01), 15–23 (2021) (in Chinese)
22. Ou, N., Yu, L., Li, H., Du, Q., Xiang, J., Gong, W.: MTAF: Shopping Guide Micro-Videos Popularity Prediction Using Multimodal And Temporal Attention Fusion Approach. In: ICASSP, IEEE International Conference on Acoustics, Speech and Signal Processing - Proceedings, 2022-May, pp. 4543–4547 (2022). https://doi.org/10.1109/ICASSP43922.2022.9746567

The Impact of Generative AI Models on Consumer Purchase Behavior in E-Commerce Platforms: Evidence from a Quasi-Natural Experiment

Jianing Xie[1], Mingqian Li[1], Rong Du[1](✉), and David M. Townsend[2]

[1] School of Economics and Management, Xidian University, Xi'an, Shaanxi, China
durong@mail.xidian.edu.cn

[2] Department of Management, Pamplin College of Business, Virginia Polytechnic Institute and State University, Blacksburg, VA, USA

Abstract. Generative AI models hold substantial potential for improving the accuracy and effectiveness of information transmission, further enhancing platform competitiveness and user satisfaction. Although platforms actively adopt generative AI models in practice, there remains a lack of empirical evidence supporting their effectiveness on e-commerce platforms. This study, grounded in cue utilization theory and employing a Difference-in-Differences (DID) method, systematically examines the impact of generative AI models on consumer purchase behavior under the moderating effect of several extrinsic cues. The findings indicate that generative AI model have significant increment on consumer purchase behavior, particularly for products with high information richness, high review inconsistency. Notably, despite conventional recommendation systems aggravate homogenized market according to the winner-take-all theory, empirical results demonstrate that generative AI model does not meet expectations. Instead, the AI model enhanced sales of the product with low brand awareness, which confirming long tail theory. This research enriches the application of cue utilization theory about the impact of generative AI model with e-commerce environment, elucidates the moderating mechanisms among multiple cues, and provides practical guidance for e-commerce platforms managers in the design of business strategies.

Keywords: Generative AI · product sales · quasi-natural experiments · cue utilization theory

1 Introduction

The year 2022 marked a pivotal moment in artificial intelligence with OpenAI's ChatGPT successfully introducing generative AI models to the public domain. In the subsequent years, the field of generative AI has experienced exponential growth, expanding across multiple modalities including text, audio, image, and video. This rapid technological advancement has catalyzed the widespread integration of generative AI across

Y. P. Tu and M. Chi (Eds.): WHICEB 2025, LNBIP 549, pp. 224–235, 2025.
https://doi.org/10.1007/978-3-031-94184-9_19

diverse industries, revolutionizing traditional practices and creating new opportunities. In healthcare systems, generative AI models can manage patient electronic medical records, review test reports, and provide regular follow-ups, thereby enhancing operational efficiency and patient care. The education industry has similarly benefited from these advancements, with AI systems now capable of personalizing learning materials based on individual student progress and learning styles, while effectively summarizing key concepts to optimize knowledge retention. The e-commerce landscape has also witnessed particularly transformative changes, with leading platforms continuously introducing innovative AI-powered features. Notably, several major platforms have implemented AI-based purchasing assistants, leveraging advanced algorithms to provide users with intelligent recommendations and support informed purchasing decisions. The AI-based purchasing assistant offers predominantly three functions: professional category and feature consultation, personalized purchasing suggestions, and product usage experience sharing (Li et al., 2022; Shi et al., 2021).

For e-commerce platforms, information asymmetry between sellers and buyers remains a persistent challenge. Consumers can only use limited information provided by platform to evaluate the quality, trustworthiness and overall appeal to products, so-called cues (Rosillo-Díaz et al., 2024). High-quality cues have been shown to mitigate customer risk and improve decision-making processes. However, existing research highlights potential drawbacks: excessive information richness can lead to information overload (Jabr & Rahman, 2022), while the inconsistency stemming from fragmented reviews may cause consumer confusion (Yin et al., 2023). In this context, generative AI models present a promising avenue for addressing these challenges. With capabilities such as professional category and feature consultations, as well as product usage experience sharing, these models have the potential to transform the way consumers interact with e-commerce platforms, making this an area ripe for further exploration and innovation.

While AI holds significant potential, it also introduces new challenges that warrant careful consideration. Although recommendations use consumers' personalized data as reference, biases may emerge due to the nature of the training data (Zhou et al., 2024). For example, brand awareness embedded in the training data could influence AI recommendations (Frenzel et al., 2020), a phenomenon that requires further investigation. Conventional collaborative filtering can lead to the Matthew effect and the long tail effect (Gu et al., 2013). And relatively few studies have affirmed AI-generated review summaries may contribute to the Matthew effect (Su et al., 2024). However, when product and user information are integrated into recommendation systems, the results could potentially change, requiring further validation.

Traditional research methodologies have predominantly relied on experimental or survey-based approaches to measure consumers' purchase intention. However, this focus on purchase intention may overlook potential shifts in consumer behavior that occur after products are added to shopping carts (Close & Kukar-Kinney, 2010). While a limited number of studies have attempted to indirectly assess purchasing behavior through metrics such as sales rankings (Su et al., 2024), research directly measuring purchase behavior through sales data is relatively scarce.

Based on this, the study at hand aims to empirically investigate the role of generative AI models on consumer purchase behavior under the moderating effects of extrinsic cues. We conducted a quasi-natural experiment from a leading international e-commerce platform. Data were collected from June 2023 to February 2024, encompassing a sample of 115 products. From the perspective of cue utilization theory, the study analyzes the performance of generative AI models across different product information characteristics, focusing specifically on the effects of product information richness, online review inconsistency and brand awareness on sales outcomes.

Our findings provide valuable insights about the mechanisms by which generative AI models function in the digital economy. Our findings also offer implications for optimizing e-commerce platforms, particularly in the context of severe information asymmetry, where the application of generative AI models can significantly enhance platform competitiveness and user satisfaction. Since consumers utilize cues that they actually notice rather than all the information provided by the sellers and the platform, the knowledge of how extrinsic cues moderate the impact of generative AI models on consumer purchase behavior can help platform manager in making product displaying and information strategies.

2 Theoretical Foundation and Research Hypothesis

2.1 Cue Utilization Theory

Cue utilization theory (CUT) explains purchasing behavior from the perspective of purchasers, assuming that consumers utilize not only the attributes sent by the sellers, but also all other attributes of the product or service that affect the consumer's decision-making process (Sun et al., 2022). According to the CUT, cues can be divided into extrinsic cues (e.g., price, brand or package) and intrinsic cues (e.g., physical attributes or ingredients) (Olson & Jacoby, 1972). While intrinsic cues, which refers to the inherent attributes of products, are hard to assess through e-commerce platform for consumers, extrinsic cues can be easily utilized to derive information and make decisions. Numerous studies have revealed consumers' perception of product value are based on a trade-off between perceived benefits (e.g., product quality) and perceived sacrifice, which are based, at least in part, on extrinsic cues (Teas & Agarwal, 2000). On the one hand, consumers evaluate the quality of products based on extrinsic cues including website quality, product reviews, brand reputation, etc. And with capabilities of professional category and feature consultations, as well as product usage experience sharing, generative AI models have the potential to increase consumers' perceived product quality. On the other hand, perceived sacrifice also affected by extrinsic cues including time and efforts, pricing and discounts, trust and risk, website usability, etc. AI-based personalized recommendation systems have the potential to address the aforementioned factors, thereby reducing consumers' perceived sacrifice.

Based on this, we propose a research model to explore the mechanism through how the generative AI model affects consumer purchase behavior and how other extrinsic cues (i.e., information richness, review inconsistency and brand awareness) play roles in this process, as illustrated in Fig. 1.

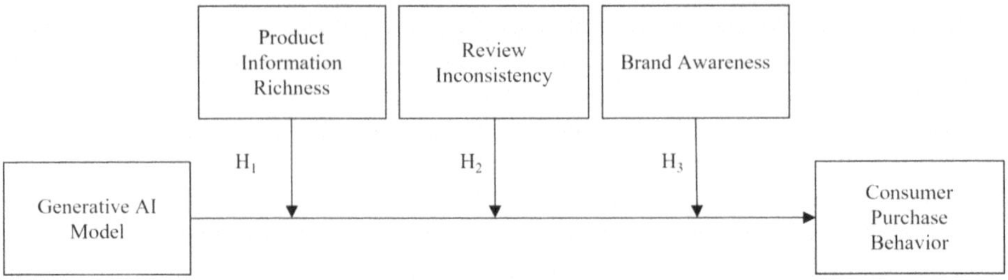

Fig. 1. Research Model

2.2 Information Richness

On the platform, consumers strive to obtain comprehensive and trustworthy information, as known as cues, for making purchase decisions. The theory of information richness posits that equivocal interactions, such as ones requiring trust, can be facilitated through communication media that transmit multiple cues interactively, which in turn diminishes ambiguity and uncertainty within the communication process (Chesney et al., 2017). However, with the plethora of multi-modal online information, consumers' cognitive demands of the purchasing task excessively high and they easily encounter the problem of information overload (Jabr & Rahman, 2022). Information overload hinders consumers from grasping the key highlights and core information provided by sellers and the platform, reduces the richness of unit information, weakens efficiency in the information transmission process, and ultimately leads to consumer impatience and diminished purchase intentions (Kakaria et al., 2023). The generative AI model offering professional category, feature consultation and personalized purchasing suggestions, acts as collaborative filtering recommendation systems, are beneficial for reducing human cognitive burden and alleviating information overload (Bollen et al., 2010). By effectively integrating internal and external information, it mitigates information asymmetry and enhances both information transparency and the quality of decisions (Zhang & Zhang, 2024). Therefore, the extent of information richness offered by the platform and sellers should not be disregarded. On the e-commerce platform, the overabundance of information may lead to consumers' information overload and decrease consumers' purchase intention, however, the increase of informativeness of description will improve the generative AI model's understanding, further enhancing capability of the AI system in decreasing consumers' uncertainty and facilitate consumer purchase behavior. Since there is limited understanding of the interaction effect of AI model and information richness on consumer purchase behavior, we propose:

Hypothesis 1: Compared to products with lower information richness on their details page, the implementation of generative AI model exerts a more pronounced influence on consumer purchase behavior for products with higher information richness.

2.3 Review Inconsistency

Online word-of-month, as kind of extrinsic cue (Tong & Zhong, 2009), such as consumer opinions, user experience and product reviews, has become increasingly popular in consumer purchase decision making and is crucial to platforms. However, two self-selection biases (i.e., acquisition bias and underreporting bias) often leads to J-shaped distribution (positively skewed, asymmetric and bimodal) of online product reviews, which are not sufficient to reveal the quality of product (Hu et al., 2017). This review inconsistency problem appears on three levels, including product level (inconsistent product ratings), review level (two-sided argument in one review) and cross-review level (disagreement for product attributes from different reviews) (Yin et al., 2023). Since consumers often read a set of featured review before purchase instead of consulting all reviews or single review, cross-review incoherence is the most significant obstacle which leads to purchase deferral even sales loss (Yin et al., 2023). Confront with this problem, platforms launch generative AI models offering the function of product usage experience sharing, which is potentially beneficial alleviating cross-review inconsistency. Unsupervised opinion summarization systems, like AI generative summary, can capture the aspects and sentiment between reviews and summaries. Moreover, though summarization, generative AI models may decrease consumer's confusion and uncertainty, especially facing products with highly inconsistent reviews, which has not been discussed in previous studies. Thus, we propose:

Hypothesis 2: For products with higher review inconsistency, the application of a generative AI model has a stronger impact on consumer purchase behavior than for products with lower review inconsistency.

2.4 Brand Awareness

Brand awareness, act as extrinsic cue or signal, often utilized in imperfect and asymmetrical information structure in market, like e-commerce platform (Bao et al., 2011). When consumers confront with uncertainty of product quality, sellers can use brand awareness improve consumers' perception on product claims, decrease their perceived risks and enhance their utility expectation (Erdem & Swait, 2001). The conventional method for assessing a seller's awareness, including aggregating feedback or ratings provided by its customers, is leading to unfair feedbacks, due to collusion between some sellers and consumers. These kind of violations of fair awareness information, such as "click farming," "cash rebate for favorable comments," and "pay-per-click," has aggravated information asymmetry and adverse selection, which cause the decrease of welfare between consumers and sellers (Hu et al., 2011). Besides, on the one hand, according to winner-take-all theory, due to factors like network effects and economies of scale, the application of standard recommendation system causes homogenized market (Molaie & Lee, 2022). On the other hand, researchers reveals that a much larger number of niche product can also succeed through recommendation systems, which lead to fragmented market, according to the long tail theory (Yin et al., 2012). This kind of seeming contradiction actually depend on the types of the product the recommendation systems prefer (Wu et al., 2011). However, since bias existing in the real world may be converted into training data, the generative AI models may become puzzled and create filter bubbles, affected by brand awareness deeply (Frenzel et al., 2020). And this may mitigate the effectiveness of personalized purchasing suggestions, further moderate the effect of the generative AI models on consumer purchase behavior. Thus, we propose:

Hypothesis 3: The impact of a generative AI model on consumer purchase behavior is more significant for products with higher brand awareness compared to those with lower brand awareness.

3 Research Method

We investigated our research questions using data collected from a leading international e-commerce platform and a third-party data service provider. The platform has launched a generative AI model, which has four major functions, including professional category consultation, personalized purchasing suggestions, product feature comparison and product usage experience sharing, according to official introduction in Fig. 2. The implementation provided a natural experimental setting, enabling us to examine the impact of the generative AI model under several extrinsic cues. Our study period spanned from June 2023 to February 2024, covering a sample of 115 products. In our analysis, we use two types of products (i.e., beauty products as experiential products and smartphones as informational products) as samples.

Fig. 2. The Introduction and Interaction Page

We measured consumer purchase behavior using product sales volume. For review inconsistency, we use sentiment analysis techniques to compute sentiment orientation values of product reviews, serving as an alternative measure to traditional product ratings. By calculating the variance value of the sentiment score of the accumulated reviews of each product before treatment, we define the top third of products with the highest variance values as products with high review inconsistency, while the rest of them are defined as products with low review inconsistency. Product information richness is measured across six dimensions: the number of product images, length of product descriptions, diversity of description themes, number of recommended products, and the inclusion of after-sales and promotional information. Through their integrated quantity, we similarly define product at top third and the rest as products with high and low information richness respectively. Previous research has often depended on consumer rankings or ratings to evaluate brand (Barone & Jewell, 2014), providing only limited detail in online settings

(Mu & Zhang, 2021). To obtain objective evidence, researchers has verified that consumers' online search behavior data can be utilized to accurately map the positioning of specific brands and their associative relationships in consumers' mental models (Jun & Park, 2017). Thus, we use "Baidu Index", an indicator analogous to "Google Trends" that measures the search popularity and attention of keywords mined from Baidu's vast data repository, to evaluate brand awareness. Specifically, we extract the value of "Baidu Index" 1 month before the implementation of generative AI models and define the top third products with higher value of "Baidu Index" as high brand awareness while the rest are low brand awareness. Definitions of key variables and descriptive statistics are presented in Table 1.

Table 1. Definitions of Variables and Summary Statistics

Variable	Definition	Mean	SD	Min	Max
Sales	The number of sales quantities for a product in a month.	11350.41	16735.48	396	191,748
Post	A dummy variable indicating whether generative AI was implemented. (1: Yes; 0: No)	0.56	0.50	0	1
Price	The average price for a product in a month.	3447.30	3205.83	100	11,699
Volume	The number of reviews for a product in a month.	80.79	89.78	1	932
Star	The average rating for a product in a month.	4.75	0.55	2	5
Review inconsistency	The degree of inconsistency in reviews for a product. (1: High; 0: Low)	0.37	0.48	0	1
Product information richness	The richness of information a product presents in the product details page. (1: High; 0: Low)	0.60	0.49	0	1
Brand awareness	The awareness for a product brand. (1: High; 0: Low)	0.50	0.50	0	1

Notes: SD is for standard deviation; Min is for minimum; Max is for maximum

4 Econometric Specification

This study employs a Difference-in-Differences (DID) model to investigate the role of generative AI models on consumer purchase behavior under the moderating effects of extrinsic cues (i.e., information richness, review inconsistency and brand awareness):

$$\ln Sales_{it} = \beta_0 + \beta_1 Post_t \times ReviewInconsistency_i + X_{it} + \mu_i + \delta_t + \varepsilon_{it}$$

$$\ln Sales_{it} = \beta_0 + \beta_1 Post_t \times ProductInformationRichness_i + X_{it} + \mu_i + \delta_t + \varepsilon_{it}$$

$$\ln Sales_{it} = \beta_0 + \beta_1 Post_t \times BrandAwareness_i + X_{it} + \mu_i + \delta_t + \varepsilon_{it}$$

The dependent variable, $Sales_{it}$, represents the sales quantity of product i in month t. The dependent variable, $ReviewInconsistency_i$, is a binary indicator where products with high review inconsistency are assigned a value of 1, and the rest are assigned a value of 0. Dependent variables, $ProductInformationRichness_i$ and $BrandAwareness_i$, are defined as same as $ReviewInconsistency_i$. $Post_t$ is a dummy variable indicating whether Generative AI was implemented. We introduce X_{it} to denote control variables, include $Price_{it}$, $volume_{it}$ and $star_{it}$. Additionally, we incorporate product fixed effects μ_i to account for inherent differences in product attributes and month fixed effects δ_t to control for potential time-varying factors.

5 Results

5.1 Moderating Role of Product Information Richness

Table 2, columns (1) and (2) represent the regression results without and with control variables, respectively. The interaction term between $Post_t$ and $ProductInformationRichness_i$ proves significant positive moderating relationship, thereby confirming Hypothesis 1. When consumers are faced with products that have high information richness (i.e., the product details pages display a large number of images, lengthy product descriptions, diverse description themes, and numerous recommended products), due to high cognitive burden, they experience information overload (Bollen et al., 2010). Thus, consumers will seek for AI models' assistance to make purchase decisions. Besides, the product with high information richness will increase the size of data source which is beneficial for generative AI model to better understand its features, further recommend it when consumers' demand is matched (Grewal et al., 2024).

5.2 Moderating Role of Review Inconsistency

From Table 3, the coefficients of the interaction terms between $Post_t$ and $ReviewInconsistency_i$ are significantly positive, indicating that the positive impact of generative AI models is more pronounced for products with high review inconsistency, thus confirming Hypothesis 2. Specifically, when products have cross-review incoherence problem, consumers suffer confusion about products. This is where generative AI models truly

Table 2. Moderating Role of Product Information Richness

Variables	(1) lnSales	(2) lnSales
Post × product information richness	0.128** (0.067)	0.104** (0.063)
Control variables	No	Yes
Product FE	Yes	Yes
Monthly FE	Yes	Yes
R-squared	0.682	0.715
Number of Obs	1035	1035

Notes: Cluster-robust standard errors in parentheses; $^{***}p<0.01$, $^{**}p<0.05$, $^{*}p<0.1$

shines. In markets characterized by information asymmetry, generative AI models can effectively reduce consumer uncertainty in the decision-making process by enhancing product recommendations and information presentation, thereby facilitating consumer purchase behavior (Mogaji & Jain, 2024). Conversely, when products' reviews have low inconsistency, consumers can independently make purchase decision through online word-of-mouth, where AI models have little increment on sales.

Table 3. Moderating Role of Review Inconsistency

Variables	(1) lnSales	(2) lnSales
Post × review inconsistency	0.146** (0.068)	0.137** (0.065)
Control variables	No	Yes
Product FE	Yes	Yes
Monthly FE	Yes	Yes
R-squared	0.682	0.7152
Number of Obs	1035	1035

Notes: Cluster-robust standard errors in parentheses; $^{***}p<0.01$, $^{**}p<0.05$, $^{*}p<0.1$

5.3 Moderating Role of Brand Awareness

Table 4 regression results indicate that the interaction term between the application of generative AI model and brand awareness remains negative ($\beta = -0.129$, $p < 0.05$), illustrating that products with lower brand awareness have more increment on AI models' impact, which rejected Hypothesis 3. This phenomenon indicates that the application of generative AI model increases the exposure rate of niche product, which confirming long tail theory (Yin et al., 2012). That is, the generative AI model enhance the total welfare between consumers and sellers, alleviating homogenized market problem caused by conventional recommendation systems (Molaie & Lee, 2022).

Table 4. Moderating Role of Brand Awareness

Variables	(1) lnSales	(2) lnSales
Post × brand awareness	-0.129^{**} (0.063)	-0.121^{*} (0.064)
Control variables	No	Yes
Product FE	Yes	Yes
Monthly FE	Yes	Yes
R-squared	0.682	0.683
Number of Obs	1035	1035

Notes: Cluster-robust standard errors in parentheses; $^{***}p<0.01$, $^{**}p<0.05$, $^{*}p<0.1$

6 Implications and Conclusions

This research provides empirical evidence on the application of generative AI models in e-commerce platforms from a cue utilization theory perspective, extending the theory's applicability in the e-commerce domain. The findings indicate that generative AI models significantly influence the purchasing intention of products with high levels of review inconsistency, high information richness and low brand awareness for consumers by reducing information asymmetry. This discovery not only deepens the understanding of the commercial applications of generative AI models but also offers new directions for future research. Generative AI models have broad applicability within e-commerce platforms, not only optimizing product recommendation systems but also enhancing overall platform performance by fostering consumer trust and simplifying the complexity of purchase decisions.

From a theoretical standpoint, this study explores how generative AI models, within the framework of cue utilization theory, influence consumer purchasing decisions by improving the accuracy and effectiveness of information transmission, providing novel empirical support, and deepening our understanding of the mechanisms by which generative AI models function in the digital economy. Practically, the findings offer strategic guidance for optimizing e-commerce platforms, particularly in contexts with severe information asymmetry, where the application of generative AI models can significantly enhance platform competitiveness and user satisfaction. These insights suggest that platform managers should consider the potential value of generative AI applications more when developing product display and information strategies. Future research could further explore the performance of generative AI models across different cultural contexts, consumer behavior preferences, and market maturity levels to uncover additional underlying mechanisms of influence. Additionally, as generative AI technology continues to evolve, integrating other advanced technologies, such as blockchain and the Internet of Things (IoT), to enhance the intelligence of e-commerce platforms warrants further investigation. Through continuous, multi-layered, and comprehensive research, we can gain a deeper understanding of the profound impact of generative AI models in the e-commerce field, providing stronger support for both theoretical development and business practice.

Acknowledgement. This research is supported by the National Natural Science Foundation of China through grant 72171187, and partially supported by the Humanities and Social Science Foundation provided by the Ministry of Education through grant 22YJA870001.

References

Bao, Y., Bao, Y., Sheng, S.: Motivating purchase of private brands: Effects of store image, product signatureness, and quality variation. J. Busi. Res. **64**(2), 220–226 (2011)

Barone, M.J., Jewell, R.D.: How brand innovativeness creates advertising flexibility. J. Acad. Market. Sci. **42**, 309–321 (2014)

Bollen, D., Knijnenburg, B.P., Willemsen, M.C., Graus, M.: Understanding choice overload in recommender systems. In: Proceedings of the Fourth ACM Conference on Recommender Systems, pp. 63–70 (2010, September)

Chesney, T., Chuah, S.H., Dobele, A.R., Hoffmann, R.: Information richness and trust in v-commerce: implications for services marketing. J. Serv. Market. **31**(3), 295–307 (2017)

Close, A.G., Kukar-Kinney, M.: Beyond buying: Motivations behind consumers' online shopping cart use. J. Busi. Res. **63**(9–10), 986–992 (2010)

Erdem, T., Swait, J.: Brand equity as a signaling. J. Cons. Psychol. **7**(2), 131–157 (2001)

Frenzel, A., Jain, S., Jia, S. J., Welck, M. V., & Langer, N.: Fighting the real AI danger: How to design virtuous AI for virtuous decision-making (2020)

Grewal, D., Satornino, C.B., Davenport, T., Guha, A.: How generative AI Is shaping the future of marketing. J. Acad. Market. Sci., 1–21 (2024)

Gu, B., Tang, Q., Whinston, A.B.: The influence of online word-of-mouth on long tail formation. Decis. Supp. Syst. **56**, 474–481 (2013)

Hu, N., Liu, L., Sambamurthy, V.: Fraud detection in online consumer reviews. Decis. Supp. Syst. **50**(3), 614–626 (2011)

Hu, N., Pavlou, P.A., Zhang, J.: On self-selection biases in online product reviews. MIS Q. **41**(2), 449–475 (2017)

Jabr, W., Rahman, M.S.: Online reviews and information overload: the role of selective, parsimonious, and concordant top reviews. MIS Q. **46**(3) (2022)

Jun, S.-P., Park, D.-H.: Visualization of brand positioning based on consumer web search information: using social network analysis. Inter. Res. **27**(2), 381–407 (2017)

Kakaria, S., Saffari, F., Ramsøy, T.Z., Bigné, E.: Cognitive load during planned and unplanned virtual shopping: evidence from a neurophysiological perspective. Int. J. Inform. Manag. **72**, 102667 (2023)

Li, X., Grahl, J., Hinz, O.: How do recommender systems lead to consumer purchases? A causal mediation analysis of a field experiment. Inform. Syst. Res. **33**(2), 620–637 (2022)

Mogaji, E., Jain, V.: How generative AI is (will) change consumer behaviour: Postulating the potential impact and implications for research, practice, and policy. J. Cons. Behav. **23**(5), 2379–2389 (2024)

Molaie, M.M., Lee, W.: Economic corollaries of personalized recommendations. J. Retail. Cons. Serv. **68**, 103003 (2022)

Mu, J., Zhang, J.Z.: Seller marketing capability, brand reputation, and consumer journeys on e-commerce platforms. J. Acad. Market. Sci. **49**(5), 994–1020 (2021)

Olson, J. C., & Jacoby, J.: Cue utilization in the quality perception process. ACR Special Volumes (1972)

Rosillo-Díaz, E., Muñoz-Rosas, J.F., Blanco-Encomienda, F.J.: Impact of heuristic–systematic cues on the purchase intention of the electronic commerce consumer through the perception of product quality. J. Retail. Cons. Serv. **81**, 103980 (2024)

Shi, S., Gong, Y., Gursoy, D.: Antecedents of trust and adoption intention toward artificially intelligent recommendation systems in travel planning: a heuristic–systematic model. J. Travel Res. **60**(8), 1714–1734 (2021)

Su, Y., Wang, Q., Qiu, L., & Chen, R.: Navigating the Sea of Reviews: Unveiling the Effects of Introducing AI-Generated Summaries in E-Commerce. Available at SSRN 4872205 (2024)

Sun, J., Li, Q., Xu, W., Wang, M.: Pay to view answers: determinants of listeners' payment decisions on social Q&A platforms. Inter. Res. **32**(4), 1401–1426 (2022)

Teas, R.K., Agarwal, S.: The effects of extrinsic product cues on consumers' perceptions of quality, sacrifice, and value. J. Acad. Market. Sci. **28**, 278–290 (2000)

Tong, Y., Zhong, Y.: Are we trapped by majority influences in electronic word-of-mouth? In: Human-Computer Interaction. New Trends: 13th International Conference, HCI International 2009, San Diego, CA, USA, July 19–24, 2009, Proceedings, Part I 13, pp. 520–529. Springer, Berlin Heidelberg (2009)

Wu, L.L., Joung, Y.J., Chiang, T.E.: Recommendation systems and sales concentration: The moderating effects of consumers' product awareness and acceptance to recommendations. In: 2011 44th Hawaii International Conference on System Sciences, pp. 1–10. IEEE (2011)

Yin, H., Cui, B., Li, J., Yao, J., & Chen, C.: Challenging the long tail recommendation. arXiv preprint arXiv:1205.6700 (2012)

Yin, D., de Vreede, T., Steele, L.M., de Vreede, G.-J.: Decide now or later: making sense of incoherence across online reviews. Inform. Syst. Res. **34**(3), 1211–1227 (2023)

Zhang, C., Zhang, H.: The impact of generative AI on management innovation. J. Indus. Inform. Integrat, 100767 (2024)

Zhou, M., Zhang, J., Adomavicius, G.: Longitudinal impact of preference biases on recommender systems' performance. Inform. Syst. Res. **35**(4), 1634–1656 (2024)

Digital Enablement and Digital Governance

Resource Utilization and Supply Chain Resilience: The Moderated Mediation Role of AI Capabilities and Technological Turbulence

Yuting Wang[1], Jinmei Yin[2](✉), Yao Chen[3], and Tianjun Qiu[4]

[1] Shanghai University, Shanghai, China
[2] Nanjing University of Aeronautics and Astronautics, Nanjing, Jiangsu, China
mayyin@nuaa.edu.cn
[3] Jiangsu University of Science and Technology, Zhenjiang, Jiangsu, China
[4] Shanghai University, Shanghai, China

Abstract. Although some research has examined the role of resource utilization in enhancing supply chain resilience, the mechanisms through which these resources contribute to resilience have been largely overlooked. Drawing on dynamic capability theory, we investigate when and how resource utilization affects supply chain resilience, focusing on the mediating role of artificial intelligence (AI) capability and the moderating role of technological turbulence. Using survey data from 137 companies in China, We find that AI capability mediates the relationship between two types of resource utilization: bricolage and R&D resource utilization, and supply chain resilience. Furthermore, technological turbulence strengthens the effect of bricolage resource utilization on supply chain resilience while weakening the effect of R&D resource utilization. These findings provide valuable theoretical and practical insights for resource management and technological adaptation in supply chain management.

Keywords: Bricolage resource utilization · R&D resource utilization · AI capability · Technological turbulence

1 Introduction

Supply chain responsiveness is critical for firms to navigate dynamic environments. Scholars have outlined five key dimensions of supply chain responsiveness: adaptability, flexibility, agility, improvisation, and resilience. Each dimension has distinct characteristics and plays a unique role in enhancing supply chain performance. The availability of diverse resources and strategic deployment have created significant opportunities to enhance supply chain resilience (SCR). SCR, defined as the ability to mitigate disruptions and restore operations swiftly, is critical for long-term growth and operational continuity in volatile environments (Atadoga et al., 2024). As disruptions increase, strategies to strengthen SCR are gaining attention. Research indicates that efficient resource utilization is key to overcoming operational constraints and enhancing resilience. However, many organizations struggle to leverage resources effectively to improve SCR (Gu et al.,

Y. P. Tu and M. Chi (Eds.): WHICEB 2025, LNBIP 549, pp. 239–251, 2025.
https://doi.org/10.1007/978-3-031-94184-9_20

2021). For example, Nokia, despite its abundant resources and efforts to develop the Symbian OS and form alliances, failed to enhance its SCR amid changing market demands. This highlights that possessing resources alone doesn't guarantee improved SCR; firms must activate the mechanisms that transform resource utilization into resilience. Yet, the understanding of these mechanisms is still limited.

Existing research has explored the link between resource utilization and SCR conceptually, but empirical evidence on the mechanisms through which resources enhance resilience remains limited. Two strategies, bricolage resource utilization (BRU) and research and development (R&D) resource utilization (RRU), address resource limitations. BRU involves innovatively repurposing internal resources (Xu et al., 2023), while RRU focuses on acquiring external resources for innovation (Nason et al., 2019). This paper states that the strategic integration of BRU and RRU is essential for addressing short-term constraints and fostering long-term growth.

Grounded in dynamic capability theory (DCT), this study proposes that AI capability, a dynamic capability enabling data-driven adaptation to environmental changes, mediates the relationship between resource utilization and SCR (Eisenhardt & Martin, 2000). AI capability enhances adaptive responses, improves decision-making, and facilitates efficient resource allocation. Moreover, resource utilization generates data that strengthens AI-driven insights, creating a feedback loop that enhances SCR (Belhadi et al., 2024). Accordingly, this study aims to address a gap in the literature by investigating the mediating role of AI capability in the relationship between resource utilization and SCR. This leads to the following research question: How does AI capability mediate the relationship between resource utilization and SCR?

Technological turbulence, characterized by rapid and unpredictable technological changes, shapes the development of dynamic capabilities (Chatterjee et al., 2023). The integration of BRU and RRU, which serves as a foundational capability, is significantly influenced by technological turbulence, challenging firms to leverage insights for AI capability development. High turbulence introduces barriers to fully realizing resource value, potentially moderating the effect of resource utilization on SCR through AI capability. This gap leads to our second research question: How does technological turbulence moderate the impact of resource utilization on SCR through AI capability? Figure 1 represents our research model.

2 Literature Review

2.1 Dynamic Capabilities Theory and Resource Utilization

DCT explains how organizations integrate, develop, and reconfigure internal and external resources to sustain competitive advantages in dynamic environments (Eisenhardt & Martin, 2000). By enabling firms to sense opportunities, seize them, and adapt their resource base, DCT enhances performance dimensions such as efficiency, quality, speed, and flexibility. It highlights the importance of continuous learning, adaptation, and resource transformation in driving organizational resilience and competitive advantage.

Within the DCT framework, BRU and RRU are conceptualized as lower-order dynamic capabilities that enable firms to respond to environmental changes through

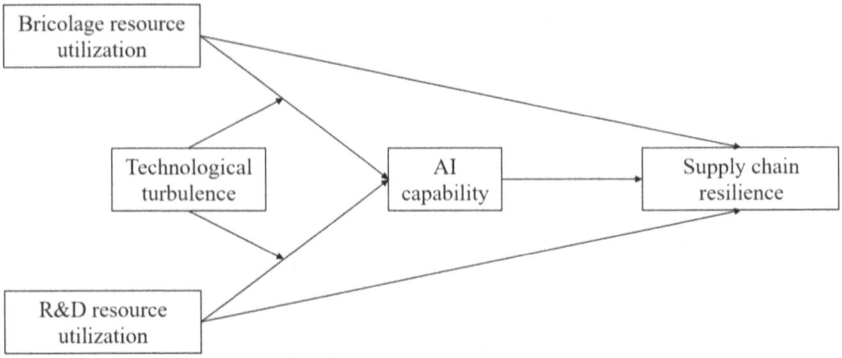

Fig. 1. Conceptual Model

learning and functional transformation. BRU involves creatively recombining and repurposing existing resources to overcome constraints and address challenges, fostering adaptability and innovation (Xu et al., 2023). It emphasizes leveraging unconventional inputs to seize opportunities and innovate despite resource limitations. In contrast, RRU focuses on the strategic employment of R&D resources to drive exploration and value creation (Nason et al., 2019). By engaging in external collaborations and accessing specialized knowledge, firms enhance innovation, mitigate risks, and develop proactive responses to market fluctuations. While R&D investments can significantly enhance firm performance, their effectiveness depends on alignment with market demands and the ability to navigate technological challenges.

Aligned with DCT's hierarchical structure, BRU and RRU, as lower-order capabilities, contribute to SCR by fostering the development of higher-order capabilities like AI capability. BRU and RRU enhance learning and innovation by generating new applications from existing and collaborative knowledge sets. In turn, AI capability synthesizes complex information, reduces uncertainty, and transforms insights into actionable strategies, ultimately driving SCR. This interplay underscores the role of lower-order and higher-order dynamic capabilities in enhancing firm adaptability, resilience, and performance in uncertain environments.

2.2 Artificial Intelligence Capability

AI capability refers to a system's ability to analyze external data, learn from it, and adjust or create new plans to respond to environmental changes (Chowdhury et al., 2023). It encompasses advanced technologies and processes that enhance efficiency and value delivery and addresses the challenges of handling large, complex datasets. By surpassing traditional analytics, AI allows firms to process complex information and predict changes in supply and demand, particularly during crises like pandemics. In supply chain management, AI is increasingly recognized for its ability to overcome information processing constraints (Lu & Zhou, 2024). For example, AI can predict disruptions, such as material shortages or transportation delays, by analyzing historical data and external factors like weather or geopolitical events. It also enhances demand forecasting by incorporating diverse variables such as social media trends and macroeconomic indicators. It optimizes logistics through intelligent routing that considers traffic, fuel costs, and delivery windows. AI capability can transform resource utilization into actionable strategies, enabling firms to adapt to dynamic environments and enhance supply chain resilience.

3 Hypotheses Development

BRU fosters improvisation and the innovative recombination of existing resources to address new challenges (Xu et al., 2023), enhancing SCR by improving agility and enabling creative solutions during disruptions. This dynamic capability helps firms maintain operations, reduce costs, and build long-term capabilities through organizational learning. We hypothesize that BRU positively affects SCR.

RRU, through continuous R&D investment, enhances a firm's adaptability and innovation, which is critical for resilience (Nason et al., 2019). It fosters agility, responsiveness, and new knowledge creation, improving a firm's ability to navigate disruptions and strengthen SCR. We hypothesize that RRU positively affects SCR. Thus, we hypothesize that:

H1: BRU has a positive effect on SCR.
H2: RRU has a positive effect on SCR.

Grounded in Dynamic Capability Theory (DCT), AI capability is a dynamic resource that helps firms make informed business decisions (Modgil et al., 2022). Both BRU and RRU enhance AI capability through different mechanisms. BRU promotes creativity and efficiency by encouraging innovative use of existing resources and data, facilitating cost-effective AI systems and broad adoption. RRU, through targeted R&D investments, advances AI algorithms and technologies, developing tailored solutions for specific challenges. AI capability strengthens SCR by analyzing data to predict disruptions and enhance decision-making with real-time visibility, enabling proactive risk management and improving supply chain resilience. In summary, we suggest that:

H3a: AI capability mediates the relationship between BRU and SCR.
H3b: AI capability mediates the relationship between RRU and SCR.

DCT emphasizes a firm's ability to integrate and reconfigure internal and external competencies to adapt to rapidly changing environments (Modgil et al., 2022). In the context of technological turbulence, BRU can strengthen AI capability by enabling firms to creatively use existing resources to develop innovative AI applications tailored to emerging trends. This approach is particularly valuable in turbulent environments, allowing for cost-effective experimentation with AI technologies. In contrast, while RRU generally enhances AI capability, high technological turbulence can weaken this relationship by introducing uncertainty and accelerating the obsolescence of R&D outcomes, making it harder to leverage these technologies effectively. To sum up, we put forward that:

H4a: Technological turbulence positively moderates the relationship between BRU and AI capability.

H4b: Technological turbulence negatively moderates the relationship between RRU and AI capability.

By integrating the above assumptions, we further proposed two moderated mediation frameworks: AI capability as a mediator in the BRU-SCR relationship and RRU-SCR relationship, and technological turbulence as a moderator. According to DCT, in high technological turbulence situations, firms are more inclined to utilize BRU and RRU to develop AI capability, thereby improving SCR. Therefore, under high technological turbulence, the mediating role of AI capability in the relationship between BRU/RRU and SCR is more significant. Specifically, the effects of BRU and RRU on SCR through AI capability are dependent on technological turbulence. To sum up, we put forward that:

H5a: The indirect effect of BRU on SCR through AI capability is positively moderated by technological turbulence.
H5b: The indirect effect of RRU on SCR through AI capability is positively moderated by technological turbulence.

4 Method

4.1 Data Collection and Sample

To test our hypothesis, we conducted a questionnaire survey with listed firms in China. China's rapid economic transformation, particularly in technological innovation and industrial upgrading, has made AI increasingly influential in supply chain operations. Additionally, the importance of supply chain resilience (SCR) became more apparent after crises like the COVID-19 pandemic. Listed firms, as pioneers in these changes, offer valuable insights into adapting to a rapidly evolving environment. Data collection through questionnaires is common in empirical research. To ensure the validity of the survey data, we adopted the items of variables used in previous studies. In the questionnaire, all constructs and items were measured using a five-point Likert scale.

We obtained contact information for listed firms and their top executives through a media firm specializing in corporate disclosures. A random sample of 200 firms from various industries was selected, and questionnaires were sent to their executives. Respondents were informed that their answers were anonymous and for academic purposes. We received 137 valid responses (response rate: 68.5%). Non-response bias was checked by comparing early and late respondents using a T-test, showing no significant differences in firm size ($t = -0.197$, $p = 0.845$), firm age ($t = 1.850$, $p = 0.070$), or ownership ($t = 0.627$, $p = 0.535$), indicating minimal non-response bias. Demographic information is summarized in Table 1.

4.2 Measurement Development

We designed the questionnaire to use a five-point Likert scale ranging from 1 (strongly disagree) to 5 (strongly agree) to measure the construct items. All the items were adopted from the existing literature. BRU was adopted by An et al. (2018). RRU adopted four items from Nason et al. (2019). AI capability was adopted by Belhadi et al. (2024). They

Table 1. Sample demographic (N = 137)

Parameters	N	Percentage (%)
Industry		
Manufacturing	56	40.90
Logistics	9	6.60
Tourism	22	15.10
Other industries	50	36.50
Firm ownership		
State-owned	40	29.20
Non-state-owned	97	70.80
Firm size		
<500	9	6.57
500–1,000	23	16.79
1,000–5,000	63	45.99
5,000–50,000	19	13.87
>50,000	23	16.78
Firm age		
<=15	17	12.41
16–20	38	27.74
21–25	48	35.04
26–30	23	16.79
> =31	11	8.02

capture a system's ability to acquire learning by analyzing the external environment's data and using acquired learnings to adjust or make new plans against environmental changes. The five items reflect the extent to which firms support and utilize AI in their production and operational activities. Technological turbulence was adopted by Nason et al. (2019). SCR was measured by four items from Ambulkar et al. (2015). In this study, we controlled firm industry, firm ownership, firm size, firm age, responders' gender, age, education, and working year, which may affect a firm's strategic decision.

4.3 Reliability and Validity

In our study, the descriptive statistics—means and standard deviations (SD) of all of the measured variables and their correlations were provided in Table 2. Several approaches were applied to examine the construct's reliability and validity. As shown in Table 3, Cronbach's alpha values of each scale ranged from 0.660 to 0.937, and the composite reliability values ranged from 0.881 to 0.952, which are higher than 0.6, thereby indicating satisfactory reliability. Then the results of confirmatory factor analysis (CFA)

Table 2. Means, Standard Deviations, and Correlations

	Mean	SD	1	2	3	4	5	6	7	8	9	10	11	12	13	14
1. BRU	3.92	0.62	**0.838**	0.56**	0.38**	0.24**	0.62**									
2. RRU	3.28	0.78	0.56**	**0.837**	0.47**	0.45**	0.55**									
3. AI capability	3.46	1.03	0.37**	0.46**	**0.893**	0.41**	0.56**									
4. TT	3.14	0.92	0.23**	0.44**	0.40**	**0.844**	0.38**									
5. SCR	3.59	0.73	0.62**	0.54**	0.56**	0.37**	**0.861**									
6. Industry 1	0.41	0.49	0.14	0.05	0.11	−0.10	0.15	**NA**								
7. Industry 2	0.07	0.25	−0.10	−0.01	−0.19*	0.11	−0.001	−0.22**	**NA**							
8. Industry 3	0.16	0.37	−0.07	0.001	0.12	0.18	0.04	−0.36**	−0.12	**NA**						
9. Firm ownership	0.29	0.46	−0.03	−0.01	0.01	0.02	−0.05	−0.18*	−0.04	0.42**	**NA**					
10. Firm size	23.04	2.05	−0.07	0.05	0.14	0.12	0.09	−0.19*	−0.15	0.49***	0.26**	**NA**				
11. Firm age	22.09	5.70	−0.17*	−0.09	−0.02	−0.06	−0.17*	−0.03	0.06	0.19*	0.11	0.30**	**NA**			
12. Gender	0.65	0.48	0.03	0.06	−0.20*	0.13	0.02	0.05	0.01	0.01	−0.03	−0.04	0.12	**NA**		
13. Age	0.11	0.31	0.020	0.11	−0.07	0.03	−0.02	0.10	0.03	−0.01	0.06	0.11	0.09	0.11	**NA**	
14. Working year	7.69	6.38	0.01	0.07	−0.02	0.001	−0.01	0.06	0.03	0.01	0.19*	0.10	0.56**	0.10	0.56***	**NA**
15. MV marker	3.42	0.63	−0.05	−0.10	−0.08	−0.17	−0.15	−0.08	−0.08	0.09	0.06	−0.03	−0.01	−0.03	−0.01	0.06

Note: The diagonal elements are the square roots of AVEs; $^{*}p < 0.05$, $^{**}p < 0.01$, $^{***}p < 0.001$. The diagonal elements are the square roots of AVEs.
Below the diagonal are the original correlations; Above the diagonal are the adjusted correlations for the common method.
Industry 1 refers to manufacturing; Industry 2 refers to logistics; Industry 3 refers to tourism; BRU refers to bricolage resource utilization; RRU refers to R&D resource utilization; AI refers to artificial intelligence; TT refers to technological turbulence; SCR refers to supply chain resilience.

revealed that the measurement model fits the data satisfactorily, thus indicating good convergent validity ($\chi^2/df = 171.904/102 = 1.685$, CFI = 0.954, NFI = 0.900, TLI = 0.939, RMSEA = 0.071). Finally, all the average variance extracted (AVE) values were higher than the threshold of 0.5 (0.700–0.798), and the square root of the AVE of each construct was greater than its correlation with any other construct, which indicated good discriminant validity (see Table 2). The one inter-construct correlation in Table 3 was higher than the threshold of 0.6, however, the highest variance inflation factor value was 1.72, less than the threshold of 3.3. Thus, multicollinearity was not a significant issue in our data.

Table 3. Results of Construct Reliability and Validity

	Items	Range of the loadings	Cronbach's alpha	Composite reliability	AVE
BRU	8	0.730–0.877	0.937	0.950	0.702
RRU	4	0.670–0.916	0.660	0.901	0.700
AI capability	5	0.835–0.920	0.936	0.952	0.798
TT	3	0.794–0.912	0.800	0.881	0.713
SCR	4	0.804–0.889	0.884	0.920	0.742

Note: AVE=Average Variance Extracted. BRU refers to bricolage resource utilization; RRU refers to R&D resource utilization; AI refers to artificial intelligence; TT refers to technological turbulence; SCR refers to supply chain resilience.

4.4 Common Method Bias

The common method bias (CMB) can be a potential threat when the data is collected in a cross-sectional survey design at the same time (Podsakoff et al., 2003). Accordingly, we carried out several methods to eliminate potential CMB. First, we adopted Harman's single-factor test to evaluate the potential impact of CMB. The results showed that the total variance explained by the first factor was 25.06%, which is less than the threshold of 40% (Podsakoff et al., 2003), indicating CMB was not a serious issue in our study. Second, following Kim (2014), we selected respondents' educational level as a method variance (MV) marker to assess CMB, which is unrelated to the main variables theoretically. The lowest positive correlation between the MV marker and other latent variables served to adjust the correlations between the constructs ($r = 0.01$). As shown in Table 2, comparing the top and bottom diagonal correlation coefficients showed that all the significant correlations remained the same after the adjustment, thereby indicating that CMB was not likely to be a serious concern in this study.

4.5 Hypothesis Testing

We tested our hypotheses using SPSS 24, with interaction terms regenerated using mean-centered independent variables to reduce multicollinearity. The results in Table 4 support Hypotheses 1 and 2, showing that BRU and RRU positively affect SCR ($\beta = 0.46$,

Table 4. Hierarchical Regression Results

Variables	AI capability			SCR			
	Model 1a	Model 2a	Model 3a	Model 1b	Model 2b	Model 3b	Model 4b
Control variables							
Industry 1	0.16	0.12	0.15	0.17*	0.13*	0.15	0.13
Industry 2	−0.10	−0.10	−0.12	0.15*	0.18**	0.18*	0.17*
Industry 3	0.14	0.14	0.09	0.15	0.10	0.06	0.05
Firm ownership	0.08	0.08	0.08	0.15*	0.12	0.08	0.10
Firm size	0.12	0.09	0.08	0.16*	0.13	0.11	0.09
Firm age	−0.16	−0.09	−0.07	−0.21**	−0.18*	−0.22*	−0.22**
Gender	0.24**	0.25**	0.31***	0.06	−0.03	−0.08	−0.06
Age	−0.06	−0.10	−0.09	−0.07	−0.03	−0.006	−0.03
Working year	0.08	0.06	0.03	0.06	0.04	0.04	0.07
Main effects							
BRU		0.14	0.20*	0.46***	0.42***		
RRU		0.38***	0.27**	0.26**	0.13†		
AI capability					0.34***	0.57***	0.54***
TT			0.26**				0.05
Interaction effects							
BRU* TT			0.27*				
RRD* TT			−0.31**				
AI capability* TT							0.18*
R^2	0.07	0.29	0.38	0.47	0.55	0.35	0.38
ΔR^2	–	0.22***	0.16***	–	0.08**	–	0.03*
F-value	2.05*	20.50***	7.37***	50.68***	23.27***	8.30***	3.94*

Note: †p < 0.10, *p < 0.05, **p < 0.01, ***p< 0.001.
Industry 1 refers to manufacturing; Industry 2 refers to logistics; Industry 3 refers to tourism; BRU refers to bricolage resource utilization; RRU refers to R&D resource utilization; AI refers to artificial intelligence; TT refers to technological turbulence; SCR refers to supply chain resilience.

Table 5. Results of bootstrapping analyses for mediation and moderated mediation

Effects	Path coefficients	*SD*	Bias-corrected 95% CI
Mediation effect			
BRU → AI capability → SCR	0.15	0.04	[0.06, 0.24]
Conditional indirect effect			
BRU → AI capability →SCR on TT (low)	0.09	0.05	[−0.03, 0.18]
BRU → AI capability →SCR on TT (high)	0.13	0.05	[0.03, 0.24]

Note. $N = 137$.

Table 6. Results of bootstrapping analyses for mediation and moderated mediation

Effects	Path coefficients	*SD*	Bias-corrected 95% CI
Mediation effect			
RRU → AI capability → SCR	0.21	0.06	[0.10, 0.33]
Conditional indirect effect			
RRU → AI capability →SCR on TT (low)	0.20	0.07	[0.07, 0.34]
RRU → AI capability →SCR on TT (high)	0.15	0.05	[0.01, 0.22]

Note. N = 137.

$p < 0.001$; $\beta = 0.26$, $p < 0.01$). Hypotheses 3a and 3b suggest AI capability mediates the relationship between BRU/RRU and SCR. Mediation analysis confirms this, supporting both hypotheses (indirect effect = 0.15, 95% CI [0.06, 0.24] for BRU and indirect effect = 0.21, 95% CI [0.10, 0.33] for RRU). Hypotheses 4a and 4b propose technological turbulence moderates the relationships between BRU/RRU and SCR, which is supported by the results ($\beta = 0.27$, $p < 0.05$ for BRU and $\beta = -0.31$, $p < 0.01$ for RRU). The effects were visualized in Fig. 2. Hypothesis 5a, testing a moderated mediation model for BRU, is supported, showing a significant indirect effect when technological turbulence is high (conditional indirect effect = 0.13, 95% CI [0.03, 0.24]). However, Hypothesis 5b, regarding RRU, is not supported as there is no significant difference between high and low technological turbulence conditions ($t = 1.13$, $p > 0.05$) (Fig. 3 and Tables 5 and 6).

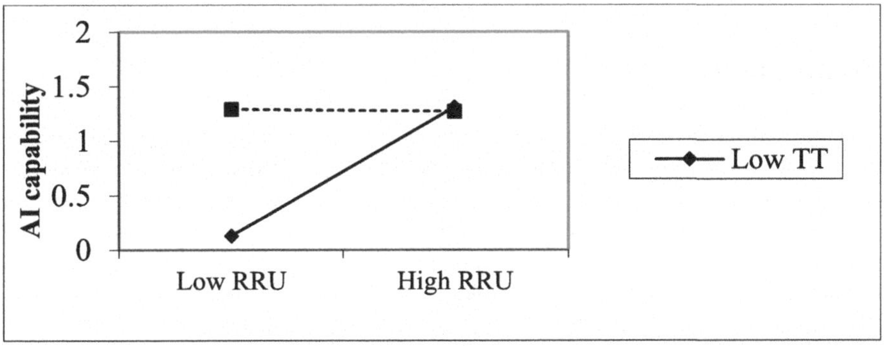

Fig. 2. The moderating role of technological turbulence (TT) on the relationship between BRU and AI capability

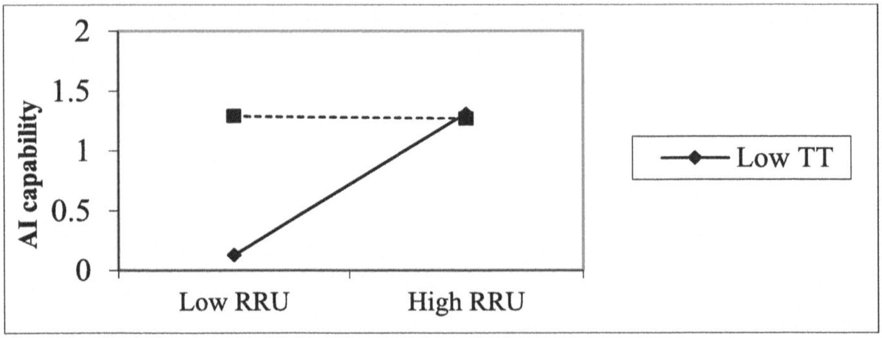

Fig. 3. The moderating role of technological turbulence (TT) on the relationship between RRU and AI capability

5 Conclusion

This study examines how Business Resource Utilization (BRU) and Resource Recombination Utilization (RRU) drive SCR through AI capability, moderated by technological turbulence, using data from 137 questionnaires distributed to listed firms in China. Our findings suggest that BRU and RRU can indeed enhance SCR through AI capability, emphasizing the importance of resource utilization in developing advanced technological capabilities. We also found that technological turbulence moderates the relationship between resource utilization and AI capability. Specifically, it strengthens the BRU-SCR relationship but weakens the RRU-SCR relationship. This suggests that different types of resource utilization impact AI usage in distinct ways. Additionally, technological turbulence positively moderates the indirect effect of AI capability on the BRU-SCR relationship but has no significant impact on the RRU-SCR relationship.

6 Implications

This study contributes to the literature by integrating the dual-resource perspective into SCR research, emphasizing the complementary roles of internal and external resources in enhancing resilience. While prior research focused on either internal capabilities or external networks, our study demonstrates the synergy of managing both types of resources. AI capability is identified as a critical mediator, clarifying how resources contribute to SCR by enabling agile, data-driven decisions. Furthermore, technological turbulence is recognized as a boundary condition, showing how rapid technological changes influence the effectiveness of resource utilization and AI capability in building resilience. This study has several limitations that must be addressed in future studies. First, we collected data from the clients of a focal firm, which may constrain the generalizability of this research. To enhance the applicability of these results, future studies could broaden their scope by collecting data from regions at various developmental stages. Second, our reliance on survey data to test hypotheses, despite efforts to ensure data reliability and validity and to mitigate CMB and endogeneity using pair-matched data, means that biases inherent in self-reported data may persist (Mikalef et al., 2020). Future studies might consider collecting secondary data to refine the measurement of variables and enhance the study's credibility (Chen et al., 2022). Third, given that resilience can manifest in various forms, subsequent research should investigate its impact across different types of resilience.

Acknowledgement. This work was supported by the Shanghai Philosophy and Social Science Fund [grant number 2024EGL014], the National Natural Science Foundation of China [grant number 72401111].

References

Ambulkar, S., Blackhurst, J., Grawe, S.: Firm's resilience to supply chain disruptions: scale development and empirical examination. J. Oper. Manag. **33**, 111–122 (2015)

An, W., Zhao, X., Cao, Z., Zhang, J., Liu, H.: How bricolage drives corporate entrepreneurship: the roles of opportunity identification and learning orientation. J. Prod. Innov. Manag. **35**(1), 49–65 (2018)

Atadoga, A., Osasona, F., Amoo, O.O., Farayola, O.A., Ayinla, B.S., Abrahams, T.O.: The role of IT in enhancing supply chain resilience: a global review. Int. J. Manag.Entrepren. Res. **6**(2), 336–351 (2024)

Belhadi, A., Mani, V., Kamble, S.S., Khan, S.A.R., Verma, S.: Artificial intelligence-driven innovation for enhancing supply chain resilience and performance under the effect of supply chain dynamism: an empirical investigation. Ann. Oper. Res. **333**(2), 627–652 (2024)

Chatterjee, S., Chaudhuri, R., Kamble, S., Gupta, S., Sivarajah, U.: Adoption of artificial intelligence and cutting-edge technologies for production system sustainability: a moderator-mediation analysis. Inf. Syst. Front. **25**(5), 1779–1794 (2023)

Chen, M., Pu, X., Zhang, M., Cai, Z., Chong, A.Y.-L., Tan, K.H.: Data analytics capability and servitization: the moderated mediation role of bricolage and innovation orientation. Int. J. Oper. Prod. Manag. **42**(4), 440–470 (2022)

Chowdhury, S., Dey, P., Joel-Edgar, S., Bhattacharya, S., Rodriguez-Espindola, O., Abadie, A., Truong, L.: Unlocking the value of artificial intelligence in human resource management through AI capability framework. Hum. Resour. Manag. Rev. **33**(1), 100899 (2023)

Eisenhardt, K.M., Martin, J.A.: Dynamic capabilities: what are they? Strateg. Manag. J. **21**(10–11), 1105–1121 (2000)

Gu, M., Yang, L., Huo, B.: The impact of information technology usage on supply chain resilience and performance: An ambidexterous view. Int. J. Prod. Econ. **232**, 107956 (2021)

Kim, D.-Y.: Understanding supplier structural embeddedness: a social network perspective. J. Oper. Manag. **32**(5), 219–231 (2014)

Lu, J.W., Zhou, X.: Disruptive events in strategy and international business research. Asia Pac. J. Manag. **41**, 1–22 (2024)

Mikalef, P., Krogstie, J., Pappas, I.O., Pavlou, P.: Exploring the relationship between big data analytics capability and competitive performance: the mediating roles of dynamic and operational capabilities. Inf. Manag. **57**(2), 103169 (2020)

Modgil, S., Singh, R.K., Hannibal, C.: Artificial intelligence for supply chain resilience: learning from Covid-19. Int. J. Logist. Manag. **33**(4), 1246–1268 (2022)

Nason, R.S., Wiklund, J., McKelvie, A., Hitt, M., Yu, W.: Orchestrating boundaries: the effect of R&D boundary permeability on new venture growth. J. Bus. Ventur. **34**(1), 63–79 (2019)

Podsakoff, P.M., MacKenzie, S.B., Lee, J.-Y., Podsakoff, N.P.: Common method biases in behavioral research: a critical review of the literature and recommended remedies. J. Appl. Psychol. **88**(5), 879–903 (2003)

Xu, S., He, J., Morrison, A.M., Su, X., Zhu, R.: The role of bricolage in countering resource constraints and uncertainty in start-up business model innovation. Eur. J. Innov. Manag. (2023)

How Enterprise Social Media Affordances Affect Employee Digital-Enabled Performance: The Moderating Role of Communication Visibility

Xinjie Yan[1], Liang Ma[1], and Feifei Hao[2](✉)

[1] Shandong University of Finance and Economics, Jinan, China
[2] Shandong University of Traditional Chinese Medicine, Jinan, China
aifeifei0210@126.com

Abstract. Drawing on affordance theory, this study investigates how enterprise social media (ESM) affordances influence employee digital-enabled performance through employee engagement and communication visibility. Analysis of survey data from 314 Chinese employees demonstrates that ESM affordances (association, visibility, persistence, and editability) enhance both task and innovative performance through employee engagement. Communication visibility exhibits differential moderating effects: negative for work engagement innovative performance relationship, but positive for organizational engagement innovative performance relationship. The findings contribute to understanding ESM's role in digital performance and suggest implications for organizational digital workplace strategies.

Keywords: ESM affordances · Employee engagement · Digital performance · Communication visibility

1 Introduction

The widespread adoption of enterprise social media (ESM) across organizations globally marks a fundamental shift in workplace interactions, transforming employee communication, collaboration, and performance patterns (Sun et al., 2024). As digital performance becomes increasingly crucial for organizational competitiveness and sustainability, understanding how ESM affordances influence employees' digital-enabled performance is particularly important.

Current research on digital performance has predominantly centered around organizational level outcomes (Zhang et al., 2025). Studies have extensively explored aspects such as the overall impact of digitalization on organizational efficiency, supply chain optimization through digital technologies, and the role of leadership in digital age organizations (Pitafi et al., 2023). However, how different ESM affordances affect employee digital performance, and what is the mediating role and moderating role is still unclear. Most previous researches have established the link between ESM affordances and performance outcomes through enhanced communication and collaboration (Chen

Y. P. Tu and M. Chi (Eds.): WHICEB 2025, LNBIP 549, pp. 252–261, 2025.
https://doi.org/10.1007/978-3-031-94184-9_21

et al., 2019). However, employee engagement represents the psychological state through which employees translate the opportunities provided by ESM affordances into actual performance, which may serve as a crucial mediating variable. Whether different ESM affordances can activate different dimensions of engagement, such as work engagement and organizational engagement, which in turn influence various aspects of digital performance, including task performance and innovative performance, is still not clear. Furthermore, high communication visibility may facilitate knowledge sharing and collaboration, amplifying the positive effects of engagement on performance. Conversely, low communication visibility may limit access to information and collaboration opportunities, reducing the effectiveness of engagement. However, it is still not clear whether communication visibility acts as a moderating variable.

Based on affordance theory, this paper investigates the relationship between ESM affordances and digital performance, and the mediator role of engagement and the moderator role of communication visibility is also considered. Understanding these mediating and moderating effects is essential for a comprehensive understanding of the complex relationship between ESM affordances and digital performance.

2 Affordance Theory

Initially, the concept of affordance was introduced within ecological psychology, as the dynamic interaction between individuals and their environment's material properties, possessing objective existence. In information systems, affordances are understood as relational and functional aspects that frame, but do not determine, potential actions. Treem and Leonardi (2013) identified four primary affordances of Enterprise Social Media (ESM): visibility (making knowledge and expertise visible), editability (allowing message modification), persistence (enabling long-term message visibility and use), and association (facilitating information relation). These affordances influence organizational processes by shaping communication and collaboration.

Affordance theory is used in this study for several reasons. First, it focuses on the interplay between technology and user perception, moving beyond technological determinism. Second, it enables analysis of ESM use by examining specific affordances rather than treating ESM as a single entity. Third, it provides a causal mechanism for exploring ESM's potential effects (Chen et al., 2019). This study operationalizes affordance theory to explain how specific ESM affordances facilitate or constrain employee actions, thus influencing engagement and subsequent digital performance.

3 Hypothesis Development

3.1 ESM Affordance and Employee Engagement

ESM affordances fundamentally shape employee interactions and organizational participation (Treem & Leonardi, 2013). The association affordance enables meaningful connections between individuals, groups, and content, facilitating organizational relationship networks and communal belonging. Chen et al. (2019) demonstrate that ESM-enabled social ties positively influence both in-role and innovative job performance, establishing a correlation between social connectivity and engagement metrics. This social infrastructure, enabled by association affordance, cultivates deeper organizational investment among employees, manifesting in enhanced engagement and commitment. The affordance framework reinforces how these technological capabilities materialize into actual behavioral outcomes, as employees actively engage with and capitalize on these connection possibilities within their work environment. Hence, we propose the following:

H1a: Enterprise social media association has a positive effect on employee work engagement.
H2a: Enterprise social media association has a positive effect on employee organizational engagement.

The affordance of visibility enables organizational transparency of employees' work, knowledge, and preferences. Task-level visibility drives work engagement by making progress observable and motivating timely task completion among team members (Ren & Sun, 2024), while organizational-level visibility fosters organizational engagement by illuminating employees' roles within the broader organizational context. Such a multi-level transparency mechanism enhances employees' understanding of their purpose and alignment with organizational objectives. This is about reshaping how employees perceive their contributions and responsibilities through the realization of the affordance. Therefore, we posit the following hypothesis:

H1b: Enterprise social media visibility has a positive effect on employee work engagement.
H2b: Enterprise social media visibility has a positive effect on employee organizational engagement.

The affordance of persistence enables enduring accessibility of platform-based communication, information, and knowledge (Treem & Leonardi, 2013). Persistence facilitates continuous learning and knowledge sharing by enabling access to past discussions and decisions, enhancing role performance and work engagement. Persistence also creates organizational memory, allowing employees to engage with institutional history and culture. Such temporal continuity in knowledge storage and retrieval strengthens employees' connection to organizational mission and values. The affordance lens supports how the persistent availability of information is actualized as employees integrate historical content into current work practices, fostering deeper organizational identification. Thus, we formulate the following assumption:

H1c: Enterprise social media persistence has a positive effect on employee work engagement.
H2c: Enterprise social media persistence has a positive effect on employee organizational engagement.

The affordance of editability allows employees to craft and refine their ESM platform communications (Treem & Leonardi, 2013). Through enhancing self-efficacy mechanisms, editability strengthens competence beliefs and work engagement. The iterative nature of editable communication encourages greater effort investment in contributions while enabling message refinement aligned with organizational standards. Moreover, participation in shaping organizational discourse through editable content cultivates ownership and involvement in organizational processes, contributing to organizational engagement. The affordance theory bolsters how the potential for content revision is actualized when employees exercise control over their communications, resulting in higher-quality contributions and deeper psychological investment in the organization's communicative ecosystem. Accordingly, we advance the following hypothesis:

H1d: Enterprise social media editability has a positive effect on employee work engagement.
H2d: Enterprise social media editability has a positive effect on employee organizational engagement.

3.2 Employee Engagement and Digital Performance

Employee engagement, encompassing emotional, cognitive, and behavioral in-vestments in work roles and organizations, serves as a significant performance predictor. Engaged employees demonstrate enhanced task effectiveness through heightened concentration, digital tool mastery, and technological resilience. Their characteristic energy, curiosity, and mental resilience promote digital technology exploration and task innovation, fostering improved digital-enabled performance outcomes. In light of this, we propose the following conjecture:

H3a: Employee work engagement has a positive effect on employee digital-enabled task performance.
H3b: Employee work engagement has a positive effect on employee digital-enabled innovative performance.

Organizational engagement reflects employees' emotional and cognitive attachment to organizational values and goals. Engaged employees leverage digital platforms for enhanced coordination and task execution aligned with strategic objectives (Leonardi et al., 2013). Within engaged organizational cultures, increased knowledge-sharing behaviors emerge, facilitating collective innovation generation and improved digital-enabled innovative performance. Consequently, we assert the following hypothesis:

H4a: Employee organizational engagement has a positive effect on employee digital-enabled task performance.
H4b: Employee organizational engagement has a positive effect on employee digital-enabled innovative performance.

3.3 The Moderating Role of Communication Visibility

Communication visibility theory posits that social media affords message transparency and network translucence, which means that ESNs make the content of others' messages accessible and employees' social networks apparent (Leonardi, 2015), potentially amplifying engagement's impact on digital-enabled performance outcomes. High communication visibility supports work-engaged employees in identifying organizational expertise and accessing task-related resources. This visibility facilitates comprehensive task understanding, collaborator identification, and workflow integration, enhancing work engagement's influence on digital-enabled performance (Fu et al., 2024). Conversely, limited communication visibility may constrain knowledge identification and collaborative opportunities. Under such conditions, employees often rely on personal knowledge and restricted networks, potentially limiting their task effectiveness and innovative capacity (Leonardi et al., 2013). Based on the above, we suggest the following proposition:

H5a: Communication visibility acts as a positive moderating role between employee work engagement and digital-enabled task performance.
H5b: Communication visibility acts as a positive moderating role between employee work engagement and digital-enabled innovative performance.

Communication visibility, as a contextual factor distinct from the visibility of technological affordances themselves, can enhance organization-engaged employees' understanding of organizational processes and opportunities (Deng, 2023). This visibility feature enables learning from coworkers' communications, supporting innovative problem-solving. Communication transparency promotes organizational alignment and informed decision-making. Communication visibility across time and space facilitates knowledge recombination for innovation. In low-visibility environments, organizational engagement's benefits may diminish. Limited visibility into colleague contributions can foster isolation, potentially reducing collaborative innovation. Employees may struggle to align engagement with organizational objectives, possibly affecting performance and innovation outcomes. We propose the following hypothesis:

H6a: Communication visibility acts as a positive moderating role between employee organizational engagement and digital-enabled task performance.
H6b: Communication visibility acts as a positive moderating role between employee organizational engagement and digital-enabled innovative performance.

The theoretical model for this study is presented in Fig. 1.

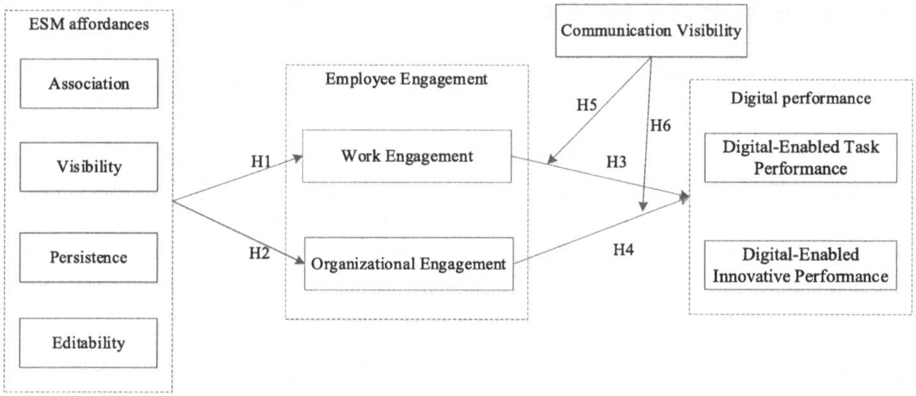

Fig. 1. Research Model

4 Research Methods

4.1 Measures

Data were collected using a structured questionnaire with items adapted from existing literature. Enterprise Social Media (ESM) Affordance, encompassing visibility, association, persistence, and editability, was measured using 12 items, taken from Sun et al. (2020). Employee Engagement (EE) was assessed through two sub-constructs: Work Engagement (WE) and Organizational Engagement (OE), each measured with three items based on Zhang et al. (2019), capturing personal investment in job responsibilities and organizational commitment, respectively. Communication Visibility (CV) was operationalized using three items adapted from Chen and Wei (2019), measuring the observability of coworker interactions facilitated by ESM. Employee Digital Performance (EDP) was also divided into two sub-constructs: Digital-enabled Task Performance (DTP) and Digital-enabled Innovative Performance (DIP), each assessed with three items, examining efficacy and creativity in leveraging digital technology. All of the above items were scored on a seven-point Likert scale ranging from 1 (strongly disagree/unlikely) to 7 (strongly agree/likely).

4.2 Data Collection

Data were collected via a professional online questionnaire platform in China (http://www.credamo.com), similar to Amazon's MTurk and Qualtrics, which is widely used in academic research and offers robust quality assurance (Zhang et al., 2019). Paid services were employed for data collection, with the platform distributing the questionnaire to the target audience. After removing incomplete and identical responses, a final sample of 314 valid questionnaires was retained for analysis. This approach ensured a rigorous and reliable data collection process.

5 Data Analysis and Results

5.1 Measurement Model

The measurement model was evaluated using Smart PLS 4.0 software. Reliability assessment yielded Cronbach's alpha values (0.721–0.796), composite reliability values (0.843–0.880), and average variance extracted values (0.642–0.710), all exceeding their respective thresholds of 0.7, 0.7, and 0.5. Factor loadings were higher than 0.7 ($p < 0.01$), suggesting appropriate convergent validity. The square root of AVE for each factor exceeded its correlation coefficients with other factors, indicating satisfactory discriminant validity. The analysis demonstrated that both convergent and discriminant validity met established thresholds, with factor loadings above 0.7 at $p < 0.01$ significance level and AVE square roots greater than factor correlation coefficients.

Common method bias analysis through variance assessment revealed substantive factor loadings averaging 0.679 and method factor loadings averaging 0.009, with predominantly non-significant method factors. This pattern suggests that common method bias may not significantly impact the study's findings. Model fit evaluation employed the standardized root mean squared residual (SRMR), yielding a value of 0.064, which falls below the recommended threshold of 0.08. These analyses suggest that the proposed model demonstrates adequate structural fit to the data while maintaining appropriate methodological controls for potential biases inherent in single-source, cross-sectional data collection approaches. The results of the structural model analysis are presented in Fig. 2.

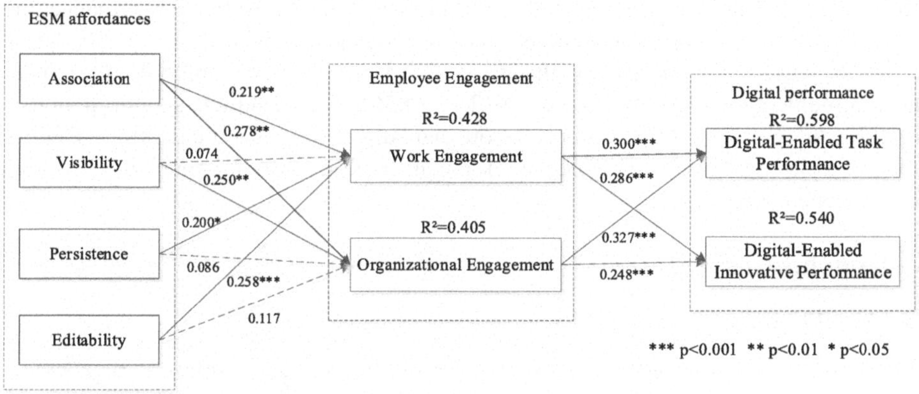

Fig. 2. Results of the structural model analysis

5.2 Structural Model

The results of the structural model analysis are presented in Fig. 2.

5.3 Mediating Effects

To examine the mediating role of employee engagement (work engagement and organizational engagement) between ESM affordances and digital performance, we employed the bootstrap method using the PROCESS SPSS macro. This approach has gained widespread acceptance among scholars for testing mediating effects (Zhang et al., 2019). We utilized both the bias-corrected and percentile methods, setting the confidence level at 95% for the confidence intervals.

These results find that all four ESM affordances influence both digital-enabled task performance and digital-enabled innovative performance through the partial mediation of work engagement and organizational engagement. This suggests that while ESM affordances have direct effects on digital performance, they also exert indirect effects by enhancing employee engagement, which in turn contributes to improved digital performance outcomes.

5.4 Moderating Effects

To examine the moderating effects of communication visibility on the relationship between employee engagement and employee digital performance, this study first established Model 1 by including work engagement (WE) and organizational engagement

(OE). Subsequently, communication visibility (CV) was incorporated into Model 2 to assess its direct impact alongside WE and OE. Finally, Model 3 was developed by adding interaction terms between WE and CV, as well as OE and CV.

Regarding digital-enabled task performance, the moderation analysis revealed that the interactions between work engagement and communication visibility ($\beta = -0.111$, $T = -1.607$) and between organizational engagement and communication visibility ($\beta = 0.116$, $T = 1.556$) were not statistically significant at the conventional $p < 0.05$ level. Thus, H5a and H6a are rejected. For digital-enabled innovative performance, the interaction between work engagement and communication visibility ($\beta = -0.185$, T = -2.866) was significant, as was the interaction between organizational engagement and communication visibility ($\beta = 0.199$, $T = 2.856$). These findings support hypothesis H6b while rejecting hypothesis H5b (opposite direction). Communication visibility moderates the relationship between work engagement and digital-enabled innovative performance negatively.

6 Conclusions

6.1 Key Findings

This study reveals relationships between ESM affordances and employee engagement forms. ESM association demonstrates positive effects on both work and organizational engagement, supporting the role of social connections in enhancing psychological attachment (Treem & Leonardi, 2013). ESM visibility significantly influences organizational engagement but not work engagement, potentially due to information overload effects on task focus. ESM persistence positively affects work engagement exclusively, likely through its facilitation of task-specific knowledge retention. Similarly, ESM editability enhances work engagement but shows no significant organizational engagement effect, suggesting content refinement primarily benefits task-related confidence. Both work and organizational engagement positively influence digital-enabled innovative performance and task performance. The study establishes a dual-path mediation model where ESM affordances influence digital performance through both engagement types, extending work on direct effects.

Regarding moderation effects, communication visibility shows no significant moderating effect on relationships between engagement forms and digital-enabled task performance, suggesting engagement's intrinsic motivation aspects may operate independently of communication tools. However, communication visibility negatively moderates the relationship between work engagement and digital-enabled innovative performance, while positively moderating the organizational engagement innovation relationship. The negative moderation contradicts traditional visualization benefit assumptions and may reflect cognitive load theory implications, where communication overload impedes individual creativity. The positive moderation indicates visualization's role in enhancing collective innovation through shared understanding and organizational trust.

6.2 Theoretical Implications

This study contributes to the digital performance literature and affordance theory by exploring the relationship between ESM affordances and digital performance. While prior research has established the link between ESM affordances and performance outcomes through enhanced communication and collaboration (Chen et al., 2019), this study extends this understanding by empirically demonstrating that specific ESM affordances positively influence both work and organizational engagement, which, in turn, enhances digital-enabled innovative performance and task performance. This perspective clarifies how different affordances can be leveraged to optimize digital performance (Ren & Sun, 2024; Sun et al., 2024).

Furthermore, both work and organizational engagement partially mediate the relationship between ESM affordances and digital performance. This contributes to the theoretical discourse on engagement mechanisms within digital contexts and underscores the importance of fostering employee engagement to realize the potential benefits of ESM implementations for organizational performance.

Finally, the study identifies communication visibility as a moderator in the relationship between employee engagement and digital performance, building on work suggesting visibility's influence on knowledge sharing and innovation. This contributes to the theoretical understanding of communication patterns within ESM contexts.

6.3 Practical Implications

Strategic implementation of enterprise social media (ESM) can enhance both work and organizational engagement, driving digital performance. Organizations should prioritize ESM features supporting association and persistence to bolster work engagement while leveraging visibility to strengthen organizational engagement by fostering connection to initiatives. ESM implementation should align with specific performance objectives. For task performance, emphasis should be placed on features streamlining workflows and improving information accessibility. For innovative performance, the focus should be on affordances facilitating knowledge sharing and cross-functional collaboration. Considering that communication visibility plays a moderating role, organizations should adopt a balanced approach to visual communication by designing ESM policies that promote knowledge sharing without overwhelming employees. This targeted strategy enables organizations to optimize digital workplace initiatives and enhance effectiveness in the digital era. Success hinges on aligning ESM implementation with performance goals and managing the moderating effects of communication visibility to maximize both employee engagement and digital performance outcomes.

6.4 Limitations and Future Research

This study, while valuable, acknowledges limitations. Firstly, the sample focusing on Chinese enterprises restricts generalizability. Future research should explore cross-cultural applications. Secondly, reliance on self-reported data may introduce bias. Future studies should incorporate objective performance metrics and multi-source data. Finally, the cross-sectional design limits longitudinal insights. Future research could investigate the impact of emerging ESM features and broader digital performance dimensions for a more comprehensive understanding.

Acknowledgments. This work was supported by the General Program of Shandong Natural Science Foundation under Project No: ZR2024MG002, and No: ZR2022QG046; 2023 Higher Education Excellent Youth Innovation Team of Shandong Province under Project No: 2023RW064; 2023 International Cooperation Research Project of Shandong University of Finance and Economics under Project No: 04; and Jinan Municipal School Integration Development Strategy Project "Digital Consumption and Manufacturing Digital Transformation Collaborative Innovation Center Construction" under Project No: JNSX2023052.

References

Chen, X., Wei, S.: Enterprise social media use and overload: a curvilinear relationship. J. Inf. Technol. **34**, 22–38 (2019)

Chen, X., Wei, S., Davison, R.M., Rice, R.E.: How do enterprise social media affordances affect social network ties and job performance? Inf. Technol. People. **33**, 361–388 (2019)

Deng, M.: Communication visibility and employee voice: mediating role of feedback-seeking. Internet Res. **33**, 531–549 (2023)

Fu, J., Sun, Y., Zhang, J.Z., Mouakket, S., Chen, P.: Creativity afforded by enterprise social media: a communication visibility perspective. Ind. Manag. Data Syst. **142**(12), 3324–3349 (2024)

Leonardi, P.M.: When flexible routines meet flexible technologies: affordance, constraint, and the imbrication of human and material agencies. MIS Q. **35**, 147–167 (2011)

Leonardi, P.M.: Ambient awareness and knowledge acquisition: using social media to learn "who knows what" and "who knows whom". MIS Q. **39**, 747–762 (2015)

Leonardi, P.M., Huysman, M., Steinfield, C.: Enterprise social media: definition, history, and prospects for the study of social technologies in organizations. J. Comput.-Mediat. Commun. **19**, 1–19 (2013)

Ma, L., Zhang, X., Ding, X.: Enterprise social media usage and knowledge hiding: a motivation theory perspective. J. Knowl. Manag. **24**, 2149–2169 (2020)

Pitafi, A.H., Rasheed, M.I., Islam, N., Dhir, A.: Investigating visibility affordance, knowledge transfer and employee agility performance. A study of enterprise social media. Technovation. **128**, 102874 (2023)

Ren, X., Sun, X.: How do enterprise social media affordances affect knowledge sharing within project teams: the social cognitive theory view. Inf. Technol. People. **37**, 2183–2202 (2024)

Sun, Y., Zhong, Y.T., Jeyaraj, A., Zhu, M.J.: The impact of enterprise social media affordances on employees' thriving at work: an empowerment theory perspective. Technol. Forecast. Soc. Chang. **198**, 122983 (2024)

Zhang, X., Ma, L., Xu, B., Xu, F.: How social media usage affects employees' job satisfaction and turnover intention: an empirical study in China. Inf. Manag. **56**, 103136 (2019)

Exploring the Dynamics of Cross-Organizational Data Sharing Processes: A Case of Railway Multi-Disciplinary Collaboration

Menghan Lv[1], Ying Wang[1](✉), Jia Wei[2], Chun Ouyang[2], and Lei Huang[1]

[1] School of Economics and Management, Beijing Jiaotong University, Beijing 100044, China
ywang1@bjtu.edu.cn

[2] Queensland University of Technology (QUT), 2 George St, Brisbane City, Australia

Abstract. This study addresses the challenge of exploring the dynamics of cross-organizational data sharing processes. The approach begins by using BPMN to model cross-organizational business processes. It then employs CPN Tools for formal modeling and simulation, thereby establishing a formal analysis framework for capturing the complexities inherent in dynamic collaborative data-sharing processes. Focusing on the railway industry, the study uses the case of handling obstructions encountered by the pantograph during high-speed train operations. This scenario exemplifies railway multi-Disciplinary collaborations, involving key stakeholders such as train operators, dispatch centers, and power supply departments. The process is characterized by stringent timeliness requirement sand complex cross-departmental collaboration. The study provides valuable insights for enhancing cross-organizational coordination efficiency and improving data sharing among multiple stakeholders.

Keywords: Cross-organizational data sharing · Railway Multi-Disciplinary Collaboration · BPMN · Colored Petri Nets

1 Introduction

In the context of globalization and digital transformation, cross-organizational business processes have become increasingly prevalent, with data sharing and collaboration emerging as significant challenges. Existing research indicates that cross-organizational data exchanges face multiple dilemmas, including fragmented information standards, difficulties in obtaining authentic data, and challenges in maintaining collaborative efficiency. This challenge is particularly critical in time-sensitive scenarios, where efficient coordination must be achieved while ensuring data security. In the handling of railway emergency incidents, the collaboration of multiple disciplines, including train operators, dispatching centers, and power supply departments, is required. In reality, there are often difficulties in cross-organizational data sharing, which leads to low collaborative efficiency. Therefore, the analysis of cross-organizational data-sharing processes in collaborative scenarios is highly necessary.

Y. P. Tu and M. Chi (Eds.): WHICEB 2025, LNBIP 549, pp. 262–273, 2025.
https://doi.org/10.1007/978-3-031-94184-9_22

However, the process of data sharing involves multiple organizations, and obtaining real data directly is often challenging due to compliance requirements. To address this issue, this study proposes using BPMN (Business Process Model and Notation) [1] and CPN [2] to model cross-organizational data-sharing processes. These formal process modeling languages can effectively capture the dynamic and complex characteristics of such processes. Furthermore, the models can be used for simulation to generate event logs under various scenarios. These logs serve as valuable inputs for analyzing the data-sharing process. To demonstrate the effectiveness of this approach, this study conducts a case study focusing on data sharing in cross-disciplinary collaborative operations within the railway sector. The results validate the applicability of the proposed method.

The remainder of this paper is organized as follows: Section 2 reviews related work in business process modeling and cross-organizational collaboration, with a particular focus on the application of Business Process Model and Notation (BPMN) and formal modeling methods. Section 3 presents our proposed method, which integrates BPMN modeling with Colored Petri Nets (CPN) analysis to enhance cross-organizational data sharing. In Sect. 4, we present a case study from the railway industry involving pantograph fault handling, which illustrates complex multi-disciplinary collaborations and their modeling results. Section 5 describes the simulation process. Section 6 provides a conclusion, summarizing the key findings of the study, and outlines potential future research directions.

2 Related Work

This section reviews the related work from three aspects: Cross-Organizational Data Sharing Processes, Railway Multi-Disciplinary Collaborations, and BPMN and Colored Petri Nets.

2.1 Cross-Organizational Data Sharing Processes

With technological advancement, forms of organizational collaboration have become increasingly diverse, encompassing both intra-organizational and cross-organizational collaboration [3]. In the context of globalization and widely applied distributed technologies, most of today's business processes must operate across organizational boundaries, with emerging internet and Web service technologies providing an essential foundation for cross-organizational cooperation [4]. However, despite rich theoretical and practical accumulation in cross-professional collaboration, several key issues remain to be resolved. In practical work scenarios, personnel with different professional backgrounds face numerous challenges in cross-departmental collaboration. Insufficient organizational willingness for data sharing leads to communication barriers and understanding gaps, affecting collaborative efficiency [5]. Data flow between departments also faces multiple obstacles, such as government departments' inherent working methods and processes causing resistance to change and lack of reform motivation; disparities in technical capabilities between departments and imbalances in data processing and security capabilities severely restrict the depth and breadth of cross-departmental collaboration [6].

2.2 Railway Multi-Disciplinary Collaborations

In the complex environment of cross-departmental collaboration, the application and optimization strategies of various models play a crucial role in enhancing collaborative effectiveness [7]. In the field of emergency management, academia has proposed several complementary model optimization approaches [8]. In BPMN model applications, researchers have conducted formal analysis of collaborative characteristics and proposed consistency modeling guidelines, providing theoretical support for the standardized application of BPMN in cross-departmental collaboration [9]. Research on the impact of modularity on BPMN model comprehensibility has deepened cross-departmental teams' understanding and application of models [10]. Notably, cross-organizational business processes must consider not only functional requirements but also the critical element of time constraints [11]. In crisis event scenarios involving cross-organizational collaboration, scholars have employed formal methods such as Petri nets for modeling and analysis, effectively constructing multiple scenarios and evaluating the practical effectiveness of crisis response systems [12]. These research achievements have driven the continuous development of model optimization strategies in cross-organizational collaboration.

2.3 BPMN and Colored Petri Nets

In business process modeling practice, clear process definitions and visual presentations can reduce communication barriers caused by professional differences and varying work habits, facilitating understanding of collaborative processes and role positioning [13]. Model-based analysis can reveal bottlenecks and potential risks in collaborative processes, providing a basis for improvement measures, such as optimizing resource allocation to enhance collaborative efficiency [14]. In this study, we propose integrating BPMN (Business Process Model and Notation) [1] with Colored Petri Nets (CPN) [2] to address the challenges of cross-organizational data sharing. BPMN provides a standardized framework for modeling business processes, while CPN offers a formal and rigorous analysis tool to simulate and validate the dynamic behavior of these processes. This integration aims to enhance the robustness and effectiveness of cross-organizational collaboration by capturing both the structural and temporal aspects of complex workflows.

3 The Method

The section illustrates our method for examining cross-organizational data sharing processes. Given the significant challenges in obtaining real cross-organizational operational data, understanding data sharing processes is crucial for improving the railway operational collaborations across multiple departments. Therefore, a model-based analysis approach becomes necessary. Our analytical framework encompasses the following steps (see Fig. 1).

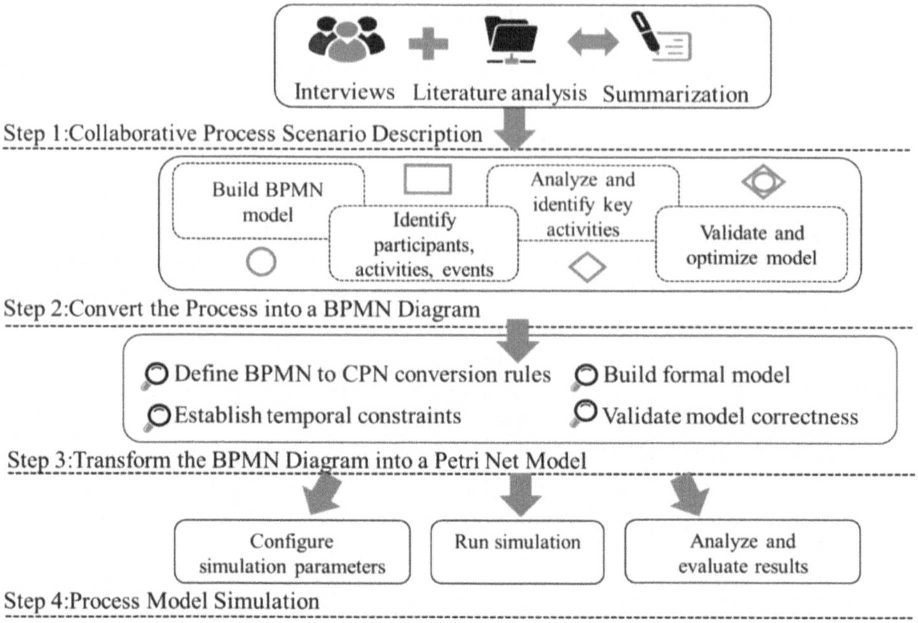

Fig. 1. The Method for Exploring Cross-organizational Data Sharing Processes

4 Case Study

4.1 Case Scenario Description: Pantograph Fault Handling

During the operation of high-speed railways, pantograph failures are typical emergency events that require coordinated efforts from multiple departments for effective handling. This study takes the handling of a pantograph failure on a specific high-speed railway line as an example to analyze the cross-organizational data sharing process. The organizations involved in the handling include the Locomotive Department (train drivers), the Dispatching Office (train dispatchers), the Rolling Stock Department (on-board mechanics), and the Power Supply Office. Each department undertakes distinct responsibilities during the failure handling process and relies on timely and accurate information exchange to ensure efficient resolution.

4.2 Multi-Pool BPMN Process Modeling

A BPMN model is developed to visualize the cross-organizational collaboration in pantograph fault handling is modelled using. The model is designed to capture both the process flow and data exchange patterns among different departments. Each pool contains a sequence of activities and events that correspond to the four phases. The BPMN model incorporates four main organizational pools corresponding to the key departments identified in the case scenario:

- Train Operation Department (train driver)

- Rolling Stock Department (on-board mechanic)
- Dispatch Center (dispatchers)
- Power Supply Center (power supply staff)

Train Operation Department Handling Process From the train driver's perspective (as shown in Fig. 2), upon detecting a pantograph fault, the driver must immediately lower the pantograph and stop the train to ensure safety, then report the fault to the dispatch center and wait for further instructions until receiving the command to resume operation.

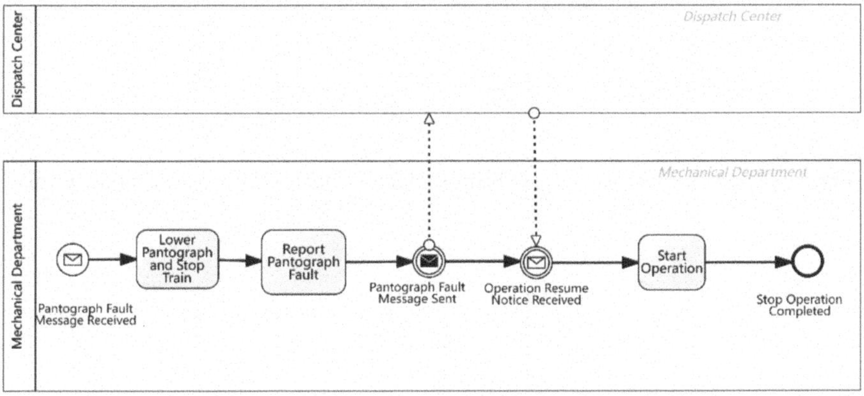

Fig. 2. BPMN View of Pantograph Fault Handling - Train Driver's Pool Focus

Rolling Stock Department Handling Process The vehicle department's workflow (as shown in Fig. 3) focuses more on specific fault handling procedures. After receiving notification, mechanics must first obtain permission to access the train roof for inspection before conducting initial fault assessment. Based on the assessment results, they will then determine the subsequent content of their report.

Dispatch Center Handling Process From the dispatch center's perspective (as shown in Fig. 4), as the coordination hub for the entire fault handling process, their work encompasses several crucial phases. Upon receiving the fault report, the dispatch center must first ensure operational safety by ordering subsequent trains to take appropriate measures. Simultaneously, they need to notify the vehicle department and implement speed restrictions in the relevant sections. As fault handling progresses, the dispatch center needs to coordinate power outages with the power supply center, approve various maintenance requests, and ultimately coordinate system recovery.

Power Supply Center Handling Process The power supply center's responsibilities (as shown in Fig. 5) primarily focus on power supply safety assurance. Upon receiving a power outage request, they need to execute the power-off operation according to procedure and confirm the completion status to the dispatch center. They remain on standby during fault handling until receiving a power restoration request. After completing power restoration, they must confirm normal system power supply status.

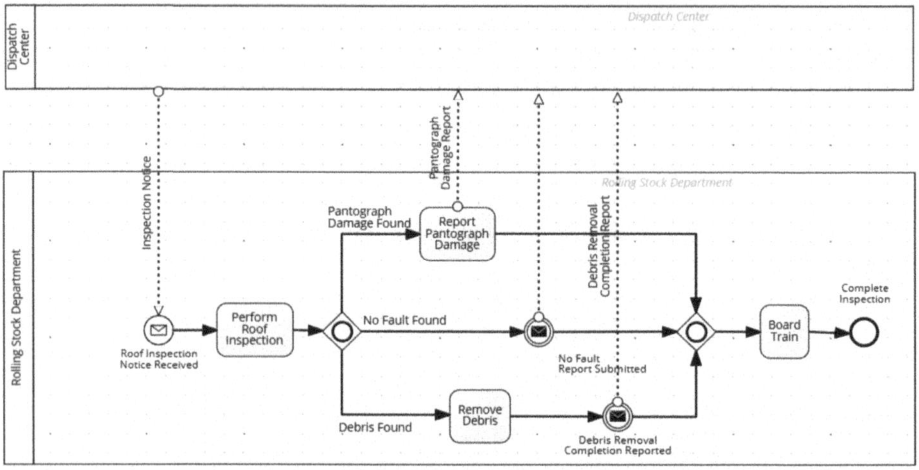

Fig. 3. BPMN View of Pantograph Fault Handling - Vehicle Department's Pool Focus

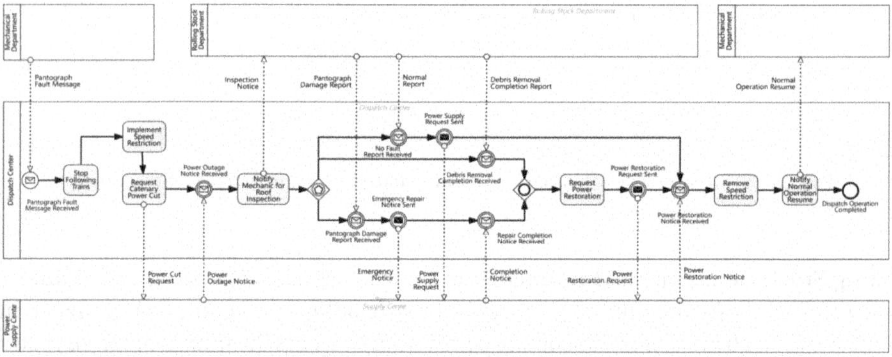

Fig. 4. BPMN View of Pantograph Fault Handling - Dispatch Center's Pool Focus

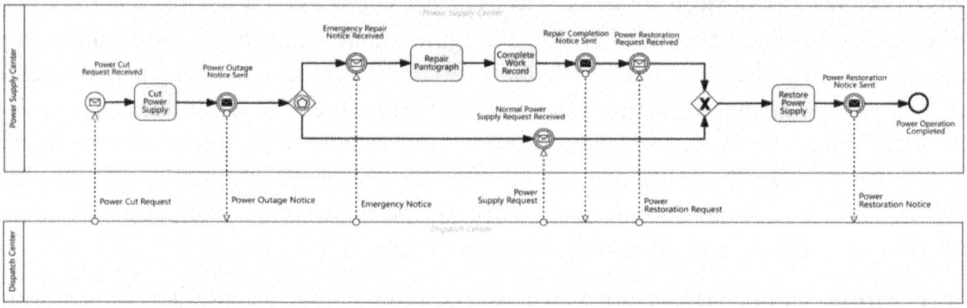

Fig. 5. BPMN View of Pantograph Fault Handling - Power Supply Center's Pool Focus

Through these four process diagrams from different perspectives, we can clearly see each department's specific responsibilities and their collaborative relationships in the pantograph fault handling process. The complete model diagrams can be accessed at: https://github.com/menghan0101/BPMN-PH-model.

4.3 CPN-Based Formal Modeling Analysis

Building upon the BPMN model presented in Sect. 4.1, we now transform the process into a Colored Petri Net (CPN) representation to enable formal analysis of the cross-organizational data sharing patterns. While the BPMN model provides an intuitive visualization of the process flow, CPN modeling allows us to examine the dynamic behavior, verify temporal properties, and identify potential bottlenecks in the data exchange process.

The transformation from BPMN to CPN focuses on three key aspects:

1. Converting organizational roles and resources into appropriate color sets
2. Mapping process activities to transitions
3. Representing message flows and data exchanges through place connections

Petri Net Modeling and Analysis of Train Operation Department The Petri net model describes the process of a train driver handling an overhead catenary fault: starting from receiving fault information and randomly selecting one of the 9 trains, which collectively triggers the train stop operation (Stop the train transition). Then, after waiting for the recovery instruction (Resume-Message place), the system transitions to the resumed operation state (Resume the ride transition). At the same time, the train status is tracked through the Train place and transitions carrying key information tuples (tid, ts, sta, st, speed, emergency). As shown in Fig. 6.

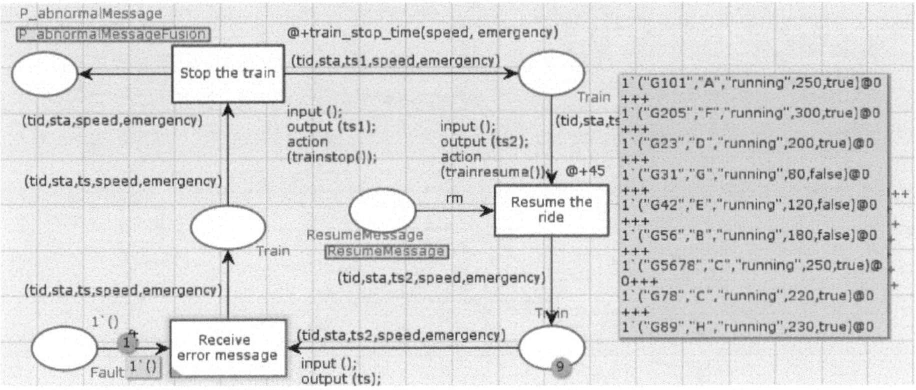

Fig. 6. CPN Model Diagram of Vehicle Department Status

Petri Net Modeling and Analysis of Rolling Stock Department Figure 7 shows the Rolling Stock Department's involvement in the fault handling process. Their responsibilities include equipment inspection, situation reporting, and maintenance coordination.

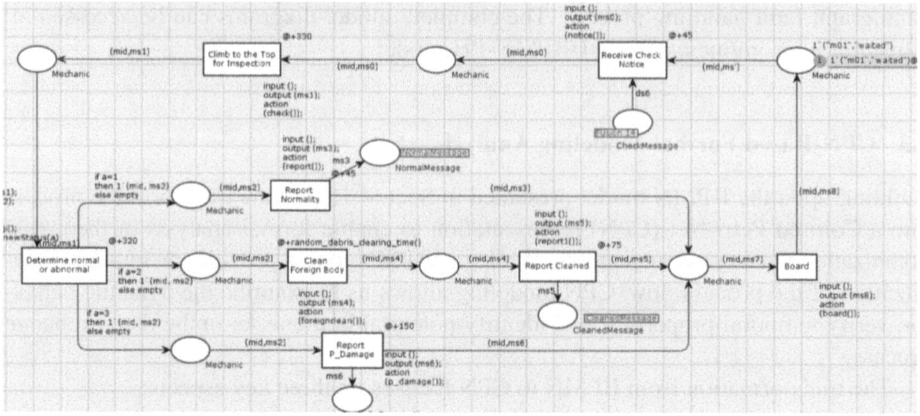

Fig. 7. Petri Net Model of the Rolling Stock Department

Petri Net Modeling and Analysis of Dispatch Center Figure 8 demonstrates the Petri net model of the Dispatch Center, illustrating its role as a key coordinator in the fault handling process. Upon receiving the pantograph abnormality information and detailed train information with pantograph faults from the driver, the dispatch center initiates multiple parallel processes.

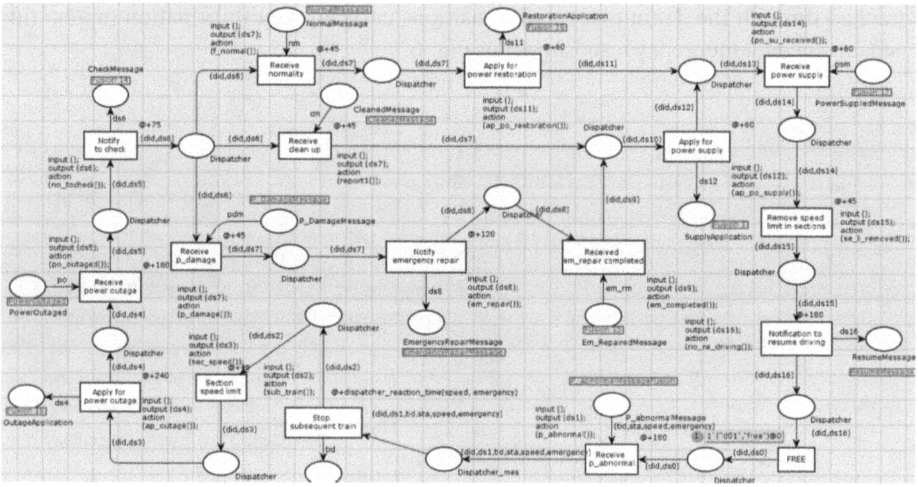

Fig. 8. Petri Net Model of the Dispatch Center

Figure 9 presents the Power Supply Center's process model, highlighting their technical response to overhead catenary system faults. It simulates the procedures of power supply staff performing power isolation, power restoration, and emergency repairs.

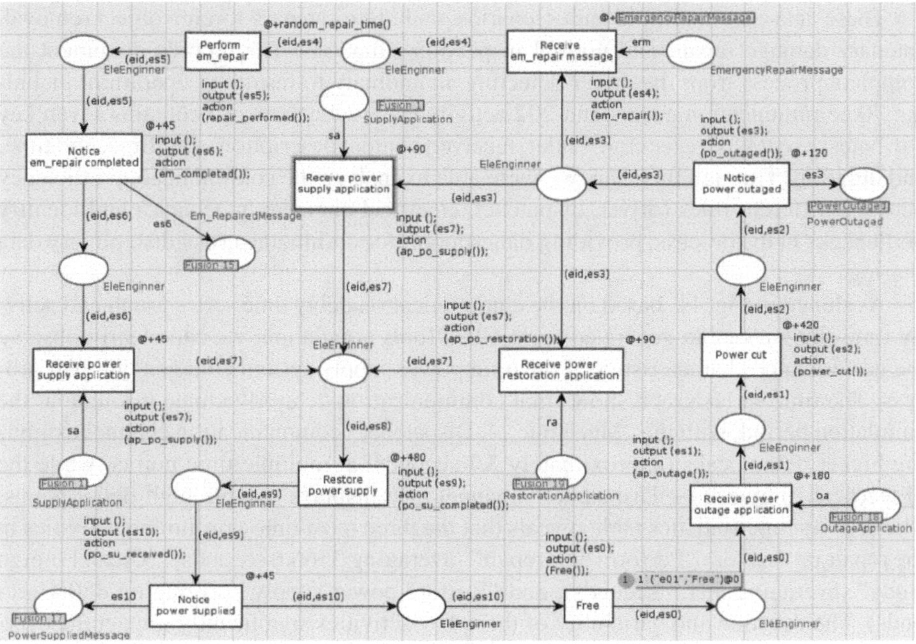

Fig. 9. Petri Net Model of the Power Supply Center

4.4 Data Sharing Process Analysis with Simulation

As shown in Fig. 10, through simulation modeling of the train power supply system emergency repair process using CPN Tools, we collected time data comprising 272 records.

Type	From	To	Content	StartTime	EndTime	Duration
Activity	Train Driver	-	Stop the train	0	91.3	91.3
Communication	Train Driver	Dispatcher	AbnormalReport	91.3	93.8	2.5
Activity	Dispatcher	-	Receive p_abnormal	93.8	273.3	179.5
Activity	Dispatcher	-	Stop subsequent train	273.3	333.1	59.8
Activity	Dispatcher	-	Section speed limit	333.1	378.4	45.3
Activity	Dispatcher	-	Apply for power outage	378.4	617.9	239.5
Communication	Dispatcher	EleEnginne	PowerOutageRequest	617.9	619.3	1.4
Activity	EleEnginner	-	Receive power outage a	619.3	800.2	180.9
Activity	EleEnginner	-	Power cut	800.2	1222.3	422.1
Activity	EleEnginner	-	Notice power outaged	1222.3	1340.7	118.4
Communication	EleEnginner	Dispatcher	PowerOutaged	1340.7	1343.1	2.4
Activity	Dispatcher	-	Receive power outage	1343.1	1522.4	179.3
Activity	Dispatcher	-	Notify to check	1522.4	1599	76.6
Communication	Dispatcher	Mechanic	CheckNotice	1599	1600.8	1.8
Activity	Mechanic	-	Receive Check Notice	1600.8	1645.9	45.1
Activity	Mechanic	-	Climb to the Topfor Insp	1645.9	1975	329.1
Activity	Mechanic	-	Determine normal or abı	1975	2292.9	317.9

Fig. 10. Simulated data

These data cover multiple fault scenarios, including catenary foreign object removal, catenary damage repair, and normal inspection situations. The records document the complete process from the driver detecting an anomaly to resuming operation, including 70 communication events and 202 activity events. Each record contains seven key attributes: event type, executor/sender, receiver, content description, start time, end time, and duration. Through this data, we were able to analyze the communication efficiency between different roles (driver, dispatcher, electrical engineer, mechanic) and identify bottlenecks in the process, providing data support for optimizing cross-disciplinary data sharing.

As shown in Fig. 11, based on the communication delay time series graph and activity time statistics table generated from CPN Tools simulation, we can clearly observe the performance characteristics of the train power supply system emergency repair process. The time series graph shows that communication delays fluctuate throughout the simulation period, with the "Mechanic → Dispatcher" communication channel exhibiting higher delay peaks (approximately 3.7 seconds) at multiple time points, while the "Electrical Engineer → Dispatcher" channel also displays notable high delay points. The activity time statistics table reveals that the three most time-consuming activities in the repair process are "Perform em_repair" (averaging 3566.6 seconds), "Clean Foreign Body" (averaging 581.3 seconds), and "Restore power supply" (averaging 480.4 seconds). The duration and variability of these key activities significantly impact the overall repair efficiency. By analyzing the communication patterns between different roles and the distribution of activity times, we can identify the time bottlenecks in the system, providing a data foundation for further optimization of train repair processes and cross-disciplinary collaboration.

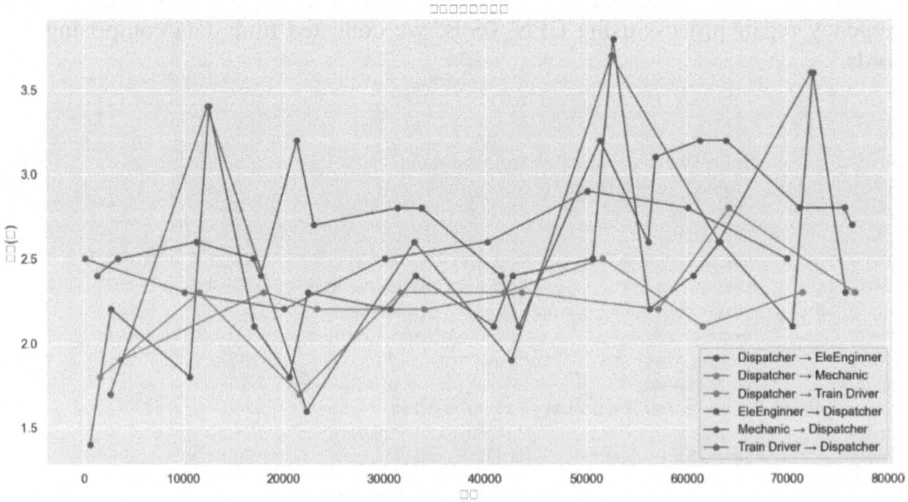

Fig. 11. Delay time series

5 Conclusion and Future Work

This study proposes an approach for exploring the dynamics within cross-organizational data sharing processes, systematically investigating a multi-departmental collaboration case in handling high-speed train pantograph faults through the combination of BPMN modeling and CPN formal analysis. The research demonstrates that the proposed method effectively captures the complexity and dynamics of cross-organizational data-sharing processes, through process modeling and simulation. The Petri net model not only analyzes the handling process of individual fault events but also identifies system bottlenecks for process optimization, providing a viable solution for optimizing cross-departmental data sharing mechanisms.

Future research will focus on utilizing Petri net models to generate simulated event log data. These data will help to better understand and analyze potential issues within the process, thereby providing important support for further optimization of cross-organizational collaboration efficiency.

Acknowledgement. This research is supported by National Natural Science Foundation of China [grant number U2268202], the Technology Research and Development Plan Program of China State Railway Group Co., Ltd.(Grant No. K2024S005(JB)).

References

1. Dumas, M., Rosa, L.M., Mendling, J., et al.: Fundamentals of Business Process Management [M]. Springer (2018)
2. Jensen, K., Kristensen, L.M., Wells, L.: Coloured Petri Nets and CPN tools for modelling and validation of concurrent systems [J]. Int. J. Softw. Tools Technol. Transfer. **9**, 213–254 (2007)
3. Adomako, S., Nguyen, N.P.: Digitalization, inter-organizational collaboration, and technology transfer [J]. J. Technol. Transf. **49**(4), 1176–1202 (2024)
4. Wang, J., Hu, H., Yu, P., et al.: Public-view and object petri net based modeling of cross-organizational process[C]. In: 2013 10th Web Information System and Application Conference, pp. 425–428. IEEE (2013)
5. Van Der Waaij, B.D., Lazovik, E., Albers, T., et al.: CO-ARCH: methodology for COllaborative ARCHitectures for cross-organizational data analysis[J]. Int. J. Model. Optim. **10**(1) (2020)
6. Mao, Z., Zhu, Y.: Tension between the safe flow of government data across organizational boundaries and fragmentations in secure collaboration: the Chinese e-government[J]. Aslib J. Inf. Manag. **76**, 629–652 (2023. (ahead-of-print))
7. Corradini, F., Morichetta, A., Muzi, C., et al.: Well-structuredness, safeness and soundness: a formal classification of BPMN collaborations[J]. J. Logic. Algeb. Meth. Program. **119**, 100630 (2021)
8. Corradini, F., Polini, A., Re, B., et al.: Consistent modelling of hierarchical BPMN collaborations[J]. Bus. Process. Manag. J. **28**(2), 442–460 (2022)
9. Turetken, O., Rompen, T., Vanderfeesten, I., et al.: The effect of modularity representation and presentation medium on the understandability of business process models in BPMN[C]. In: Business Process Management: 14th International Conference, BPM 2016, Rio de Janeiro, Brazil, September 18-22, 2016. Proceedings 14, pp. 289–307. Springer International Publishing (2016)

10. Peña, L., Andrade, D., Delgado, A., et al.: An Approach for Discovering Inter-organizational Collaborative Business Processes in BPMN 2.0[C]. In: International Conference on Process Mining, pp. 487–498. Springer Nature Switzerland, Cham (2023)
11. Yang, X., Yu, T., Xu, H.: A novel framework of using petri net to timed service business process modeling[J]. Int. J. Softw. Eng. Knowl. Eng. **26**(04), 633–652 (2016)
12. Ha, S., Suh, H.W.: A timed colored Petri nets modeling for dynamic workflow in product development process[J]. Comput. Ind. **59**(2–3), 193–209 (2008)
13. Köpke, J., Franceschetti, M., Eder, J.: Analyzing data-flow implementations for distributed execution of inter-organizational processes[C]. In: Proceedings of the 19th International Conference on Information Integration and Web-based Applications & Services, pp. 502–510 (2017)
14. Mendling, J., Weber, I., Aalst, W.V.D., et al.: Blockchains for business process management-challenges and opportunities [J]. ACM Trans. Manag. Inform. Syst. (TMIS). **9**(1), 1–16 (2018)

The Impact of Text-Photo Sentiment Disparity on Review Helpfulness from a Cognitive Dissonance Perspective

Qian He, Maomao Chi(✉), Xinyi Xie, and Yuyan Shen

China University of Geosciences, Wuhan, China
chimaomao@vip.163.com

Abstract. With the increasing popularity of multimodal information on e-commerce platforms, the impact of text-photo sentiment disparity on online consumer behavior has grown increasingly significant. Based on Cognitive Dissonance Theory, this study explores the underlying mechanism through which text-photo sentiment disparity affects the perceived helpfulness of online reviews. By analyzing secondary data from the Ctrip platform and conducting four laboratory experiments, we find the sentiment disparity between images and text significantly boosts the perceived helpfulness of reviews. This effect is mediated through the perception of cognitive dissonance. Additionally, we explore the moderating effect of the Need for Cognition (NFC) during information processing, showing that for individuals with a high NFC, the impact of cognitive dissonance on review helpfulness is more salient. These findings promote the application of multimodal information processing and Cognitive Dissonance Theory, offering valuable insights for e-commerce platforms to optimize review systems and marketing strategies effectively.

Keywords: Text-photo sentiment disparity · Cognitive dissonance · Review helpfulness · Need for cognition · Multimodal information

1 Introduction

In recent years, online reviews have increasingly integrated text and images. Consumers use textual and visual cues to comprehensively assess products. This combination enriches the means of expression but also brings challenges. Especially, discrepancies between the emotions in images and text may occur. For example, a beautiful text description might be paired with an image of a disorderly and shabby room, conveying an ironic and intricate meaning.

This phenomenon of text-photo sentiment disparity has complex implications. On the one hand, they render it arduous for potential consumers to distill valuable information from conflicting data, thereby instilling doubts regarding the reviewers' attitudes and the authenticity of their evaluations. On the other hand, such disparities can arouse consumers' curiosity, compelling them to engage in a more in-depth interpretation of

Y. P. Tu and M. Chi (Eds.): WHICEB 2025, LNBIP 549, pp. 274–285, 2025.
https://doi.org/10.1007/978-3-031-94184-9_23

reviews in an attempt to discern the true stance. Such phenomenon poses novel challenges and research directions for traditional online review research.

Existing studies primarily examine textual features (e.g., sentiment polarity, detail level) and their impact on review helpfulness [1]. However, systematic research on multimodal interactions (text and images) in shaping consumer cognition remains limited.

While the role of emotional consistency in information processing has been extensively studied, emotional inconsistency's potential value has been overlooked. Conventional wisdom suggests that emotional consistency is more easily embraced by consumers, augmenting the persuasive power of information [2]. However, according to the Cognitive Dissonance Theory, inconsistent information can trigger cognitive dissonance among individuals, prompting deeper thinking and information processing [3]. This study explores how text-photo sentiment disparities can induce cognitive dissonance and impact review helpfulness, presenting a new perspective on the research of emotional complexity.

Prior research often applied cognitive dissonance to analyze consumer regret, conflict, or attitude change. This study extends the application of Cognitive Dissonance Theory to the context of text-photo sentiment disparities, providing new insights into the cognitive mechanisms underlying multimodal information processing.

Based on this, this paper centers on the following key research questions: (1) How does text-photo sentiment disparity affect the perceived usefulness of online reviews? (2) Does text-photo sentiment disparity indirectly influence the perceived usefulness of reviews by affecting consumers' perception of cognitive dissonance? (3) Does consumers' Need for Cognition moderate the relationship between cognitive dissonance and the perceived usefulness of reviews?

To answer these questions, this study utilizes hotel review data from the Ctrip platform, integrating machine learning, secondary data analysis, and laboratory experiments. Four research hypotheses are proposed and validated at multiple levels. The study aims to disclose the complex relationship between text-photo sentiment disparity and review helpfulness, offering novel insights for the application and theoretical research of multimodal information.

2 Literature Review and Hypothesis Development

2.1 Cognitive Dissonance Theory

Festinger first proposed the Cognitive Dissonance Theory, which is crucial for understanding individuals' psychological and behavioral responses to conflicting information. According to this theory, when individuals notice contradictions among cognitive elements like beliefs, attitudes, and behaviors, cognitive dissonance occurs. This discomfort prompts them to modify their cognition or behavior to reduce the dissonance [3].

The theory has been widely applied in consumer behavior research. For example, Whelan et al. [4] found that when product choices fail to meet expectations, cognitive dissonance increases, leading consumers to take corrective actions such as seeking extra information or justifying their purchasing decisions.

The Cognitive Dissonance Theory offers a framework for understanding how emotional differences affect consumers. Disparities between the emotions in images and text can cause psychological discomfort among consumers, which may drive them to closely examine review content, enhancing the depth and quality of information processing.

Moreover, the degree of cognitive dissonance is influenced by various factors, such as the individual's Need for Cognition (NFC). High-NFC individuals actively resolve discrepancies [5], amplifying dissonance effects and driving deeper information processing. This shows that cognitive dissonance is not only a result of information conflict but can also drive consumers to process information more actively.

2.2 Text-Photo Sentiment Disparity

Information inconsistency is a key topic in information dissemination research, which means the state where information elements are inharmonious in sentiment and content. Previous studies have shown that information consistency can enhance processing fluency, resulting in more positive product attitudes and stronger persuasive effects. On the other hand, information differences may reduce processing fluency, but due to novelty and uniqueness, they may also attract more attention and trigger more complex cognitive processing, thus improving attitude evaluations (e.g., humorous advertisements) [6]. For example, Li and Xie [7] pointed out that moderate differences can lead to greater decision utility as consumers view conflicting info as multi-perspective. Given that online reviews have become an important form of product promotion, understanding the inconsistency of customer-generated information is equally important.

In customer-generated content, attitudes and emotions are crucial as they reflect customers' subjective experiences and opinions. When the information in a review conveys the same sentiment (either positive or negative), other customers can sense the reviewer's consistent attitude towards the product [8]. When the information in a review is inconsistent, especially when there is a sentiment difference between the review text and the image, it can significantly affect customer behavior, although the specific mechanism remains unclear.

The text-photo sentiment disparity essentially indicates the difference in the valence of opinions expressed in the review text and the photos [8]. When the visual and textual information conflicts, consumers may experience internal conflict and dissonance. This cognitive dissonance phenomenon has been verified in many information processing contexts [5]. According to the Cognitive Dissonance Theory, individuals' perception of dissonance activates deeper cognitive processing to resolve contradictions and conflicts. For consumers, reviews with text-photo sentiment disparity are more attractive than those with emotional consistency, thus increasing the helpfulness of the review.

Therefore, the following hypotheses are proposed.

H1. Greater disparity between the sentiment in the photo and in the text of a review increases the perceived helpfulness of a review.
H2. Greater disparity between the sentiment in the photo and in the text of a review increases the perceived cognitive dissonance.
H3. The effect of text-photo sentiment disparity on helpfulness is due to the positive effect of disparity on perceived cognitive dissonance.

2.3 Need for Cognition

Need for Cognition (NFC) refers to an individual's personality trait of a tendency to engage in and enjoy effortful cognitive activities [9]. Individuals with higher NFC are more willing to conduct in-depth information processing and tend to seek meaning from complex and conflicting information.

Previous study [10] shows that when consumers face emotional differences, those with higher NFC may resolve the differences through more thinking and analysis, thus enhancing the credibility of the information and the helpfulness of the review. In those with low NFC, cognitive dissonance may cause neglect of info and lower review helpfulness perception.

Therefore, the following hypotheses are proposed.

H4. NFC positively moderates the influence of cognitive dissonance on the perceived helpfulness of reviews.

3 Research Design

To ensure external and internal validity, we test our predictions in one secondary data study and in four experiments to examine the proposed theoretical model (see Fig. 1). Study 1 provides real-world evidence for our core prediction: greater photo–text sentiment disparity is associated with greater helpfulness. Next, Study 2a validates algorithm-based similarity judgments with similarity assessments of human judges. We then replicate our core finding across several experimental studies using Ctrip reviews (Studies 2b, 3, and 4). Study 3 examines the psychological mechanism of cognitive dissonance using mediation. Finally, Study 4 investigates the moderating effect of the need for cognition. We provide an overview of studies and findings in Fig. 2.

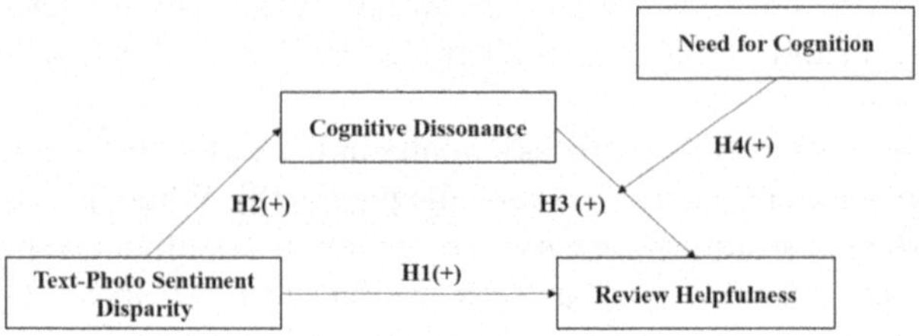

Fig. 1. Research Model

3.1 Study 1

In Study 1, we use field data to investigate the relationship between text-photo sentiment disparity and review usefulness.

Data. We analyzed 1,336,745 Ctrip hotel reviews (2021–2024) from Beijing, including text, ratings, photos, and helpful votes. Reviewer/hotel metadata (e.g., travel type, hotel rating) were controlled.

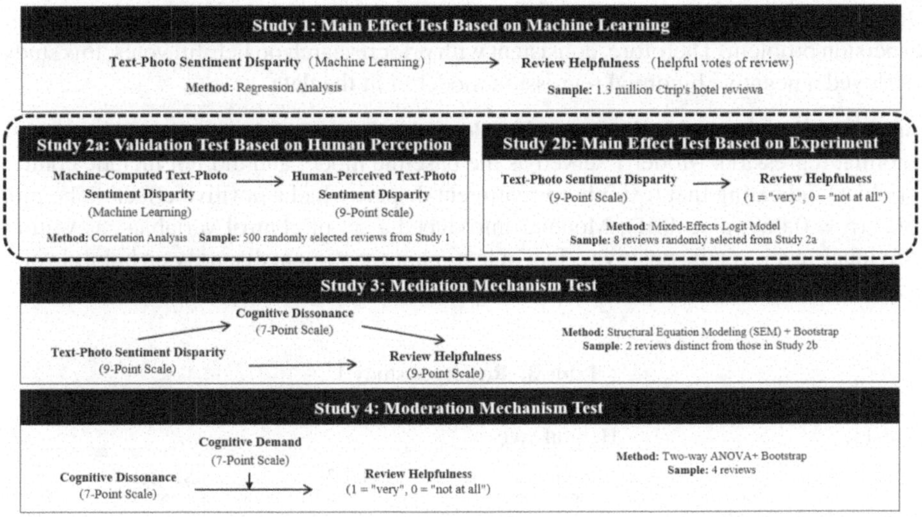

Fig. 2. Overview of studies.

Variables and Measurement. The dependent variable in this study is the number of helpful votes received by the review, and the independent variable is the sentiment disparity score between the review's text and images.

Measuring Text-Photo Sentiment Disparity. The open-source project Chinese-Multimodal-Sentiment-Analysis is used for multimodal sentiment analysis. For text feature extraction, the model utilizes the BERT architecture, applying Masked Language Modeling and Next Sentence Prediction tasks to learn the semantics and sentiment of the text. For image feature extraction, the model uses contrastive learning, similar to CLIP-Vision Transformer, and combines ResNet and Vision Transformer technologies.

For the image-side training dataset and training effectiveness, the image feature extraction model training uses the CH-SIMS dataset. On the validation set, the model achieved an accuracy of 77.20% and a weighted F1 score of 0.7775, with good performance and stable accuracy across sentiment categories.

The text-photo sentiment disparity of a review is calculated by taking the absolute difference between the sentiment scores of the text and the image and then summing the resulting values.

Control variables include hotel rating, popularity, review length, reviewer expertise, and travel type. Definitions of related variables are provided in Table 1.

Descriptive Statistics. Table 2 displays the mean, standard deviation, and correlation coefficients for all variables in Study 1. The average number of helpful votes per review was 0.355, suggesting that most reviews received few evaluations. Helpful votes were positively correlated with text–photo sentiment disparity($r = 0.013,\ p < .001$). The values of the variance inflation factor ranged from 1.00 to 1.18, all of which were below 3. Thus, Study 1 was not affected by multicollinearity.

Analysis Strategy. Due to the non-negative count nature of the dependent variable (i.e., helpful votes), a standard multiple regression technique was deemed inappropriate.

Moreover, the mean of helpful votes was smaller than the variance resulting in an over-dispersion problem. Therefore, consistent with prior research on helpful votes, this study employed a negative binomial regression model to fit the data.

Empirical Results and Robustness Check. Table 3 presents the results of the negative binomial regression. Model 1 served as the baseline model and did not include control variables, indicating that text–photo sentiment disparity had a positive effect on helpful votes ($b = 0.069$, $p < .001$). Model 2 introduced a set of control variables, as well as individual-level, yet the positive effect of text–photo sentiment disparity on helpful votes remained significant ($b = 0.027$, $p < .001$). Therefore, H1 was supported.

Table 3. Results of study 1.

Variable	Helpful votes		
	Model 1	Model 2	Model 3
Independent variable			
Disparity	0.069***	0.027***	0.057***
Control variable			
Hotel popularity		−0.000***	0.000***
Review length		0.007***	−0.026***
Reviewer expertise		0.003***	−0.011***
Intercept	−1.121***	1.128***	−0.533***
Travel type	N	Y	Y
Hotel rate	N	Y	Y
Log-likelihood	−166,413.99	−160,353.20	−161327.05
Pseudo R2	0.001	0.037	–
Observations	244,099	244,099	244,099

Notes: Standard errors are in parentheses. *$p < .05$, ** $p < .01$, *** $p < .001$.

For robustness check, this study modified the modeling approach to reanalyze the data. Given that the dependent variable had predominantly zero counts, a zero-inflated negative binomial regression model was adopted as an alternative modeling approach. A reanalysis of the dataset using this model confirmed that the significance of the results remained unchanged ($b = 0.057$, $p < .001$; Model 3).

Discussion. Study 1 confirmed that text-photo sentiment disparity enhances review helpfulness (H1 supported). However, secondary data limitations (e.g., correlation vs. causation) necessitate controlled experiments, detailed next.

Table 1. Description of Study 1's variables.

Variable	Description
Dependent variable	
Helpful votes	Number of helpful votes a review receives.
Independent variable	
Disparity	The text–photo sentiment disparity score is calculated by machine learning.
Control variable	
Hotel rate	Overall average score each hotel receives.
Hotel popularity	Number of reviews each hotel receives.
Review length	Number of words in a review.
Reviewer expertise	Number of cumulative reviews posted by the reviewer before the current review.
Travel type	The categorical variable includes the reviewer's travel type, such as solo, business.

Table 2. Descriptive statistics.

Variable	1	2	3	4	5	6
1.Helpful votes	1					
2.Disparity	0.013***	1				
3.Hotel rate	−0.032***	−0.042***	1			
4.Hotel popularity	−0.001	0.047	0.276***	1		
5.Review length	0.178***	0.030***	0.026***	0.065***	1	
6.Reviewer expertise	0.014***	0.022***	−0.032***	0.019***	0.046***	1
Mean	0.355	22.227	4.642	1642.036	74.737	7.736
SD	1.942	1.020	0.245	1711.785	82.956	17.144
VIF	–	1.18	1.17	1.09	1.06	1.01

Notes: VIF represents the variance inflation factor, and "—" represents no value. ***$p < .001$.

3.2 Study 2a

We expect the algorithmic metric to align with human judgments. To test this, human judges assess the sentiment disparity between the review's photo and text, and we compare these ratings with the algorithm-based disparities from Study 1.

Method. *Experimental Materials.* We randomly selected five samples of 100 reviews each from Study 1, all containing a photo. The overall sentiment disparity score was 2.53 (SD = 1.38), and the random samples closely aligned with this.

Participants. We recruited 500 participants (48.6% male, 51.4% female) to evaluate text-photo sentiment disparity. Each assessed 10 reviews from one of five samples, with each review rated by 10 judges.

Experimental Procedure. Evaluators first rated the question "Based on the image in the review, what emotional attitude do you think the consumer holds towards the hotel?" (1 = negative, 9 = positive). Then, they rated the review text with the question "Based on the text, what emotional attitude do you think the consumer holds towards the hotel?" (1 = negative, 9 = positive). The absolute difference between these scores was the human-perceived process-based text-photo sentiment disparity, which aligns with the machine-calculated disparity. Evaluators then assessed the outcome score with the question "How much does the emotional attitude conveyed by the image differ from the text?" (1 = "not at all," 9 = "very ").

Results. A significant positive correlation was found between the algorithm-based disparity and human evaluators' process-based perception ($r(500) = .129$, $p < .01$). The relationship with outcome-based perception was significant ($r(500) = .303$, $p < .01$).

Discussion. The findings show that algorithm-based and human-perceived disparities are consistent, indicating the algorithm captures human perception of emotional disparity.

3.3 Study 2b

Method. *Experimental Materials.* we used 8 reviews from Study 2a as the experimental materials, with 4 showing high and 4 showing low difference, with difference scores close to the mean ± 1 standard deviation.

Participants. 392 participants were recruited. The sample size was determined based on the effect size ($d = 0.31$) and 90% statistical power.

Experimental Procedure. Participants viewed all eight reviews in random order, in two rounds. First, they rated the usefulness of all reviews (1 = "useful", 0 = "not useful"). Then, they rated all reviews based on the questions used in Study 2a.

Results. *Perceived Disparity.* We conducted two independent mixed-effects models, regressing each disparity score (process-based and outcome-based) onto the disparity condition (1 = high, −1 = low), with random intercepts for participants. As expected, reviews in the high disparity condition scored significantly higher on outcome disparity ($M_{disparity}$=6.63, M_{parity}=2.38; b=2.13, SE=0.02, $t(1,390)$=111.77, p<.001) and process-based disparity ($M_{disparity}$=5.12, M_{parity}=2.38, b=1.52, SE=0.02, $t(1,390)$=75.61, p<.001). These results confirm the effectiveness of our manipulation.

Perceived Usefulness. We used usefulness judgments (1 = useful, 0 = not useful) as the dependent variable, disparity condition (1 = high disparity, −1 = low disparity) as the independent variable, and random intercepts for participants in a mixed-effects logistic regression model. Results showed that participants in the high disparity condition were more likely to consider the review useful($M_{disparity}$=5.12, M_{parity}=2.38, b=1.52, SE=0.02, $t(1, 390)$=75.61, p<.001)

Replacing the experimental condition with continuous disparity scores, both process and outcome perception disparity were positively correlated with usefulness votes($r_{\text{useful - outcome}}(392)$ =0.53, p<.001; $r_{\text{useful - process}}(392)$ =0.47, p<.001).

Discussion. By manipulating the differences in real reviews from Study 2a, we provided causal evidence for the effect of emotional disparity on perceived usefulness.

3.4 Study 3

Method. *Experimental Materials.* Study 3a used a between-subjects design with two conditions (high vs. low emotional disparity). The hotel review sample was drawn from the subset in Study 2a, containing two reviews with different emotional disparity, distinct from those in Study 2b. The selection process followed previous methods.

Participants. A total of 358 participants were recruited (55.5% female, 44.4% male).

Experimental Procedure. Participants were randomly assigned to one of two conditions. The experiment consisted of three phases: Firstly, participants read the reviews and rated the perceived usefulness (1 = "not at all", 9 = "very"). Next, participants completed a cognitive dissonance perception scale to assess psychological conflict (1 = "not at all", 7 = "very"; $\alpha = .92$).Last, participants read the reviews again and rated the emotional disparity between image and text.

Results. *Perceived Disparity.* Participants perceived a greater emotional disparity in the high disparity condition (M = 6.09, SD = 1.98) than in the low disparity condition (M = 4.41, SD = 2.02; b = .179, SE = .021, $t(397) = 8.391$, $p < .001$).

Perceived Usefulness. Supporting H1, participants in the high disparity condition (M = 5.18, SD = 1.74) rated the review as more helpful than those in the low disparity condition (M = 3.17, SD = 1.76; b = .69, SE = .04, $t(397) = 17.026$, $p < .001$).

Cognitive Dissonance. Supporting H2, participants in the high disparity condition (M = 4.84, SD = 1.60) reported more conflict and inconsistency than those in the low disparity condition (M = 3.14, SD = 1.52; b = .84, SE = .10, $t(397) = 8.39$, $p < .001$).

Mediating Mechanism. To test H3, we used Hayes' Model 4 to examine whether the effect of emotional disparity on perceived usefulness was mediated by cognitive dissonance. Supporting H3, we found a significant indirect effect of image-text emotional disparity on perceived usefulness through cognitive dissonance (b_indirect = .38, SE = .06, 95% CI = [.2671, .5117]). (see Fig. 3).

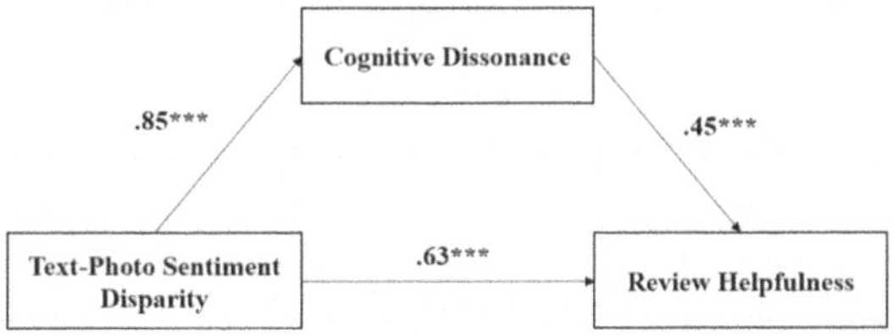

Fig. 3. A Mediation Model

Discussion. Study 3 supports H1 with causal evidence from ecologically valid stimuli and shows that higher emotional disparity between image and text increases cognitive dissonance, which in turn enhances perceived review usefulness.

3.5 Study 4

Method. *Participants and Grouping.* 360 participants, with sample size determined by an effect size (d = 0.32) and at least 90% statistical power. Prior to the experiment, participants NFC was measured using the NFC scale [9] ($\alpha = .88$), and divided into high NFC (top 50%) and low NFC (bottom 50%) groups.

Experimental Materials. Four text-only reviews were chosen to manipulate cognitive dissonance: two high and two low dissonance reviews.

Experimental Procedure. A 2 (Cognitive Dissonance: high vs. low) × 2 (NFC: high vs. low) between-subjects design was used. The experiment consisted of two steps: 1) Participants rated review usefulness, verifying the indirect effect of emotional disparity on usefulness. 2)Participants completed a cognitive dissonance scale ($\alpha = .89$) to assess perceived dissonance while reading the reviews.

Results. A two-way ANOVA showed a significant main effect of cognitive dissonance on perceived usefulness ($F(3, 316) = 559.77, p < .001$). Participants in the high cognitive dissonance condition (M = 5.11, SD = 0.68) rated the review as more useful than those in the low cognitive dissonance condition (M = 2.18, SD = 0.39). Additionally, the interaction between cognitive dissonance and NFC was significant ($F(3, 316) = 15.85$, $p < .001$), with high NFC participants rating high cognitive dissonance reviews as more useful.

Discussion. Study 4 confirmed that cognitive dissonance positively affects perceived review usefulness moderated by NFC, supporting H4.

4 Conclusion

This study demonstrates that text-photo sentiment disparity enhances online review helpfulness. Analysis of Ctrip reviews reveals that greater disparity increases perceived helpfulness, supported by causal evidence from four experiments. Furthermore, Need for Cognition (NFC) moderates this relationship: individuals with higher NFC exhibit stronger positive effects of cognitive dissonance on review helpfulness.

4.1 Theoretical Implications

First, this study broadens the multimodal information research framework. Unlike existing studies mainly focusing on information consistency, this research emphasizes how text-photo sentiment disparity affects consumer cognition and information evaluation.

Second, this study extends Cognitive Dissonance Theory to the text-photo sentiment disparity context. While often linked to negative emotions, it finds that cognitive dissonance can enhance in-depth review processing and review helpfulness in some cases, expanding the theory's application. Third, this study proposes and tests the mediating mechanism of text-photo sentiment disparity on review helpfulness through cognitive dissonance. Five studies provide solid evidence, deepening the understanding of multimodal information processing.

Lastly, this study explores the moderating role of NFC in information processing. It shows that for individuals with a high NFC, cognitive dissonance has a more significant impact on review helpfulness, providing new theoretical explanations for individual differences in information processing.

4.2 Practical Implications

Our study generates several practical implications for e-commerce platforms. First, platforms can use technology to detect text-photo sentiment disparity and optimize review order, recommendations, or filters to enhance perceived helpfulness.

Secondly, for platform creators, they can strategically craft reviews with text-photo sentiment mismatches to evoke curiosity and emotional engagement, enhancing review appeal.

Thirdly, for personalized recommendations based on the NFC, platforms can recommend more in-depth reviews to users with high NFC and simpler ones to those with low NFC. This can improve the perceived helpfulness of reviews and user satisfaction.

4.3 Limitations and Future Research

As with any research, this study is subject to a few limitations. First, generalizability may be constrained by Ctrip hotel data. Future research should test cross-domain (e.g., Taobao, Amazon). Second, lab experiments may not match real e-commerce. Future work could be supplemented with field trials tracking click/purchase behavior. Finally, sentiment analysis tools may overlook nuanced emotions, warranting advanced deep-learning models.

Acknowledgement. This research was supported by the grant from the National Natural Science Foundation of China (No. 72272138 and 71801104), and the grant from the Humanities and Social Sciences Fund of the Ministry of Education of China (No. 22YJA630009).

3References

1. Lee, J., Cho, M.: The (in)congruency effects of message framing and image valence on consumers' responses to green advertising: focus on issue involvement as a moderator. J. Mark. Commun. **28**(6), 617–636 (2021)
2. Pang, B., Lee, L.: Opinion Mining and Sentiment Analysis. Foundations and Trends in Information Retrieval: Vol. 2: No. 1–2, pp 1–135
3. Festinger, L.: A Theory of Cognitive Dissonance, 1st edn. Stanford University Press, Stanford (1957)
4. Whelan, J., Hingston, S.T.: Pathogens, privilege, and purity: how pathogen threat and childhood socioeconomic status influence consumers' condemnation of purity violations. J. Bus. Res. **142**, 636–647 (2022)
5. Vaidis, D.C., Bran, A.: Respectable challenges to respectable theory: cognitive dissonance theory requires conceptualization clarification and operational tools. Front. Psychol. **10**, 249 (2019)

6. Lee, Y.H., Mason, C.: Responses to information incongruency in advertising: the role of expectancy, relevancy, and humor. J. Consum. Res. **26**(2), 156–169 (1999)
7. Li, J., Xie, X.: Exploring the boundary conditions of emotional inconsistencies in visual–textual information. Mark. Lett. **33**(2), 267–283 (2022)
8. Li, H., Ji, H., Liu, H., Cai, D., Gao, H.: Is a picture worth a thousand words? Understanding the role of review photo sentiment and text-photo sentiment disparity using deep learning algorithms. Tour. Manag. **92**, 104559 (2022)
9. Cacioppo, J.T., Petty, R.E.: The need for cognition. J. Pers. Soc. Psychol. **42**(1), 116–131 (1982)
10. Lin, C.L., Lee, S.H., Horng, D.J.: The effects of online reviews on purchasing intention: the moderating role of need for cognition. Soc. Behav. Personal. Int. J. **39**(1), 71–81 (2011)

A Fine-Tuned LLM Method to Explore Corporate Policy-Attention Themes in the New Energy Vehicle Sector

Huiru Jia, Hanfei Li, Jiajia Cai, Daqing Yin, Shengyuan Yin, Yue Han, and Zhen Zhu(✉)

School of Economics and Management, China University of Geosciences, Wuhan, China
zhuzhen2008@gmail.com

Abstract. To improve the accuracy and authenticity of a large language model (LLM) in identifying Policy-Attention themes, this study proposes a method for constructing a domain-specific LLM using LoRA fine-tuning technology. The main steps are as follows: constructing a directive dataset for automotive companies' responses to new energy policies; LoRA fine-tuning of the ChatGLM4-9B model results in ChatGLM-LoRA-NEVPR; evaluating the model through objective, human, and intelligent assessments. Experimental results show that the proposed method improves the accuracy by 12% compared to the baseline model. Additionally, the results from both human and intelligent evaluations further validate the effectiveness of the method across various dimensions. The paper develops ChatGLM-LoRA-NEVPR, and fine-tuning large language models can significantly enhance its accuracy and authenticity in recognizing policy-attention themes within the new energy vehicle sector.

Keywords: LLM · Corporate Policy-Attention Themes · LoRA · New Energy Vehicle Sector

1 Introduction

The current socio-economic development is confronted with a complex policy environment, where enterprises, as key drivers of high-quality growth, are significantly influenced by policy changes. Anticipating enterprises' responses to policies is crucial for enhancing policy coordination and achieving related policy objectives. This study proposes leveraging a large language model (LLM) to assist governments in identifying enterprises' responses to policies. While general-purpose LLMs are typically trained on extensive public datasets and capable of addressing a wide range of generic problems, these datasets often lack the domain-specific expertise and technical details necessary for specialized applications. As a result, general models may exhibit limitations in accuracy and specificity when identifying enterprise responses to industrial policies.

To address this gap, by focusing New Energy Vehicles (NEVs) Policy-Attention in China, this paper develops ChatGLM-LoRA-NEVPR, a domain-specific large model

Y. P. Tu and M. Chi (Eds.): WHICEB 2025, LNBIP 549, pp. 286–297, 2025.
https://doi.org/10.1007/978-3-031-94184-9_24

to explore corporate Policy-Attention themes in the NEVs sector. Using web scraping techniques, we obtained the full annual reports of 201 listed corporation in new energy vehicle sector and constructed a directive dataset focused on their responses to new energy industrial policies. This dataset was used to fine-tune the model via LoRA and apply quantization for optimized performance. Subsequently, the fine-tuned model underwent comprehensive evaluation through objective assessments, human evaluations, and intelligent evaluations. The results demonstrate that fine-tuning LLM can significantly enhance the accuracy and reliability of policy-attention themes in the NEV domain.

2 Related Work

2.1 Natural Language Processing in Policy Themes

Natural Language Processing (NLP) technologies offer a novel perspective for understanding policy-related themes through text mining and semantic analysis. Existing studies demonstrate the diverse applications of NLP across various policy domains. For instance, Dong employed the Latent Dirichlet Allocation (LDA) model to perform topic modeling on policy literature related to smart cities and artificial intelligence, identifying key themes such as "service transformation," "community engagement," and "sustainable development goals." [1]. Zhou analyzed public support for policy instruments, revealing that policy effectiveness, political trust, and policy knowledge are critical factors influencing public attitudes [2]. Similarly, Gutiérrez Domínguez utilized social media data to evaluate public opinion on the reform of the European Common Agricultural Policy (CAP), further highlighting the potential of NLP in monitoring policy dynamics and analyzing public sentiment [3].

2.2 LLMs and Fine-Tuning for Text Understanding

Large language models (LLMs), trained on massive textual data, excel in NLP tasks and demonstrate emergent abilities like in-context learning [4]. Despite their billion-parameter architectures enabling complex pattern recognition, LLMs face critical limitations: high hardware demands, domain knowledge gaps, and hallucination risks. To mitigate LLMs' domain-specific inaccuracies and unreliable outputs, fine-tuning is widely adopted. However, extreme parameter scales impose prohibitive costs. Addressing this, Microsoft proposed LoRA [5], a parameter-efficient method that freezes pretrained weights and trains low-rank matrices, guided by natural language instructions. Leveraging this framework, this study implements instruction fine-tuning on domain-specific datasets to develop a specialized LLM for corporate policy attention analysis.

2.3 ChatGlm Model and Lora Fine-Tuning

With the rapid advancement of pretrained language models, current mainstream architectures primarily include auto-encoding models (e.g., BERT [6]),auto regressive models (e.g., GPT [7]), and encoder-decoder models (e.g., T5 [8]). However, none of these frameworks achieves optimal performance across three major task categories: natural language understanding, unconditional generation, and conditional generation. To address this limitation, the GLM model proposed by Zhipu AI and Tsinghua University's KEG Laboratory introduces an auto regressive blank infilling framework. Although GLM demonstrates superior performance in large-scale pretraining, its effectiveness in domain-specific applications remains constrained by insufficient integration of domain prior knowledge.

To enhance model adaptability in vertical domains, conventional full-parameter fine-tuning methods suffer from excessive computational resource demands and significant hardware overhead. Recent parameter-efficient fine-tuning approaches (e.g., LoRA and P-Tuning v2) substantially reduce resource consumption through optimized training mechanisms. Specifically, Low-Rank Adaptation (LoRA)embeds trainable low-rank decomposition matrices within Transformer modules, enabling performance maintenance through minimal parameter updates. This methodology effectively reduces GPU memory requirements and enhances training efficiency by freezing pretrained weights and minimizing gradient computation [9], thereby providing a practical technical pathway for real-world deployment of large language models [10].

2.4 Corporate Policy-Attention in NEV Sector

Previous research has predominantly focused on policies in NEV sector, examining their impact on industry development. However, studies on corporate responses to these policies remain relatively limited and have primarily relied on survey-based approaches [11]. While traditional NLP techniques can extract policy-relevant information, they often lack the capability for deep understanding and reasoning [12]. In recent years, the development of LLMs has introduced new opportunities for studying policy attention, as these models demonstrate significant potential in comprehending complex textual data. Nonetheless, LLMs face certain limitations, such as challenges in handling ambiguous queries or appropriately rejecting unreasonable requests. To address these challenges, this study employs fine-tuning techniques to enhance the model's ability to understand and reason over policy texts, providing a more effective tool for analyzing corporate responses to policies.

3 Methodology

3.1 Overall Framework

This study introduces an instruction fine-tuning technique based on the ChatGLM-4-9B large language model, aimed at improving the model's performance in responding to corporate policies within the vertical domain of NEV enterprises. This approach effectively addresses the limitations of traditional NLP techniques in terms of deep understanding and reasoning capabilities, while also overcoming certain constraints of LLMs in domain-specific applications. The specific technical steps are as follows:

Step 1: Construction of Instruction Dataset. Using BERT technology, a policy theme keyword lexicon is extracted from policy texts and corporate annual reports, followed by the construction of an instruction-supervised fine-tuning dataset.

Step 2: Instruction Fine-tuning of ChatGLM-4-9B Large Language Model. LoRA fine-tuning is applied to obtain ChatGLM-LoRA-NEVPR.
Step 3: ChatGLM-LoRA-NEVPR Evaluation. The fine-tuned model is subjected to objective evaluation, manual evaluation, and intelligent evaluation (Fig. 1).

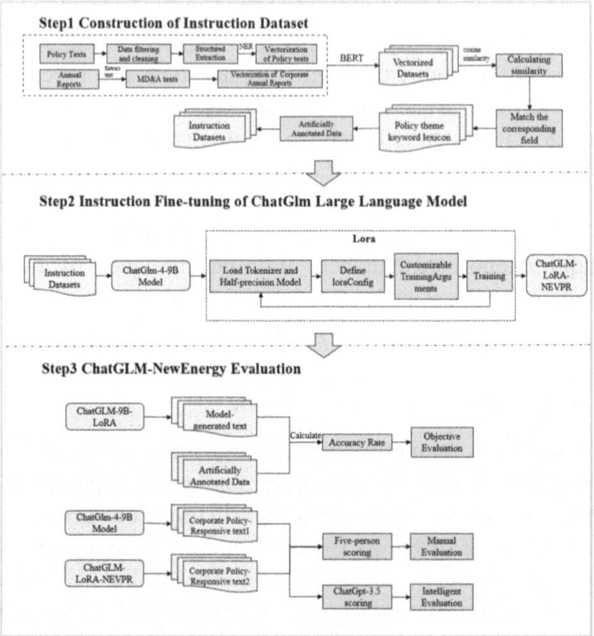

Fig. 1. Overall framework

3.2 Parameter-Efficient Model Fine-Tuning

Parameter-efficient fine-tuning, or lightweight fine-tuning, reduces the number of parameters requiring training, aiming to maintain performance close to full fine-tuning. This study uses low-rank fitness fine-tuning as a primary technique for large models.

LLMs have over-parameterized, high-dimensional matrices, yet research reveals low intrinsic rank during task adaptation. LoRA addresses this by adding a low-rank decomposition matrix to approximate parameter updates, reducing the parameters needed for adaptation. The model parameter matrix W is updated as follows:

$$W = W_0 + \Delta W \tag{1}$$

where W_0 is the original parameter matrix and ΔW is the updated gradient matrix. The basic idea of LORA is to freeze the initial matrix $W_0 \in R^{H \times H}$ and approximate the parameter update matrix $\Delta W = A \bullet B^T$ by the low-rank decomposition matrices $A \in R^{H \times R}$ and $B \in R^{H \times R}$, where $R \ll H$ is the reduced rank. During fine-tuning, the original matrix parameters W_0 are not updated and the low-rank decomposition matrices A and B are trainable parameters for adaptation to downstream tasks. During forward propagation, the original formula for calculating the intermediate state $h = W_0 \bullet x$ can be expressed as follows:

$$h = W_0 \bullet x + A \bullet B^T \bullet x \tag{2}$$

After the training is completed, the updated parameter matrix is further obtained by merging $W = W_0 + A \bullet B^T$ the original parameter matrix W_0 with the weights A and B obtained from the training. Therefore, the model obtained by LORA fine-tuning does not add extra overhead in the decoding process.

As LLMs gain prominence, LoRA has emerged as an efficient fine-tuning method that reduces training costs without sacrificing performance. It has been successfully applied to open-source models like LLaMA and BLOOM. Evaluation of fine-tuning techniques shows LoRA's superiority, requiring fewer parameters and simplifying implementation. Therefore, this study uses LoRA for fine-tuning ChatGLM.

4 Dataset Construction

In this study, 284 listed corporations' annual reports from 2011 to 2022 were labeled to identify and categorize policy themes into seven main categories: green emission reduction, technological innovation, infrastructure investment, demonstration projects, financial incentives, market regulation, and market access [13]. Each report was annotated with the policy theme, response logic, impact, and the firm's position in the industrial chain. This annotated text-data set aids understanding of corporate policy attention and supports the training and evaluation of the ChatGLM-LoRA-NEVPR model. The next section will detail the dataset construction methodology.

4.1 Retrieve Corporate Annual Reports

This study examines listed companies in the Shanghai and Shenzhen A-share markets across the upstream, midstream, and downstream sectors of the NEV industry. According to Avery Consulting, the industry includes raw materials, batteries, motors, vehicle manufacturing, and charging services. The upstream sector covers materials like lithium and nickel, while the downstream focuses on automotive finance and recycling. Excluding sectors without listed companies, seven categories were analyzed: raw materials, batteries, motors, electronic control, parts, vehicle manufacturing, and charging services.

Using Python web scraping, stock codes and business profiles for 282 listed companies were gathered from the Flush website with keywords such as "new energy vehicles" and "electric vehicles." From 2011–2022, 247 relevant companies were identified, with 46 excluded due to financial risks or being listed for less than a year. A total of 201 annual reports from this period were analyzed, as summarized in Table 1.

This study analyzes corporate managerial attention by extracting MD&A sections from annual reports using a Python program that identifies these sections based on their periodic chapter distribution patterns. The text underwent standard preprocessing including stop word removal and tokenization.

Table 1. Industry Distribution of Sample

Listed Company	Upstream			Midstream	Downstream
	Raw Materials	Battery	Other	Vehicle Manufacture	Charging and switching services
Sample size/	19/	48/	86/	27/	21/
Percentage	9.45%	23.88%	42.79%	13.43%	10.44%

4.2 Selection of MD&A Texts

To ensure the representativeness and generalizability of the instruction dataset, we systematically selected 11 enterprises from 201 NEV industry listed companies, stratified according to the proportional distribution of industrial chain sectors (70% upstream, 20% midstream, 10% downstream). The sample comprises:

1. Upstream: Raw material producers (Tianqi Lithium, Yunhai Metal), three electric system suppliers (Guoxuan High-Tech, Founder Motor, Inovance Technology, Jiangte Electric), and component manufacturers (Nanfang Bearing)
2. Midstream: Vehicle manufacturers (SAIC Motor, Zhongtong Bus)
3. Downstream: Charging infrastructure providers (Tgood Electric, Wanma Shares)

Using 2023 market capitalization data, enterprises were classified into three tiers: large (>CNY 50 billion: SAIC Motor, Inovance Technology, Tianqi Lithium, Tgood Electric), medium (CNY 5–50 billion: Guoxuan High-Tech, Wanma Shares, Yunhai Metal, Zhongtong Bus), and small (<CNY 5 billion: Founder Motor, Nanfang Bearing, Jiangte Electric). This stratification enables systematic analysis of scale-dependent policy responsiveness,large enterprises predominantly align with strategic innovation policies, whereas small enterprises demonstrate heightened sensitivity to cost-oriented regulations such as subsidy mechanisms.

4.3 Constructing Instruction Datasets

A manual construction of a 284-instruction fine-tuning dataset was undertaken following an in-depth analysis of the annual report data of these 11 companies. This dataset is both representative and universal in content and can provide effective support for the training of LLMs and achieve good training results.

As illustrated in Fig. 2, a prototype data sample is presented, comprising two primary components: input and output, accompanied by comprehensive task de-scription texts for each 'input-output' data pair. These descriptive texts are intended to clarify the goal of the task and its related contextual information, thus enhancing the ability of the large language model to follow instructions and improve its generalization across different tasks. In the output section, key phrases such as 'policy theme of the attention', 'logic of the policy response', 'impact of the policy response', and 'company's industry chain location' have been manually authored. This information helps the model to more accurately understand and reflect the response mechanism of listed corporation in NEV sector to policy changes. The construction of the command dataset, as illustrated in the figure, can provide high-quality training materials for the subsequent fine-tuning of the large language model.

System:[You are a policy analysis expert responsible for identifying corporate response strategies to new energy vehicle policies from listed companies' annual reports and conducting an in-depth exploration of how different levels of policy attention impact corporate development.]

Input: [insert policy text]

Output:[**"Responsive policy themes"**:[Insert policy theme]
"Logic of policy response":[Insert text]
"Impact of policy responses":[Insert text]]

Fig. 2. Instruction Dataset

4.4 Data Imbalance Handling Strategy

Preliminary analysis identified significant class imbalance, with technological innovation representing the dominant category (36.27%) and market access management the least frequent (5.99%). To address this skew, we implemented a dual strategy combining oversampling of minority classes and an inverse-frequency weighted loss function. The weighting scheme assigned dynamically adjusted coefficients ranging from 0.5 (for high-frequency classes like technological innovation) to 1.5 (for rare classes such as market access management). This synergistic approach compensates for underrepresented categories through synthetic sample generation while rebalancing gradient updates via loss recalibration, thereby enhancing model sensitivity to minority patterns without compromising generalization through over-optimization on resampled data.

5 Experiment Settings

5.1 ChatGLM-4-9B Model

In this study, we utilized ChatGLM-4-9B as the base model. ChatGLM-4-9B is an open-source bilingual dialogue model developed by the Knowledge Engineering and Data Mining Group at Tsinghua University. Built upon the GLM architecture, it consists of 9 billion parameters. GLM is an autoregressive, masked token prediction framework that allows for arbitrary sequential prediction spans and enhances task adaptability by adjusting the number and length of masked tokens. Under equivalent model size and data conditions, ChatGLM-4-9B demonstrates superior performance compared to BERT, T5, and GPT in various tasks. The model employs a single Transformer architecture, refines the ordering of layer normalization and residual connections, uses the Gaussian Error Linear Unit (Gelu) activation function, and supports deployment on consumer-grade Graphics Processing Unit (GPUs) through quantization techniques. Addition-ally, GLM-4 can handle up to 128 K tokens in conversational context, making it well-suited for the long annual report texts explored in this research, and significantly reducing inference costs.

5.2 LoRA Fine-Tuning Process

To ensure that the results obtained are not affected by changes in the cue words, we used a uniform cue word when fine-tuning the ChatGlm-4-9B model for LoRA. See appendix for specific LLM prompt settings.

In this study, five companies, excluding the aforementioned 11, were selected as training samples for the model training process. These samples included three upstream companies, one midstream company, and one downstream company. The training data were collected from the annual reports of these companies spanning the years 2011 to 2022, resulting in a total of 60 training samples. Upon completing the training process, the final model parameters are presented in Table 2.

Table 2. Third round parameters

Parameters	Numerical value
r	16
lora_alpha	64
lora_dropout	0.2
batch_size	5
Epochs	3

Notes: r: The rank of the low-rank matrix; lora_alpha: A scaling factor that adjusts the integration ratio between the low-rank matrix and the original weights; lora_dropout: A dropout probability value to prevent overfitting; batch_size: The number of samples fed into the model during each training step; Epochs: The total number of complete training cycles over the entire dataset.

The experimental results summarized the three aspects of "responsive policy themes," "logic of the policy response," and "impact of the policy response," with the generated content demonstrating a high degree of alignment with corporate annual reports. However, to more comprehensively and objectively evaluate the model's performance and verify its generalization capability across different datasets, we will further introduce a validation set for evaluation.

5.3 Results and Analyses

In this study, three distinct evaluation methods were employed to assess the performance of the models: objective evaluation, manual evaluation, and intelligent evaluation. Objective evaluation provides a quantitative measure of accuracy, manual evaluation assesses the semantic quality, logical consistency, and fluency of generated responses, while intelligent evaluation leverages a language model to evaluate content from multiple dimensions efficiently. Using all three methods ensures a comprehensive assessment, accounting for both precision and content quality, while minimizing subjective biases and the labor-intensive nature of manual assessments.

Objective Evaluation

In this study, accuracy was adopted as the evaluation metric to assess the model's performance on question-answering tasks, quantifying the proportion of correctly predicted answers. Specifically, accuracy is determined by calculating the ratio of correctly predicted samples to the total number of samples. For the specific context of this study, the evaluation primarily focused on the model's accuracy in classifying policy attention themes within corporate annual reports. The accuracy before and after fine-tuning is shown in Table 3. After fine-tuning, the model achieved an accuracy of over 70%, demonstrating satisfactory performance in identifying policy attention themes from corporate annual reports.

Table 3. Comparison of accuracy

Model	ChatGlm-4-9B	ChatGLM-LoRA-NEVPR
correct identification	45	54
Aggregate	76	76
Accuracy	0.59	0.71

Manual Evaluation.
Although objective evaluation can quantitatively measure the accuracy of generated content, it cannot assess factors such as semantic quality, logical consistency, and fluency. Therefore, this study designed a human evaluation experiment to conduct blind testing on the generated content, ensuring the objectivity of the assessment.In the human evaluation phase of this study, five evaluators with a detailed understanding of new energy policies were selected. The evaluators scored the generated text based on three key dimensions: the accuracy of policy attention theme classification in corporate annual reports (Accuracy), the rationality of the policy response logic (Reasonableness), and the authenticity of the policy response impact (Validity). The 3-point Likert scale was conducted with a 3 point for excellent, a 2 point for average, and 1 point for poor. To ensure the objectivity and fairness of the evaluation, a blind testing setup was adopted, meaning that the evaluators were unaware of the source of the generated content during the scoring process.

The results of the human evaluation indicate that the ChatGLM-LoRA-NEVPR model, after fine-tuning, performs more accurately in the task of policy attention theme classification in corporate annual reports. The model effectively identifies and classifies different policy attention themes, and the generated policy response logic and impacts are consistent with the corporate annual reports and their context, avoiding any baseless speculations or fabrications (Table 4).

Table 4. Results of manual assessments

Model	Accuracy	Reasonableness	Validity
ChatGlm-4-9B	1.2	1.6	1.9
ChatGLM-LoRA-NEVPR	2.6	2.8	2.6

Intelligent Evaluation.
To overcome the labor costs and the influence of subjective factors in human evaluation, this study also employs an intelligent evaluation method. We use the large language model ChatGPT-3.5 for the intelligent evaluation of the generated text. ChatGPT-3.5, leveraging its natural language processing capabilities, evaluates the generated content from multiple dimensions. The criteria for the intelligent evaluation are the same as those used in human evaluation, focusing on three aspects. The specific evaluation instructions are shown in Table 5.

Table 5. Intelligent Evaluation Command Set

Num	Instruction
1	Please evaluate the generated corporate responses to new energy policies based on the provided corporate annual report texts.
2	Please assess the accuracy of the policy theme classification in the generated corporate responses to new energy policies using the corporate annual report texts as a reference.
3	Please evaluate the generated corporate responses to new energy policies in terms of both the accuracy of the policy theme classification and the logical consistency of the policy attention, based on the corporate annual report texts.
4	Please rate the generated corporate responses to new energy policies using the provided corporate annual report texts. The evaluation should focus on the following three aspects: (1) The accuracy of the policy theme classification in the corporate annual report. (2) The logical consistency of the policy attention. (3) The authenticity of the impact of the policy response.

Based on the above instructions, 50 samples randomly selected from the test set were evaluated, and the average scores for the generated text content from each model were calculated.

As shown in the table, ChatGLM-LoRA-NEVPR excels in multiple evaluation dimensions, particularly demonstrating a significant advantage in the accuracy of policy attention topic classification in corporate annual reports. This indicates that ChatGLM-LoRA-NEVPR is capable of accurately classifying and analyzing policy attention topics (Table 6).

Table 6. Results of Intelligent Assessment with AI Tools

Model	Instruction1	Instruction2	Instruction3	Instruction4
ChatGlm-4-9B	1.3	1.5	1.7	1.4
ChatGLM-LoRA-NEVPR	2.6	2.7	2.8	2.5

6 Conclusion and Future Work

This study integrates ChatGLM-4-9B with LoRA fine-tuning technology to construct a new energy policy instruction dataset and successfully implement the locally deployed ChatGLM-LoRA-NEVPR after fine-tuning. A vertical-domain large language model for the NEVs policy themes was thus established. Preliminary validation demonstrated that fine-tuning LLM significantly improves the accuracy and authenticity of policy attention recognition in the new energy domain, highlighting the potential of localized LLM deployment in future applications.

Future research will focus on following two directions. First, we will refine the instruction dataset by meticulously annotating policy attention texts from corporate annual reports and introducing diverse prompt patterns to further enhance the model's professionalism and flexibility. Second, we will introduce data argumentation methods to explore more effective result enhancement strategies, and leverage the latest large language model technologies such as GPT-4 to optimize the quality and diversity of the training data, thereby improving the comprehensiveness and accuracy of the generated responses.

Appendix

LLM Prompt

If you are a researcher in macro economics management and need to conduct a tracking analysis of how listed companies in NEV industrial respond to national renewable energy policies, please follow the specified analytical requirements below based on company information and annual report disclosures.

Specific Requirements:

1.Identify the response types of listed companies to NEV industrial policy themes :

Detailed requirements: Analyze the types of policy responses disclosed in the annual reports. Select one or more of the most relevant policy themes from the following seven types, without creating additional themes:

- Green low-carbon emission reduction
- Technological innovation and development
- Infrastructure investment
- Demonstration and promotion projects
- Fiscal incentive measures
- Market regulation optimization
- Market access management

2.Conduct a logical analysis of the company's responses to NEV industrial policy themes:

Detailed requirements: Based on the listed company's information, summarize the specific measures disclosed in the annual reports that reflect the company's response to renewable energy policies. For example, strategies such as increased R&D investment, technological innovation, and market expansion should be evaluated for their alignment with policy requirements.

3.Analyze the impact of the company's responses to NEV industrial policies (optional):

Detailed requirements: If feasible, analyze the specific impacts of the company's responses on its strategy, market position, and competitiveness, with a focus on evaluating their contribution to the company's long-term development.

4.Output Format Requirements:

Strictly follow the format below for the output:

•**"Policy Themes Responded to"**: (Content: Select one or more of the most relevant policy themes from the seven types listed above. Do not create new themes.)

•**"Policy Response Logic"**: (Content: Summarize the specific measures dis-closed in the annual reports that respond to renewable energy policies.)

•**"Impact of Policy Response"**: (Content: Analyze the impacts of the company's policy response based on the annual report disclosures. If no explicit im-pact analysis is available, this section can be omitted.)

The output must be complete, concise, and consistent with the input data and context, without omitting any critical analytical points.

Company Information: XXXX
Annual Report Disclosure:
Year: 2010
Annual Report Disclosure:

References

1. Dong, L., Liu, Y.: Frontiers of policy and governance research in a smart city and artificial intelligence: an advanced review based on natural language processing. Front. Sustain. Cities. **5**, 1199041 (2023)
2. Zhou, L., et al.: What is policy content and how is the public's policy support? A policy cognition study based on natural language processing and social psychology. Front. Psychol. **13**, 941762 (2022)
3. Domínguez, A.G., et al.: Natural language processing of social network data for the evaluation of agricultural and rural policies. J. Rural. Stud. **109**, 103341 (2024)
4. Guu, K., et al.: Retrieval augmented language model pre-training. In: International Conference on Machine Learning, pp. 3929–3938. PMLR (2020)
5. Hu, E.J., et al.: Lora: low-rank adaptation of large language models. ICLR. **1**(2), 3 (2022)
6. Devlin, J., et al.: Bert: pre-training of deep bidirectional transformers for language understanding. In: Proceedings of the 2019 Conference of the North American Chapter of the Association for Computational Linguistics: Human Language Technologies, pp. 4171–4186 (2019)
7. Brown, T., et al.: Language models are few-shot learners. Adv. Neural Inf. Proces. Syst. **33**, 1877–1901 (2020)
8. Raffel, C., et al.: Exploring the limits of transfer learning with a unified text-to-text transformer. J. Mach. Learn. Res. **21**(140), 1–67 (2020)
9. Xin, C., et al.: Beyond full fine-tuning: Harnessing the power of LoRA for multi-task instruction tuning. In: Proceedings of the 2024 Joint International Conference on Computational Linguistics, Language Resources and Evaluation, pp. 2307–2317 (2024)
10. Houlsby, N., et al.: Parameter-efficient transfer learning for NLP. In: International Conference on Machine Learning, pp. 2790–2799, PMLR (2019)
11. Zhao, M., Sun, T.: Dynamic spatial spillover effect of new energy vehicle industry policies on carbon emission of transportation sector in China. Energy Policy. **165**, 112991 (2022)
12. Zhang, L., Qin, Q.: China's new energy vehicle policies: evolution, comparison and recommendation. Transp. Res. A Policy Pract. **110**, 57–72 (2018)
13. Liu, Y., et al.: Constructing policy domain dictionary generated by DTM-embeddings to identify policy response features of listed companies in electric vehicle industry. In: Proceedings of 23thWuhan International Conference on E-business, pp. 408–420. Springer (2024)

Digital Innovation and Social Impact

Does Internationalization Promote Enterprise Digital Technology Innovation? – A Study on the Impact of Internationalization Degree on the Quality of Enterprise Digital Technology Innovation

Lin Wang[1,2](✉) and Congrui Fu[1]

[1] School of Information Management, Wuhan University, Wuhan 430072, China
Lwang@whu.edu.cn

[2] E-Commerce Research and Development Center, Wuhan University, Wuhan 430072, China

Abstract. In the era of the digital economy, digital technology innovation and internationalization are indispensable components of national policy guidelines. R&D innovation and expanding international development have become key to strategic management of enterprise. Based on this background, this paper selects samples of A-share listed companies and employs the High-Dimensional Fixed Effects Model to empirically test the relationship between the internationalization degree and the quality of digital technology innovation. The study finds that: First, the internationalization of enterprises can significantly improve the quality of their digital technology innovation; Second, an increase in the degree of enterprise internationalization increases the number of executives with overseas backgrounds, enriching the heterogeneity of the executive team, thereby compensating for the limited rationality of individual or similar managers, and promoting the improvement of enterprise digital technology innovation quality; Third, an increase in the degree of enterprises internationalization will significantly encourage institutional investors to increase their holdings, enabling enterprises not only to raise funds for R&D but also to send a positive signal of upward development and favor by institutional investors to internal employees and the external market, thereby promoting the improvement of their digital technology innovation quality.

Keywords: Enterprise Internationalization · Digital Technology Innovation Quality · Executive Characteristics · Institutional Investor Holdings

1 Introduction

With the continuous deepening of economic globalization and the internationalization process of enterprises, innovation has become an important source for enterprises to create and maintain competitive advantages in the global market [1]. Along with the advancement of the internationalization process, the digital economy era has arrived, and digital technologies represented by big data, AI, cloud computing, and blockchain are

Y. P. Tu and M. Chi (Eds.): WHICEB 2025, LNBIP 549, pp. 301–313, 2025.
https://doi.org/10.1007/978-3-031-94184-9_25

rapidly iterating and deeply integrating with the real economy [2]. Digital technology innovation is not only a crucial path for the digital transformation and high-quality development of traditional enterprises but also key to enhancing the competitiveness and influence of digital economy.

Against this backdrop, how can digital technology innovation become a new engine for driving high-quality enterprise development? The impact of internationalization on enterprise digital technology innovation becomes particularly critical to explore. This is not only crucial for digital transformation but also has profound significance for expanding new frontiers in economic development and aiding the rise of enterprises on the global stage.

Previous literature has extensively studied the impact of enterprise internationalization behavior on the effectiveness of business management and the quality of enterprise digital technology innovation. However, few studies have explored the causal relationship between the two, how the degree of enterprise internationalization affects the improvement of digital technology innovation quality through what transmission mechanisms, and whether this causal relationship varies in heterogeneous samples. This paper attempts to explore the impact of the degree of internationalization on the quality of enterprise digital technology innovation through empirical research. On the theoretical level, this paper focuses on the internationalization behavior of Chinese listed companies, with their digital technological innovation quality indicators as the explained variable. It empirically tests the relationship, transmission paths, heterogeneity, and robustness between the two using empirical data, enriching the literature in the field and providing a reference for cross-disciplinary research between international management and innovation management. On the practical level, the empirical research results of this paper help to present the economic effects of multinational management and operational behaviors of listed companies from the perspective of digital technology innovation quality.

2 Literature Review

2.1 Definition and Measurement of Digital Technology Innovation Quality and Internationalization Degree

Digital technology innovation involves the process and outcomes of enterprises or organizations creating entirely new products, processes, organizational structures, and business models based on digital technologies [3]. Digital technologies include information, computation, communication, and connectivity technologies and their combinations, such as AI, big data, cloud computing, and blockchain. The quality of digital technology innovation can be measured from the perspective of the innovation quality concept model proposed by E. Haner, which posits that assessing the innovation quality of an economy involves three areas: the products or services provided by companies to the market, the production and manufacturing processes of the companies, and the innovation strategies within the management philosophy of the companies [4]. Based on this framework, J. M. Juran further defines innovation quality as the degree to which innovation outcomes meet customer needs and the ability to avoid adverse situations. Patents are one aspect of measuring the quality of technological innovation. Academics believe that granted patents reflect an enterprise's technological innovation quality more than those not granted, and patents with high citation rates can effectively enhance enterprise value [5]. Specifically digital technology-related patent information can identify the digital technology innovation achievements of enterprises and portray the quality of digital technology innovation [6].

In terms of internationalization, multinational enterprises can establish specific advantages in imperfectly competitive markets to obtain monopoly profits [7]. P. Buckley's internalization theory posits that enterprises can internalize external markets through international actions such as FDI, thereby improving overall efficiency [8]. The Eclectic Theory further indicates that multinational enterprises can leverage the unique locational advantages to extend their core competencies and resources to overseas markets [9]. In summary, international actions such as FDI, internalization advantages, and locational advantages all contribute to improving of enterprise performance and fostering enterprise innovation. In measuring enterprise internationalization, previous studies have mainly used ratios such as overseas main business revenue to total main business revenue, overseas assets to total assets, overseas employee numbers to total employee numbers, the number of overseas subsidiaries, the number of countries and regions where overseas subsidiaries are distributed, and the amount of outward direct investment to calculate. This paper focuses on the depth of internationalization, which refers to the proportion of overseas sales to total sales or overseas assets to total assets, reflecting the degree of dependence on overseas operations [10].

2.2 Enterprise Internationalization and Digital Technology Innovation

Enterprise technological innovation is driven by two primary sources: internal R&D investment and external knowledge acquisition. Internationalization enhances innovation capabilities by enabling firms to absorb global knowledge, diversify intellectual resources, and improve innovation performance. It also strengthens R&D, production, and sales systems through valuable cross-border information exchange and participation in value-creating activities. Thus, internationalization serves as a key driver of technological innovation, fostering advancements and elevating innovation quality.

Specifically, in digital innovation, highly internationalized firms leverage digital technologies to streamline production cycles and enhance internal communication [11]. Given the complexity and risks of international business, digital tools prove instrumental in problem-solving.

In summary, prior studies have examined how enterprise internationalization influences management effectiveness and digital innovation quality. However, few have explored the causal relationship between them, the transmission mechanisms involved, or how this relationship varies across different samples.

3 Theoretical Analysis and Hypothesis

3.1 Resource-Based View: The Impact of Internationalization of Enterprises on the Quality of their Digital Technology Innovation

The Resource-Based View (RBV) theory, proposed by Wernerfelt, posits that a enterprise's competitive advantage stems from its unique resources. Acquisition of these resources is primarily achieved through three avenues: organizational learning, knowledge management, and external communication. Organizational learning drives internal knowledge acquisition, knowledge management optimizes resource allocation, and external communication—via strategic alliances and cross-border activities—facilitates technological learning. Extending RBV, the resource acquisition perspective argues that internationalization enhances access to diverse knowledge and complementary resources, overcoming domestic constraints, boosting technological innovation, and improving efficiency [12]. Internationalization also exposes firms to varied market demands and cultural practices, creating unique learning environments.

Additionally, greater internationalization aids in integrating global resources, expanding markets, achieving scale economies, and accelerating innovation benefits [13].

In summary, this paper proposes Hypothesis 1: An increase in the degree of enterprise internationalization has a positive impact on the quality of enterprise digital technology innovation.

3.2 Upper Echelon Theory: Internationalization of Enterprises, Overseas Background of Executives and Quality of Technology Innovation

Hambrick and Mason's Upper Echelons Theory posits that in complex environments, managers, constrained by incomplete information and limited decision-making capacity, engage in selective observation. Their cognitive abilities, values, and psychological traits influence strategic decisions, thereby affecting firm performance. As these traits are difficult to quantify, research often focuses on measurable factors like managers' educational and professional backgrounds [14].

Studies extending this theory reveal that executive teams with diverse overseas experience enhance radical innovation and patent activity. Such executives also boost digital innovation quality through optimized HR structures, increased R&D investment, and technology spillovers, ultimately elevating firm innovation performance.

In summary, this paper proposes Hypothesis 2: An increase in the degree of enterprise internationalization increases the number of executives with overseas backgrounds, enriching the heterogeneity of the executive team, thereby compensating for the limited rationality of individual or similar managers, and promoting the improvement of enterprise digital technology innovation quality.

3.3 Signaling Theory: Internationalization of Enterprises, Shareholding Ratio of Institutional Investors and Quality of Digital Technology Innovation

Spence's signaling theory posits that in asymmetric information settings, informed entities send signals to facilitate understanding and streamline market transactions. Based on this, studies show that institutional investment positively impacts enterprise digital innovation. Interaction with industry stakeholders enhances knowledge flow and identifies innovation opportunities [15]. Specifically, a positive link exists between institutional ownership and digital patent applications, with long-term investors exhibiting stronger effects than short-term ones. Venture capital further elevates innovation quality by aiding new product and technology development. These insights highlight how executives' overseas experience and institutional investment bolster digital innovation.

In summary, this paper proposes Hypothesis 3: An increase in the degree of enterprise internationalization will significantly encourage institutional investors to increase their holdings, enabling enterprises not only to raise funds for R&D but also to send a positive signal of upward development and favor by institutional investors to internal employees and the external market, thereby promoting the improvement of their digital technology innovation quality.

4 Data Construction and Research Design

4.1 Sample Selection and Data Source

This study selects A-share listed companies from 2007 to 2023 as the research sample, excluding observations with missing key variables, from the financial sector, and those that were specially treated as ST, *ST, PT, etc. This ensures that the listed companies included in the study are consistent in terms of financial index and information disclosure, resulting in a total of 5565 company-year panel data. The control variable data used in this paper, including Return on Invested Capital (ROIC), Intangible Asset Ratio (IA), Fixed Asset Ratio (FA), Book-to-Market Ratio (BM), Industry Herfindahl-Hirschman Index (HHI5), and Regional Per Capita GDP (GDP_PERP), as well as the explanatory variable of Enterprise Internationalization Degree Index (INTER), are sourced from the CSMAR database. The dependent variable, Enterprise Technology Digital Innovation Quality (DTIQ), is sourced from PatSnap.

4.2 Model Design and Variable Definition

To verify the impact of enterprise internationalization on digital technology innovation quality and its mechanisms, this paper employs a High-Dimensional Fixed Effects Model for empirical analysis, denoted as Model (1):

$$dtiq_{itch} = \beta_0 + \beta_1\ inter_{itch} + \lambda\ Z_{itch} + \mu_t + v_c + \gamma_h + \varepsilon_{itch} \quad (1)$$

The dependent variable $dtiq_{itch}$ represents the innovation quality achieved by the ith company in industry h and region c in year t. This paper measures the innovation quality achieved by the company in that year using the natural logarithm of the number of invention patents obtained or authorized plus 1 [21].

The explanatory variable $inter_{itch}$ represents the degree of internationalization of the ith company in industry h and region c in year t. The coefficient β_1 represents the net impact of companies increasing their degree of internationalization on their digital technology innovation quality, measured by the proportion of overseas main business revenue to total main business revenue.

Additionally, the model controls for time fixed effects μ_t, region fixed effects v_c, and industry fixed effects γ_h, with ε_{itch} as the random disturbance term. Z_{itch} includes control variables at three levels: micro-level (ROIC, IA, FA, BM), industry-level (HHI5), and city-level (GDP_PERP, UTL). Variable definitions are provided in Table 1.

Table 1. Variable Definition

Type		Name	Symbol	Variable Definition
Dependent variable		Digital technology innovation quality	dtiq	Ln(Total number of digital technology-related invention patents granted or authorized +1)
Explanatory variable		Internationalization degree	inter	Overseas main business revenue / Total main business revenue
Grouping variable		Internal control deficiency	isdefic	Categorical variable, coded 1 represents internal control deficiencies, coded 2 represents no internal control deficiencies
		Geographic location(east, center, west)	isecw	Categorical variable, coded 1 represents the eastern region; coded 2 represents the central region; coded 3 represents the Western region
		Geographic location(north, south)	isns	Categorical variable, coded 1 represents the northern region; coded 2 represents the southern region
		Property rights nature	soe	Categorical variable, coded 1 represents state-owned enterprises, coded 2 represents private enterprises, coded 3 represents Chinese-foreign joint ventures
Control variable	Firm level	Leverage ratio	lev	Total liabilities / Total assets
		Return on invested capital	roic	(net profit + financial expenses) / (Total assets - current liabilities + notes payable + short-term borrowings + long-term debt due within one year)
		Return on assets	roa	Net profit / average total assets; average total assets = (Total assets at the end of the period + Total assets at the beginning of the period) / 2
		Intangible asset ratio	Ia	Net bal. of intangible assets / Total assets
		Fixed asset ratio	fa	Net fixed assets / Total assets

(continued)

Table 1. (*continued*)

Type		Name	Symbol	Variable Definition
		Cash ratio	cashr	Cash and cash equivalents at the end of the period / current liabilities
		Total asset turnover	tat	Operating income / average total assets; average total assets = (Total assets at the end of the period + Total assets at the beginning of the period) / 2
		Capital intensity	capin	Total assets / operating income
		Book-to-market ratio	bm	Book value / market value
		Enterprise size	size	Ln(Total assets)
		Enterprise age	age	The difference between the year of the statistical cutoff date and the year of the enterprise's establishment
		Equity balance degree	estrict	The combined shareholding ratio of the second to fifth largest shareholders / the shareholding ratio of the largest shareholder
		Independent director ratio	indep	Number of independent directors / Total number of board members
	City level	Regional per capita GDP	gdp_perp	Regional gross product / Total population at the end of the year
		Urban Technology level	utl	Local fiscal expenditure on scientific affairs / local fiscal budgetary expenditure
	Industry level	Herfindahl-Hirschman index	hhi5	The sum of the squares of the shareholding ratios of the top five circulating shareholders

4.3 Descriptive Statistics

Table 2 presents the descriptive statistics for the main variables. The dependent variable (dtiq) has a mean of 1.505 and a median of 1.386, indicating a left-skewed distribution. This suggests that the digital technology innovation quality of most listed companies is relatively low. The explanatory variable (inter) has a mean of 0.227, with maximum and minimum values of 1.000 and −0.008, respectively. This indicates that while most A-share listed companies operate domestically, some are fully or partially engaged in international business. Control variables include enterprise-level (age, cashr), industry-level (main business sector), and city-level (gdp_perp) factors, all of which are continuous variables. Notably, the distributions of age, cashr, and gdp_perp are highly dispersed, reflecting significant variability across observations.

Table 2. Descriptive Statistics

Symbol	Number	Mean	Standard Deviation	Minimum	Medium	Maximum
dtiq	5565	1.505	1.434	0.000	1.386	8.048
inter	5565	0.227	0.238	−0.008	0.138	1.000
lev	5565	0.386	0.201	0.007	0.373	1.685
roic	5565	0.061	0.094	−1.639	0.062	1.106
roa	5565	0.053	0.075	−0.690	0.049	0.969
ia	5565	0.044	0.041	0.000	0.035	0.589
fa	5565	0.197	0.128	0.001	0.173	0.730
cashr	5565	1.239	3.765	0.002	0.452	167.500
tat	5565	0.614	0.371	0.036	0.542	5.038
capin	5565	2.182	1.482	0.198	1.846	28.070
bm	5565	0.870	1.189	0.030	0.540	17.760
size	5565	22.130	1.309	19.560	21.910	28.610
age	5565	17.210	5.954	1.420	17.080	51.670
estrict	5565	0.801	0.632	0.012	0.640	3.922
indep	5565	0.378	0.058	0.222	0.364	0.800
gdp perp	5565	10.761	4.791	0.000	11.023	25.691
utl	5565	0.047	0.049	0.001	0.044	1.000
hhi5	5565	0.073	0.102	0.000	0.022	0.670

5 Empirical Result Analysis

5.1 Baseline Regression Analysis

Table 3 presents the baseline regression results examining how the internationalization degree of listed companies impacts their innovation quality. Column (1) shows that without control variables, the coefficient of internationalization (inter) is 0.311, significant at the 5% level (adjusted $R^2 = 0.566$). Column (2) confirms this effect remains robust (coefficient = 0.315, $p < 0.05$) after controlling for variables such as ROIC, IA, FA, BM, HHI5, and GDP_PERP, with an improved adjusted R^2 of 0.737. These findings support Hypothesis 1, indicating that increased internationalization significantly enhances digital innovation quality.

This effect is driven by two mechanisms. First, internationalization diversifies executive teams by recruiting managers with overseas experience, mitigating individual managerial limitations and optimizing management practices through strategic adjustments in human resource structures, risk management, and R&D investment. Second, increased internationalization attracts institutional investors, signaling positive growth prospects to internal employees and external markets, thereby fostering innovation quality improvements.

Table 3. Baseline Regression and Mechanism Test Results

Variable	Without Control Variables	With Control Variables	Executive Overseas Background Mechanism	Institutional Holding Ratio Mechanism
	(1)	(2)	(3)	(4)
	dtiq	dtiq	oseabnum	insinvest
Inter	0.311** (2.256)	0.270** (2.063)	0.801*** (5.100)	6.441*** (2.641)
Constant	1.576***	−7.421***	−1.028	−111.375***
	(36.635)	(−7.850)	(−1.048)	(−8.488)
Control variables	NO	YES	YES	YES
Year fixed	YES	YES	YES	YES
Industry fixed	YES	YES	YES	YES
City fixed	YES	YES	YES	YES
N	5548	5548	5522	5543
Adj-R2	0.566	0.737	0.402	0.414

t-statistics in parentheses (*** $p<0.01$, ** $p<0.05$, * $p<0.1$)

5.2 Influence Mechanism Test

Internationalization of enterprises, overseas background of executives and quality of technological innovation. In the process of participating in international operations, domestic enterprises will cultivate and attract outstanding management talent from developed countries to enrich their executive teams, leading to a natural increase in the number of executives with overseas backgrounds. Column (3) of Table 3 shows that after controlling for fixed effects and covariates, the degree of internationalization (inter) positively affects digital innovation quality at the 1% significance level ($\beta = 0.801$). This occurs as internationalization increases executives with overseas experience, mitigating individual managerial limitations. These findings support Hypothesis 2.

The Internationalization of Enterprises, Shareholding Ratio of Institutional Investor, and Digital Technology Innovation Quality. Column (4) of Table 3 reveals a positive correlation between internationalization and institutional investor shareholding ratio (insinvest) at the 1% level. Greater internationalization encourages institutional investment, providing R&D funding while signaling growth potential to stakeholders. This dual mechanism—resource provision and signal enhancement—boosts innovation quality, thereby supporting Hypothesis 3.

5.3 Heterogeneity Test

Property Rights Nature. Columns (6), (7), and (8) of Table 4 report the results of the subgroup tests for samples divided into three groups based on property rights nature.

The data indicate that increased internationalization does not significantly affect digital innovation quality in state-owned or private enterprises but is significant at the 5% level for Chinese-foreign joint ventures, aligning with prior studies.

Table 4. Heterogeneity Test Results

Variables	Internal Control Deficiency		Division by Geographic Location			Division by Property Rights Nature		
	(1)	(2)	(3)	(4)	(5)	(6)	(7)	(8)
	Defective	Non-Defective	Eastern Region	Central Region	Western Region	State-Owned Enterprises	Private Enterprises	Joint Ventures
	dtiq	dtiq	dtiq	dtiq	dtiq	dtiq	dtiq	dtiq
Inter	−0.333	0.273*	0.381***	0.423	1.521**	−0.465	−0.121	0.746**
	(−1.195)	(1.842)	(2.612)	(0.937)	(2.404)	(−1.294)	(−0.710)	(2.091)
Constant	−10.614***	−6.230***	−7.680***	−4.147**	−15.108***	−8.583***	−6.119***	−2.256
	(−5.815)	(−5.111)	(−6.867)	(−2.022)	(−5.183)	(−4.686)	(−4.445)	(−0.905)
Control variables	YES	YES	YES	YES	YES	YES	YES	YES
Year fixed	YES	YES	YES	YES	YES	YES	YES	YES
Industry fixed	YES	YES	YES	YES	YES	YES	YES	YES
City fixed	YES	YES	YES	YES	YES	YES	YES	YES
N	1343	3801	4146	754	502	1477	3179	706
Adj-R2	0.362	0.232	0.226	0.384	0.459	0.409	0.228	0.380

t-statistics in parentheses (*** $p<0.01$, ** $p<0.05$, * $p<0.1$)

Geographic Location. Following the classification standards of the National Bureau of Statistics for eastern, central, and western provinces, this paper divides the samples into three groups for testing, with results as shown in columns (3), (4), and (5) of Table 4. The regression results for the nine central provinces are not statistically significant, but correlations are significant in eastern (99% CI) and western regions (95% CI), consistent with existing literature.

Quality of Internal Control. This paper collected data on whether there are defects in internal control within the samples and conducted subgroup tests accordingly. Columns (1)–(2) indicate that internationalization positively impacts innovation quality only in firms without internal control defects ($p < 0.10$), supporting previous findings.

5.4 Robustness Test

Changing the Regression Model. Since the total number of digital innovation-related invention patents is a count variable, which fits a Poisson distribution, but the data distribution is quite dispersed (mean = 1.505, variance = 2.056), and the difference is relatively large, a high-dimensional negative binomial regression model is used for robustness testing. The results, as shown in column (1) of Table 5, is consistent with the baseline regression results of this paper.

Table 5. Robustness Test Results

Variable	(1)	(2)	(3)
	High-Dimensional Negative Binomial Regression Model	Changing the Dependent Variable	Introducing the Lagged Independent Variable
	dtiq	dtiq1	dtiq
Inter	0.212***	0.070**	–
	(3.691)	(1.972)	–
L.inter	–	–	0.394**
	–	–	(2.263)
Constant	−4.648***	0.044	−7.874***
	(−10.760)	(0.157)	(−6.512)
Control variables	YES	YES	YES
Year fixed	YES	YES	YES
Industry fixed	YES	YES	YES
City fixed	YES	YES	YES
N	5565	4364	3316
Adj-R2		0.396	0.581

t-statistics in parentheses (*** $p<0.01$, ** $p<0.05$, * $p<0.1$)

Changing the Dependent Variable. This paper now uses the square root of the ratio of invention patents obtained or authorized in the digital technology field to the total number of patents obtained or authorized to measure the digital technology innovation quality of listed companies. Since the independent R&D capabilities of companies are in a constant state of development, using the relative value of the number of relevant invention patents to the total number of patents better reflects the enterprise's digital technology innovation quality. This adjustment, addressing sparse patent changes and dynamic R&D capabilities, maintains a significant positive link between internationalization and innovation quality (Column 2).

Introducing the Lagged Independent Variable. Considering that the acquisition of new knowledge and technology, this paper replaces the original independent variable with a lagged one-period sample for regression analysis. The results, as shown in column (3) of Table 5, still show a significantly positive relationship between the internationalization behavior of listed companies and their digital technology innovation quality, indicating that the empirical results are robust.

6 Research Conclusions

This paper selects samples of A-share listed companies from 2007 to 2023 and employs the High-Dimensional Fixed Effects Model to empirically test the relationship between the degree of internationalization of listed companies and the quality of their digital technology innovation. The study finds that:

- The internationalization of enterprises can significantly improve the quality of their digital technology innovation, indicating that the internationalization of enterprises leads to an increase in the number of executives with overseas backgrounds, enriching the heterogeneity of the executive team, thereby compensating for the limited rationality of individual or similar managers, and optimizing management details through specific measures such as adjusting the enterprise's human resource structure, improving the enterprise's risk response capabilities, and increasing R&D investment, thereby enhancing the enterprise digital technology innovation quality; at the same time, an increase in the degree of internationalization of enterprises can attract institutional investors to increase their holdings, helping the enterprise to raise funds for development, and also sending a positive signal of upward development and favor by institutional investors to internal employees and the external market, thereby promoting the improvement of enterprise digital technology innovation quality.
- The impact of the internationalization of enterprises on their digital technology innovation quality varies among enterprises with different property rights, geographical locations, and internal control qualities, and this causal relationship is significantly established in samples of Chinese-foreign joint ventures, enterprises in the eastern and western regions, and enterprises with no internal control deficiencies.

References

1. Filatotchev, I., Piesse, J.: R&D, internationalization and growth of newly listed firms: European evidence. J. Int. Bus. Stud. **40**, 1260–1276 (2009)
2. Vial, G.: Understanding digital transformation: a review and a research agenda. In: Managing Digital Transformation, pp. 13–66. Routledge (2021)
3. Nambisan, S.: Digital entrepreneurship: toward a digital technology perspective of entrepreneurship. Entrep. Theory Pract. **41**, 1029–1055 (2017)
4. Haner, U.-E.: Innovation quality—a conceptual framework. Int. J. Prod. Econ. **80**, 31–37 (2002)
5. Parida, V., Wincent, J., Oghazi, P.: Transaction costs theory and coordinated safeguards investment in R&D offshoring. J. Bus. Res. **69**, 1823–1828 (2016)
6. Liu, Y., Dong, J., Mei, L., Shen, R.: Digital innovation and performance of manufacturing firms: an affordance perspective. Technovation. **119**, 102458 (2023)
7. Hymer, S.H.: The International Operations of National Firms, a Study of Direct Foreign Investment. Massachusetts Institute of Technology (1960)
8. Buckley, P.J., Casson, M.: The Future of the Multinational Enterprise. Springer (2016)
9. Dunning, J.H.: Explaining International Production (Routledge Revivals). Routledge (2014)
10. Schwens, C., Zapkau, F.B., Bierwerth, M., Isidor, R., Knight, G., Kabst, R.: International entrepreneurship: a meta–analysis on the internationalization and performance relationship. Entrep. Theory Pract. **42**, 734–768 (2018)

11. Lecerf, M., Omrani, N.: SME internationalization: the impact of information technology and innovation. J. Knowl. Econ. **11**, 805–824 (2020)
12. Hitt, M.A., Hoskisson, R.E., Kim, H.: International diversification: effects on innovation and firm performance in product-diversified firms. Acad. Manag. J. **40**, 767–798 (1997)
13. Kafouros, M.I., Buckley, P.J., Sharp, J.A., Wang, C.: The role of internationalization in explaining innovation performance. Technovation. **28**, 63–74 (2008)
14. Hambrick, D.C., Mason, P.A.: Upper echelons: the organization as a reflection of its top managers. Acad. Manag. Rev. **9**, 193–206 (1984)
15. Kohli, R., Melville, N.P.: Digital innovation: a review and synthesis. Inf. Syst. J. **29**, 200–223 (2019)

The Impact of Artificial Intelligence on Total Factor Productivity in the Service Industry and Its Mechanism Research

Shu Zhao[1(✉)] and Yan Tu[1,2]

[1] Central University of Finance and Economics, Beijing 100872, China
zszs0411@163.com
[2] China Academy of Internet Economics, Beijing 100081, China

Abstract. Artificial intelligence(AI) has great potential to solve the problems of uneven and insufficient development of China's service industry. This paper takes a micro-firm perspective and starts from the perspective of new quality productivity to examine the impact of AI on the total factor productivity (TFP) of service firms and its underlying mechanisms. The study finds that the application of AI helps to improve the TFP of service firms. The mechanism analysis shows that the application of AI enhances the TFP of firms through the key channel of promoting new quality productivity development. The heterogeneity analysis shows that the TFP of production service firms is more significantly affected by AI than that of life service firms. This paper refines and enriches the theoretical understanding of the impact mechanism of AI practical implications for promoting the healthy development of service firms, driving service innovation, accelerating the development of new quality productivity, and achieving high-quality economic growth.

Keywords: Artificial Intelligence · Service Industry · Total Factor Productivity · New Quality Productivity

1 Introduction

With China's rapid social and economic development, the principal contradiction in our society in the new era has been transformed into the contradiction between unbalanced and inadequate development and the people's ever-growing needs for a better life. Nowadays, people's needs for a better life are mostly closely related to the consumption of services, such as culture, education, and medical care. The problem of unbalanced and inadequate development in these service areas is still prominent, mainly reflected in the backward development of the service industry in rural areas and the mismatch between the supply and demand of personalized services. Artificial intelligence(AI) has great potential in solving the above problems: On the one hand, AI technology can effectively break the barrier of time and space, improve the inclusive nature of resources, and then solve the problem of unbalanced development of the service industry; On the other hand,

Y. P. Tu and M. Chi (Eds.): WHICEB 2025, LNBIP 549, pp. 314–325, 2025.
https://doi.org/10.1007/978-3-031-94184-9_26

the application of AI technology can improve service efficiency, enhance service experience, meet diversified and personalized needs, and then solve the problem of inadequate development of the service industry.

The characteristics of the service industry, which is mainly based on the provision of labor services and cannot be traded over long distances, have led to the lack of momentum for the traditional factors to improve the productivity of the service industry. Compared with traditional productivity, the new quality productivity is a qualitative transition and has higher efficiency based on the integration of the digital economy era and emerging technologies [1], which can effectively solve the problems such as the lack of momentum of traditional factors to improve the productivity of the service industry. As an advanced productivity tool, AI helps service enterprises to more accurately grasp market demand and consumer behavior, and achieve more efficient and intelligent services. Against the backdrop of the transformation of economic growth patterns and the prominent role of AI, studying the impact AI on the TFP of the service industry can help clarify its significant role in promoting the development of the service industry and provide a scientific basis for formulating policies and measures to promote sustained and healthy economic development. There are numerous studies on the impact of AI on productivity, but due to differences in environmental and institutional conditions among countries, as well as the use of different samples and research methods, no consensus has been reached.

At present, studies on the relationship between AI and TFP generally have two viewpoints: positive impact and negative impact. Scholars with a positive impact view believe that AI can improve TFP by optimizing factor allocation, reducing enterprise costs, and improving enterprise R&D and innovation capabilities [2]. AI can achieve long-term productivity improvement and labor cost reduction through the complementarity of robotization, innovation, digitalization, and human capital [3]. Some scholars also hold negative views on the above research conclusions, believing that the effect of AI on productivity improvement at the current stage is not obvious, and the fundamental reason is that there is a long lag effect between the application of breakthrough technology and productivity improvement [4]. Moderate application of AI is conducive to improving labor productivity, but excessive application will cause labor productivity loss due to man-machine mismatch [5]. Driven by the development of AI, new quality productivity shows the intellectualization of subject labor, the intellectualization of labor tools, and the digitalization of production factors [6]. The new quality productivity emphasizes the transformation of the "quality" of productivity, that is, the profound transformation of the production factor endowment and its combination mode to promote the substantial increase of t TFP. Therefore, the impact of AI on TFP can be investigated from the perspective of new quality productivity.

To sum up, there are abundant research achievements on AI and TFP. From the perspective of experience, whether AI technology has a positive effect on TFP is still controversial in the academic community. The existing literature has not deeply revealed the mechanism of AI affecting the improvement of TFP, especially for the service industry, there is still a large space for exploration. In view of this, this paper focuses on the micro-enterprise level and conducts an empirical analysis on how AI affects the TFP of service enterprises from the perspective of new quality productivity.

2 Theoretical Analysis and Research Hypothesis

The total factor productivity (TFP) was first proposed by Solow (1957), reflecting not only the technical level, but also the knowledge level in production, management skills, corporate governance strategies, resource allocation ability and many other factors [7]. At present, the productivity growth of the service industry obviously lags behind that of the manufacturing industry, but new forms, new services and new models driven by AI continue to emerge, and a number of data-intensive service enterprises are gradually formed, making the service fields such as accommodation and catering, transportation, wholesale and retail not only achieve more effective and accurate supply and demand matching, but also break through the time and space constraints of services. It has changed the non-storage and non-tradable characteristics of the service industry, and fundamentally solved the problem of low efficiency of the traditional service industry. First, AI can break through the bottleneck of human capital through factor substitution and synergy effect. Generative AI can help businesses expand their products and increase the productivity of their employees, while knowledge workers and information workers can also use these tools to increase their labor productivity [8]. Second, AI reconstructs the path of value creation through service process reengineering. For example, the online education platform realizes the separation of time and space of service delivery with the help of AI dual-teacher system, which combines AI technology and the teaching experience of offline teachers to improve the learning effect and experience of students. Third, through big data analytics and machine learning algorithms, companies can better understand market trends, consumer needs and competitive dynamics to optimize strategic planning and resource allocation. Fourth, AI can process massive data, generate multiple resource allocation schemes based on data analysis results, and evaluate the pros and cons of each scheme through simulation. The following hypothesis is proposed:

H1: The application of AI can improve the TFP of the service industry.

As advanced scientific and technological productivity and new elements, AI is an important component of the key core of new quality productivity (scientific and technological innovation). Driven by the development of AI, human labor is mainly shifted from physical labor to mental labor, labor tools are shifted from general machines to intelligent machines, and the direct object of labor is shifted from material entities to data, information and knowledge [6]. First, the development of AI helps to improve the quality of workers. On the one hand, the new generation of artificial intelligence can serve as an assistant to employees, enhancing work efficiency. For instance, medical diagnosis support systems increase the processing capacity of doctors, and knowledge graphs shorten the time for consultants to prepare plans. On the other hand, the new generation of artificial intelligence may also completely replace certain jobs, thereby improving the overall efficiency of the economy. By using technologies such as robotic process automation and intelligent customer service to replace repetitive labor (such as data entry and basic consultation), the proportion of human resource costs can be reduced. Second, AI can help to greatly optimize labor data. AI is a highly automated intelligent machine that can replace humans in repetitive, mechanical tasks and complete tasks autonomously in complex and changing environments. Finally, the application of AI has changed the object of labor. In the age of intelligence, the object of labor is no longer a traditional, tangible material carrier, but a large amount of information and data. The production process is simplified as the subject converts the labor object and process into the numerical input of the intelligent machine, which is then automatically solved by the intelligent machine, and can sum up experience, feedback information and optimize itself in the production process. The following hypothesis is proposed:

H2: AI can improve the TFP of the service industry by promoting the development of new quality productivity.

3 Empirical Design

3.1 Panel Model Setting

In this paper, data of listed service companies in China from 2012 to 2022 are selected to build a panel model to analyze the impact of AI on the TFP of the service industry, in order to verify hypothesis 1. The panel model is set as follows:

$$TFP_{it} = \beta_0 + \beta_1 AI_{it} + \sum \varphi Controls + year + id + \varepsilon_{it} \quad (1)$$

In order to verify hypothesis 2, it is necessary to test the impact mechanism of AI on the TFP of the service industry. The model is set as follows:

$$Npro_{it} = \beta_0 + \beta_1 AI_{it} + \sum \varphi Controls + year + id + \varepsilon_{it} \quad (2)$$

Where subscripts i and t represent region and year respectively, TFP represents TFP, Npro represents new quality productivity, AI represents AI application, Controls is the control variable, ε is the error term, year and id represent annual fixed effect and individual fixed effect respectively.

3.2 Variable Selection

Explained variable: Total factor productivity (TFP) is calculated using the LP method. Specifically, the total output, capital input, intermediate product input and labor input of the enterprise are measured by the operating income, net fixed assets, cash paid by the enterprise for purchasing goods and receiving services, and the number of employees of the enterprise respectively. The subsequent robustness test was replaced by OP method and OLS method.

Core explanatory variable: Artificial Intelligence (AI). From the perspective of text analysis, Yao (2024) uses machine learning methods to generate an a AI dictionary, constructs a micro-enterprise-level AI index [9], and examines the application of AI in enterprises from a more comprehensive perspective. This paper uses the "jieba" word segmentation module to extract the natural logarithm of the number of AI keywords plus 1 in the annual report of listed companies as an enterprise AI index.

Intermediate variable: New quality productivity (Npro), which is an innovation-led advanced productivity, so this paper starts from the three elements of productivity, considering the role of workers, labor objects and labor materials on productivity. Referring to the research framework of Zhang et al. (2024) [10], this paper analyzes the new quality workers, new quality labor objects and new quality labor materials from three dimensions, and adopts the entropy method for quantitative calculation. Specific indicators are shown in Table 1.

Table 1. New quality productivity indicators

Variable	Factor	Subfactor	Indicator	Indicator Definition
New quality productivity	New quality labour force	Staff quality	Proportion of R&D personnel	Number of R&D personnel/employees
			Proportion of highly educated personnel	Number of graduate students or above/number of employees
		Management quality	Management digital background	Whether the executive team has a digital background
			CEO functional experience richness	CEO functional experience counts
	New quality labor materials	Scientific and technological labor materials	Enterprise innovation level	Ln (number of patent applications +1)
		Green labor materials	Green technology level	Ln (number of green patents applied by enterprises +1)
			Proportion of green patents	Number of enterprises applying for green patents/number of enterprises applying for patents
		Digital labor data	Intelligent level	Ln (intelligent horizontal word frequency + 1)
			Proportion of digital assets	Total digital-related assets/intangible assets
	New quality object of labor	Future development	Proportion of fixed assets	Fixed assets/total assets
			Robot permeability	Robot penetration rate at enterprise level
		Ecological environment	Environmental performance	Environmental scores in the ESG scoring system of China securities

Control variable: Asset-liability ratio (lev), corporate performance (roa), cashflow, growth, equity concentration (top1) and property right nature (soe) are respectively used as control variables. The asset-liability ratio is measured by dividing total liabilities by total assets at the end of the year. Business performance is measured by dividing net profit by the average balance of total assets; Cash flow is measured by dividing net cash flows from operating activities by total assets; Growth is measured by dividing the current year's operating income by the previous year's operating income −1; Ownership concentration is measured by the proportion of the number of shares held by the largest shareholder to the total number of shares; Property rights of state-owned holding enterprises are 1, and others are 0.

3.3 Data Source

In this paper, listed service companies in Shanghai and Shenzhen stock markets of China that published financial reports from 2011 to 2022 are selected as empirical research samples to study the impact of AI on TFP. The annual financial statement data of listed companies comes from Guotai 'an database, Sina financial website and Wind database. In order to ensure the validity of the data and eliminate the influence of abnormal values on the empirical test, this paper makes the following treatments for the selected samples: (1) The listed companies that issue both A-shares and B-shares are excluded; (2) Companies with ST and *ST in the sample range are excluded; (3) Companies with abnormal data and serious data missing are excluded; (4) Reduce the tail of the data by 1%. Ultimately, the unbalanced panel data includes 730 publicly traded companies with 5,242 annual observations.

4 Empirical Results and Analysis

4.1 Baseline Regression Results

Table 2 shows the results of baseline regression. Among them, column (1) is the regression results without introducing control variables and fixed effects; Column (2) shows the regression results with only the control variables introduced; Column (3) shows the regression results for all control variables and annual and individual fixed effects. It can be found that in all regressions, the coefficient of explanatory variable AI is significantly positive, indicating that the application of AI has a promoting effect on the improvement of the TFP of enterprises, and verifies the hypothesis H1.

4.2 Robustness Test

In order to test the robustness of the results, this paper uses the enterprise TFP measured by OP method and OLS method as the proxy variable of the explained variable. The application of AI in the service industry is mainly reflected in the number of AI patents and introduction of intelligent robots, such as humanoid robots, care robots, etc., so the number of AI patents and penetration of industrial robots replace the original core explanatory variable [11]. From column (1)–(4) in Table 3, it can be found that the

Table 2 Results of baseline regression

Variable	(1)	(2)	(3)
	TFP	TFP	TFP
AI	0.1973*** (20.92)	0.1852*** (20.54)	0.2041*** (9.06)
Constant	8.2007*** (186.28)	7.3869*** (119.52)	7.7384*** (47.07)
Control variable	No	Yes	Yes
Year/individual fixed effect	No	No	Yes
N	5242	5241	5241
R^2	0.1035	0.2298	0.2367

Note: The values in brackets are t statistics, *, **, and *** indicate that the estimated coefficients are significant at the 10%, 5%, and 1% levels, respectively. The following table is the same.

coefficient of AI is significantly positive at the level of 1%, indicating that after replacing variables, the application of AI still helps to promote the improvement of enterprise TFP, and the conclusion is still valid.

Considering the impact of the stock market crash in China (2015) and the Asian financial crisis (2018), in order to avoid the observation error caused by irresistible factors, this study excluded the samples of enterprises in 2015 and 2018, and re-tested the benchmark regression. The results are shown in column (5) of Table 3. The AI coefficient

Table 3. Robustness test results

Variable	(1)	(2)	(3)	(4)	(5)
	TFP_OP	TFP_OLS	TFP_LP	TFP_LP	TFP
AI	0.1651*** (7.66)	0.2428*** (9.86)	–		0.2183*** (9.30)
Penetration of industrial robots	–	–	0.0096*** (5.06)		
Number of AI patents				0.0111** (2.17)	
Constant	6.2448*** (39.52)	9.7263*** (49.97)	8.0475*** (46.22)	8.2110*** (43.49)	7.6739*** (45.32)
Control variable	Yes	Yes	Yes	Yes	Yes
Year/individual fixed effect	Yes	Yes	Yes	Yes	Yes
N	5241	5241	5241	4612	4329
R^2	0.1981	0.2746	0.14	0.1946	0.2466

is significantly positive at the level of 1%, and the conclusion that the application of AI can improve the TFP of enterprises is still valid.

4.3 Endogenous Processing

In order to avoid endogenous bias caused by missing variable error and two-way causation, AI lag of one stage is selected as instrumental variable (IV). The estimation results of the instrumental variable 2SLS are shown in columns (1) and (2) of Table 4. Column (1) is the regression result of the first stage. It can be found that the instrumental variable IV is significantly positive at the level of 1%, and the selected instrumental variable is positively correlated with AI, satisfying the condition that the instrumental variable is correlated with the original explanatory variable. Column (2) is the regression result of the second stage, and the AI coefficient is significantly positive, indicating that after fully considering the endogeneity problem, the application of AI still has a significant promoting effect on the TFP of enterprises, which is consistent with the benchmark regression result. In order to avoid the endogeneity bias caused by sample self-selection, selection propensity score matching (PSM) can alleviate the endogeneity problem as much as possible. The enterprises whose AI index is not 0 are classified as the experimental group and defined as Treat 1, and the other enterprises are classified as the control group and defined as Treat 0. The balance test results showed that the difference between the experimental group and the control group was no longer obvious, and the matching effect was good. After the feature difference between the experimental group and the control group was greatly reduced, the matched samples were used for regression. The results were shown in column (3) of Table 4. The regression coefficient of AI was still significantly positive, indicating that the research conclusion of improving the TFP of enterprises by AI remained robust after alleviating the endogenous problem.

Table 4. Endogenous processing results

Variable	(1)	(2)	(3)
	AI	TFP	TFP
AI		0.1649*** (13.99)	0.2138*** (7.87)
L.AI	0.9115*** (149.55)		
Constant	0.4627*** (11.83)	6.3307*** (102.03)	7.6717*** (40.43)
Control variable	Yes	Yes	Yes
Year/individual fixed effect	Yes	Yes	Yes
N	4229	4229	4106
R^2	0.8458	0.3573	0.2288

4.4 Mechanism Analysis

This paper further examines the mediating role of new quality productivity, and the specific regression results are shown in Table 5. Column (1) is the regression result of AI on new quality productivity, and the coefficient of AI is significantly positive, indicating that the application of AI is conducive to the development of new quality productivity, and hypothesis 2 is verified.

Because the development of new quality productivity is multi-dimensional, for example, the development of new quality productivity can be reflected in the improvement of the quality of labor force, or the improvement of labor materials, or the change of labor objects. Therefore, we further investigate the different effects of the application of AI on the secondary indicators of new quality productivity. Columns (2)–(4) show the regression results of AI on the three elements of new quality productivity respectively, and the coefficients of AI are significantly positive. First of all, the improvement of the quality of the labor force by artificial intelligence is reflected in the introduction of new technologies such as humanoid robots and care robots, replacing traditional manual services, and helping enterprises to make more scientific and reasonable decisions through a more complex logical thinking process. Secondly, the improvement of labor data by AI is reflected in the introduction of new technologies to the automatic transformation of the production process. Taking intelligent medical care as an example, the "AI health butler" launched by Alipay provides more than 30 services such as finding doctors, reading reports, accompanying patients, asking medical insurance, and managing health. Finally, the change of AI on the object of labor is reflected in the increase of enterprise digital assets and the responsibility for environmental protection. The application of AI is based on the analysis and calculation of massive data, which will inevitably lead to the increase of enterprise digital assets. AI can also greatly improve management efficiency and organizational efficiency, and realize the intelligent and green process of economic activities. Among them, the impact on new quality means of production is the most significant, indicating that AI mainly promotes the development of new quality productivity through improving labor means, and then improves the TFP of enterprises.

Table 5. Regression results of mediation mechanism

Variable	(1)	(2)	(3)	(4)
	Npro	Npro_Labor	Npro_Tool	Npro_Object
AI	0.0272*** (17.22)	0.0112** (2.55)	0.0387*** (55.56)	0.0053** (2.28)
Constant	0.0956*** (11.45)	0.1745*** (7.82)	0.0323*** (9.00)	0.2604*** (18.44)
Control variable	Yes	Yes	Yes	Yes
Year/individual fixed effect	Yes	Yes	Yes	Yes
N	5241	5241	5241	5241
R^2	0.1833	0.0088	0.6864	0.0094

4.5 Heterogeneity Analysis Based on the Nature of Service Industry

The productivity effects of AI may vary across industries. Enterprises are grouped according to the Statistical Classification of Producer Services and Statistical Classification of Living Services formulated by the National Bureau of Statistics. The results of grouping regression are shown in column (1) (2) of Table 6. The productivity effect of AI is mainly concentrated in producer services. In the productive service sector, AI can handle large volumes of data and optimize processes, such as risk assessment in finance and route optimization in logistics. These tasks are highly structured and easy to automate, and AI can significantly enhance efficiency. However, in the consumer service sector, which is more about face-to-face services requiring emotional interaction and immediate response, AI may be difficult to replace or the replacement cost could be high. The application of AI in the field of living service industry is relatively late. Due to the time-lag effect of production efficiency improvement caused by technological progress, the improvement of TFP of active service industry enterprises by AI is relatively not obvious.

In order to further verify the above ideas, the samples were divided into two groups according to the median level of AI, and the influence of AI on the TFP of different service enterprises under different application levels was compared respectively, as shown in columns (3) to (6) of Table 6. In the case of low application level, the impact of AI on the TFP of producer service enterprises is significantly higher than that of domestic service enterprises. In the case of high application level, there is no significant difference in the impact of AI on the TFP of the two kinds of firms. The results show that with the wide application of AI, the positive impact on domestic service enterprises has gradually emerged, and the TFP has been greatly improved.

Table 6. Heterogeneity analysis

Variable	(1)	(2)	(3)	(4)	(5)	(6)
	Consumer services	Producer services	Low level of AI		High level of AI	
			Consumer services	Producer services	Consumer services	Producer services
AI	0.150*** (7.47)	0.199*** (19.43)	0.193*** (3.16)	0.282*** (5.04)	0.133*** (2.94)	0.149*** (10.29)
Constant	7.736*** (64.62)	7.351*** (100.94)	7.681*** (55.73)	7.344*** (63.24)	7.462*** (33.13)	7.729*** (81.23)
Control variable	Yes	Yes	Yes	Yes	Yes	Yes
Year/individual fixed effect	Yes	Yes	Yes	Yes	Yes	Yes
N	1594	3647	1163	1350	431	2297
p	0.072*		0.081*		0.355	

5 Research Conclusions and Suggestions

The main conclusions are as follows: (1) The application of AI is helpful to improve the TFP of service enterprises. (2) The application of AI can improve the TFP of enterprises by promoting the development of new quality productivity, which is mainly through improving labor materials to improve the TFP of enterprises. (3) Compared with the domestic service industry, the TFP of producer service enterprises is more significantly affected by AI. Based on the above conclusions, the following suggestions are put forward:

Guide enterprises to firmly intelligent strategic direction. China's service industry is accelerating the development of digital intelligence, and government policies are closely coordinated with market development. Digital intelligent transformation needs to promote the integration of AI with digital infrastructure, data elements, in-depth industrial transformation, and people's better life, strengthen scientific and technological innovation, especially original and subversive scientific and technological innovation, stimulate the vitality of production factors, open up and develop new industries and new business forms and models, and cultivate new drivers of high-quality development.

According to the actual production needs and production levels of different departments, artificial intelligence is appropriately introduced to carry out intelligent production transformation. In order to grasp the rationality of human capital investment, we should pay attention to avoid the "buyout" mode of talent introduction in the region and avoid the polarization of labor employment structure. While promoting the research and development and innovation of artificial intelligence technology, we should pay attention to improving the market-oriented allocation of factors, promoting the efficient allocation and flow of factors, actively guiding the flow of skilled production factors to high-growth industries, and improving TFP.

Strengthen technical exchanges between enterprises. Small and medium-sized enterprises are at a disadvantage when it comes to competing with large enterprises in terms of capital, technology and market share, which limits their growth opportunities and can even lead to a "Matthew effect" in the market, where the strong get stronger and the weak get weaker. Governments can limit the concentration of market dominance by creating policies that level the playing field. Monitor unfair competition practices, review corporate mergers and acquisitions, increase market transparency, and promote data sharing to ensure fair competition in the AI market.

The innovation and research significance of this paper are as follows: First, the existing literature generally studies the impact of AI on the manufacturing industry, ignoring the importance of the service industry. In the context of changing the mode of economic growth and the prominent role of AI, the study of the impact of AI on the TFP of the service industry can help clarify the important role of AI in promoting the development of the service industry, and provide a scientific basis for the formulation of policies and measures to promote the sustainable and healthy development of the economy. Second, most existing studies regard the service industry as a homogeneous whole, or only distinguish the technology intensity, while this study reveals the industry heterogeneity of AI impact through the binary framework of producer/consumer service industry. Third, as for the mechanism of AI's impact on TFP, the existing literature may focus more on labor substitution or process automation. This paper finds that AI improves TFP by improving labor data, which supplements the mechanism research.

This study has three limitations: at the data level, it relies on simplified indicators, making it difficult to capture the differences among various sub-technologies of artificial intelligence; in terms of theoretical mechanisms, it focuses on a single mediating path and fails to fully deconstruct the multi-dimensionality and negative effects of new productive forces; and in terms of contextual embedding, it neglects the moderating roles of institutional environments and market competition, thus limiting its universality. Future research can address these issues by constructing a multi-dimensional artificial intelligence indicator system, expanding the theoretical exploration of heterogeneous paths of artificial intelligence's effects, and exploring the institutional-technological synergy mechanism to verify the theoretical boundaries. Additionally, it is necessary to pay attention to the threshold effect and ethical challenges of AI technology diffusion, and to build an analytical framework that takes into account both productivity improvement and social welfare, providing more refined theoretical support and practical guidance for the digital transformation of the service industry.

Acknowledgement. This research was supported by Beijing Social Science Fund Decision Consulting Project "Research on Optimal Allocation Strategy of Beijing Science and Technology Innovation Resources" (No. 24JCB015).

References

1. Su, X., Sun, J.: Fostering new quality productive forces for the overall revitalization of Northeast China: internal logic, key direction and practical path. Soc. Sci. J. **1**, 126–133 (2024)
2. Du, C., Cao, X., Ren, J.: Research on the mechanism and effect of artificial intelligence on total factor productivity in China. Nankai Econ. Stud. **02**, 3–24 (2024)
3. Ballestar, M.T., Camiña, E., Díaz-Chao, Á., et al.: Productivity and employment effects of digital complementarities. J. Innov. Knowled. **6**(3), 177–190 (2021)
4. Cai, Y., Chen, N.: Artificial intelligence and high-quality growth & employment in the era of new technological revolution. J. Quant. Technol. Econ. **36**(05), 3–22 (2019)
5. Hu, S., Wang, L., Zhao, H.: Artificial intelligence application, human-machine collaboration and labor productivity. Chinese journal of population. Science. **05**, 48-62+127 (2021)
6. Xiao, F., He, J.: New quality productivity: a new direction of productivity development in the intelligent era. J. Nanchang Univ. Human. Soc. Sci. **54**(06), 37–44 (2023)
7. Lu, X., Lian, Y.: Estimation of total factor productivity of industrial enterprises in China: 1999—2007. China Econ. Q. **11**(02), 541–558 (2012)
8. Brynjolfsson, E., Li, D., Raymond, L.: Generative AI at work. SSRN Electron. J. (2023)
9. Yao, Z., Zhang, K., Guo, L., et al.: How does artificial intelligence improve firm productivity? Based on the perspective of labor skill structure adjustment. J. Manag. World. **40**(02), 101–116+133+117–122 (2018)
10. Zhang, X., Wang, W., Yu, Y.: Research on the influence of digital intelligence transformation on the new quality productivity of enterprises. Stud. Sci. Sci., 1–19 (2024)
11. Wang, Y., Dong, W.: How the rise of robots has affected China's labor market: evidence from China's listed manufacturing firms. Econ. Res. J. **55**(10), 159–175 (2019)

Does the Attention of Small and Medium - Sized Investors Affect Corporate Green Innovation?

Junyao Wu[1] and Yan Tu[2(✉)]

[1] Central University of Finance and Economics, Beijing 100872, China
[2] China Academy of Internet Economics, Beijing 10081, China

Abstract. Amid growing environmental and resource constraints, green development has become a strategic priority for national and governmental progress. Green innovation is increasingly recognized as vital for companies aiming to achieve sustainability and meet carbon peak and neutrality goals. This study, based on data from Shanghai and Shenzhen A-share listed companies (2010–2021), investigates the impact of small and medium investors' (SMIs) green attention on corporate green innovation. Results indicate that SMIs' green attention significantly enhances both substantive and strategic green innovation, with a stronger effect on substantive innovation. These findings remain robust across various tests. Heterogeneity analysis shows that SMIs' green attention has a more significant impact on state-owned enterprises, non-high-tech firms, and non-heavily polluting companies. In terms of governance, the effect is stronger in firms with environmentally conscious executives, low media attention, and a high proportion of institutional investors. This study categorizes corporate green innovation by motivation, offering a deeper understanding of the concept, and highlights how SMIs' attention drives innovation. The findings provide valuable insights for companies aiming to attract environmentally conscious investors and foster green innovation.

Keywords: Investor Attention · Corporate Green Innovation · Substantive Innovation · Strategic Innovation

1 Introduction

Transitioning to a greener development model is central to global sustainable growth efforts. In China, this goal aligns with the 14th Five-Year Plan for Industrial Green Development, which emphasizes energy efficiency, carbon reduction, and integrating green innovation with low-carbon transformation. This strategy also supports the development of new productivity paradigms, which highlight the integration of green and digital technologies to build a modern industrial system. Corporations, as key drivers of China's dual carbon goals, are central to this strategy, facing increasing pressure to balance economic growth with environmental sustainability.

Green innovation, which aims to enhance the environmental quality of products while expanding sustainable functionalities, plays a pivotal role in this transition. It can be categorized into two types: substantive green innovation and strategic green innovation [1]. Substantive green innovation involves advancements in green technologies and

Y. P. Tu and M. Chi (Eds.): WHICEB 2025, LNBIP 549, pp. 326–340, 2025.
https://doi.org/10.1007/978-3-031-94184-9_27

process improvements, directly enhancing corporate competitiveness, profitability, and sustainability [2]. By aligning environmental objectives with operations and products, this approach generates long-term value and is a primary focus of existing research. In contrast, strategic green innovation emphasizes meeting external expectations, such as government policies or investor demands, without necessarily addressing fundamental environmental issues [3, 4],. This often results in superficial or formalized practices that may leave firms unprepared for stricter environmental regulations and competitive pressures.

However, green innovation faces challenges, including high R&D costs, uncertain outcomes, and insufficient patent protections. Its development is influenced by external factors, such as government regulations, media attention, and investor focus, as well as internal factors like corporate resources, industry characteristics, and executive environmental awareness.

Investors, particularly small and medium-sized investors (SMIs), play a significant role in driving corporate innovation. Empowered by online interaction platforms launched by the Shenzhen and Shanghai Stock Exchanges, SMIs have increased their influence in corporate governance. While existing studies recognize that investor green attention can positively impact corporate green innovation [5], they often overlook how SMIs specifically influence different types of green innovation. Moreover, there is limited research exploring how companies respond differently to SMIs' green attention based on substantive versus strategic motives.

This study aims to address these gaps by examining the impact of SMIs' green attention on corporate green innovation, focusing on analyzing the manifestation of heterogeneity between substantive and strategic green innovation. The findings will provide valuable insights into the drivers of corporate green innovation and contribute to the development of strategies to attract environmentally conscious investors.

2 Literature Review

2.1 Influencing Factors of Corporate Green Innovation

Factors influencing corporate green innovation can be divided into external pressures and internal drivers.

External pressures mainly arise from government regulations and media attention. Government regulations, both command-based (such as subsidies, tax incentives, and environmental tools) and market-based (like emissions trading systems), play a crucial role in promoting green innovation. Research indicates that command-based regulations have an inverted U-shaped effect on green innovation strategies, while incentive-based policies have a significantly positive impact [2, 6]. Media attention also influences corporate green innovation by enhancing transparency and improving corporate reputation. Media coverage provides information on ecological issues, regulatory violations, and environmental disclosures, which in turn encourages investments in green technologies and fosters improved green innovation performance as companies seek to meet sustainability expectations [7].

Internal factors include organizational characteristics, resources and capabilities, and executives' environmental awareness. Organizational characteristics such as firm size and industry type affect green innovation. Larger firms often have the resources for sustainable practices, while smaller firms may achieve higher returns on green innovation due to greater flexibility [8]. Resources like technological expertise, R&D investment, and knowledge management are critical for pursuing green innovation [6]. Finally, executives' environmental awareness is a key driver, as leaders who understand environmental issues can better align corporate strategies with sustainability goals, ensuring the advancement of green innovation within the company [9].

2.2 The Impact of Investor Attention on Corporate Innovation

Investor attention serves as a crucial external governance mechanism for listed companies. As a limited resource, attention prioritizes specific information, influencing investment decisions. Research highlights that investor attention alleviates financing constraints, reduces information asymmetry, and enhances information disclosure, directly affecting a firm's cost of capital, reputation, and market competitiveness.

The growing focus on investor attention has spurred extensive research on its impact on corporate innovation. Studies indicate that investor attention significantly improves green innovation performance, enhancing both the quantity and quality of green initiatives in listed companies [5, 10, 11]. However, the findings remain inconclusive. While some research suggests that investor attention effectively promotes corporate innovation [10–12], others argue that limited attention can hinder innovation levels.

Traditional metrics used to assess investor attention, such as trading volume, media coverage, and search indices [11], often provide indirect insights. Recently, interactive platform data has emerged as a more effective proxy, reflecting direct communication between investors and companies [5, 12]. This study adopts question-and-answer data to measure investor attention, aiming to explore the impact of investors' green focus on corporate green innovation, with an emphasis on how investor attention can drive sustainable development.

3 Theoretical Analysis and Research Hypothesis

Small and medium-sized investors (SMIs) play a crucial role in motivating companies to adopt environmentally friendly practices. Failing to engage in green innovation can lead to criticism from investors and stakeholders, damaging a company's reputation and financial performance. As environmental concerns rise, SMIs increasingly demand proactive measures from companies.

Due to information asymmetry, investors rely on innovation signals to make investment decisions, which affect capital market pricing [13]. To attract investment, companies use strategic green innovation as a cost-effective way to signal their commitment to sustainability. Unlike substantive green innovation, which focuses on technological progress and competitiveness, strategic green innovation aims to create a positive green image [1] This helps attract government subsidies and external investments. These benefits encourage companies to adopt strategic green innovation, which in turn captures the attention of SMIs. As a result, SMIs allocate funds to companies aligned with sustainability, promoting strategic green innovation. Thus, we propose:

H1: SMIs' green attention promotes corporate strategic green innovation.

In addition to providing financial support, SMIs' attention helps ensure funds are effectively used for substantive green innovation. Externally, increased investor attention improves governance by enhancing interaction between investors and companies, reducing information asymmetry, and providing effective oversight of green initiatives. According to Porter's "push" hypothesis, SMIs act as external monitors, ensuring meaningful green innovation [14]. Their oversight prevents misuse of funds and guides companies to focus on substantive green innovation. This ensures authenticity and reduces over-reliance on strategic innovation. Internally, SMIs influence corporate governance by opposing short-term profit motives. When management focuses on strategic over substantive innovation, SMIs engage through platforms to ensure resources are allocated to impactful green initiatives. This strengthens green innovation efforts and fosters sustainable growth [3]. Therefore, we propose:

H2: SMIs' green attention promotes corporate substantive green innovation.

4 Research Design

4.1 Samples and Data

This study examines all A-share listed companies in Shanghai and Shenzhen from 2010 to 2021 to analyze the impact of small and medium-sized investors' green attention on corporate green innovation. Data sources include Q&A records from interactive platforms and green patent data. Specifically, we used Python to extract 12 years of data from Shenzhen Stock Exchange's "Interactive-Easy" and Shanghai Stock Exchange's "E-Interactive" platforms, covering over 4.25 million Q&A interactions between investors and corporate managers. Green patent data was sourced from the CSMAR database's green patent research module.

To refine the dataset, we excluded financial firms, ST or ST* firms, and companies with missing control variables. After matching and merging the Q&A and patent data, the final sample comprised 26,836 observations from 2048 companies. Winsorizing was applied to mitigate the influence of outliers.

4.2 Variables

Dependent Variables and Independent Variable

The dependent variables of this paper are strategic green innovation and substantive green innovation. Green patents serve as indicators of corporate green innovation. Drawing on prior studies [1], strategic green innovation is measured by the natural logarithm of the total number of green utility model and design patent applications plus one. Substantive green innovation is measured by the natural logarithm of green invention patent applications plus one.

The independent variable of this paper is green attention of small and medium-sized investors. Investor questions on Shenzhen Stock Exchange's "Interactive-Easy" platform and Shanghai Stock Exchange's "E-Interactive" platform reflect small and medium-sized investors' concerns. The frequency of questions about "green" and "green innovation" indicates their level of green attention [12].

Using methods from Pan Hongbo et al. [12], we conducted text analysis on investor questions from 2010 to 2021. A lexicon of 340 green-related keywords was constructed by analyzing government green governance policies and employing the Word2Vector algorithm. Words with a similarity score above 0.45 and frequency over 50 were included. Python was used to identify green-related questions, resulting in 371,386 records (8.7% of all questions). This highlights significant investor interest in green innovation among China's A-share companies. The final green attention indicator measures the number of green-related investor questions per company-year.

Control Variables

According to relevant studies, we included 16 control variables. These encompass six variables representing firm characteristics, such as size, and ten governance-related variables, such as operating income growth and board structure. Fixed effects for industry and year were also applied.

4.3 Model

Drawing on the research method of Pan Hongbo and Yang Haixia [12], this paper constructs the following model to test the impact of green attention of small and medium investors on the level of green innovation of corporate:

$$Gresub_{i,t}(Grestra_{i,t}) = \beta_0 + \beta_1 * GQR_{i,t} + \gamma * Controls_{i,t} + Ind_i + Year_t + \varepsilon_{i,t} \tag{1}$$

where $Gresub_{i,\,t}$ denotes the substantive green innovation of corporate, $Grestra_{i,\,t}$ denotes the strategic green innovation of corporate, and $GQR_{i,\,t}$ denotes the green attention of small and medium investors, $Controls_{i,\,t}$ are control variables, Ind_i and $Year_t$ are the control industry and year dummy variables, respectively. The regression is robust to the standard errors of the model.

5 Empirical Analysis

5.1 Basic Regression

The regression results in Table 1 examine the impact of small and medium-sized investors' green attention on corporate green innovation. Columns (1), (3), and (5) use substantial innovation (Gresub) as the dependent variable, while columns (2), (4), and (6) use strategic innovation (Grestra). All regressions employ clustered standard errors by firm.

Columns (1) and (2) present univariate results, indicates that green attention significantly promotes corporate innovation. Columns (3) and (4) include basic firm characteristics and fixed effects for year and industry, columns (5) and (6) add corporate governance variables, with coefficients for Gresub and Grestra still positive and significant at the 1% level. Notably, the effect size for substantial innovation (Gresub) exceeds that of strategic innovation (Grestra).

Table 1 Green attention of SMIs and Green Innovation of Corporate

	(1)	(2)	(3)	(4)	(5)	(6)
	Gresub	Grestra	Gresub	Grestra	Gresub	Grestra
GQR	0.015***	0.016***	0.004***	0.004***	0.004***	0.004***
	(17.819)	(18.608)	(6.356)	(5.466)	(6.288)	(5.465)
size			0.600***	0.571***	0.619***	0.566***
			(34.261)	(33.574)	(32.395)	(31.089)
Lev			−0.353***	−0.026	−0.040	0.200**
			(−4.128)	(−0.295)	(−0.429)	(2.154)
REC			0.0722	−0.0159	0.0453	−0.0312
			(1.027)	(−0.232)	(0.619)	(−0.436)
INV			−0.186***	−0.222***	−0.206***	−0.229***
			(−6.112)	(−6.760)	(−6.672)	(−6.787)
soe			0.160***	0.079*	0.201***	0.128***
			(3.769)	(1.934)	(4.496)	(2.987)
age			−0.128**	−0.110**	−0.110**	−0.088
			(−2.411)	(−2.026)	(−2.066)	(−1.607)
Growth					−0.002	−0.015
					(−0.067)	(−0.636)
ROA					1.312***	1.180***
					(6.441)	(5.419)
cfps					−0.006	−0.008
					(−0.465)	(−0.570)
TobinQ					0.018**	−0.016**
					(2.464)	(−2.226)
Dual					0.033	0.014
					(1.159)	(0.475)
Indp					−0.288	−0.237
					(−1.074)	(−0.908)
Topz					−0.001	−0.003**
					(−1.098)	(−2.263)
Supln					0.029	−0.006
					(0.350)	(−0.074)
Mshare					0.187**	0.292***

(*continued*)

Table 1 (*continued*)

	(1)	(2)	(3)	(4)	(5)	(6)
	Gresub	Grestra	Gresub	Grestra	Gresub	Grestra
					(2.211)	(3.190)
Mfee					1.737***	0.850***
					(6.638)	(3.308)
Cons	1.711***	2.014***	11.860***	10.013***	12.982***	10.113***
	(71.514)	(76.985)	(−19.243)	(−9.796)	(−24.389)	(−9.711)
Year	No	No	Yes	Yes	Yes	Yes
Ind	No	No	Yes	Yes	Yes	Yes
Adj. R2	0.041	0.041	0.433	0.468	0.439	0.471
N	26,836	26,836	26,836	26,836	26,836	26,836

These findings confirm that small and medium-sized investors' green attention significantly enhances both types of green innovation, with a stronger effect on substantial innovation. This supports hypotheses H1 and H2.

5.2 Robustness Test

Adjusting the Measurement of Independent and Dependent Variables
To ensure robustness, alternative measures for both independent and dependent variables were employed, with regression results summarized in Table 2.

Table 2. Robustness test results for replacing independent and dependent variables

	Alternative independent variables		Alternative dependent variables	
	Gresub	Grestra	Gresub_Award	Grestra_Award
GQR_LSTM	0.013***	0.011***		
	(8.135)	(6.563)		
GQR			0.003***	0.003***
			(4.632)	(5.205)
Year	Yes	Yes	Yes	Yes
Ind	Yes	Yes	Yes	Yes
Adj. R2	0.441	0.472	0.373	0.470
N	26,836	26,836	26,836	26,836

For the independent variable, green attention of small and medium investors, a pre-trained BERT-based LSTM model was used to classify whether investor questions reflect green attention. The total number of green-related questions (GQR_LSTM) for each firm-year was calculated and used as an alternative independent variable. Regression analysis with GQR_LSTM confirms a significant positive relationship with both substantive (Gresub) and strategic green innovation (Grestra).

For dependent variables, the number of granted green invention patents plus one was used to measure substantive green innovation (Gresub_Award), while the sum of granted green utility model and design patents plus one was used for strategic green innovation (Grestra_Award). Regression results consistently support the robustness of the findings, as shown in Table 2.

Other Robustness Test

To verify robustness, the paper also adopts the tests of expanding the regression period and replacing the regression model. The approach of lagging the independent variables by one period (LGQR) and two periods (L2GQR), and the use of a firm fixed effects model to fix the firms, industries and years were adopted. The results of the robustness tests are shown in Table 3 and are consistent with the results of previous studies.

Table 3. Other robustness test results

	Expanding the regression period				Replacement of regression model	
	Gresub	Grestra	Gresub	Grestra	Gresub	Grestra
LGQR	0.005***	0.004***				
	(6.376)	(5.406)				
L2GQR			0.004***	0.003***		
			(5.502)	(4.441)		
GQR					0.002***	0.002***
					(3.842)	(4.082)
Year	Yes	Yes	Yes	Yes	Yes	Yes
Ind	Yes	Yes	Yes	Yes	Yes	Yes
Adj. R2	0.440	0.471	0.445	0.474	0.229	0.230
N	21,961	21,961	18,542	18,542	26,836	26,836

5.3 Endogeneity Test

Instrumental Variable Analysis

Mutual causality exists between the green attention of small and medium investors (SMIs) and corporate green innovation. To address endogeneity, we adopt an instrumental variable (IV) approach, referencing prior studies. The selected IVs include: (1) the number of executive roles held by the company secretary (IV1), (2) the national Internet penetration rate (IV2), and (3) the lagged one-period investor attention variable (IV3). These were estimated using the least squares method.

First, the company secretary, often answering SMIs queries on online platforms, can provide targeted information if they hold multiple executive roles. This reduces SMIs' information acquisition costs but is unrelated to corporate green innovation. Second, Internet penetration facilitates SMIs' access to corporate news without directly affecting green innovation. Lastly, past investor attention influences current attention but does not directly impact firms' green innovation decisions. Thus, these IVs meet the requirements of relevance and exogeneity.

Table 4 report regression results for substantive and strategic green innovation, respectively. The first-stage regressions show all IVs are significantly correlated with SMIs green attention at the 1% level, passing validity tests. Second-stage results indicate positive and significant coefficients, confirming robustness and supporting hypotheses H1 and H2.

Table 4. Results of a two-stage least squares regression of corporate green innovation

	Gresub				Grestra			
	First-IV GQR	Second-IV1	Second-IV2	Second-IV3	First-IV GQR	Second-IV1	Second-IV2	Second-IV3
GQR		0.080***	0.056***	0.017***		0.156***	0.064***	0.018***
		(3.96)	(6.32)	(19.14)		(4.37)	(6.22)	(17.60)
IV1	3.000***				3.000***			
	(4.33)				(4.33)			
IV2	0.151***				0.151***			
	(7.91)				(7.91)			
IV3	0.784***				0.784***			
	(85.72)				(85.72)			
Year	Yes	Yes	Yes	Yes	Yes	Yes	Yes	Yes
Ind	Yes	Yes	Yes	Yes	Yes	Yes	Yes	Yes
N		15,680	8206	6522		15,680	8206	6522

Heckman Two-Stage Test

This study addresses potential sample selection bias using Heckman two-stage regression. In the first stage, a Probit model is used to regress whether a company has small and medium-sized investors' green-related questions and calculate the Inverse Mills Ratio (IMR). In the second stage, IMR is included in the regression model. The result shows that significant IMR coefficients at the 1% level confirm sample selection bias, and the Green Attention of Small and Medium-sized Investors remains positively significant, showing the robustness of the original results.

Propensity Score Matching Method

To address endogeneity due to omitted variables, Propensity Score Matching (PSM) is also applied. Companies are matched based on green attention from small and medium-sized investors, with control variables from the main regression model. Nearest Neighbor Matching (NNM) results in 12,617 valid matched samples. Regressing on these samples yields consistent results, further confirming the robustness of the findings.

5.4 Heterogeneity Analysis

Nature of the Corporate

To examine how different corporate nature influence the role of small and medium-sized investors' (SMIs) green attention in promoting corporate green innovation, this paper conducts a heterogeneity analysis across three dimensions: ownership, technology level, and industry attributes.

First, based on ownership, firms are classified as state-owned (SOE = 1) or non-state-owned (SOE = 0). State-owned enterprises (SOEs) are typically more influenced by policies and inclined toward green innovation, while non-SOEs focus more on short-term profits. Therefore, SMIs' green attention is expected to have a stronger impact on SOEs. Regression results confirm this inference.

Second, firms are categorized as high-tech (HighTech = 1) or non-high-tech (HighTech = 0) based on their technology level. High-tech firms already lead in green innovation, making SMIs' influence weaker. Conversely, non-high-tech firms depend more on green innovation to enhance competitiveness and thus benefit more from SMIs' green attention. Regression findings support this distinction.

Finally, firms are divided into heavily polluted (Pollute = 1) and non-heavily polluted industries (Pollute = 0), following the Guidelines for Industry Classification of Listed Enterprises. Heavily polluted firms face greater environmental pressures, limiting SMIs' influence on their green innovation. Non-heavily polluted firms, with lower environmental impacts, are more likely to adopt sustainable strategies, amplifying SMIs' role. Regression results validate these observations.

In conclusion, the findings highlight that the green concern effect of SMI is more pronounced in SOEs, non-high-tech firms and non-heavy polluting firms. (Please refer to Appendix 3 for specific empirical results).

Corporate Governance

From a corporate governance perspective, this study analyzes the heterogeneity of small and medium-sized investors' (SMIs) green attention on the promotion of corporate green innovation under the three dimensions.

First, executives' environmental awareness, measured by the frequency of environmental terms in decision-making [15], reflects their attention to green issues. A higher frequency indicates stronger awareness. Empirical analysis indicates that higher executive environmental awareness amplifies the effect of SMIs' green attention on corporate green innovation. Further subgroup regression based on awareness levels demonstrates that SMIs' green attention has a stronger impact on both substantive and strategic green innovation in firms with high executive environmental awareness.

Second, media attention influences the transparency and reputation of firms [7]. Higher media coverage provides investors with more information, reducing their reliance on interactive platforms. Using media attention scores, a dummy variable Media (1 for above-average attention) is introduced into the model. Results show that SMIs' green attention has a stronger effect on firms with lower media attention, as these firms are more motivated to signal their green innovation efforts through disclosure, enhancing both substantive and strategic innovation.

Lastly, institutional investor ownership, a proxy for governance quality, is crucial for corporate oversight. Institutional investors, with superior expertise and financial strength, monitor corporate activities more effectively. A dummy variable InsInvestor (1 for above-average ownership) is used in the model. Results show that SMIs' green attention has a significant positive impact on substantive green innovation in firms with higher institutional investor ownership, but no heterogeneity effect is observed for strategic green innovation.

In summary, the findings highlight that the effects of SMIs' green attention are more pronounced in firms with high executive environmental awareness, low media attention, or high institutional investor ownership, emphasizing the critical roles of internal and external governance mechanisms. (Please refer to Appendix 3 for specific empirical results).

6 Conclusion and Discussion

This paper investigates the impact of small and medium-sized investors' green attention on the green innovation level of A-share listed companies in Shanghai and Shenzhen from 2010 to 2021. Utilizing Q&A data from the "Interactive-Easy" and "E-Interactive" platforms and green patent data, the study finds that green attention from small and medium-sized investors significantly promotes both substantive and strategic green innovation, with a stronger effect on substantive innovation. These findings hold even after robustness and endogeneity tests. In order to deeply analyze the heterogeneity effect of small and medium-sized investors' green attention on enterprises' green innovation level, this paper carries out the heterogeneity test from two major parts: enterprise nature and corporate governance. The results show that, from the perspective of enterprise nature, in state-owned enterprises, non-high-tech enterprises and non-heavily polluted enterprises, the green attention of small and medium-sized investors has a more significant promotion effect on the level of green innovation of enterprises; from the perspective of corporate governance, in enterprises with high awareness of environmental protection by executives, low media attention and large proportion of shares held by institutional investors, the green attention of small and medium-sized investors has a more significant promotion effect on the level of green innovation of enterprises. Promotion effect is more significant.

The study also has limitations, including its focus on only two platforms. Future research could incorporate additional platforms, such as the Panorama Investor Relations platform and others, to broaden the understanding of small and medium-sized investors' role in promoting green innovation. Furthermore, the lack of a standardized lexicon for green innovation impacts the measurement of green attention; future studies could explore deep learning models to enhance this measurement.

Based on these findings, the paper offers four recommendations: (1) Prioritize engagement with small and medium-sized investors' environmental concerns via interactive platforms to foster trust and drive green innovation. (2) Increase investments in substantive green R&D, focusing on core technologies, talent cultivation, and systemic innovation capabilities. (3) Develop industry-specific approaches: polluting industries should accelerate clean technology adoption and eco-product development, while state-owned enterprises (SOEs) align green initiatives with policy frameworks. (4) Strengthen green branding by actively implementing carbon-neutral practices, enhancing environmental accountability disclosures, and aligning operations with the "dual-carbon" agenda to attract sustainability-focused investments. These measures aim to balance ecological goals with market competitiveness, ensuring long-term growth through strategic green transformation.

Acknowledgement. This research was supported by Beijing Social Science Fund Decision Consulting Project "Research on Optimal Allocation Strategy of Beijing Science and Technology Innovation Resources" (No.24JCB015).

Appendices

Appendix 1. Descriptive Statistics

The descriptive statistics result reflects the current low-level problem of A-share-listed enterprises in China's green innovation. The statistical results of other control variables are kept within a reasonable range, providing reliable data support for the subsequent analysis and research.

Table A1. Descriptive statistics

Varname	OBS	Mean	SD	P25	Median	P75	Min	Max
GQR	25,369	11.157	21.104	1.000	4.000	11.000	0.000	133.000
Gresub	25,369	1.871	1.513	0.693	1.792	2.944	0.000	6.057
Grestra	25,369	2.185	1.657	0.693	2.303	3.401	0.000	6.174
size	25,369	22.083	1.264	21.170	21.884	22.762	19.929	26.139
Lev	25,369	0.402	0.205	0.235	0.389	0.551	0.049	0.884
REC	25,369	0.265	0.241	0.090	0.205	0.364	0.001	1.206
INV	25,369	0.340	0.559	0.108	0.191	0.332	0.000	3.876
Growth	25,369	0.182	0.379	−0.008	0.122	0.288	−0.522	2.238
ROA	25,369	0.039	0.064	0.015	0.040	0.070	−0.272	0.198
cfps	25,369	0.466	0.885	0.049	0.326	0.747	−2.026	4.408
TobinQ	25,369	2.955	2.169	1.545	2.258	3.566	0.886	12.910

(*continued*)

Table A1. (*continued*)

Varname	OBS	Mean	SD	P25	Median	P75	Min	Max
Dual	25,369	0.321	0.467	0.000	0.000	1.000	0.000	1.000
Indp	25,369	0.376	0.053	0.333	0.364	0.429	0.333	0.571
Topz	25,369	7.664	12.242	1.710	3.347	7.676	1.003	80.341
Supln	25,369	1.205	0.220	1.099	1.099	1.099	1.099	1.946
Mrshare	25,369	0.125	0.184	0.000	0.005	0.224	0.000	0.670
Mfee	25,369	0.089	0.067	0.045	0.073	0.112	0.009	0.392
soe	25,369	0.288	0.453	0.000	0.000	1.000	0.000	1.000
Firmage	25,369	2.859	0.350	2.639	2.890	3.091	1.792	3.526

Appendix 2. Relevance Analysis

Relevance analysis result shows the matrix of correlation coefficients of the main variables of the model in this paper. From the results, it can be seen that the independent variable green attention of small and medium-sized investors (GQR) and the dependent variables substantial green innovation (Gresub) and strategic green innovation (Grestra) are significant at 1% level, which can support the hypothesis of this paper preliminarily.

Table A2. Correlation coefficient matrix

	GQR	Gresub	Grestra
GQR	1	0.260***	0.253***
Gresub	0.205***	1	0.709***
Grestra	0.206***	0.724***	1

Appendix 3. Heterogeneity Analysis Results

Table A3. Heterogeneity analysis of the nature of corporate

	Nature of ownership		Technology levels		Industry attributes	
	Gresub	Grestra	Gresub	Grestra	Gresub	Grestra
GQR	0.003***	0.003***	0.006***	0.005***	0.005***	0.004***
	(8.077)	(6.760)	(8.877)	(7.240)	(10.448)	(8.804)
GQR*SOE	0.002**	0.001*				
	(2.396)	(1.764)				
GQR*High-Tech			−0.003***	−0.002***		
			(−3.649)	(−2.931)		
GQR*Pollute					−0.002**	−0.002**
					(−2.368)	(−2.344)
Year	Yes	Yes	Yes	Yes	Yes	Yes
Ind	Yes	Yes	Yes	Yes	Yes	Yes
Adj. R2	0.439	0.470	0.439	0.471	0.439	0.470
N	25,241	25,241	25,241	25,241	25,241	25,241

Table A4. Heterogeneity analysis of the corporate governance

	Executives' environmental awareness		Media attention		Institutional investors' shareholdings	
	Gresub	Grestra	Gresub	Grestra	Gresub	Grestra
GQR	0.003***	0.002***	0.006***	0.006***	0.003***	0.003***
	(5.731)	(3.939)	(10.008)	(9.085)	(6.541)	(5.852)
GQR*MAN _AWA	0.001**	0.002**				
	(2.063)	(2.492)				
GQR*Media			−0.003***	−0.003***		
			(−3.896)	(−4.451)		
GQR* InsInvestor					0.002**	0.001
					(2.535)	(1.282)
Year	Yes	Yes	Yes	Yes	Yes	Yes
Ind	Yes	Yes	Yes	Yes	Yes	Yes
Adj. R2	0.439	0.471	0.439	0.470	0.439	0.470
N	25,369	25,369	25,369	25,369	25,369	25,369

References

1. Li, W., Zheng, M.: Is it substantive innovation or strategic innovation? ———impact of macroeconomic policies on micro-enterprises' innovation[J]. Econ. Res. **51**(4), 60–73 (2016) in Chinese
2. Xiao, H.: Research on the influence of financial subsidy on green technology innovation of enterprises[J]. Technol. Econ. Manag. Res. **2023**(1), 32–37 (2023) in Chinese
3. Wang, Y., Li, X.: Promoting or inhibiting: the impact of Government R&D Subsidies on the green innovation performance of firms [J]. China Indus. Econ. **2023**(2), 131–149 (2023) in Chinese
4. Tong, T.W., He, W., He, Z.L., et al.: Patent regime shift and firm innovation: evidence from the second amendment to China's patent law[J]. Acad. Manag. Proc. **2014**(1), 14174 (2014)
5. Xiong, X., Di, J., Gao, Y.: The influence of green concerns on the green innovation of listed companies—based on the investor interactive platforms[J]. Syst. Eng. Theor. Pract. **43**(7), 1873–1893 (2023) in Chinese
6. Cao, H., Chen, Z.: The driving effect of internal and external environments on corporate green innovation strategies: the moderating role of executives' environmental awareness. Nankai Bus. Rev. **20**(6), 95–103 (2017) in Chinese
7. Ban, Q., Fan, X.: Mandatory social responsibility disclosure and corporate green innovation: evidence from green patents of listed companies[J]. Financ. Rev. **15**(1), 23–43+122 (2023) in Chinese
8. Lin, W.L., Cheah, J.H., Azali, M., et al.: Does firm size matter? Evidence on the impact of the green innovation strategy on corporate financial performance in the automotive sector[J]. J. Clean. Prod. **229**, 974–988 (2019)
9. Martin, R., Muûls, M., de Preux, L.B., et al.: Anatomy of a paradox: management practices, organizational structure and energy efficiency[J]. J. Environ. Econ. Manag. **63**(2), 208–223 (2012)
10. Han, G., Gan, Y.: Can investors' attention promote green innovation performance? The mediating effect of financing constraints and the moderating effect of environmental regulation[J]. Sci. Technol. Progr. Countermeasur. **40**(8), 89–98 (2023) in Chinese
11. Zhang, W., Jin, X.: Investor attention, financing costs, and corporate innovation. World. Econ. Rev. **2022**(3), 85–102 (2022) in Chinese
12. Hand, J.R.M.: The value relevance of financial statements in the venture capital market[J]. Account. Rev. **80**(2), 613–648 (2005)
13. Porter, M.E., van der Linde, C.: Toward a new conception of the environment-competitiveness relationship[J]. J. Econ. Perspect. **9**(4), 97–118 (1995)
14. Pan, H., Yang, H.: Can stakeholders' attention to innovation improve corporate innovation? Evidence from irm.cninfo.com.cn under SSE[J]. Nankai Bus. Rev. **25**(3), 85–96 (2022) in Chinese
15. Duriau, V.J., Reger, R.K., Pfarrer, M.D.: A content analysis of the content analysis literature in organization studies: research themes, data sources, and methodological refinements[J]. Organ. Res. Methods. **10**(1), 5–34 (2007)

Gamification Competition Mechanisms and Goal Gradient Effect on Online Fundraising Platforms for Charity

Manning Li(✉), Miaomiao Li, Xiaoying Li, Qian Wan, and Xinyue Wang

School of Business Administration, Northeastern University, Shenyang, China
mnli@mail.neu.edu.cn

Abstract. How to increase users' support for charity projects through appropriate gamification mechanisms on Online Fundraising Platforms for Charity (OFPC) has recently harvested significant attention in practice but not yet been systematically studied. Hence, this study examines the impact of gamification competition mechanisms on users' intention to donate and repost on OFPC. Through an empirical experiment, we verified the impact of goal gradient effect by exploring how different gamification competition mechanisms on these platforms drive users' motivation under different goal progress levels, thus affecting their intention to donate and repost. The results show that when goal-progress is high, cooperative competition mechanisms work better in increasing users' perceived reputation, perceived social identity, perceived warm glow, and perceived altruism, which in turn improves users' intention to repost and donate for charity projects.

Keywords: Online Fundraising Platforms for Charity · Goal Gradient Effect · Gamification Competition Mechanisms · Donation Intentions · Repost Intentions

1 Introduction

The rapid advancement of information and communication technologies has not merely enabled a means for those grappling with desperate circumstances, such as severe illnesses, natural disasters, or poverty, to solicit assistance online, it has also ignited the public's enthusiasm for engaging in charity donations. Online fundraising platforms represent a convenient and highly promising approach for charity involvement, especially when traditional offline charity organizations frequently face public doubts and scrutinization. As a result, a number of online charity initiatives embodied the effective design of online interactive systems such as games to engage the netizens.

Gamification, defined as "the use of game design elements in non-game environments" [1], has enlightened the design of a number of OFPC. While previous studies have explored the value of gamification for online donation, few studies have considered the impact of different gamification competition mechanisms on these platforms. As one of the popular gamification mechanisms adopted on many OFPC, such as Tencent and Weibo Charity platforms, competition is a highly popular and interesting phenomenon.

Y. P. Tu and M. Chi (Eds.): WHICEB 2025, LNBIP 549, pp. 341–352, 2025.
https://doi.org/10.1007/978-3-031-94184-9_28

Besides, goal gradient effect suggests that users' support for a charity project will drastically increase with goal proximity [2]. These interesting findings motivate us to explore further how goal gradient effect impacts users under different gamification competition mechanisms. Therefore, this research examines the impact of different gamification competition mechanisms (regular competition vs. cooperative competition) on user donation and repost intentions on OFPC, while taking into account the donation progress, through investigating the following research questions:

1. How do gamification competition mechanisms affect users' donation motivations, and donation and repost intentions on OFPC?
2. How does goal progress moderate the above relationships?

2 Theoretical Background

2.1 Donation Motivations in Online Charity Projects

Online fundraising platforms for charity, which provides comprehensive and real time information related to the progress and goal of charity projects, has become increasingly popular among donors, who can conveniently support a project via online payments [3]. While analyzing what drives users' donation and repost intentions, we classify users' backing motivations into two types: altruistic and social recognition motivations [4–6]. Donors motivated by altruism are more associated with self-sacrifice, the interests of others, unselfishness, and virtues; whereas social motives are associated with egoism, selfishness, self-interest, reciprocity, social motivation, and social pressure [7]. As such, we analyze two types of motivations for charity donations: (1) social recognition motivations (perceived reputation and perceived social identity) and (2) altruistic motivations (perceived warm glow and perceived altruism).

Among social recognition motivations, reputation helps individuals achieve and maintain their status in a community [8]. Jiao [9] proposed that reputation is an individual's expectation of reputational feedback generated by donations to charity projects. People often prefer their donations to be known [10]. Besides, social identity serves as a significant impetus for pro-social behavior, meaning that an individual has a clear awareness of the social group to which they belong and holds a high level of esteem for the members within that group. For altruistic motivations, we examine perceived warm glow and perceived altruism. Perceived warm glow to a large extent reflects the sense of spiritual fulfillment that is brought about when an act of kindness is performed. Hou et al. [11] claimed that the enjoyment of helping others is one of the most important motivations in life. In contrast, perceived altruism focuses more on the subjective feeling of an individual that his/her behavior is motivated by a genuine concern for the well-being of others, without any expectation of personal gain or reward [9], and altruism is the primary motivation for giving [12]. Consequently, perceived warm glow and altruism are examined as altruistic motivations in this study.

2.2 Gamified Charity and Competition

Gamified charity emphasizes the strategic use of gamification mechanisms in promoting socially responsible behaviors [13]. Ye et al. [13] argued that the characteristics of gamified charity applications (including functional transparency, interactive graphical user interface, and accessibility) encouraged charitable intentions from individuals. Behl et al. [14] showed that gamification in a fundraising platform for disaster relief operations increases donor engagement in fundraising channels. Golrang and Safari [15] demonstrated that the use of gamification mechanisms successfully enhanced user engagement in a charitable giving platform. Chen et al. [16] analyzed the giving behavior of Chinese millennial donors using WeChat, and found that gamification elements must be carefully designed to avoid negative effects. Gomez-Leyva and Giannini [17] conducted a study in the context of a new global coronavirus. The results suggest that the implementation of gamification (e.g., rewards, feedback, etc.) in nonprofit organizations can benefit organizations by improving their engagement, donations, and volunteer actions. Based on goal-framing theory, Lv et al. [18] found that autonomy support and achievement visibility can help to achieve users' hedonic, gainful, and normative goals, while competition and interaction positively satisfy users' revenue goals. Lee et al. [19] explored how design features of progress bars (including bar dynamics, color, and additional information) increase intention to support fundraising projects. It is also found that gamification elements enhance public engagement and bring about fun and competition, which generate positive impacts on individual donations [16]. While most existing research shows gamification is promising for OFPC, studies surrounding the rationale for incorporating competition mechanisms with different goal proximity conditions still lack empirical support on these platforms.

2.3 Goal Gradient Effect in Charitable Giving

The motivations and behaviors of potential donors in competitions can be heavily influenced by the progress of a charity project, especially when it is close to the funding goal. Liberman [20] argued that goal gradient effect works in fundraising because people perceive a higher sense of impact when approaching completion, and this sense of impact influences people's donation intentions. The goal gradient effect also occurs when a visualized goal is used because when people see visualizations of progress, they are better motivated to work towards the goal. Research by Cryder et al. [21] showed that people are more willing to help someone who is close to achieving a goal; and that people derive satisfaction from the fact that they are having an impact on solving a social problem; the perceived impact of this contribution increases later in the project, and this impact produces satisfaction that explains goal-gradient helping. Jin [22] found that there is a strong herding effect, which produces a sustained acceleration to reach the fundraising goals in the final stages of a fundraising project. Li and Wang [23] demonstrated that goal proximity drives a significant surge in supporter backing that usually occurs within a few hours, owing to their pro-social motivation. Thus, we delve further into whether goal gradient effect manipulates the impact of gamification competition mechanisms on user donation and repost intentions in the online charity context.

3 Hypotheses Development

3.1 Gamification Competition Mechanisms and Donation Motivations

Perceived Reputation (PR).
Perceived reputation refers to individuals' subjective perceptions of their social status or public image during charitable contributions [9]. On OFPC, competition mechanisms are implemented by providing feedback on how much users contribute compared with others individuals or groups. By integrating these mechanisms, people are often motivated to compete for leading others, gaining attention, and attaining status [24]. In cooperative competition settings, users join a pre-formed donation group and compete with other groups collectively, which leads to upward social comparison in-group and motivates them to pursue higher status [25]. Overall, when users donate together, their desire for reputation increases, as the glory of success is shared by the whole team rather than a single person. Thus, we hypothesize:

H_1: On OFPC, users generate a lower sense of perceived reputation under regular competition mechanisms compared with cooperative competition mechanisms.

Perceived Social Identity (PSI).
Perceived social identity reflects individuals' sense of belonging to donation groups, as well as their emotional attachment to other group members [26]. On OFPC, users can naturally form groups based on common interests, adopt group norms and identify their roles through frequent social interactions. Morschheuser et al. [27] studied the effects of three gamified conditions, including competitive, cooperative, and inter-team competitive gamification, and found that inter-team competitions can invoke the social identification processes and enhance users' emotional connection. In such teams, even if users are not personally acquainted, they internalize group membership and align their behavior with collective expectations [28]. Moreover, the visibility of contributions further amplifies this effect, leading to a contest of generosity. Thus, we hypothesize:

H_2: On OFPC, users generate a lower sense of perceived social identity under regular competition mechanisms compared with cooperative competition.

Perceived Warm Glow (PWG).
Perceived warm glow refers to the feelings of pleasure and self-satisfaction derived from participating in online charity projects [13]. This concept aligns with research on altruistic behavior, where individuals experience emotional rewards, such as happiness and fulfillment, from engaging in prosocial activities. In regular competition settings, users donate to highlight their own contributions, which may shift their focus away from the altruistic motivations for charitable giving. In contrast, cooperative competition settings offer a different dynamic. Here, participants work together towards a clear goal and experience a stronger "warm glow" effect, as their contributions to the group are perceived as more valuable and meaningful [29]. This environment promotes a sense of collective success and personal satisfaction from being part of a larger, altruistic project. Thus, we hypothesize:

H_3: On OFPC, users generate a lower sense of perceived warm glow under regular competition mechanisms compared with cooperative competition.

Perceived Altruism (PA).
Perceived altruism is defined as the belief that a person's charitable actions are motivated purely by the willingness to help others, without any expectation of personal gain [7]. Altruism is often regarded as a pivotal driver of prosocial behavior, where individuals voluntarily engage in activities that benefit others, even at a personal cost. Prior research has shown that cooperative gamification mechanisms can promote altruistic behavior by strengthening collective responsibility among participants and encouraging joint efforts towards the fundraising goals [30]. In regular competition mechanisms, however, social pressure from the competitive environment can lead to a crowding-out effect, as the intense desire for personal achievement often overshadows the altruistic motivations to help others. Thus, we hypothesize:

H_4: On OFPC, users generate a lower sense of perceived altruism under regular competition mechanisms compared to cooperative competition.

3.2 User Donation Motivations and Behavioral Intentions

Donation intentions refer to users' willingness to donate money for a project on OFPC, while repost intentions refer to users' willingness to share a project from OFPC to their social platforms. Online charity platforms provide multiple possibilities for users to showcase their prosocial behavior, allowing them to publicly demonstrate their support for charitable events [31]. Research indicates that users are more motivated to support charitable projects when they believe that donating money or sharing project information will improve their social reputation [9]. Thus, we hypothesize:

H_5: On OFPC, perceived reputation positively impacts user donation intentions.
H_6: On OFPC, perceived reputation positively impacts user repost intentions.

Social identity plays an important role in online charitable giving. Individuals are often motivated by a sense of belonging to charity platforms or communities, which strengthens their identification with the group. This sense of social connectedness can enhance their commitment and positively influence their behavioral intentions, ultimately leading to increased engagement in charitable events [32]. Thus, we hypothesize:

H_7: On OFPC, perceived social identity positively impacts user donation intentions.
H_8: On OFPC, perceived social identity positively impacts user repost intentions.

Perceived warm glow is an emotional experience derived from engaging in charitable behavior [13]. Unlike external incentives such as social recognition or monetary rewards, warm glow serves as an internal motivator that drives prosocial actions. Research suggests that the more individuals give, the stronger "warm glow" effect they experience, which in turn increases their willingness to support the charitable activities [29]. At the same time, people engage in prosocial behaviors not only for external recognition but also for emotional gratification. This emotional reward fosters a positive feedback loop, in which individuals participate in charitable activities to sustain their feelings of fulfillment and happiness. Thus, we hypothesize:

H_9: On OFPC, perceived warm glow positively impacts user donation intentions.
H_{10}: On OFPC, perceived warm glow positively impacts user repost intentions.

Perceived altruism plays a crucial role in shaping individuals' willingness to help others on online charity platforms [33]. People who are driven by pure altruistic motivations are typically more prosocial and inclined to engage in behaviors that benefit others. These individuals are not only more likely to donate but also to engage in other forms of pro-social behavior, such as sharing charitable projects to raise broader awareness. Overall, when users are motivated by altruism, they are more likely to seek out ways to help those in need and actively contribute to charitable events on OFPC. Thus, we hypothesize:

H_{11}: On OFPC, perceived altruism positively impacts user donation intentions.
H_{12}: On OFPC, perceived altruism positively impacts user repost intentions.

3.3 The Moderating Role of Goal Progress

Goal progress, defined as the percentage of the charitable project completed, is selected as a moderating variable in this study to explore how gamification competition mechanisms affect user donation motivations under different goal proximity conditions. Cryder et al. [21] proposed the concept of "goal-gradient helping behavior", which posits that individuals are more likely to donate as a charitable event approaches its fundraising goals. Furthermore, prior research has found that people often evaluate the significance of their contributions based on timing [34]. In particular, when a project is nearing completion, the final contributions from group members can be decisive. As a result, those who donate at the final stage are recognized as key contributors to the project's success, even though their donation amounts are relatively small. In light of this, within the context of online charitable giving, participants may experience a higher sense of social recognition and emotional satisfaction from knowing their actions contribute to a greater impact. This suggests that compared with regular competition settings, users in cooperative competition settings may experience stronger donation motivations under high goal progress levels. Thus, we hypothesize:

H_{13}: On OFPC, goal progress levels moderate the relationship between gamification competition mechanisms and user donation motivations (PR, PSI, PWG, and PA).

Based on the above hypotheses, the research model is presented in Fig. 1.

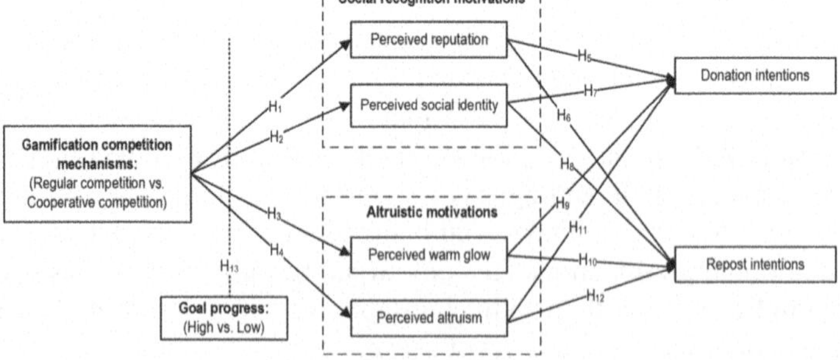

Fig. 1. Research model.

4 Research Design

This research examines how gamified competition mechanisms influence donation and repost intentions, examining the mediating role of donation motivations and the moderating effect of goal progress. To achieve this goal, a 2 (gamification competition mechanisms: regular vs. cooperative) × 2 (goal progress: low vs. high) between-subjects experiment was carried out.

First, we conducted a pilot test with 16 participants to gather feedback on the experimental procedure, scenario design, and questionnaires. Then, 491 participants were recruited online for the formal experiment and randomly assigned to one of the four treatment conditions. They were instructed to interact with the system (Fig. 2), complete the tasks and fill out the questionnaires.

Fig. 2. Examples of experimental interfaces.

The measurement scales used in this study were adapted from previous research: PR (Jiao et al. [9]), PSI (Wang et al. [26]), PWG (Ye et al. [13]), PA (Chen et al. [7]), donation intentions (Hou et al. [11]), and repost intentions (Chen et al. [7]). All items were rated on a 7-point Likert scale. The experiment lasted around 5 minutes. After data collection and screening, 315 valid responses are included for further analysis (64.2% response rate). Among these respondents, 192 (61%) were female and 123 (39%) were male; 248 (78.7%) had prior experience with OFPC; 210 (66.7%) stated that they would only participate in charity donations if prompted by others.

5 Data Analysis and Results

AMOS 24.0 was used to analyze the structural equation model. The model fit indexes ($\chi^2/df = 3.678$, GFI = 0.634, NFI = 0.702, IFI = 0.897, TLI = 0.872, CFI = 0.896, RMSEA = 0.093) indicated that the model was acceptable [35]. Following this, a path analysis of the model was conducted. Table 1 presented a summary of the analysis results, and the structural equation model diagram was shown in Fig. 3.

The data analysis results showed that: Compared with regular competition mechanisms, users perceived significantly higher reputation ($\beta = 0.398$, $p < 0.01$), social identity ($\beta = 0.351$, $p < 0.01$), warm glow ($\beta = 0.223$, $p < 0.05$) and altruism ($\beta =$

Table 1. Results of the path coefficients

Hypothesized Paths	β	S.E.	P	Results
H1: GCM → PR	0.398	0.124	0.001 (***)	Supported
H2: GCM → PSI	0.351	0.125	0.005 (***)	Supported
H3: GCM → PWG	0.223	0.113	0.049 (**)	Supported
H4: GCM → PA	0.358	0.121	0.003 (***)	Supported
H5: PR → DI	−0.363	0.101	0.000 (***)	Not supported
H6: PR → RI	−0.376	0.149	0.012 (**)	Not supported
H7: PSI → DI	−0.175	0.117	0.135 (n.s.)	Not supported
H8: PSI → RI	−0.298	0.153	0.051 (*)	Not supported
H9: PWG → DI	0.779	0.115	0.000 (***)	Supported
H10: PWG → RI	0.659	0.145	0.000 (***)	Supported
H11: PA → DI	0.892	0.118	0.000 (***)	Supported
H12: PA → RI	1.258	0.186	0.000 (***)	Supported

Note:*P<0.1, **P<0.05, ***p<0.01; n.s.: non-significant

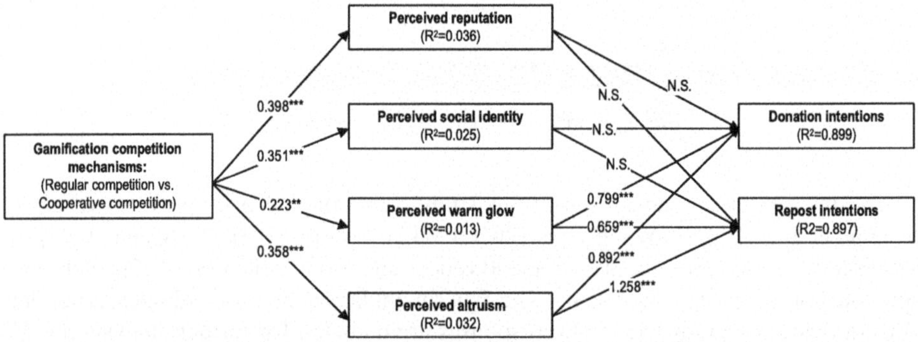

Fig. 3. Structural equation model results. Note:*p<0.1, **p<0.05, ***p<0.01; N.S.: Not Supported

0.358, $p < 0.01$) in cooperative competition mechanisms. Thus, H_1, H_2, H_3, and H_4 were supported. Perceived reputation negatively impacted donation intentions ($\beta = -0.363$, $p < 0.01$) and repost intentions ($\beta = -0.376$, $p < 0.05$), so H_5 and H_6 were not supported. Perceived social identity had no significant effect on donation intentions ($\beta = -0.175$, $p > 0.1$), but has a negative marginally significant impact on repost intentions ($\beta = -0.298$, $p < 0.1$), thus both H_7 and H_8 were not supported. Altruistic motivations (perceived warm glow and altruism) had a significant positive influence on both donation intentions and repost intentions, supporting H_9-H_{12}.

In addition, a multivariate analysis of variance (MANOVA) was conducted to examine the interaction effects of competition mechanisms and goal progress on donation motivations. The results revealed significant interaction effects on perceived reputation ($F = 10.025$, $p < 0.01$), perceived social identity ($F = 4.256$, $p < 0.05$), perceived warm glow ($F = 3.470$, $p < 0.1$) and perceived altruism ($F = 4.771$, $p < 0.05$). Further, a simple effects analysis was performed and the results (Table 2) indicated that: Under high goal progress, users in cooperative competition mechanisms perceived higher reputation ($M = 5.70$ vs. $M = 4.86$, $p < 0.01$), social identity ($M = 5.78$ vs. $M = 5.17$, $p < 0.01$), warm glow ($M = 5.90$ vs. $M = 5.44$, $p < 0.05$) and altruism ($M = 5.72$ vs. $M = 5.07$, $p < 0.01$) compared with regular competition mechanisms; Under low goal progress, the effects of competition mechanisms on perceived reputation ($M = 5.45$ vs. $M = 5.52$, $p > 0.1$), perceived social identity ($M = 5.76$ vs. $M = 5.72$, $p > 0.1$), perceived warm glow ($M = 5.91$ vs. $M = 5.94$, $p > 0.1$), perceived altruism ($M = 5.70$ vs. $M = 5.61$, $p > 0.1$) were not significant. Therefore, H_{13} was partially supported.

Table 2. Results of the simple effects analysis

Dependent Variables	Goal Progress	Competition Mechanisms	M	SD	P
Perceived reputation	Low	Regular competition	5.52	0.203	0.725 (n.s.)
		Cooperative competition	5.45		
	High	Regular competition	4.86	0.204	0.000 (***)
		Cooperative competition	5.70		
Perceived social identity	Low	Regular competition	5.72	0.194	0.817 (n.s.)
		Cooperative competition	5.76		
	High	Regular competition	5.17	0.194	0.002 (***)
		Cooperative competition	5.78		
Perceived warm glow	Low	Regular competition	5.94	0.186	O.855 (n.s.)
		Cooperative competition	5.91		
	High	Regular competition	5.44	0.187	0.015 (**)
		Cooperative competition	5.90		

(continued)

Table 2. (*continued*)

Dependent Variables	Goal Progress	Competition Mechanisms	M	SD	P
Perceived altruism	Low	Regular competition	5.61	0.183	0.643 (n.s.)
		Cooperative competition	5.70		
	High	Regular competition	5.07	0.184	0.000 (***)
		Cooperative competition	5.72		

Note:*P<0.1, **P<0.05, ***p<0.01; n.s.: non-significant

6 Conclusion and Discussion

This paper examined the effect of gamification competition mechanisms on users' donation motivations and behavioral intentions. Through an empirical experiment, we found that cooperative competition mechanisms are more effective in triggering social recognition and altruistic motivations on OFPC. However, contrary to our expectations, social recognition motivations were not found to have significant impacts on donation and repost intentions. A possible explanation is that such extrinsically driven motivations reduce users' sincerity in their charitable behavior, which in turn triggers users' emotional aversion. Furthermore, the study explored the moderating effect of goal progress and found that high goal progress boosted the influence of competition mechanisms on donation motivations.

From a theoretical perspective, through scrutinizing goal gradient effect in the context of charitable giving, the study reveals the more effective competition mechanisms for different goal progress levels, which enlightened future research related to user engagement on OFPC. Moreover, this paper contributes to literature through providing a deeper understanding of how different competition mechanisms impact user donation motivations and further influence user behavioral intentions on OFPC. Precisely speaking, we focus on regular and cooperative competition mechanisms, which are important but have not been widely explored in research in the gamified charity area.

For practice, the research emphasizes the significance of gamification in enhancing users' donation motivations and further promoting users' charity support intentions. Specifically, group-based competition mechanisms were found to be more effective, especially in high goal progress situations. This suggests that platforms can use both competition mechanisms in the early stages to cater for different user preferences. However, as the project progresses, platforms should adopt cooperative competition mechanisms to maximize their impact on potential donors. It is also worth noting that gamification serves merely as an incentive, not a coercive tool. The crucial impact of gamification should always be grounded in respect for users' autonomy and moral agency.

It should also be noted that there are some limitations that future researchers should be aware of while interpreting the results of this current study. Due to time and resource limitations, our experiment setting is constrained to the "donate for the education of children in rural areas charity" context. In the future, we plan to collect data across a wide range of charity contexts and use multi-methodologies to improve the validity and generalizability of the findings. As a further investigation to our current cross-sectional research, future studies could also examine the long-term effects of gamification competition mechanisms on user donation behavior on OFPC. Finally, future researchers could also examine whether our findings also apply to other interesting online fundraising scenarios such as fundraising for new start-up companies or innovative products.

Acknowledgement. This work was supported by the National Natural Science Foundation of China (No. 72371064).

References

1. Deterding, S., Dixon, D., Khaled, R., Nacke, L.: From game design elements to gamefulness: defining "gamification". In: Proceedings of the 15th International Academic MindTrek Conference: Envisioning Future Media Environments, pp. 9–15 (2011)
2. Popescul, D., Radu, L.D., Pavaloaia, V.D., Georgescu, M.R.: Psychological determinants of investor motivation in social media-based crowdfunding projects: a systematic review. Front. Psychol. **11** (2020)
3. Zhang, Y., Tan, C.D., Sun, J., Yang, Z.: Why do people patronize donation-based crowdfunding platforms? An activity perspective of critical success factors. Comput. Hum. Behav. **112**, 106470 (2020)
4. Bock, D.E., Eastman, J.K., Eastman, K.L.: Encouraging consumer charitable behavior: the impact of charitable motivations, gratitude, and materialism. J. Bus. Ethics. **150**, 1213–1228 (2016)
5. Hong, Y., Hu, Y., Burtch, G.: Embeddedness, Prosociality, and social influence. MIS Q. **42**, 1211–A1214 (2018)
6. Chen, X., Song, D., Shou, Y., Pan, Y.: Altruism or social motives? Evidence from online charitable giving in China. Enterp. Inf. Syst. **16**, 566–588 (2021)
7. Zhang, X., Liu, S., Deng, Z., Chen, X.: Knowledge sharing motivations in online health communities: a comparative study of health professionals and normal users. Comput. Hum. Behav. **75**, 797–810 (2017)
8. Jiao, H., Qian, L., Liu, T., Ma, L.: Why do people support online crowdfunding charities? A case study from China. Front. Psychol. **12**, 582508 (2021)
9. Bekkers, R., Wiepking, P.: A literature review of empirical studies of philanthropy. Nonprofit Volunt. Sect. Q. **40**, 924–973 (2010)
10. Hou, T., Hou, K., Wang, X., Luo, X.: Why I give money to unknown people? An investigation of online donation and forwarding intention. Electron. Commer. Res. Appl. **47**, 101055 (2021)
11. Steele, W.R., et al.: The role of altruistic behavior, empathetic concern, and social responsibility motivation in blood donation behavior. Transfusion. **48**, 43–54 (2008)
12. Ye, Q., Rafique, Z., Zhou, R., Asmi, F., Anwar, M.A., Siddiquei, A.N.: Embedded philanthropic CSR in digital China: unified view of prosocial and pro-environmental practices. Front. Psychol. **12**, 695468 (2021)

13. Behl, A., Dutta, P.: Engaging donors on crowdfunding platform in Disaster Relief Operations (DRO) using gamification: a Civic Voluntary Model (CVM) approach. Int. J. Inf. Manag. **54**, 102140 (2020)
14. Golrang, H., Safari, E.: Applying gamification design to a donation-based crowdfunding platform for improving user engagement. Entertain. Comput. **38**, 100425 (2021)
15. Chen, Y.-R.R.: Strategic donor engagement on mobile social networking sites for mobile donations: a study of millennial WeChat users in China. Chin. J. Commun. **11**, 26–44 (2017)
16. Gomez-Leyva, A., Giannini, R.: Gamification Techniques Implemented to Increase Engagement and Donations in the nonProfit sector in Los Angeles to Counteract the Negative Effects of the Global Pandemic, Covid-19. Master thesis in digital marketing. Geneva Business School (2021)
17. Lv, J., Xu, J., Du, H.S.: How Gamification Affordances Drive Micro Public Welfare, p. 187. PACIS (2021)
18. Lee, Y., Coyle, J.R., Chen, A.N.K.: Improving intention to back projects with effective designs of progress presentation in crowdfunding campaign sites. Decis. Support. Syst. **147**, 113573 (2021)
19. Liberman, A.: Charitable Giving: How Framing Amount Raised Influences Donations. Vanderbilt University (2019)
20. Cryder, C.E., Loewenstein, G., Seltman, H.: Goal gradient in helping behavior. J. Exp. Soc. Psychol. **49**, 1078–1083 (2013)
21. Jin, Y., Ding, C., Duan, Y., Cheng, H.K.: Click to success? The temporal effects of Facebook likes on crowdfunding. J. Assoc. Inf. Syst. **21**, 1191–1213 (2020)
22. Li, G., Wang, J.: Threshold effects on backer motivations in reward-based crowdfunding. J. Manag. Inf. Syst. **36**, 546–573 (2019)
23. Jia, Y., Liu, Y., Yu, X., Voida, S.: Designing leaderboards for gamification. In: Proceedings of the 2017 CHI Conference on Human Factors in Computing Systems, pp. 1949–1960 (2017)
24. Wiepking, P., Heijnen, M.: The giving standard: conditional cooperation in the case of charitable giving. Int. J. Nonprofit Volunt. Sect. Mark. **16**, 13–22 (2011)
25. Wang, T., Li, Y., Kang, M., Zheng, H.: Exploring individuals' behavioral intentions toward donation crowdfunding: evidence from China. Ind. Manag. Data Syst. **119**, 1515–1534 (2019)
26. Morschheuser, B., Hamari, J., Maedche, A.: Cooperation or competition—when do people contribute more? A field experiment on gamification of crowdsourcing. Int. J. Human-Comput. Stud. **127**, 7–24 (2019)
27. Tajfel, H.: Experiments in intergroup discrimination. Sci. Am. **223**, 96–103 (1970)
28. Duffy, J., Kornienko, T.: Does competition affect giving? J. Econ. Behav. Organ. **74**, 82–103 (2010)
29. Riar, M., Morschheuser, B., Hamari, J., Zarnekow, R.: How Game Features Give Rise to Altruism and Collective Action? Implications for Cultivating Cooperation by Gamification. HICSS (2020)
30. Ernst, C.-P.H., Hock, C.: Factors Driving Prosocial Online Behavior. AMCIS (2017)
31. Jiao, H., Tang, W., Liu, T., Wang, X., Ma, L.: How do IT affordances support behavioral intention in charitable crowdfunding? The mediating effects of donor perceptions and motivations. Kybernetes. **51**, 3172–3200 (2021)
32. Lee, G., Lee, W.J.: Altruistic traits and organizational conditions in helping online. Comput. Hum. Behav. **26**, 1574–1580 (2010)
33. Ziano, I., Pandelaere, M.: Late-action effect: heightened counterfactual potency and perceived outcome reversibility make actions closer to a definitive outcome seem more causally impactful. J. Exp. Soc. Psychol. **100**, 104290 (2022)
34. Wu, M.: Structural Equation Modeling: AMOS Operation and Application. Chongqing University Press, Chongqing (2009)

The Impact of Sustained Digital Innovation on Economic Development from the Perspective of Complex Networks: A Case Study of the Nine Inland Cities in the Guangdong-Hong Kong-Macao Greater Bay Area

Yiming Guo[1], Jianming Zhu[1(✉)], and Yuanqing Wen[2]

[1] School of Information, Central University of Finance and Economics, Beijing 100081, China
zjm@cufe.edu.cn

[2] Law School, Beijing Normal University, Beijing 100091, China

Abstract. This study focuses on digital innovation in the nine inland cities of the Guangdong-Hong Kong-Macao Greater Bay Area, exploring the mechanisms of regional collaborative innovation and the flow of innovative resources driven by the digital innovation. Using digital economy-related patent data from 2014 to 2023, a spatial association network of digital innovation is constructed, and complex network analysis methods are employed to examine the network structure characteristics and its dynamic evolution patterns. The research finds that sustained innovation investment has a significant positive impact on economic development, with network scale and degree centrality acting as mediators in this relationship. Additionally, network density and centrality moderate the influence of sustained innovation investment on economic development. This study provides a new theoretical perspective for understanding the mechanisms through which the digital economy empowers regional economic coordination and offers theoretical support for regional policy-making.

Keywords: Complex Networks · Regional Economic Coordination · Greater Bay Area · Sustained Digital Innovation · Innovation Network

1 Introduction

Urban agglomerations have become essential spatial units for enhancing regional competitiveness in the global economy. As hubs for capital, technology, and talent, they drive economic transformation and high-quality development. The Guangdong-Hong Kong-Macao Greater Bay Area (GBA), comprising Hong Kong, Macao, and nine inland cities in Guangdong Province, is one of China's most dynamic and globally significant urban clusters. In recent years, China has actively advanced regional coordinated development, with the GBA playing a key role in Chin's economic development and innovation.

Y. P. Tu and M. Chi (Eds.): WHICEB 2025, LNBIP 549, pp. 353–364, 2025.
https://doi.org/10.1007/978-3-031-94184-9_29

Amid the rapid rise of the digital economy, digital technologies have become critical factors of urban agglomerations' competitiveness. In the GBA's inland cities, digitalization has mitigated traditional geographical constraints through knowledge spillovers and network effects, fostering industrial transformation and strengthening regional economic linkages. Innovation, particularly sustained investment in digital innovation, is fundamental to this process. Understanding the spatial structure and evolution of digital innovation networks is thus essential for uncovering the mechanisms of resource flows and intercity collaboration.

Existing research on digital innovation in urban agglomerations primarily focuses on overall innovation performance or individual cities, overlooking the internal spatial network structure and its evolution. Given the GBA's active digital innovation ecosystem and significant spatial linkages, identifying its network structure and dynamics is crucial for understanding how digitalization fosters regional economic development and collaborative innovation. This study employs complex network analysis and digital patent data (2014–2023) to construct a spatial association network of digital innovation among the nine inland cities of the GBA. By analyzing its structural characteristics, this study aims to reveal how digital innovation drives regional economic development, contributing to theoretical advancements and informing policy decisions.

2 Literature Review

Sustained innovation is a crucial driving force behind modern economic development. Brynjolfsson and McAfee (2014) argue that digital technologies and innovation not only facilitate industrial transformation but also boost global productivity [1]. Digital technologies optimize resource allocation and accelerate information flow, while sustained investment in digital innovation promotes technological progress, transforms traditional industries, and fosters emerging digital sectors—thereby significantly impacting economic growth. Yang and Yang (2025) found that digital transformation continuously increases patent outputs and enhances innovation quality within firms [2].

With the development of digital technologies, the digital economy has begun to transcend traditional geographic boundaries, especially exhibiting significant spatial effects within regional economies. Li et al. (2020) explored the spatial effects of the digital economy in the Greater Bay Area and found that the region, through technological innovation and industrial cooperation, has overcome traditional geographic limitations and promoted economic integration within the region [3]. Wang et al. (2021) demonstrated that the spatial spillover effects of the digital economy have led to close connections between urban agglomerations within the Greater Bay Area in terms of industrial collaboration and technological innovation, thereby facilitating the optimization of regional resource allocation [4]. Tian and Guo (2024) further noted that the development of the digital economy has significantly promoted the coordinated development of regional economies, providing new momentum for economic coordination through collaborative division of labor among cities and alleviating issues of regional imbalance and insufficient development [5].

A substantial body of literature has explored the pathways through which the digital economy influences regional development. Mediation and moderation effect models reveal that technological innovation, industrial restructuring, and improved resource allocation drive economic growth. Meanwhile, spatial econometric models capture inter-regional spillover effects, showing that the digital economy not only directly boosts local growth but also strengthens economic synergy in surrounding areas via technology spillovers and factor flows. However, traditional models—largely based on static causal analyses—offer limited insights into dynamic spatial changes and multidimensional network relationships. In contrast, complex network analysis, grounded in graph theory and statistical physics, employs concepts such as nodes, edges, centrality, and density to quantify system structure and better capture evolving spatial relationships [6].

In recent years, due to its ability to quantify spatial relationships, reveal heterogeneous interactions, and trace dynamic evolution, complex network analysis has gradually been applied to studies on regional spatial structure evolution, enriching the research perspective of regional economics. Wang et al. (2024) constructed a spatial association network for new quality productivity and found that new quality productivity exhibits stronger connections in eastern regions and weaker connections in western regions [7]. Similarly, Wang et al. (2024) arrived at similar conclusions in their study of the spatial distribution of the digital economy [8]. This consistency indicates a significant similarity in the spatial structure between new quality productivity and digital economy. As two key factors driving regional economic development, both new quality productivity and digital economy reflect the importance of resource flow and collaborative innovation between regions. Thus, the introduction of complex network analysis not only helps to uncover their networked distribution characteristics, reflecting the imbalance of regional economic development, but also offers a new research perspective for exploring the internal connections between the two. This demonstrates that complex network methods can effectively describe the node relationships, resource flows, and network characteristics between regions, making them a powerful tool in studying the spatial evolution of the digital economy.

As one of China's most economically developed regions, the Greater Bay Area has a highly active digital innovation landscape. Existing research shows that the development of the digital economy in the Greater Bay Area has promoted the transformation and upgrading of regional industries. Liu and Huang (2021) further discussed the development of the digital economy in the Greater Bay Area, pointing out that while digital innovation activities have made significant progress, the innovation cooperation and spatial association effects between cities within the region have yet to be fully explored [9]. Mao (2024) argued that as the Greater Bay Area continues to develop, closer regional innovation collaboration—particularly in transportation infrastructure, cross-border data flows, and standard mutual recognition—will emerge as key drivers of innovation [10]. Although previous studies have documented the impact of digital innovation on the region's economic development, few have examined its spatial effects and network structure in depth. Most existing research focuses on overall innovation levels or on the performance of individual cities, lacking detailed analysis of inter-city spatial associations. Therefore, this study constructs a spatial association network of digital innovation among the nine inland cities of the Greater Bay Area from a complex network perspective. It analyzes the network's structural characteristics and influencing factors, thereby enriching our understanding of the mechanisms and pathways through which the digital economy supports regional development.

3 Research Design and Data Processing

This study focuses on the nine inland cities of the Guangdong-Hong Kong-Macao Greater Bay Area. By collecting patent data related to the digital economy from these nine cities, a digital innovation spatial association network is constructed, with cities as nodes and city relationships as edges. Specifically, the study first constructs the digital innovation spatial association network of the nine inland cities in the Greater Bay Area and analyzes its structural characteristics. Subsequently, an adjusted mediation model is used to test the research hypotheses and explore the impact paths of digital innovation on economic development.

3.1 Research Design

Innovation input is one of the core driving forces behind the sustained development of the digital economy. According to the study by Chen et al. (2017), technological innovation can influence economic development by improving production efficiency and enabling technological spillover effects. Moreover, continuous innovation input is a core factor for the steady development of the digital economy [11]. Research by Zhao et al. (2017) also indicates that Chinese enterprises exhibit certain characteristics of continuous innovation [12]. Based on this, this study posits that continuous innovation input accelerates the diffusion of knowledge and technology, enhances the cohesion and innovation capabilities of regional economies, and thus provides strong support for promoting the sustainable growth of regional economies. Therefore, the following hypothesis is proposed:

H1: Continuous innovation input (*IIP*) has a significant positive effect on economic development.

In social network analysis and complex network theory, individual network characteristics such as network size, degree centrality, and structural holes have been proven to have significant effects on information flow, resource sharing, and technological spillover [13]. Network size reflects the coverage of innovation resources, with larger networks facilitating more technological spillover and knowledge dissemination, thereby promoting economic development. The degree of a node reflects its centrality within the regional innovation network. Generally, nodes with higher degree centrality play a pivotal role in innovation networks and can accelerate the spread of innovation results and resource flow. Structural holes refer to regions in the network that lack direct connections, and nodes occupying these structural holes possess informational and control advantages [14]. Based on this, the study suggests that individual network characteristics such as network size, degree centrality, and structural holes are key factors in determining whether a network can effectively promote innovation and economic development. These individual network characteristics (network size, degree centrality, structural holes) mediate the relationship between continuous innovation input and economic development, leading to the following hypotheses:

H2a: Network size (*Size*) mediates the relationship between continuous innovation input and economic development.
H2b: Degree centrality (*Degree*) mediates the relationship between continuous innovation input and economic development.
H2c: Structural hole (*Structural hole*) mediates the relationship between continuous innovation input and economic development.

Overall network structural characteristics such as network density and centrality are considered key factors influencing network efficiency and innovation diffusion. Network density refers to the ratio of actual connections to potential connections in the network. Networks with higher density typically indicate more resource and information flow, which facilitates innovation diffusion [15]. Network centrality quantifies the extent to which a few central nodes dominate the network structure, and it is calculated using the centralization index, which measures the disparity between the most central node and the others in the network. This study argues that overall network structural characteristics, including density and centralization, moderate the relationship between continuous innovation input and economic development, leading to the following hypotheses:

H3a: Network density (*Density*) moderates the effect of continuous innovation input on economic development.
H3b: Network centrality (*Centralization*) moderates the effect of continuous innovation input on economic development (Fig. 1).

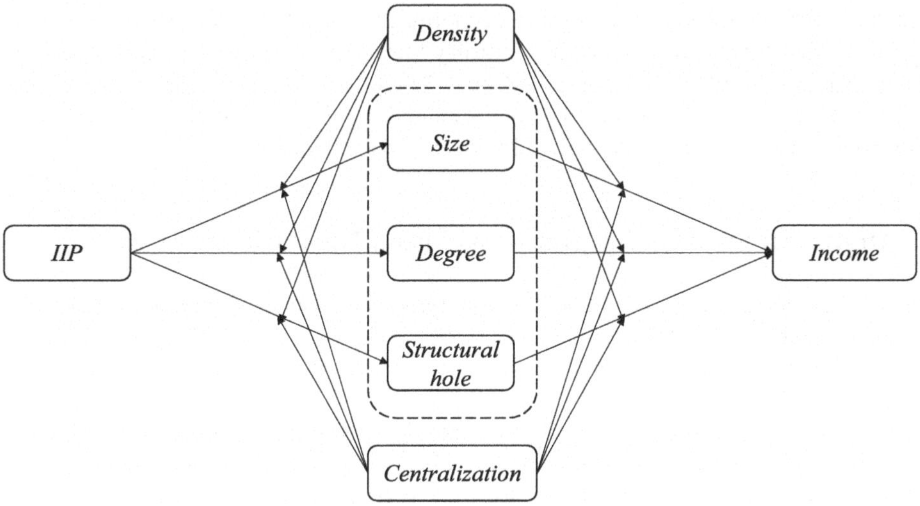

Fig. 1. Design Framework.

3.2 Research Object and Data Processing

Dependent Variable. The dependent variable in this study is the level of economic development, which can be measured and represented in various ways, such as per capita GDP or per capita disposable income. In this study, per capita disposable income is used as a representation of regional economic development.

Independent Variable. This study uses continuous innovation input as the independent variable, which is represented by continuous R&D investment. The measurement of continuous innovation input follows the approach of Zhao et al. (2023) [12]. Specifically, continuous innovation input for each region is measured by the ratio of the sum of R&D investment in years *t-1* and *t* to the sum of R&D investment in years *t-2* and *t-1*, multiplied by the sum of R&D investment in years *t-1* and *t*. The specific calculation formula is as follows:

$$IIP_t = \frac{IIP_t + IIP_{t-1}}{IIP_{t-1} + IIP_{t-2}} \times (IIP_t + IIP_{t-1}) \tag{1}$$

Control Variables. The development of the digital economy is influenced by various factors. This study adopts variables closely related to digital economy development as control variables in order to minimize the impact of unobserved factors on the results.

Industrial Structure (*Industry*): The ratio of the value-added of the tertiary industry to regional GDP is used as a representation of industrial structure.

Labor Force (*Labor*): The number of employees in information transmission, software, and information technology service industries, which are closely related to the digital economy, is used as a representation of labor force.

Data Sources. The patent data required to construct the digital innovation spatial association network in this study comes from the China Economic Network Digital Economy Database. Patents related to the digital economy are collected based on the standards of the "Digital Economy and Its Core Industry Statistical Classification (2021)" issued by the National Bureau of Statistics of China. The time span for the data is from 2014 to 2023. Other data are sourced from the "Guangdong Province Statistical Yearbook," with some missing data supplemented by local statistical yearbooks.

4 Digital Innovation Spatial Association Network Analysis

Based on patent data from 2014 to 2023, this study constructs the digital innovation spatial association network for the nine inland cities of the Guangdong-Hong Kong-Macao Greater Bay Area (GBA). The analysis focuses on individual network characteristics for the years 2014, 2018, and 2023.

From Fig. 2, it can be observed that network density (green line) shows a generally consistent upward trend from 2014 to 2022, though with minor fluctuations. In 2014, network density was relatively low, but it rose rapidly in the early phase and then continued to increase steadily from 2016 onward, eventually stabilizing after 2020. This indicates that, over the study period, intercity connections within the GBA's digital innovation network have continually strengthened, collaboration has expanded, and the overall network's closeness has improved.

In contrast, centralization (blue line) was at a relatively high level in 2014, suggesting that certain core cities initially dominated regional digital innovation activities. Centralization then declined until 2016, followed by a moderate rebound from 2016 to 2019, and

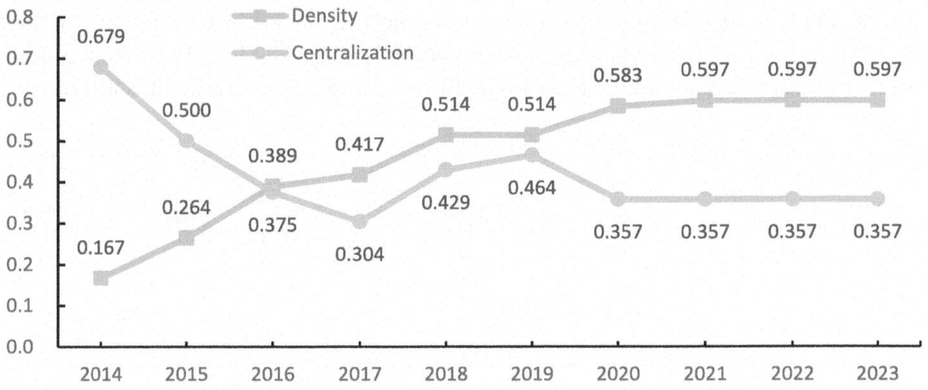

Fig. 2. Trends in Network Density and Centrality.

continued to rise slightly through 2021–2022. After 2022, centralization shows a notable drop, indicating a shift in the network structure away from a "core-periphery" model toward a "multi-center collaboration" model, in which digital innovation resources and cooperative relationships are more broadly distributed among cities.

Overall, the increase in network density reflects more frequent intercity collaboration and the intensified flow of innovation resources, which facilitates knowledge spillover and technological diffusion. Meanwhile, the evolving pattern of centralization suggests that although a few core cities once held significant influence, the network is progressively moving toward a more balanced and decentralized structure. This trend may help mitigate innovation imbalances and promote collaborative economic development throughout the region.

To illustrate the evolution of intercity digital innovation linkages, we focus on the years 2014, 2018, 2021, and 2023, which represent distinct phases in the GBA's development trajectory. Specifically, 2014 captures the early stage of network formation, 2018 marks a period of rapid growth in intercity collaboration, 2021 reflects a further consolidation of multi-center innovation, and 2023 offers insight into the most recent advanced stage of full-scale cooperation.

From Fig. 3, it is evident that the spatial association network of the GBA's nine inland cities became more tightly connected over time, with an increasing number of edges and progressively complex intercity linkages. In 2014, the network was relatively loose, featuring a typical "core-periphery" structure in which innovation resources were concentrated in a few developed cities. Shenzhen, for instance, established significant connections with other cities, while most remained on the periphery. By 2018, network density had grown substantially, and mid-level cities like Foshan and Zhongshan gained importance, suggesting an emerging multi-core collaboration. In 2021, further consolidation occurred, as more cities actively engaged in digital innovation exchanges, bridging the gap between core and peripheral nodes. Collaboration among mid-level cities became more frequent, suggesting that the region was transitioning toward a more balanced distribution of innovation resources. By 2023, the network displayed a high level of connectivity and multi-directional ties, reflecting an advanced stage of collaborative innovation. At this point, the "core-periphery" pattern had largely faded, replaced by a more integrated structure that facilitated widespread resource sharing and synergy.

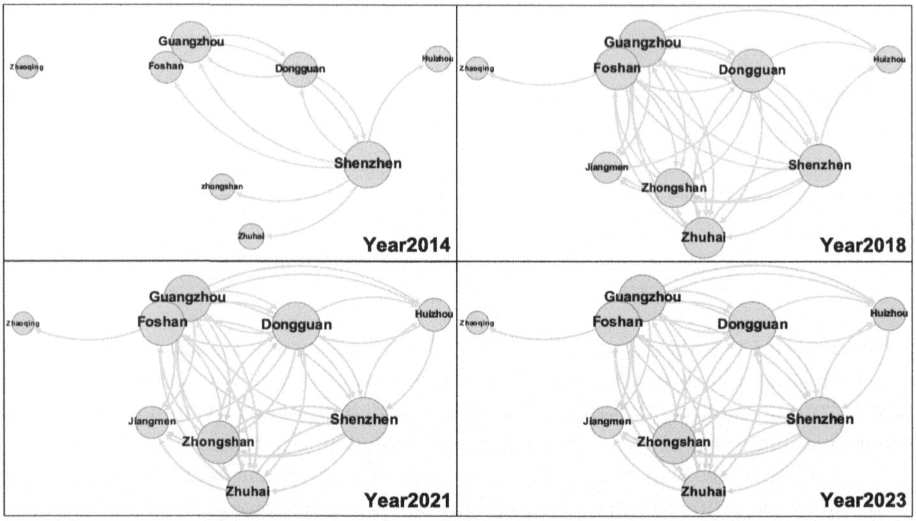

Fig. 3. Digital Innovation Spatial Association Structure of the Nine Inland Cities in the Greater Bay Area.

Overall, this evolutionary trend—from a loose network with a strong "core-periphery" characteristic in 2014 to a highly interconnected system by 2023—demonstrates the deepening of regional collaborative innovation. It also underscores the increasing role of digital innovation activities in driving regional economic development, providing essential support for the GBA's coordinated and high-quality integration.

5 The Impact of Sustained Digital Innovation on Economic Development

5.1 Empirical Analysis

To explore the impact of sustained digital innovation on the economic development of the nine inland cities of the Greater Bay Area, this section tests the hypotheses proposed earlier and identifies the impact pathways.

Table 1 presents the empirical results, indicating that sustained digital innovation input (*IIP*) has a significant positive effect on regional economic development. Across models 1–8, the IIP coefficients remain positive and significant, confirming Hypothesis *H1*. This aligns with the innovation-driven growth paradigm, underscoring the critical role of continued R&D and investment in fostering high-quality regional economic expansion.

Table 1. Regression Results of Digital Innovation and Economic Development

Variables	Model 1	Model 2	Model 3	Model 4	Model 5	Model 6	Model 7	Model 8
IIP	0.444***	0.362***	0.342***	0.437***	0.237***	0.308***	0.236***	0.258***
Size		0.029***			−0.031***			
Degree			0.020***				−0.019***	0.030**
Structural hole				0.022**				
Density							1.651***	
Centrality						−0.731*		−1.010**
*IIP*Density*					−0.180***			
*IIP*Centralization*						0.133		
*Size*Density*					0.075***			
*Size*Centralization*						−0.019		
*Degree*Density*							0.010*	
*Degree*Centralization*								−0.027
Labor	−0.009	0.004	−0.005	−0.002	0.008	0.011*	0.010*	0.001
Industry	2.793***	1.951***	1.898***	2.657***	1.905***	0.420**	0.430*	1.743***
R^2	0.914	0.936	0.936	9.919	0.941	0.984	0.983	0.945

Note: ***, **, and * indicate significance at the 1%, 5%, and 10% levels, respectively.

Models 2–4 introduce individual network characteristics (*Size, Degree,* and *Structural Hole*) as mediating variables. The findings support Hypotheses *H2a* and *H2b*, as larger network size and higher degree centrality significantly enhance economic growth. However, while the *Structural Hole* coefficient is significant, further bootstrap tests do not confirm its mediating role. This suggests that its effect may be contingent on complex network mechanisms beyond the current model's scope. The linear analysis in the current model and data may not fully capture its characteristic impact. Given the lack of significance in the mediation path, moderation tests were conducted only for *Size* and *Degree*.

Models 5–8 incorporate overall network characteristics (*Density* and *Centralization*) as moderating variables. Network density significantly moderates the impact of innovation input, with a negative coefficient for the interaction term (*IIP*Density*). This suggests that while higher density facilitates resource sharing, excessive density may introduce inefficiencies due to information redundancy, partially suppressing the marginal benefits of innovation. Hypothesis *H3a* is thus supported. Network centrality exhibits a significant negative main effect, indicating that excessive resource concentration in certain core cities can hinder balanced regional development. However, its moderating effect on innovation input is insignificant, implying that the central nodes in the Greater Bay Area network may not yet fully exert their influence. Consequently, Hypothesis *H3b* receives partial support.

These findings highlight the nuanced role of network structures in shaping the economic impact of digital innovation, emphasizing the balance between connectivity and resource allocation efficiency.

5.2 Discussion of Results

This study empirically confirms the significant impact of sustained digital innovation on the economic development of the nine inland cities in the Greater Bay Area and further elucidates its underlying mechanisms at both the individual and overall network levels. The discussion is structured around two key dimensions: direct effects and moderating effects.

Direct Effects at the Individual Network Level. At the individual network level, sustained digital innovation positively influences economic development through network size (*Size*) and degree centrality (*Degree*). A larger network size facilitates resource sharing and knowledge exchange among cities, fostering regional economic growth. Similarly, the significance of degree centrality highlights the pivotal role of highly connected cities in allocating digital innovation resources. This "hub" effect is particularly evident in cities like Shenzhen and Guangzhou, which efficiently attract and redistribute resources, enhancing regional collaboration. Conversely, structural holes did not exhibit a significant mediating effect, suggesting that the potential benefits of non-redundant information in the Greater Bay Area's digital innovation network remain underutilized. This may be attributed to the region's strong spatial ties and direct resource flows, which reduce reliance on intermediary nodes. Future research could explore the role of structural holes under different network configurations to assess their potential impact.

Moderating Effects at the Overall Network Level. At the overall network level, structural characteristics significantly moderate the relationship between digital innovation and economic development. Network density (*Density*) positively influences economic growth by strengthening intercity connections and promoting resource sharing. However, the negative interaction effect suggests that excessive density may lead to resource congestion, diminishing the marginal benefits of innovation input. This finding implies a possible inverted U-shaped relationship, emphasizing the need for an optimal level of density in regional network development. Moreover, the negative main effect of network centrality (*Centralization*) indicates that an overly centralized network structure may exacerbate regional disparities by concentrating resources in a few core cities (e.g., Shenzhen, Guangzhou), thereby limiting the growth potential of peripheral cities. Although the interaction term (*IIP*Centralization*) was not significant, the main effect underscores the importance of balanced resource distribution in regional policy design to ensure more equitable economic development.

6 Conclusion and Outlook

Using digital economy patent data (2014–2023) from nine inland cities in the Greater Bay Area, this study constructs a spatial correlation network of digital innovation and examines the relationship between sustained innovation input and regional economic development from a complex network perspective. The key findings are as follows:

First, sustained digital innovation input significantly promotes regional economic growth. At the individual network level, network size and degree centrality mediate this effect, with larger networks enhancing resource sharing and high-connectivity cities playing a pivotal role in aggregating and diffusing innovation resources.

Second, at the overall network level, network density positively moderates the innovation–growth relationship, reinforcing the role of strong intercity linkages. However, excessive density may lead to resource congestion, diminishing marginal benefits. The negative effect of network centrality suggests that over-concentration of resources in core cities may widen regional disparities, limiting the development potential of peripheral cities. Structural holes did not show significant mediating effects, likely due to strong direct innovation linkages reducing reliance on intermediaries.

From a theoretical perspective, this study deepens the understanding of digital innovation networks' role in regional economic development, emphasizing both individual network attributes and overall structural characteristics. It highlights the need to balance network density and centrality to maximize innovation-driven growth. From a policy standpoint, the findings offer insights for enhancing regional collaborative innovation in the Greater Bay Area. Governments should foster regional collaboration through innovation platforms and cross-city partnerships while maintaining moderate network density to avoid overconcentration.

Despite these contributions, the study has certain limitations. First, it does not differentiate network characteristics across industries, which may affect the generalizability of the findings. Second, external influences such as policy frameworks and institutional factors that shape digital innovation networks were not explicitly considered. Future research could extend this analysis by incorporating industry-specific dynamics and policy interventions, further enriching the theoretical and empirical discourse on digital innovation networks and regional economic development.

References

1. Brynjolfsson, E., McAfee, A.: The Second Machine Age: Work, Progress, and Prosperity in a Time of Brilliant Technologies. W. W. Norton & Company (2014)
2. Yang, R., Yang, M.: Persistent innovation effect of digital transformation. J. Quant. Technol. Econ. **42**(02), 109–129 (2025) in Chinese
3. Li, J., Wang, Y., Zhang, Q.: Digital economy and regional development in the Greater Bay Area: mechanisms and effects. J. Econ. Geogr. **40**(3), 48–62 (2020)
4. Wang, Z., Zhang, L.: Regional integration and innovation network in the Guangdong-Hong Kong-Macau Greater Bay Area. Reg. Stud. **54**(10), 1348–1360 (2020)
5. Tian, Y., Guo, L.: Digital economy and shared development of the region—based on the perspective of regional economic coordinated development. Inq. Econ. Issue. **45**(02), 1–16 (2024) in Chinese
6. Albert, R., Barabási, A.L.: Statistical mechanics of complex networks. Rev. Mod. Phys. **74**(1), 47–97 (2002)
7. Wang, Q., Wang, N., Wang, J.: Evolution of spatial correlation network structure and influencing factors of new quality productivity in Chinese cities. World Region. Stud., 1–19 (2024) in Chinese
8. Wang, S., Teng, T., Hu, S., Li, W.: Evolution and driving factors of spatial network structure of digital economy in China. Sci. Geogr. Sin. **44**(5), 743–753 (2024) in Chinese
9. Liu, Z., Huang, H.: The role of digital innovation in the economic transformation of the Greater Bay Area. Chin. Econ. Rev. **61**, 101482 (2021)
10. Mao, Y.: New trend and promotion path of integrated development in the Guangdong-Hong Kong-Macao Greater Bay Area. People Trib. **33**(24), 40–45 (2024) in Chinese
11. Chen, Y., Jin, Y., Liu, X.: The impact of digital innovation on economic growth: evidence from China's industrial sector. Tech. Anal. Strat. Manag. **29**(6), 653–666 (2017)
12. Zhao, Y., Qi, N., Yan, R., Meng, Q., Li, Z.: Structural embeddedness, absorptive capacity, and firms' sustainable innovation: evidence from an alliance innovation network of high-tech firms. J. Indus. Eng. Eng. Manag. **37**(04), 85–98 (2023) in Chinese
13. Borgatti, S.P., Everett, M.G.: Models of core/periphery structures. Soc. Networks. **21**(4), 375–395 (2000)
14. Burt, R.S.: Structural holes and good ideas. Am. J. Sociol. **110**(2), 349–399 (2004)
15. Newman, M.E.: The structure and function of complex networks. SIAM Rev. **45**(2), 167–256 (2003)

Research on the Configuration Causes of Users' Intention to Adopt Information in Health Rumor-Refuting Videos

Zewei Fang[1,2,3,4], Chuane Huang[2,3,5], Pei Pan[2], Jiani Wu[6], Yanming Chen[7], Qiuqi Xie[7], and Qiping Liu[8](✉)

[1] Center for Studies of Information Resources, Wuhan University, Wuhan 430072, China
[2] School of Information Management, Wuhan University, Wuhan 430072, China
[3] Big Data Institute, Wuhan University, Wuhan 430072, China
[4] Wuhan Institute of Data Intelligence, Wuhan 430072, China
[5] National Demonstration Center for Experimental Library and Information Science Education, Wuhan University, Wuhan 430072, China
[6] Wuhan Children's Library, Wuhan 430014, China
[7] Hubei Standardization and Quality Institute, Wuhan 430061, China
[8] School of Information Management, Hubei University of Economics, Wuhan 430205, China
1043531305@qq.com

Abstract. To reveal the multiple configuration patterns influencing users' adoption toward health rumor-refuting videos, and to provide theoretical guidance for the effective dissemination of such content. Based on the Elaboration Likelihood Model, this study extracted 11 ante-dependent variables from three levels: content quality characteristics, dissemination subject characteristics and public characteristics. And by using the fsQCA to analyze the data of health rumor-refuting videos on Bilibili, the complex causal mechanisms of characteristics influencing users' adoption for such videos are identified. The analysis reveals three primary configurations of antecedent factors that contribute to high adoption: (1) High-Quality Viral Original Videos; (2) Highly Interactive Original Videos with Consistent Bullet Comment Sentiment; and (3) Hot-Topic Health Rumor-Refuting Videos. The findings offer valuable theoretical insights into enhancing users' willingness to adopt information in health rumor-refuting videos and provide practical strategies for optimizing the production and dissemination of such content.

Keywords: Information Adoption · Health Rumor Refute · fsQCA

1 Introduction

In the post-truth era, advancements in internet technology have significantly reduced the barriers and costs associated with the dissemination of health rumors. According to the *2024 Annual Rumor Governance Report* released by Toutiao, over 5 million false rumors were reported in 2024 alone, with health rumors being the most covert and variable in form [1]. Simultaneously, health information disseminated via social media

Y. P. Tu and M. Chi (Eds.): WHICEB 2025, LNBIP 549, pp. 365–375, 2025.
https://doi.org/10.1007/978-3-031-94184-9_30

has witnessed explosive growth, with new media becoming the primary source for public health information acquisition. Among these, video-based health information stands out due to its visual appeal, higher information density, and superior dissemination potential. Moreover, existing studies [2] have demonstrated that public adoption directly influence the effectiveness of information dissemination.

Therefore, this study constructs an indicator framework based on the Elaboration Likelihood Model (ELM), wherein content quality characteristics represent the central route, and characteristics of the information dissemination subject represent the peripheral route. Additionally, this study innovatively incorporates public characteristics of the information to analyze health rumor-refuting videos on Bilibili video platform, a prominent platform for knowledge-sharing, where knowledge-related content accounts for a significant portion of total views, with science content experiencing rapid growth. By employing fuzzy-set Qualitative Comparative Analysis (fsQCA), the study explores the cognitive motivations behind users' adoption of health rumor-refuting videos and reveals the synergistic effects of characteristic indicators.

2 Literature Review

2.1 Health Rumor-Refuting Information

Rumor refutation refers to a short-term response that counteracts widely disseminated misinformation through media and other communication channels using refuting information [3]. Its core objective is to mitigate the potential negative impacts of health rumors. Text-based refutations on platforms like Twitter and Weibo dominate existing research, but video-based refutations on platforms such as YouTube and Bilibili better align with public information preferences, playing a pivotal role in advancing health rumor-refutation systems and offering novel research perspectives. In addition, Previous studies have primarily focused on the structural mechanisms of health rumor-refuting information [4] and the evaluation of refutation effectiveness [5], with limited exploration of individual adoption and behaviors.

2.2 Adoption of Health Rumor-Refuting Information

Information adoption is a decision-making process in which users actively and purposefully select, evaluate, accept, and utilize information [6], and this process ultimately influences subsequent behaviors. The factors influencing the adoption of health rumor-refuting information primarily revolve around two dimensions: information content characteristics (e.g., information quality, topic type) and information source characteristics (e.g., credibility, influence of the information publisher). However, the role of public characteristics, such as the degree of user interaction and emotional polarity on social media, in influencing sharing and adoption has been largely overlooked. Additionally, the diverse factors influencing adoption operate not in isolation but through complex interdependencies [7]. There is still a need for in-depth research into health rumor-refuting information adoption behavior from the perspective of complex configurations.

2.3 Elaboration Likelihood Model

The Elaboration Likelihood Model (ELM) explains how individuals process information through a central route, involving deep cognitive engagement with information quality, and a peripheral route, relying on heuristic cues such as source credibility [8]. ELM has been applied to online health information adoption but remains underexplored in rumor-refuting studies. Existing research primarily emphasizes content and source characteristics, overlooking factors like topic relevance, user interaction, and emotional polarity, which strongly influence information adoption. To bridge this gap, this study extends the ELM framework by integrating public characteristics for a more comprehensive understanding of health rumor-refuting video adoption.

3 Research Design

3.1 Model

This study takes the health rumor-refuting information on the Bilibili as the research object, leveraging the ELM to classify content quality characteristics as the central route requiring deep processing, dissemination subject characteristics as the peripheral route involving simple decision-making, and combines the public characteristics to analyze the configuration effects of these three antecedent variables on adoption. The conceptual model is shown in Fig. 1.

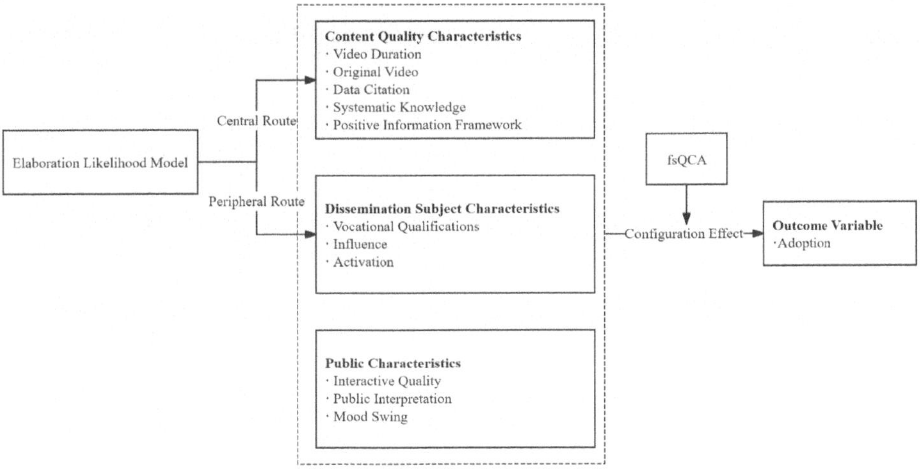

Fig. 1. Conceptual model of research

3.2 Variable Definition

User interactions, such as likes, coins, and favorites, reflect their attention and recognition of video information [9] and can be used to evaluate adoption. Principal Component

Analysis (PCA) is employed to integrate like rate, coin rate, and favorite rate into a comprehensive continuous indicator, serving as the outcome variable for adoption.

Information adoption behavior is influenced by subject factors, object factors, and interpersonal influence factors. Drawing on previous research and the specific characteristics of the study object [6, 10], 11 antecedent variables of adoption are identified (see Table 1) and preprocesses the data using binary classification, sentiment analysis, PCA, and z-score normalization.

Table 1. Variable Definition and Measurement Method

Variable Category		Variable Name	Definition and Measurement
Outcome variable		Adoption (Ap)	Measured by like rate, coin rate, and favorite rate, using PCA for aggregation.
Antecedent variables	Central route - content quality characteristics	Video duration (VD)	Represented by the duration of the video in seconds.
		Original video (OV)	Indicates whether the video is original; 0 = non-original, 1 = original.
		Data citation (DC)	Indicates whether the video cites supporting data; 0 = no data citation, 1 = data citation present.
		Systematic knowledge (SK)	Indicates whether the video provides systematic health knowledge; 0 = non-systematic (focused on single-point knowledge), 1 = systematic.
		Positive information framework (PF)	0 = adopts a negative framing to avoid positive outcomes; 1 = emphasizes positive outcomes.

(*continued*)

Table 1. (*continued*)

Variable Category		Variable Name	Definition and Measurement
	Peripheral route - Dissemination subject characteristics	Vocational qualifications (VQ)	Indicates whether the creator holds relevant professional credentials; 0 = no credentials, 1 = possesses credentials.
		Influence (IN)	Measured by the creator's follower count, cumulative likes and cumulative plays across uploaded videos, using PCA for aggregation.
		Activation (AC)	The creator's update frequency; measured as the ratio of the total number of historical submissions to the time span of the creator's submission activity (calculated from the first submission to the present).
	Public characteristics	Interactive quality (IQ)	Measured by the repost rate, comment rate, and bullet comment rate, using PCA for aggregation.
		Public interpretation (PI)	Indicates whether the video topic aligns with currently discussed health issues; determined by the average daily Baidu index value within 15 days of the video's publication.
		Mood swing (MS)	Measured by the variance in sentiment score of bullet comments, capturing the degree of emotional fluctuation.

3.3 Data Collection and Calibration

On January 18, 2023, the study used the keyword "health rumor refuting" to search on the Bilibili, and sorted the results by views. After excluding non-health-related videos, the top 100 videos were selected as the research sample. The study collected 100,323 bullet comments and extracted 18 feature datasets for each samples. Direct calibration was used to transform variables into fuzzy sets ranging from 0 to 1 (see Table 2), with the 95th, 50th, and 5th percentiles set as thresholds for full membership, crossover, and full non-membership, respectively.

Table 2. Descriptive Statistics and Calibration of Variables

Variable		Max	Min	M	SD	full membership	crossover	full non-membership
Outcome variable	Ap	5.95	−1.61	0	1.30	2.45	−0.42	−1.38
Antecedent variables	VD	1540	20	269.03	260.37	725.6	190	28
	OV	1	0	0.89	0.31	1	/	0
	DC	1	0	0.19	0.39	1	/	0
	SK	1	0	0.09	0.29	1	/	0
	PF	1	0	0.11	0.31	1	/	0
	VQ	1	0	0.26	0.44	1	/	0
	IN	10.63	−0.59	0	1.67	1.57	−0.49	−0.59
	AC	5.00	0.00	0.5	0.96	3.01	0.22	0.04
	IQ	5.53	−1.59	0	1.22	2.38	−0.24	−1.25
	PI	9.18	−0.15	0	1	−0.09	−0.14	−0.15
	MS	1	0	0.23	0.19	0.59	0.17	0.04

4 Data Analysis and Results

4.1 Necessity Test

In fsQCA, a condition is deemed necessary if it consistently leads to the outcome. Consistency levels were used to evaluate the necessary conditions for high adoption. A consistency score above 0.9 indicates a necessary condition. As shown in Table 3, the consistency level of non-systematic knowledge exceeds 0.9, identifying it as a necessary condition for high adoption.

4.2 Configuration Analysis

Configuration analysis (i.e., sufficiency analysis) was conducted to explore the combinations of antecedent conditions leading to high adoption. Following recommended

Table 3. Necessity Test for Individual Conditions

Condition	Consistency	Coverage
VD	0.724890	0.747030
~VD	0.598831	0.528496
OV	0.889359	0.475067
~OV	0.110641	0.478182
DC	0.189100	0.473158
~DC	0.810900	0.475938
SK	0.089418	0.472333
~SK	0.910583	0.475714
PF	0.136724	0.590909
~PF	0.863276	0.461135
VQ	0.229907	0.420385
~VQ	0.770093	0.494743
IN	0.587745	0.688227
~IN	0.690961	0.553013
AC	0.498980	0.587440
~AC	0.823689	0.656832
IQ	0.708651	0.753860
~IQ	0.627479	0.539342
PI	0.608549	0.645464
~PI	0.701920	0.604770
MS	0.691004	0.683812
~MS	0.662165	0.605862

standards, the raw consistency threshold was set at 0.8, and the case frequency threshold at 2, based on sample size [11]. Complex, parsimonious, and intermediate solutions were yielded after counterfactual analysis. By comparing their nested relationships, the study identified core and peripheral conditions for each solution.

Seven configurations (Ap1a, Ap1b, Ap1c, Ap2a, Ap2b, Ap2c, Ap3) were identified for high adoption. Configurations sharing the same core conditions were categorized into three distinct high adoption-effect types: Ap1, Ap2, Ap3. The analysis results are shown in Table 4.

4.3 Robustness Test

To ensure robustness, the study raised the consistency threshold from 0.8 to 0.85. This adjustment resulted in six configurations, fewer than the original results due to logical simplifications of the overall configurations, which did not affect the interpretation of the

Table 4. Configurations Leading to High Adoption in Health Rumor-Refuting Videos

Condition	Ap1			Ap2			Ap3
	Ap1a	Ap1b	Ap1c	Ap2a	Ap2b	Ap2c	
VD	●	●	●	●	⊗	⊗	⊗
OV	●	●	●	●	●	●	⊗
DC	⊗	⊗	⊗	●	●	⊗	⊗
SK	⊗	⊗	⊗	⊗	⊗	⊗	⊗
PF	⊗	⊗	⊗	⊗	⊗	⊗	⊗
VQ	⊗	⊗	⊗	⊗	⊗	⊗	⊗
IN	⊗	⊗	●	⊗	⊗	●	●
AC	⊗	⊗	⊗	⊗	⊗	●	●
IQ	●	⊗	–	●	●	●	⊗
PI	⊗	●	⊗	●	⊗	●	●
MS	–	–	●	⊗	⊗	⊗	●
Consistency	0.9420	0.7839	0.9086	0.9655	0.9336	0.8427	0.9790
Raw coverage	0.1504	0.1351	0.1422	0.0648	0.0591	0.0755	0.0294
Unique coverage	0.0303	0.0349	0.0425	0.0292	0.0236	0.0212	0.0294
Overall solution consistency	0.8416						
Overall solution coverage	0.3734						

Note: "●" and "●" indicate the presence of a specific condition, while "⊗" and "⊗" denote its absence. "●" and "⊗" represent core conditions, whereas "●" and "⊗"indicate secondary conditions. The symbol "-" signifies that the corresponding condition variable may either be present or absent.

results. All six configurations retained "non-systematic knowledge" as a core condition, with "non-positive information framework" and "no vocational qualifications" as auxiliary conditions, which is consistent with the original Ap1, Ap2, and Ap3 configuration types. These findings confirm the robustness of the study results, as the antecedent configurations for user adoption toward health rumor-refuting videos remained consistent under stricter thresholds.

5 Conclusions and Enlightenments

5.1 Configuration Types Analysis

Configuration Type 1: High-Quality Viral Original Videos. Ap1 emphasizes high video duration and originality. Users are less concerned about data verification or the frequency of creator activity. Ap1a and Ap1b primarily involve UGC content, where creators' influence is relatively low, and high adoption stems from strong interactivity and trending topics. Ap1c highlights high creator influence, featuring health rumor-refuting videos by professional creators with noticeable emotional fluctuations in bullet comments, sparking public discussion. Even when the video is not a trending topic, users still exhibit high adoption. Comparing Ap1a and Ap1b reveals that "high interactive quality" and "public interpretation" are substitutable conditions within this type.

Configuration Type 2: Highly Interactive Original Videos with Consistent Bullet Comment Sentiment. Ap2 emphasizes high video interactivity, consistent sentiment in bullet comments, and originality. In this type, original health rumor-refuting videos achieve high adoption through high rates of sharing, commenting, and bullet chatting. The consistent sentiment in bullet comments influences viewers' emotional engagement during video consumption. Ap2a, Ap2b, and Ap2c further enhance adoption through high video duration, data verification, and influential creators, respectively.

Configuration Type 3: Hot-Topic Health Rumor-Refuting Videos. Unlike the first two types, Ap3 considers non-original videos as a core condition and requires the video topic to align with current public health concerns. High-profile, highly active professional creators capitalize on trending topics by reposting or authorizing non-original videos. Despite low video duration, lack of data verification, and limited interactivity, significant emotional fluctuations in bullet comments still result in high user adoption.

5.2 Comprehensive Analysis

This study extends the ELM framework by incorporating the public characteristics, and comprehensively examines the seven configurations to analyze the complex causal relationship between the three types of characteristics and user adoption.

Content Quality Characteristics. Apl seven configurations emphasize "non-systematic knowledge" as a core condition, indicating that users on video platforms prefer fragmented knowledge that directly addresses specific rumors over systematic explanations. This preference aligns with the fragmented knowledge acquisition behavior typical of video platforms [12]. Furthermore, the auxiliary condition of "non-positive information framing" highlights the importance of emphasizing the health risks posed by rumors, which enhances adoption. Core and auxiliary conditions in multiple configurations also underscore the significance of video duration and originality in boosting adoption [13].

Dissemination Subject Characteristics. No configuration identifies creator authority, influence, or activity level as core conditions, suggesting that on content-driven video platforms, these characteristics are secondary [14]. Even professional creators must produce high-quality content that aligns with users' needs to achieve better adoption.

Public Characteristics. Public characteristics of the information significantly impact adoption. Many configurations highlight the importance of high interactivity, popularity, and sentiment scores. High rates of sharing, commenting, and bullet interactions stimulate public discussion, thereby enhancing adoption. Besides, health rumor-refuting videos that align with trending topics can achieve high adoption despite shortcomings in content quality (e.g., Ap3) or dissemination subject characteristics (e.g., Ap1b, Ap2a). Emotion also influences adoption: high sentiment consistency in bullet comments can serve as a core condition by evoking consistent emotional responses, while significant sentiment fluctuations can act as auxiliary information cues, fostering the spread and adoption of refutation information [15].

5.3 Enlightenments

This study innovatively highlights the critical role of public characteristics in health rumor-refuting videos while underscoring the declining influence of dissemination subject characteristics in the big data era. It identifies three configuration types driving high adoption: high-quality viral original videos, highly interactive original videos with consistent bullet comment sentiment, and hot-topic health rumor-refuting videos. The findings suggest that original videos presenting multiple single-point facts, aligned with social hotspots, and emphasizing the health risks or psychological impacts of rumors are more likely to be adopted. Furthermore, video creators can strategically guide bullet comment sentiment to shape and enhance adoption outcomes.

Acknowledgements. This research was supported by the National Natural Science Foundation of China (NO. 72274146), the S&T Plan Projects of the State Administration for Market Regulation (NO. 2023MK088), the Hubei Provincial Social Science Fund (NO. 23ZD195), and the Fundamental Research Funds for the Central Universities.

References

1. Beijing Youth Daily, https://news.qq.com/rain/a/20250114A06VSO00, last accessed 14 Jan 2025
2. Song, S.J., Zhao, Y.X., Yao, X.L., et al.: Serious information in hedonic social applications: affordances, self-determination and health information adoption in TikTok. J. Doc. **78**(4), 890–911 (2022)
3. Paek, H.J., Hove, T.: Mediating and moderating roles of trust in effective risk rumor management: a test case of radiation-contaminated seafood in South Korea. Risk Anal. **39**(12), 2653–2667 (2019)
4. Li, X., Wang, Y., Han, W., et al.: Research on the content, quality and optimization of health rumor-refuting information. Inform. Document. Serv. **43**(03), 84–93 (2022)
5. Chen, J.H., Ma, H.C., Yang, S.: SEIOR rumor propagation model considering hesitating mechanism and different rumor-refuting ways in complex networks. Mathematics. **11**(2), 283 (2023)
6. Chen, Y., Zhou, X.Y., Yue, L.X., et al.: Influencing factors of users' health information adoption behavior intention in mobile UGC communities. Knowled. Lib. Inform. Sci. **39**(05), 82–95 (2022)
7. Song, X.Y., Wang, P.: Research on the concept and influencing factors of information adoption behavior. Inform. Sci. **28**(05), 760–762 + 767 (2010)
8. Petty, R.E., Cacioppo, J.T.: The effects of involvement on responses to argument quantity and quality: central and peripheral routes to persuasion. J. Pers. Soc. Psychol. **46**(1), 69–81 (1984)
9. Li, Z.M., Zhang, Q., Du, X.Y.: Research on rumor-refutation effectiveness based on the interactions and popular comments' emotional tendencies of the rumor-refuting microblogs: taking rumor-refuting microblogs related with COVID-2019 as an example. J. Intelligence. **39**(11), 90–95 + 110 (2020)

10. Han, Y., Jiang, B., Guo, R.: Factors affecting public adoption of COVID-19 prevention and treatment information during an Infodemic: cross-sectional survey study. J. Med. Internet Res. **23**(3), e23097–e23097 (2021)
11. Schneider, C.Q., Wagemann, C.: Set-Theoretic Methods for the Social Sciences: a Guide to Qualitative Comparative Analysis. Cambridge University Press, Cambridge (2012)
12. Liu, S., Zeng, X.: Research on the key elements and communication logic of knowledge-based short videos: based on the qualitative comparative analysis (QCA) of knowledge-based short videos on Bilibili. J. Mass Commun. Month. **02**, 30–39 + 48 (2022)
13. Zhao, W., Jiang, J., Weng, J., et al.: Comparing Twitter and traditional media using topic models. Advances in Information Retrieval. ECIR 2011. Lecture Notes in Computer Science, vol 6611. Springer, Berlin, Heidelberg, 338–349 (2011).
14. Yang, C.: The current situation, characteristics and strategies of the short-video dissemination of public policies: taking the garbage classification on the Douyin platform as an example. Media. **389**(24), 46–48 + 50 (2022)
15. Bai, H., Li, T.: The adoption tendency of comments in online peer-review: from the perspective of emotional experience. Open Educ. Res. **26**(04), 95–101 (2020)

Author Index

Y. P. Tu and M. Chi (Eds.): WHICEB 2025, LNBIP 549, pp. 377–380, 2025.
https://doi.org/10.1007/978-3-031-94184-9

The manufacturer's authorised representative in the EU is Springer Nature Customer Service Centre GmbH, Europaplatz 3, 69115 Heidelberg, Germany. If you have any concerns regarding our products, please contact ProductSafety@springernature.com

Printed and bound by CPI Group (UK) Ltd, Croydon, CR0 4YY
01/10/2026
02225951-0018